John Gill And Justification From Eternity

A Tercentenary Appreciation 1697-1997

John Gill And Justification From Eternity

A Tercentenary Appreciation

George M. Ella

Go *publications*

Go Publications
Gibb Hill Farm, Ponsonby, Cumbria, CA20 1BX, ENGLAND.

© Go Publications 1998
First Published 1998

This Edition 2018

British Library Cataloguing in Publication Data available

ISBN 978-1-908475-14-5

Printed and bound in Great Britain by
Lightning Source UK Ltd

Dedication

This book is dedicated to Joe and Balinda Skoda of Waukomis, Oklahoma; a brother and sister who thrill my heart. The grace in their lives is so catching that after fellowshipping with them, mountain moving seems so much easier.

JOHN GILL D.D. 1697 — 1771

6

Table of Contents

Foreword

The apostle Paul prayed to God on behalf of the Christians in Ephesus that they might come 'to know the love of Christ which passeth knowledge … ' (Ephesians 3:19). What Paul prayed may sound like a contradiction—that individuals would come to 'know' the love of God which 'passeth knowledge'. The apostle wanted the Ephesians to know the unknowable, to grasp the unreachable, to comprehend the incomprehensible. It is as if Paul is saying to all who contemplate God's love for the elect in Christ Jesus, 'Meditate to your heart's delight on the love of God for His people, consider with all your might the love of Christ for His bride, devote all your energy to fathom the breadth, length, depth, and height of His great love, but know this also that you will come as close to really comprehending His love as a man really comes close to emptying the ocean by dipping out water with a teaspoon.'

The love of God which passes knowledge is an eternal love, 'I have loved thee with an everlasting love' (Jeremiah 31:3). Because God is eternal and the love of God flows from His nature, His love for sinners also must be eternal. 'But', some may ask, 'does not God's eternal love conflict with His justice?' 'Doth the Almighty pervert justice?' (Job 8:3). 'Is justice sacrificed for the sake of His love?'

The answer to these questions is found in the doctrine of the eternal union of Christ with His elect and the eternal justification of the elect by the Father. If you are unfamiliar with these themes, you are in for a treat. The book you now hold, *John Gill And Justification From Eternity: A Tercentenary Appreciation* will help you understand the most God-glorifying, Christ-exalting, soul-comforting teaching found in all of the Bible.

John Gill was, in this pastor's opinion, the greatest evangelical theologian and pastor of the eighteenth century. His mighty ministry flowed from experiential and theological knowledge of God's love. Just as the flock he led were richly blessed, so too, thousands of others who turn to his prodigious writings discover a powerful example in Gill's testimony of how much a man can learn of God. John Gill was born 300 years ago and this book celebrates the occasion by bringing to twenty-first century Christians a well-written examination and appreciation of Gill's teaching of God's eternal love for His elect and the eternal justification of sinners. I hope you read it with the same pleasure and delight as I did.

I was first introduced to Gill's writings through the preaching ministry of C. H. Spurgeon, successor to and admirer of the great Dr Gill. I have long used Gill's *Exposition of the Old and New Testaments* and believe them to be the best Bible commentaries available today. Imagine my pleasure to discover that Dr George Ella, a recent acquaintance as a result of an earlier biography, was soon to release a biography of Gill himself.

As soon as a copy of *John Gill and The Cause of God and Truth* reached me I read it with delight. I had in my possession a lengthy, sympathetic biography of the man I long had considered a model for my own ministry. The people I shepherd have often heard me quote from Gill, and now I could put something in their hands that told them about his life and ministry.

My friendship with Dr Ella has grown over the past few years and bonds of Christian love and fellowship were cemented during his recent visit to the United States. I wanted the people of Emmanuel Baptist Church in Enid, Oklahoma to be introduced to Dr Ella. When I picked him up at the airport, he had been sharing Christ with a young Jewish person who had been seated next to him on the plane. His warmth to this stranger was no act and testifies to the same evangelistic ardour that took him in earlier years to be a missionary of the gospel to the Lapp people of Norway and Sweden. His love for the Lord and heart-felt desire to witness for Him meant that in turn, my own family and my church took him to their hearts.

I feel it is necessary to commend the author of this book as well as the book itself because of the efforts which have been made by some leading evangelicals of our day to discredit my friend and his writing. One such leader, the editor of an American journal, wrote me a letter stating that Ella was 'subtle and theologically dangerous'. He went on to say that he was 'repulsed' by Ella and that others were too. Interestingly, this fellow says such things about a man he has never met. Dr Ella is accused of being 'a Hyper-Calvinist', 'an Antinomian', and 'a denier of human responsibility', an earlier work is described as a 'very dangerous book' written by an 'equally dangerous author'.

Yet, how can one describe a man who spends years serving as a missionary on the frozen tundra of Norway and Sweden as a Hyper-Calvinist? How can one construe a man who believes everyone to be responsible to his Creator to keep the law perfectly as Antinomian? How can one say that a man denies human responsibility when, in fact, he believes that sinners receive death for just one violation of God's eternal Law unless covered by the righteousness of Christ? I may not agree with everything George Ella believes, I have yet to meet a man who believes everything I do! But I certainly know enough of him personally to commend him to you as a man who loves Christ, bows before the Scriptures, and deeply respects the people of God. Dr Ella's theology is orthodox, evangelical and honouring to Christ. He not only understands that the theology of John Gill is the theology of the Bible, he believes it.

George Ella is a scholar par excellence. His numerous degrees are a testimony to his erudition and scholarly discipline. However, his secular education does not blind him to the fact that the classroom where Christ is the teacher, with the Bible as the textbook is the only place where eternal wisdom can be gained. John Gill, on the other hand, was a man of little formal education (though he received an honorary degree from Aberdeen University for research into the Hebrew language), but one who learned the deep things of God by sitting at the feet of Christ. George Ella understands this and in his own scholarly manner, he shows us that the wisdom of Gill is the wisdom of heaven.

It is for these reasons I believe there to be no better author to give *A Tercentenary Appreciation Of John Gill And His Doctrine Of Eternal Justification*.

Read the book again and again. I believe your soul will be nourished greatly as you meditate on the everlasting love of God. I feel sure that as you read Dr Ella's appreciation of John Gill and his doctrine, you will discover the comfort of God's eternal love for His people. In fact, if by the grace of God your eyes are opened to the tremendous truth that God eternally justifies His elect in Christ, you will begin to know what it means to rest in the finished work of Christ for your eternal salvation. Put another way, you will begin to know 'the love of Christ which passeth knowledge'.

Pastor Wade Burleson
Emmanuel Baptist Church,
Enid, Oklahoma, USA.

Introduction

A Return To An Old, Reliable Path

I make no claim to be the author of this book. I see myself rather as an editor preparing a compendium of John Gill's excellent and Scriptural thoughts on the subject of justification and its relation to God's eternal plan of salvation for His elect. John Gill was second to none in guiding the sinner along the straight path to heaven following the footsteps of Christ. As there is no better way than that shown us by Christ and to which Gill testified, it would be ridiculous to attempt anything new. The aim of this book is therefore, plainly and simply, to present the good old path leading to full pardon and justification in the courts of God as taught by John Gill (1697-1771). Gill wrote literally volumes on the subject of justification as it was, to him of vital saving importance and ought to be central to any preaching of the gospel. Summing up his thoughts on the importance of this doctrine in 1769, Gill affirms:

> The doctrine of justification by the righteousness of Christ is a doctrine of great importance; the apostle speaks of it as if the essence of the gospel lay in it; and calls the opposite to it, justification by the works of the law, another gospel; see Galatians 1:6, 7 and 3:8. It is a fundamental article of the gospel; some have called it, the basis of Christianity; it was the great doctrine of the Reformation; what our first reformers made their

chief study; and by it cut the sinews of popery, the antichristian doctrines of penance and purgatory, of pardons and indulgences, of the merit of good works, works of supererogation, &c.. Luther used to call it, *articulus stantis val cedentis ecclesiiae*, the article of the church, by which it stands or falls; as this is, the church is. If this obtains,[1] the church is in a well-settled and prosperous state; but if this loses ground, and is rejected, it is in a ruinous one: if this is a rule to judge by, it may be easily discerned, in what case the church, and interest of religion, now are. This doctrine is the ground and foundation of all solid joy, peace, and comfort, in this life, and hope of eternal glory hereafter.[2]

Justification is, once again, the most neglected of doctrines
Sadly, what Gill has to say about justification is not only the most neglected part of his teaching but this doctrine is demonstrably the most neglected part of gospel preaching today. We have no shortage of preachers that tell us that we must turn and embrace God who is extending His arms to us in patient hope and love. We have many preachers who, on more Biblical grounds, preach the commands of God to be reconciled to Him and repent and believe. Few of today's preachers, however, seem to have a call to preach justification to either sinners or saints. This is obviously because today's preaching in the generality of our churches is mostly based on what man is expected to do. He must display love to God, he must be reconciled, he must repent, he must believe. It really seems that preaching justification would be something of an embarrassment to modern evangelists as this would imply rejecting that agency of man which so many preachers, Reformed or otherwise, feel is indispensable in accepting the gospel. We must preach to man, they believe, in a way that allows him to muster up the capacities he has to accept the offer of salvation. Justification is the one doctrine which of all doctrines emphasises the sovereignty of God alone in salvation. Justification reminds us perhaps too much of a judge who

---

[1] 'To obtain' carried the meaning 'to be prevalent' or 'to hold fast to' in Gill's day.
[2] *Body of Divinity*, vol. ii, Book III, Chap. 8, p. 797, 1769 Subscription edition. Readers using the 1839 one volume edition or its reprint by the Baptist Standard Bearer will find the quote in Gill's essay *On Justification*, p. 503.

takes the entire initiative in choosing the one to be justified according to a scheme of justice which appals sinful man. Many thus leave this uncomfortable doctrine entirely out of their preaching programme, explaining to those who miss the inclusion of this vital subject that it belongs to the secret, un-revealed will of God and is thus not part of the gospel.

A new need for reform
This state of affairs will strike many a sound Christian as being urgently in need of reform. For those who see justification emphasised all through both the Old and New Testaments, the quite faulty logic of this thinking will be apparent. It will also be clear to them that we are as little called upon to exercise a work of reconciliation, repentance or belief ourselves in order to secure our salvation as we are required to perform a work of justification. The Scriptures tell us that 'For if, when we were enemies, we were reconciled to God by the death of his Son, much more, being reconciled, we shall be saved by his life.'[3] In other words, our reconciliation has already been accomplished by a fiat of God's grace.

Repentance, we are told time and time again in Scripture, can be of two kinds. The term is used for the human, selfish kind of repentance which man displays when he realises that he has lost a benefit through breaking the law. Such a repentance is so strong that it can drive a man to suicide, as it did in the case of Judas. But such repentance can save no one. This is not that repentance which is given the elect and associated with belief which we know as evangelical, gospel or saving repentance, according to our Reformed linguistic traditions. Such God given repentance opens the heart to belief. Similarly, in the Scriptures, belief is never shown to be a product of man's agency but always as a product of God's grace. Furthermore, and this shows how essential it is to preach justification, there is no reconciliation, no chance of repentance and no sign of belief unless a man be justified by grace. Unless a man is declared pardoned, free of guilt and righteous before God, all talk of the other benefits of the gospel is in vain as it is only God's justified ones who come into such benefits. Only justified people have saving faith and without faith no man shall see God.

---

[3] Romans 5:10.

Modern sound works on justification are extremely rare

All this was very clear to Gill. He recognised that the great deliverance which came in the Reformation was a re-discovery of that great gospel truth of justification by faith which had been rejected by the Roman pontiffs. By Gill's time, however, though faith was written large in teaching and preaching, justification was only mentioned, as it were, in small print. Indeed, when studying the systematic writings of many an evangelical theologian after the Reformation blaze had died down somewhat, we really do find the doctrine of justification mentioned merely in the small print of footnotes or as dependent on the other doctrines of grace which are thought to be more fundamental to salvation. Our modern times have become quite barren of works on justification, the last major treatise on the subject being penned by Dr James Buchanan as long ago as 1866.[4] If there is a modern work which has bettered it, that work will be well-worth reading, but, I fear, none exists. This neglect of justification is also apparent in the commentaries and collection of sermons published by evangelical leaders throughout the last three hundred years.

Even where these leaders do take up the doctrine of justification in a more positive sense, it is often to depart widely from the Scriptural sources. We are now becoming used to nominally Reformed evangelists telling us that justification is a feast spread by God before us and all we have to do is grasp out and take it. They tell us that 'justification and eternal life are *absolutely given, granted, and promised*, to all who hear the gospel.'[5] If we followed this teaching, we could go a long, easy way in emptying hell as it would mean that all who came under the sound of the gospel would be automatically saved. These words were the basis for Andrew Fuller's duty-faith preaching, but true to his temperament of always reserving the freedom to change his mind for himself and the right to redefine his words, he tells us elsewhere that 'God justifies the ungodly' means that God justifies ungodly believers.[6] Those that God justifies are ungodly people who have, nevertheless, what Fuller called a 'holy disposition'. This is a novel interpretation which Fuller uses to

---

[4] (1804-1870). Buchanan's work was entitled *The Doctrine of Justification.*
[5] My emphasis. Fuller's *Works*, The Gospel Worthy of All Acceptation, vol. ii, p. 338.
[6] Ibid., vol. iii, *Remarks on God's Justifying the Ungodly*, p. 714 ff.

show how God's purpose and man's agency are combined in salvation. Justification and eternal life are given to the ungodly but holy person who manages, in spite of his ungodliness to believe and thus secure the 'gift, grant and promise'.

The doctrine of justification under fire
Another feature of this modern lack of teaching on justification is that, so often, where the doctrine is dealt with, it is done so in a negatively critical mood, striving to prove what justification is not rather than what it is. Such views will be dealt with as the argument of this book progresses. Sufficient be it to say at this point that, though modern critics of Gill reject his doctrine of justification as part of his 'strong Hyper-Calvinism', they do not refute it by establishing a more Biblical pattern but start what they call their 'assault on Hyper-Calvinism' by invariably quoting those who stand the Biblical doctrine of justification on its head, maintaining that God's decrees are fulfilled when the necessary human conditions are performed.[7] It could be said that we are almost as untaught today as to what justification really means, and its relationship to faith, as we were before Luther came on the scene and our preaching and teaching is all the poorer for this inexcusable ignorance.

Gill's practical teaching on justification could save us from church-splitting extremes
Anyone who has read my book *John Gill and The Cause of God and Truth* will realise that I think Gill is a most balanced scholar, pastor and evangelist who, thinking mainly of professing Calvinists at the moment,

---

[7] See Robert Oliver's article *Historical Survey of English Hyper-Calvinism*, Foundations, Issue No. 7, 1981, p. 8. ff. for a typical example of such folly. Oliver repeatedly in his articles, seeks to make Fuller, his chief Hyper-Calvinist-slayer, more respectable by associating him with Abraham Booth. Actually, Booth disagreed with Fuller on all the essentials of the gospel so that, according to Fuller, Booth thought he was lost. Oliver uses both Ivimey and Booth as evidence to show how Hyper-Calvinistic Gill was, yet Ivimey defends Gill, at times vigorously, against traditional criticisms of Hyper-Calvinists, though he does criticise him in other areas. Also, according to Ivimey, Booth was careful to explain that 'the doctrines of Calvinism according to the views of Dr Gill and Mr Brine' were not Antinomian, though Booth thought (wrongly) that William Huntington's were. See Joseph Ivimey, *History of the English Baptists*, vol. iv, pp. 76, 77.

steers clear of the cold, merely forensic, metaphysical and philosophical Calvinism of the more theoretical Supralapsarians on the one side and modern Fullerites or so-called 'Moderate Calvinists', with their religion of metaphors, on the other. Both these forms cannot compete with Gill's experimental, practical religion with its feet on the rock of God's Word without having its head in the scholastic and the symbolic, speculative theological clouds of those to its right and left. I do honestly believe that Gill's views on justification which I shall strive to present in a concentrated yet easily-digestible form, will assist the cause of God and truth in showing how the doctrine of justification gives us deeper insight into human needs and divine methods of meeting them. Gill introduced the subject of justification into most of his teaching and preaching because he saw that only a person who was acquitted from all his guilt could begin to live freely for Christ and rely on His righteousness. We cannot preach the gospel without showing sinners how to be rid of their sins and guilt and we cannot live out the gospel until we experience that Christ has perfectly redeemed us and clothed us with His righteousness. These factors are made clear in the preaching of justification more than any other doctrine.

A request for prayerful consideration

I would ask my fellow-Christians to consider the message of this book prayerfully as I outline Gill's doctrine of justification from eternity. I am sure that no Christian could reject this doctrine in its entirety, and all will find some comfort and instruction in it. Although I equally acknowledge that few Christians are prepared to accept it in its entirety today. I have been long persuaded myself that, as far as we can understand things clearly through the infirmities of our mortal bodies and the fact that we yet see in part only, the doctrine of justification from eternity is the only way of looking at this act and work[8] of God which provides us with clear gospel insight into how God accounts man just.

---

[8] It is usually maintained that justification is a mere *act* of God, declaring man merely *pro-forma* 'just' yet not effecting anything in him which, they explain, would be a 'work'. I have found no teacher of justification from eternity who would hold to this distinction which merely artificially separates one aspect of salvation from another.

The tercentenary of Gill's birth

John Gill was born on November 23, 1797. This means we are celebrating his tercentenary. His qualifications were considerable. Though not able to take up an academic career because of denominational prejudice at the time, Gill became a Greek and Hebrew scholar second to none. We see this in the way he was tackled by Wesley, no mean linguist himself. The Arminian tried to argue Gill into submission with his 'improvements' on the Authorized Version based on the best Greek and Hebrew he could muster. Gill told him that he was arguing like a first-year student whose zeal was greater than his knowledge and quickly out-Greeked and out-Hebrewed Wesley so the Methodist lost all his linguistic pride and retired from the battle with the best possible opinion of Gill's skills. Gill was a Baptist and worthy of all honour amongst that particular group as he was the best theologian they have ever had. He was the one who kept the whole Particular Baptist denomination free from the troubles that the General Baptists were going through for half a century. The banner Gill raised was quickly pulled down by his denomination in later years when they joined hands doctrinally with the General Baptists, but his successors in his Goat Yard, Carter Lane ministry still treasured his testimony up to the days of Spurgeon. The Evangelicals of the Anglican church as witnessed by Toplady, Hervey, Middleton, Maddox[9], Moses Brown, Jones and Venn, welcomed Gill and his theology with open arms so that he became one of the few Baptists to be greatly admired as a scholar and preacher outside of his denomination. Indeed, Gill's work in promoting fellowship among all the major denominations has yet to be adequately praised. And what shall we say of the tremendous written production which earned for Gill the title of Mr Voluminous?

A Festschrift indeed

Readers may doubt the practicability, and relevance of Gill's writings to deep Christian experience in view of a commonly held misunderstanding that Gill spent so much time in his study that he had no time for pastoral care. He was thus a theorist, it is maintained, and not a writer of experimental religion. This study will show that such fears are easily dispelled and Gill will be seen to be thoroughly reliable

---

[9] Sometimes spelt Maddock.

as a practical shepherd and a wise chronicler of experimental religion. All Gill's theological works were first preached before they were published and reflect a true pastoral heart and are full of good advice for facing the problems of living a life pleasing to God. Gill faithfully pastored the same flock for fifty-two years. A feat almost unknown amongst today's churches. His flock loved him so deeply and were so moved by every word that fell from his shepherding lips, that even when Gill became weak and feeble with old age, his people refused to appoint a new pastor at his earnest wish. They felt very strongly that what Gill could still give them was more precious than the words of any other pastor.

When I started on this work on Gill two years ago, I also had my misapprehensions because of the reserves just mentioned. I feared that what would be seen as a festschrift by many, might still be received as a streitschrift by some. Happily, now more and more are coming to read Gill for themselves and not merely the works of later influential writers who chose to contend with him. Gill is obviously coming back to his own again and this new and well deserved popularity has resulted in his works becoming freely available and at an extraordinary good price for solid hardbacks. Various news groups and historical symposiums on the Internet, numbering many hundreds if not several thousand of participants, have also been greatly instrumental in furthering a positive knowledge of Gill's life and works. Works by Gill's pen can now be downloaded from many web-sites. Indeed, a common love for Gill is now helping to heal former divisions amongst Reformed men and those Baptist churches which love the doctrines of grace but chose not to use the title 'Reformed' for historical reasons. Modern commentators such as Tom Nettles, Timothy George, Thomas Ascol, Gregory Wills and Sharon James have all produced highly positive works on Gill during the last few years which show him to be a spiritual giant and a mighty shepherd of souls. It is refreshing to know that lovers of the doctrines of grace in all the main protestant denominations are showing a renewed and marked interest in Gill's pastoral message. Thus, I trust that my present book will now be received as a festschrift indeed, in the full sense of the word i.e. as a celebration of the work and life of a great man of God who has a special message for these times.

This book has been chiefly written with Christians in view who are still marvelling at the work of God in their lives and His gracious love to them and are open and willing to lend an ear to good men of God in the past who may be able to help them in their walk of faith and in coming to a deeper knowledge of their Saviour's work on their behalf. The work is intended for the one who realises his own vileness before God and cannot possibly imagine, in the words of John Newton, that God could save a wretch like him. The aim is simply to show how salvation is all of grace and that God graciously fits out those whom He justifies to be eternal, heavenly citizens and to share the very inheritance that Christ took over at His ascension and is keeping habitable for us until we join Him for ever there. I believe that seldom has one been so mightily equipped by God for this task than John Gill. Few, as he, have been able so clearly to show sinners how to become right with God. Please bear prayerfully with me as I lay before you Gill's account of the badly neglected doctrine of justification from eternity and ask God for a blessing as you read. In this way, I am sure such a blessing will become yours and you will thus vouchsafe that Gill's labour, and thus also mine in compiling this book, has not been in vain in the Lord.

Chapter One

On Justifying Justification

Many years ago, I read an interesting booklet in the Swedish language entitled, when translated, *How Can the Reconciled be Reconciled?* It was an attempt to bring brethren together who were at loggerheads over the subject of how God reconciles sinners to Himself. It seems that the modern counterpart of this church-splitting debate now runs under the heading *How Can the Justified Justify Justification?* Since the Reformation revived the crucial doctrine of justification by faith, there have been far more views of justification propagated than there are denominations. The matter of justification may have caused our Reformers little difficulty but nowadays believers are burdened with countless more or less Calvinistic interpretations, a multiplicity of Lutheran interpretations, numerous Arminian interpretations and an enormous amount of Neonomian and Socinian ideas on the subject that are being disguised as 'evangelical' and even as 'evangelical Calvinist'. One might think that such a variety of views only makes Christian debate more attractive and that, in spite of minor differences, there is a large area of the debate where all Christians find common ground. For instance, it is difficult to imagine Christians questioning the need for justification or not viewing justification in relationship to the other benefits believers have in Christ. Human nature, however, finds disagreements far more interesting than agreements, as if disagreements made life more purposeful. The clear trend seems to be, however, that

23

the further away from the Reformation, the less Biblical content the
theories of justification have.

Early Reformed Attempts To Define Justification

The Thirty-Nine Articles
One of the earliest attempts to reach a consensus of opinion amongst
English-speaking Reformed believers and present an authoritative
definition of justification was Article XI of the 1563 Anglican *Thirty-
Nine Articles*, entitled 'Of the Justification of Man'. This stated:

> We are accounted righteous before God, only for the merit of
> our Lord and Saviour Jesus Christ by Faith, and not for our own
> works or deservings. Wherefore, that we are justified by faith
> only is a most wholesome doctrine, and very full of comfort, as
> more largely is expressed in the Homely of Justification.[10]

The benefit of this definition is its terseness and brevity, and that it
indicates where further teaching is available. It shows that justification
is an expression of faith in being accounted righteous, irrespective of
one's own deserts and this is due to the merits of Christ. The very
brevity of this definition is, however, its weakness. We are not told *who*
is accounted righteous nor *what* the merits of Christ are, nor *how* faith
is obtained, nor *when* justification takes place.

A Particular Baptist definition
In 1644 the London Particular Baptists produced an equally brief
definition of justification which, however, answered some of the points
left open by the Anglican creed. Article XXVIII reads:

> That those which have union with Christ, are justified from
> all their sinnes, past present and to come, by the bloud of Christ;
> which justification wee conceive to be a gracious and free
> acquittance of a guiltie, sinfull creature, from all sin by God

---

[10] Part of the *Homely on Salvation*. Philip Schaff *The Creeds of Christendom* vol. iii
(Michigan, 1990) p. 494.

through the satisfaction that Christ hath made by his death; and this applied in the manifestation of it through faith.[11]

Here we are told *who* the justified are, namely, those who have union with Christ. This would imply that justification does not bring union with Christ but that justification is given to those who are already united to Christ. According to Article III this union was established *from everlasting* by the immutable decree of God, thus answering the question *when*. We also see here *how* this justification becomes the sinner's, namely by the sacrificial satisfaction wrought out by Christ on the cross which is applied and manifested to the sinner by faith. This admirable piece of theological precision was, however, the work of a mere handful of London Baptist churches and sadly never found general approval amongst Christians in the major denominations.

The Westminster Confession
In order to establish such a general consensus of doctrine, the major denominations sent a number of their best thinkers, writers and preachers to take part in the Westminster Assembly which sat from 1643-46 in London, producing the famous *Westminster Confession*. This confession not only influenced the theological development of the Anglicans, Presbyterians and Independents but also led the London Particular Baptists to completely re-write their articles to tally with the *Westminster Confession*. Nowhere was this change more radical than in the 1644 Article on justification. In the *Second London Particular Baptist Confession* of 1677, it was completely scrapped and substituted by the very lengthy, but far less precise, Article on justification taken verbatim from the *Westminster Confession*.

The *Westminster Confession* reads:

> 1. Those whom God effectually calleth, he also freely justifieth: not by infusing righteousness into them, but by pardoning their sins, and by accounting and accepting their persons as righteous; not for anything wrought in them, or done by them, but for Christ's sake alone; not by imputing faith itself,

---

[11] William L. Lumpkin, *Baptist Confessions of Faith* (Valley Forge, 1969) p. 164.

the act of believing, or any other evangelical obedience to them, as their righteousness; but by imputing the obedience and satisfaction of Christ unto them, they receiving and resting on him and his righteousness by faith; which faith they have not of themselves, it is the gift of God.

2. Faith, thus receiving and resting on Christ and his righteousness, is the alone instrument of justification; yet is not alone in the person justified, but is ever accompanied with all the other saving graces, and is no dead faith, but worketh by love.

3. Christ, by his obedience, and death, did fully discharge the debt of all those that are thus justified, and did make a proper, real, and full satisfaction to his Father's justice in their behalf. Yet insomuch as he was given by the Father for them, and his obedience and satisfaction accepted in their stead, and both freely, not for anything in them, their justification is only of free grace; that both the exact justice and rich grace of God might be glorified in the justification of sinners.

4. God did, from all eternity, decree to justify all the elect; and Christ did, in the fulness of time, die for their sins and rise again for their justification: nevertheless they are not justified until the Holy Spirit doth, in due time, actually apply Christ unto them.

5. God doth continue to forgive the sins of those that are justified; and although they can never fall from the state of justification, yet they may by their sins fall under God's fatherly displeasure, and not have the light of his countenance restored unto them, until they humble themselves, confess their sins, beg pardon, and renew their faith and repentance.

6. The justification of believers under the Old Testament was, in all these respects, one and the same with the justification of believers under the New Testament.[12]

The definition of the *Westminster Confession* provides a good amount of detail which the Anglican definition lacks. It states *who* is accounted righteous, *what* the merits and work of Christ in the work of justification are and *how* these are imparted to the believer. The

---

[12] Philip Schaff op. cit. pp. 626-628. See Hendry's *The Westminster Confession for Today*.

relationship between faith and justification is established and it is clearly stressed that this justifying faith is a gift of God and in no way dependent on the merits of the sinner who is justified. This is all excellent material and worthy of all praise. There is, however, a marked piece of uncertainty reflected regarding *when,* or rather *from whence,* justification comes.

The problem of consensus-seeking
Clearly, what might be thought to speak against any doctrine of justification from eternity is Section 4 where the justification wrought out at Christ's death and resurrection does not become the sinner's until applied by the Holy Spirit in time. Thus the sinner is in one sense justified and in another sense not justified. Furthermore, there is no reference to union with Christ as being the basis for justification. This, for our purpose, rather unsatisfactory situation can be explained by viewing the circumstances under which the *Westminster Confession* was compiled. In its earliest stages, it was an illicit enterprise in the eyes of many as it was expressly carried out against the wishes of the King. Thus several very good men, such as Bishop Ussher, refused to join the committee responsible, arguing that it was an unlawful gathering. Furthermore, those members who did accept invitations were of exceedingly different theological backgrounds ranging from the high Calvinism of Twisse, who was its first Prolocutor to the surprisingly large body of what were called 'hypothetical universalists' and Neonomians led by Calamy with Seaman, Marshall and Vines assisting him. Indeed, according to the Scotsman Baillie, a committee member, the views of Amyraut were often aired in the debates and put forward as a basis for the confession. Perhaps this is one of the reasons why a few modern writers such as Dr Alan C. Clifford are arguing that genuine Reformed doctrine is Amyraldian which is tantamount to saying genuine Reformed doctrine is not Reformed. Baillie also confesses that the vast majority of committee members never said a word during the debates, but we know from the records that Calamy and his men were very verbal.

A number of debates which went on during the Westminster committee meetings must sound very contemporary to modern ears. Several members with Samuel Rutherford, circa 1600, as their spokesman, wished to include a clause concerning the universality of the offer of the gospel. This thrilled Calamy who quickly asserted that a universal redemption is requisite to give verity to the universal offer. So we see here that the Council of Dort meaning of 'to offer = to present' was already being altered and used as a reference to a universal atonement. This was a change in meaning against which Gill rightly protested and has earned for him the unfair tag of Antinomian ever since. However, Rutherford denied the logic of Calamy's suggestion, but given the changed meaning of 'offer', Calamy's logic cannot be denied, though his theology might be ever so poor. Seaman backed Calamy up here, arguing that Christ died to make all men salvable, as Adam had made all men damnable. Warfield comments, 'which one cannot believe was much of an aid to the cause he was advocating, as it involved a seriously low view of the effect of Adam's fall as well of Christ's redemption.'[13] Be this as it may, this low view of the effect of Adam's fall and of Christ's redemptive act is once again being traded as 'Strict Calvinism' and its proponents claim that they have the backing of the Council of Dort and the *Westminster Confession*. Perhaps this is why the *Second London Particular Baptist Confession* of 1677, which followed the *Westminster Confession* closely, wisely altered Article X 'Of the Gospel' with the words 'God … doth freely offer this salvation to all men in the gospel', placing the term 'offer' under Chapter VII 'Of God's Covenant'. Here salvation is offered within the covenant of grace with reference to 'all those that are ordained unto eternal life.' Chapter X thus became 'Of Effectual Calling'. 'Of the Gospel' is placed in Chapter XX and refers to the revelation of the gospel to the elect and not to a general offer to all sinners.

The Orthodox Creed
On January 30, 1678 fifty-four representatives of the Midland General Baptists met to form a defence against the heresies being spread in their churches by followers of Matthew Caffyn. A further aim was to offer

---

[13] See Warfield's, The Making of the Confession in his *The Westminster Assembly and its Work*, p. 141. For my remarks here, I am relying mainly on Warfield's, *The Westminster Assembly and its Work*, Hendry's *The Westminster Confession for Today*, Reid's *Memoirs of the Westminster Divines*, Lumpkin's *Baptist Confessions*, see Lumpkin op. cit. pp. 259, 260. Bicknell's *The Thirty-Nine Articles* and Thomas' *The Principles of Theology*. See Bibliography.

the right hand of fellowship to other churches, including the Calvinists, and also combat the errors of Rome. This gave rise to *An Orthodox Creed, or a Protestant Confession of Faith, Being an Essay to Unite and Confirm All True Protestants In the Fundamental Articles of the Christian Religion, Against the Errors and Heresies of Rome*. The authors do not disguise the fact that the creed is intended as an improvement on the *Westminster Confession*. Sensitive of the Arianism in both the Establishment and Dissent, the *Orthodox Creed* stresses the value of the Apostles', Nicene and Athanasian creeds. The compilers were most thorough in their work and added two Articles on Justification, one in relation to saving faith and one in relation to the work of Christ. Article XXIV 'Of Justification' by Christ reads:

Justification is a declarative, or judicial sentence of God the father, whereby he of his infinite love, and most free grace, for the alone and mediatorial righteousness of his own son, performed in our nature and stead, which righteousness of God man, the father imputing to us, and by effectual faith, received and embraced by us, doth free us by judicial sentence from sin and death, and accept us righteous in Christ our Surety, unto eternal life; the active and passive obedience of Christ being the accomplishment of all that righteousness and sufferings the law, or justice of God required, and this being perfectly performed by our mediator, in the very nature of us men, and accepted by the father in our stead, according to that eternal covenant-transaction, between the father and the son. And hereby we have deliverance from the guilt and punishment of all our sins, and are accounted righteous before God, at the throne of grace, by the alone righteousness of Christ the mediator, imputed, or reckoned unto us through faith; for we believe there are six necessary causes of man's justification, or salvation; viz.

First, The efficient cause of our justification, is God's free grace.
Secondly, The meritorious cause is the blood of Christ.
Thirdly, The material cause is Christ's active obedience.
Fourthly, The imputation of Christ, his obedience for us, is the formal cause.
Fifthly, The instrumental cause is faith.

Sixthly, God's glory, and man's salvation, is the final cause.

Now we principally apply the first and last to God the father; the second and third to Christ the mediator; the fourth and fifth to the blessed comforter, the holy ghost; hence it is we are baptized in the name of the father, of the son, and holy ghost, and so we worship a trinity in unity, and unity in trinity.[14]

Perhaps no other statement by leading Arminians ever came nearer to the Reformed faith and the truth that is in Jesus as this excellent declaration of faith. It is certain that this Arminian document is far more Calvinistic than much that is taught under the name of 'Evangelical Calvinism' today. It would be interesting to know when the act of grace on God's part referred to took place and again, astonishingly but encouragingly for an Arminian creed, Article IX 'Of Predestination and Election', speaks of predestination to life in the eternal purpose of God of those whom he elected in the mystical body of Christ before the foundations of the world and placed in an eternal covenant.[15] One can only conclude that those who compiled the *Orthodox Creed* believed in justification as an eternal decree of God. It is also interesting to note that although the authors speak dangerously of the sinner's 'improving on common grace', there is no talk of a 'universal offer' as such.

The Antinomian-Neonomian Controversy
By the time of the *Second London Confession*, the great Antinomian-Neonomian Controversy which grew out of these confessional debates was at its height in Britain. Herman Witsius (1636-1708) of Holland was invited to take on the role of Moderator as he was respected by all sides. This gave rise to Witsius' work *Conciliatory Animadversions on the Controversies agitated in Britain under the Names of Antinomians*

---

[14] William L. Lumpkin, *Baptist Confession of Faith*, p. 314, 315.
[15] I am in no way endorsing all that the *Orthodox Creed* maintains but must point out that this Arminian creed was in a number of doctrines more Reformed than the so-called Calvinistic creeds. Indeed, Ivimey, in his *History of the English Baptists*, confessed that he thought the *Orthodox Creed* was a Calvinistic creed. See Lumpkin p. 295 ff. for *Orthodox Creed*.

and Neonomians.[16] Witsius was surprised by the lack of Biblical understanding shown both by the alleged Antinomians and their alleged Neonomian brethren, particularly regarding election and justification. Both sides had seemingly no Biblical idea of eternity and had looked upon eternal election as God's will declared in an age before our age or in some other form of past time. They could not conceive as Witsius and Scripture that God is working His purpose out from eternity and this purpose is manifested in God's all-presence in time. Witsius was especially astonished that such a great intellect and theologian as Twisse could say in his *Vindiciis Gratiae* 'that it is not necessary directly to believe, that what is said to be before the foundation of the world, signifies to be before all time; but only before many ages.' Thus Twisse actually rejects the idea of election from eternity, placing election in time, arguing that this is the meaning of 'from the beginning' in 2 Thessalonians 2:13. Witsius hopes that Twisse will not apply this strange exegesis to the eternity of the Logos as the Socinians do.[17]

It must be regarded as something of a miracle that, given the conditions which included a great deal of political pressure to have things done quickly, the *Westminster Confession* resulted in such a masterful Body of Divinity. It was, however, a compromise from the start and obviously did not represent fully the views of any party, whether right or wrong.

The rule of three
Since those far off days, the churches have striven to work out better definitions but few improvements have ensued and we are left today with a large percentage of Anglicans, Presbyterians, Independents and Baptists who shy away from any 'definitions' and cannot even accept the simple creeds of their fathers as a basis of faith. Traditionally speaking amongst Reformed theologians, justification is almost always viewed in three parts, although these parts vary. Scholars speak, for instance, of justification being *effected* as a direct decision of God;

---

[16] I have not been able to date this moderating work exactly but it probably occurred in 1685 when Witsius was for a short time chaplain to the embassy of the Dutch Provinces in London.

[17] I am chiefly dependent on Witsius' *The Economy of the Covenants Between God and Man* for his views concerning eternity. See especially vol. i, Book III, Chap. IV, p. 333 and Book II, Chap. III, p. 177 ff.

declared when the sinner is made aware of the fact in his conscience and consciousness; and *operated* in its outworking in faith and through the inner work of the Holy Spirit. Others speak of the *ground of justification*; seen variously as Christ's obedience unto death for the sake of His elect and in the imputed righteousness of Christ; the *nature of justification* which is seen as pardon or non-imputation of guilt and being accepted as righteous and the *condition of justification*. There are many varieties of the latter from the passive and active obedience of Christ to exercising duty faith, according to how 'high' or 'low' one is along the Calvinist line. Those who have crossed the Calvinistic line completely into Arminian and Socinian domains speak of the condition of justification being faith as standing in lieu of perfect obedience. Another group of three, represented by Louis Berkhof, places the *means of justification* where others place the conditions and see this as 'man is justified freely by that faith which receives and rests in Christ only for salvation.'[18] A common Anglican view of a three-fold understanding of justification looks to the related meaning of justification and righteousness in the Biblical languages. They thus see the entire work of justification as: a. To be justified, which is God's decision in a person's favour to free him from penalty and give him a claim to an eternal inheritance; b. To be accounted righteous because Christ stands in the stead of all believers and c. To receive the gift of righteousness in the form of Christ's righteousness imputed to the justified sinner.[19] Robert Traill (1642-1716) taught that there is a. 'a decreed justification from eternity, particular and fixed, as to all the elect;' b. 'a virtual, perfect justification of all the redeemed, in and by the death and resurrection of Jesus Christ;' and c. 'a sinner, for his actual justification, must lay hold on and plead this redemption in Christ's blood by faith.'[20] John Gill also saw justification in a three-fold capacity which he explained as a. an eternal, immanent act in God; b. as a declarative act to and upon the conscience of the believer through the instrument of faith; and c. as the final confirmation declared to men and angels at the

---

[18] Louis Berkhof, *Systematic Theology*, p. 512.
[19] See the chapter 'Justification, according to the New Testament', in *Synonyms of the Old Testament: Their Bearing in Christian Faith and Practice*, R. B. Girdlestone, Longmans, Green & Co., 1871.
[20] The Doctrine of Justification Vindicated from the Charge of Antinomianism, p. 318. *Works of the Late Rev. Robert Traill*, vol. i, 1795.

last judgment.[21] Gill sees justification as fitting the elect out for their never-ending inheritance. It begins in timeless eternity from whence God always decrees and acts and it continues in eternity when the elect receive the heavenly estate reserved for the justified. He thus calls this doctrine appropriately *justification from eternity*.

Witsius on justification

Gill, along with a team of multi-denominational friends, re-introduced the works of Herman Witsius (1636-1708) into England and this Dutch scholar has strongly influenced British and American Reformed theology in the past. Witsius offers perhaps the most complicated system of justification of all Reformed writers.[22] He maintains that justification is an essential part of the covenant of grace which is secured in Christ outside of time, that is, in eternity. This eternal decree is operated in time from eternity in various dispensations or periods in the history of salvation. He counts no less than seven such periods, the first two being the *general* justification of the elect and the succeeding five periods signify *particular* justification. The first period refers to justification through the 'suretyship of Christ, whereby he took upon himself all the sins of the elect, and on account of which God declared, he never intended to exact them from any of his chosen; because, on admitting a Surety, the principle debtor is freed from all obligation to make satisfaction. And this is the first effect of Christ's suretyship, the declaration of that counsel of God, by which he had purposed to justify the ungodly; and not impute sin to those who are inserted as heirs in the testament.' Witsius argues that this part of the divine plan of justification was effected when it was needed, i.e. after the fall. It was an infralapsarian plan which was effected as soon as man sinned. Witsius argues in this way as there was no need for justification to absolve man until man sinned in Adam his federal head. Witsius' second period of general justification was when 'God was in Christ, reconciling the world unto himself, not imputing their trespasses unto them' (2 Corinthians 5:19). Witsius takes 'the world' here to be the world of the elect, and non-imputation is, for him, justification. The third period for Witsius is at conversion when the elect person receives

[21] *Sermons and Tracts*, vol. ii, pp. 459, 460.
[22] See vol. i *Economy of the Covenants*, chap. VIII Of Justification.

a living faith and the application of justification reserved for him in Christ. He is now declared pardoned in the court of heaven and free from God's wrath and placed in God's special favour. The fourth stage is the outworking of the gift of faith on the conscience of the pardoned one so that the believer knows, feels and experiences that he is justified. The believer has been now actively justified when he was yet ungodly and passively justified when faith was given him. This is an important factor to note as modern Hyper-Calvinist hunters look upon the doctrine of passive and active justification as a symbol of Supralapsarianism and thus Hyper-Calvinism. Both Witsius and Gill, however were sub or infralapsarians, yet they held to an active and passive doctrine of justification. The fifth stage for Witsius comes when the believer is admitted to a 'familiar converse with God' and real joy in believing ensues. The sixth stage arrives when at death, the elect are received by God and the seventh follows at the day of judgment when the elect will be publicly justified and declared heirs of eternal life. One could sum up Witsius' view of justification in the words, 'God is always justifying His elect.' It appears that Gill leaned heavily on Witsius in his treatment of justification but strove to simplify him on the tripartite lines of traditional British Reformed thinking.

Louis Berkhof on justification

One of the most acceptable Reformed definitions of justification in the English-speaking churches of more recent times is that of Louis Berkhof, a theologian of Dutch descent whose *Systematic Theology*[23] became the bestselling hardback of any the Banner of Truth produced. It has also been my own constant companion for thirty-eight years. I was brought up in a Holiness Mission background, and have no complaints about the sweet fellowship of those brethren but when my young eyes read Berkhof, I began to see the true depth and breadth of God's mercies. Berkhof says on the subject:

> Justification is a judicial act of God, in which He declares, on the basis of the righteousness of Jesus Christ, that all the claims of the law are satisfied with respect to the sinner. It is unique in the application of the work of redemption in that it is a judicial

---

[23] First issued 1941. Re-issued in 1959 by the Banner of Truth Trust.

act of God, a declaration respecting the sinner, and not an act or process of renewal, such as regeneration, conversion, and sanctification. While it has respect to the sinner, it does not change his inner life. It does not affect his condition, but his state, and in that respect differs from all the other principal parts of the order of salvation. It involves the forgiveness of sins, and restoration to divine favour. The Arminian holds that it includes only the former, and not the latter; but the Bible clearly teaches that the fruit of justification is much more than pardon. They who are justified have 'peace with God', 'assurance of salvation', Romans 5:1-10, and an 'inheritance among them that are sanctified', Acts 26:18.[24]

This is meat indeed, but the men of Berea amongst us would still like to know the relationship between justification and faith and where justification can be placed in God's programme of salvation. Berkhof does not disappoint us. Though he explains what the grounds, nature and means of justification are, he looks at the doctrine from the active standpoint of God in what he terms 'His tribunal' and then from the passive side as man experiences the gifts of God. He thus speaks of:

1. Active or objective justification
This is justification in the most fundamental sense of the word. It is basic to what is called subjective justification, and consists in a declaration which God makes respecting the sinner, and this declaration is made in the tribunal of God. This declaration is not a declaration in which God simply acquits the sinner, without taking any account of the claims of justice, but is rather a divine declaration that, in the case of the sinner under consideration, the demands of the law are met. The sinner is declared righteous in view of the fact that the righteousness of Christ is imputed to him. In this transaction God appears, not as an absolute Sovereign who simply sets the law aside, but as a righteous Judge who acknowledges the infinite merits of Christ as a sufficient basis for

---

[24] All quotes from Berkhof are taken from his *Systematic Theology* p. 510 ff. and his *The History of Christian Doctrine*, Banner of Truth Trust, 1969, p. 204 ff. Much of the material overlaps.

justification, and as a gracious Father who freely forgives and accepts the sinner. This active justification logically precedes faith and passive justification. We *believe* the forgiveness of sins.

2. Passive or subjective justification
Passive or subjective justification takes place in the heart or conscience of the sinner. A purely objective justification that is not brought home to the sinner would not answer the purpose. The granting of a pardon would mean nothing to a prisoner, unless the glad tidings were communicated to him and the doors of the prison were opened. Moreover, it is exactly at this point that the sinner learns to understand better than anywhere else that salvation is of free grace. When the Bible speaks of justification, it usually refers to what is known as passive justification. It should be borne in mind, however, that the two cannot be separated. The one is based on the other. The distinction is simply made to facilitate the proper understanding of the act of justification. Logically, passive justification follows faith; we are justified by faith.[25]

Here, Berkhof clearly states that the objective activation of justification must be before faith as it proceeds from God's declared will. What God wills is done, this is why the Christian, in keeping with this divine attribute, prays 'Thy will be done on earth *as it is in heaven.*' This is an important factor to note as Berkhof's view of God's active, objective will in justification is being seriously challenged at the present time in the very circles who jubilantly promoted his works in the late fifties and sixties. This doctrine, however, is certainly truly Calvinistic and is very much part of John Gill's doctrine of justification. This is no surprise as Berkhof obviously built on the faith of his fathers.

Berkhof on the timing of God's blessings in Christ
There is, however, still a tiny question in the Berean mind as to the timing of justification. We now know that we must view justification as being activated objectively in the mind and will of God and it is thus before faith but when does this take place in relation to the other

---

[25] *Systematic Theology*, p. 517.

benefits we have in Christ? Obviously such thinking is rather pointless as we are thus expecting God, who is in eternity, to conform Himself to thinking in time relationships. Nevertheless, Berkhof seeks to find a starting-point for the mind of God at work in redemption. In his *History of Christian Doctrines*, he has weighed the Lutheran order of salvation and found it wanting in certain aspects and then goes on to say under the title 'The Reformed Order of Salvation':

> In Reformed theology the *ordo salutis* acquired a somewhat different form. This is due to the fact that Calvin consistently took his starting-point in an eternal election and in the mystical union established in the *pactum salutis*. His fundamental position is that there is no participation in the blessings of Christ, except through a living union with the Saviour. And if even the very first of the blessings of saving grace already presupposes a union with Christ, then the gift of Christ to the Church and the imputation of His righteousness precedes all else. In the Council of Peace a union was already established between Him and those who were given unto Him by the Father, and in virtue of that union, which is both legal and mystical, all the blessings of salvation are ideally already the portion of those who are of Christ. They are ready for distribution and are appropriated by them through faith.
>
> From this fundamental position several particulars follow.

> The salvation of the elect is not conceived atomistically, since they are all eternally in Christ, and are born out of Him, who is the Head, as members of His mystical body. Regeneration, repentance, and faith are not regarded as mere preparations, altogether apart from any union with Christ, nor as conditions to be fulfilled by man, either wholly or in part, in his own strength. They are blessings of the covenant of grace, which already flow from the mystical union and the grant of Christ to the Church. Penitence assumes a different place and character than in the Lutheran order. Calvin recognized a repentance preceding faith, but saw in it merely an initial fear, a legal repentance that does not necessarily lead to faith and cannot be regarded as an absolutely essential preparation for it. He stresses the repentance that flows from faith, that is possible only in communion with

Christ, and that continues throughout life. Moreover, he does not regard it as consisting of *contritio* and *fides*. He recognises the close connection between repentance and faith, and did not consider the former possible without the latter, but also pointed out that Scripture clearly distinguishes the two, and therefore ascribed to each of them a more independent significance in the order of salvation.[26]

Berkhof thus sees our inheritance in Christ starting from the doctrine of eternal election and in the mystical union which he sees as a living union with the Saviour in which all the blessings of salvation are already the portion of the elect. Here we have the doctrine of salvation from eternity, including every single blessing that Christ has in store for us. It is interesting that there is a slight criticism of Calvin's doctrine of repentance employed in Berkhof's account of the order of salvation and indeed it is Calvin's doctrine of repentance (claimed by some to be too 'legal') that is seen today, paradoxically enough, as a sign of Hyper-Calvinism. Gill shared Berkhof's mild censure of Calvin here and applied the same active and passive factors regarding repentance that he did justification, now looking at it from the active, objective side, now the operative, subjective side. Berkhof is in full agreement with Gill here that all the blessings of Christ centre on God's initial act of eternal election.

Berkhof outlines various arguments, including his own, against justification from eternity
Though Berkhof outlines the order of salvation and all its blessings in the section he has reserved for justification as being an act of God's election of His people to salvation, the word justification is conspicuous by its absence in the passage. All Berkhof is prepared to say on justification after the above quote is that he sees it as a single act of God. We presume that this is in conjunction with the act that provides all the blessings of salvation referred to above but Berkhof does not expressly say so. His reason can be inferred from the following pages where he outlines his fears of Antinomianism and in his section on 'The Time of Justification' in his *Systematic Theology*. Though Berkhof's

---

[26] *History of Christian Doctrine*, op. cit. p. 219, 220.

doctrine of justification, as also salvation is so close to Gill's, what he says concerning Antinomians has been automatically taken up as a criticism of John Gill because Berkhof says these Antinomians believe in the doctrine of justification from eternity, which is the name Gill gives to his own doctrine of justification. Berkhof explains that 'Some reformed theologians also speak of justification from eternity, but at the same time refuse to subscribe to the Antinomian construction of this doctrine.'

Such warnings from Berkhof's pen against tarring all with the same brush because they define God's eternal, active, and objective act (with which Berkhof agrees) as justification from eternity (a term which Berkhof chooses not to use), fall on remarkably deaf ears nowadays and there is a small group of nominal Calvinists who are campaigning to declare the doctrine of justification from eternity as heretical because they strongly feel it is Antinomian and Hyper-Calvinistic. This group have chosen John Gill, with William Huntington running a close second, as their proto-type of an Antinomian. In combating such men, however, it is becoming increasingly clear that they are, in reality, revising the whole doctrine of justification which has been staunchly held by traditional Calvinists, including Berkhof, from the Reformation until today. In principle it is a contra-Reformation movement. As there is no doctrine of salvation which is not linked to justification as an act of God's will, all the Five Points of Calvinism are being reviewed and revised in the name of 'Evangelical Calvinism' or 'Moderate Calvinism' with the result that the traditional Calvinistic views of not only justification but atonement, ransom, redemption, imputation, satisfaction, reconciliation, sanctification and the work of the Holy Spirit are being re-defined, one by one as 'Hyper-Calvinist'. Meanwhile, as this group, in their zeal, revise doctrine after doctrine, they distance themselves from not only Calvinism but the great saving doctrines of the Bible. Once these doctrines are given up, man's fallen rationalism knows no end until now we find teaching that Jesus had a different will to His father and that the Bible is full of paradox and irreconcilable contradictions.[27] This movement, though it contains

---

[27] See article by David Gay, *Banner of Truth*, Issue 371-372, p. 42 ff. and Gay's review of Iain Murray's work of historical revisionism entitled 'Spurgeon versus Hyper-Calvinism' *Evangelical Times*, August, 1996, p. 19.

some of the once most respected men in Reformed circles, has now dropped its normal church ministry and has become merely a *Society For the Suppression of Antinomianism* which is rapidly changing into a *Society for the Promotion of Amyraldianism.* They have allowed themselves the freedom of keeping their definitions of Antinomianism and Neonomianism so open and elastic and so indefinite that they always mean to them 'those who disagree with us'.

With this in mind, it is very important that we note how Berkhof feels Antinomianism is usually defined before going on to his own rather uncertain view both of which in no way can be seen as a criticism of John Gill's well-founded doctrine of justification. First Berkhof gives generally held views of the relationship between Antinomianism, justification and righteousness.

1. Antinomians hold that the justification of a sinner takes place in eternity or in the resurrection of Christ.

2. They confuse justification with the eternal decree of election, or with the objective justification of Christ when he was raised from the dead.

3. They do not distinguish properly between the divine purpose in eternity and its execution in time.

4. Nor in the work of Christ in procuring, and that of the Holy Spirit in applying the blessings of redemption.

5. Justification, for Antinomians, comes in its entirety before belief and faith simply declares this fact to us.

6. The Antinomian doctrine of imputation makes Christ a sinner and ourselves inherently righteous.

Berkhof sums up all these arguments in affirming that the Antinomians fail to distinguish between the counsel of God and its execution.

Berkhof shows a surprising amount of sympathy with these views, outlining their alleged Biblical basis but concludes 'It is hardly correct, however, to speak of justification as an *actus immanens* in God; it is rather an *actus transiens*, just as creation, incarnation and so on.' Berkhof allows that his supposed Antinomians do distinguish between the intention of God in the divine decree and the enacting of it. This confession rather weakens the above definition of Antinomianism and obviously shows that Berkhof does not wish to appear one-sided or over-dogmatic. Berkhof now goes on to add his own criticisms of

Antinomians which again weaken the above definitions and suggest that Berkhof has really no strong arguments against justification from eternity at all apart from his associating *some* Antinomians with that doctrine.

He argues:

1. Justification takes place by faith or out of faith according to its being viewed actively or passively. Antinomians accept this only in part as they represent it as meaning that man merely becomes conscious of what God has done in eternity when faith comes. Berkhof says that it is impossible to separate the active and passive outworkings of justification. He then surprisingly adds, 'except in the case of children'. This is because of Berkhof's own very private and most extraordinary view that whereas adults must be justified with faith, children are justified without it. One can imagine Gill raising his hands with horror at such a distinction!

2. In Romans 8:29, 30 justification stands between calling and glorification. Calling, Berkhof maintains, begins in time and glorification ends in eternity, therefore justification can only be viewed in time. Gill would argue here, as will be explained at length later, that effectual calling is a matter of God acting from eternity.

3. What took place in eternity in what Berkhof calls the *pactum salutis*, cannot be identified with what results from it. (Presumably here, the author means 'results in time'.) This is a strange argument indeed as it postulates no identification between cause and effect. Light came because God said, 'Let there be light!' Surely the light was in the mind of God and His will at least as He spoke those creative words in eternity. Berkhof then adds 'All imputation is not justification. Justification is one of the fruits of Christ's redemptive work, applied to believers by the Holy Spirit. But the Spirit did not and could not apply this or any other fruit of the work of Christ from eternity.'[28]

---

[28] See *Systematic Theology*, p. 514, 517-520.

Where Berkhof's arguments might touch Gill

In the process of this work, Gill's doctrine of justification will be compared with Berkhof's from time to time as it will be compared with his traducers'. Sufficient be it to say at this point that if Gill were to be called upon to view Berkhof's arguments critically, he would find a great deal with which he could agree wholeheartedly, a few points where he would give Berkhof the benefit of the speculative doubt but also point out that Berkhof, on occasions, is letting his philosophical view of time and eternity confuse the Biblical issue. He would also, in true pastoral and caring strictness, tell Berkhof that he ought to make up his own mind on the issue before beating about the bush in the open forum of a book.

This present work on Gill's doctrine of justification will show that Berkhof's strictures concerning Antinomians only touch Gill in a few areas where Gill is quite able to defend his point adequately, which in his case means, Biblically. Berkhof has admitted that the belief in justification from eternity does not automatically make one an Antinomian and the belief in a substitutionary justification with Christ at the resurrection, though not Gill's view stated in such terms, is such a widespread view even amongst critics of Antinomianism that it can hardly be considered a commonly recognised feature of law-haters. Gill's view of election, one would think is quite akin to Berkhof's though Berkhof obviously formally disagrees with this point against supposed Antinomians as the above quote on eternal election from his works shows.

Election is not a vessel in which one finds everything necessary to salvation

Gill, as we shall see, is very cautious of using election as a vessel in which he finds everything, so that there is virtually no need for the atoning death of Christ, reconciliation and the work of the Holy Spirit. In his own day, he criticised those who saw sanctification as a work proposed and finished in the decree of God with no operative and applying function in the believer and likewise criticised those who profanely thought the Holy Spirit was unemployed. Modern Don Quixotes who spot the windmill of Antinomianism around every corner and charge at it in full power, vociferously argue that Gill sees faith as but 'a notion' but Mrs Alexander's little book which received so much praise from Dr Martyn Lloyd-Jones, who supplied the Foreword, shows that unquestionably, the faith that Gill, Romaine, Toplady, Huntington, Gadsby, Philpot and others with whom Lloyd-Jones was not ashamed to associate himself was 'More than Notion' as Joseph Hart (himself a Gillite) says in his truly experimental hymn. At times, it appears that Berkhof sees justification in exactly the same way as Gill, arguing that 'Justification is essentially an objective declaration respecting the sinner in the tribunal of God, but it is not merely that, it is also an *actus transiens*, passing into the consciousness of the believer.'[29] This 'consciousness' for both Gill and Berkhof refers not to mere notions but a true faith in union with the Lord Jesus Christ based on a conviction of forgiven sins and favour with God.

Problems concerning Berkhof's view of imputation, active and passive justification, 'fruit' and chronology

Berkhof's statement concerning imputation is something of a *non sequitur*. The very idea of imputation is that one is considered under the demerits or the merits of another, thus ruling out that Christ died for His own sins (what a blasphemous thought!) and that the sinner is saved because of his own righteousness (what a hopelessly ridiculous thought!). Nevertheless, all Christians, one would expect, are united in believing that when God looks on the elect, He finds no sin in them as they are clothed with Christ's justifying righteousness. If God still considers a sinner in his sins, then that sinner is not justified.

When we come to Berkhof's own arguments against Antinomians we find him more speculative than Biblical. His argument that it is impossible to distinguish between God's active and passive justification, raises the question why he, himself has done so. For Gill, it is not at all impossible to see justification from eternity as being an effective product of eternity yet justification by faith as its operative outcome in time. If we are to distinguish between time and eternity, and it is certainly Biblically and philosophically impossible not to, then we must accept that whatever happens in time for our salvation, God has worked it out in eternity. Berkhof is perhaps unwise to refer so often to justification as a 'fruit'. A fruit normally grows out of something and is a product of it, whereas justification is an original declaration of God

---

[29] See *Systematic Theology*, p. 315.

saying that this man is pardoned and judged guiltless, therefore he is justified. This is an act of grace rather than a fruit of such an act. Being justified, however, ought to bear its rightful fruit in living a God-honouring life, which Gill is always eager to teach.

Berkhof's supposed chronological list of Christ's blessings (calling, justifying, glorifying) being given one after the other over a period of time falls quite flat, as we shall see when Gill takes up this argument, as even Paul gives a different order to these events in several cases elsewhere according to the emphasis he wishes to make, which rarely seems to be a chronological one.

Most puzzling is again, Berkhof's words concerning imputation in his own arguments against his obvious 'paper' Antinomians. His words 'All imputation is not justification' could only be applied as a criticism of justification if Berkhof's supposed Antinomians argued for imputed justification. The only place they could possibly argue for this would be if Antinomians claimed that God's justification of Christ at the resurrection was imputed to the elect. Berkhof, however, says that Antinomians look upon this as 'objective justification'. Gill certainly believed in imputed righteousness as the grounds of his justification but he saw justification as being actual because of this and not as a further imputation.

Where Berkhof agrees with Gill

Berkhof's final argument concerning the work of the Holy Spirit also falls quite flat in Gill's case as he preaches forcefully, faithfully and often on the work of the Holy Spirit in convicting sinners and building up the saints. Here again, Berkhof is apparently contradicting himself as he says elsewhere in his *Systematic Theology* concerning justification and sanctification, 'While the meritorious cause of both lies in the merits of Christ, there is a difference in the efficient cause. Speaking economically, God the Father declares the sinner righteous, and the Holy Spirit sanctifies him.'[30] This is *exactly* Gill's view on the matter. He sees the work of the entire Trinity in redemption and views the Spirit as applying to the believer what has already been wrought out for him but also looks to the Holy Spirit for sanctification which Gill argues is different from justification. This doctrine may not be

---

[30] See *Systematic Theology*, p. 514.

acceptable to all but the fact that James Hervey held it, though he did not believe in what he called 'eternal justification', shows how careful we should be in our use of the term 'Antinomian'. A personal confession of this writer is perhaps in place here. I have been an avid reader of theological works throughout four decades, but must confess that I have never, ever found one single believer whose ideas correspond to the scores of paper Antinomians I have seen defined throughout this period. It seems to me that God, in His grace, permits and uses these definitions to keep us from becoming castaways and they thus serve a very good purpose.

Reconciling the Antinomian-hunters
Dealing with these various ideas of what Antinomianism might be reminds me of my university lectures on the Hebrew text of Isaiah at Uppsala university. Our lecturer was certain that Isaiah had a multiple authorship but all the evidence he gave us was so chaotic, no two 'scholars' agreeing on who wrote what and when, so that the whole critical exercise became a farce. This is most surely true of the modern theological fashion of Antinomian-bashing. These people invariably see Antinomianism and Hyper-Calvinism as synonyms though definitions of the one are as elusive as the other. The one says it is 'Hyper' to believe in the eternal love of God for His elect, the other protests against this definition and says that a Hyper-Calvinist does not believe in human ability. The inability of a human being to do anything towards his own salvation is, however, accepted as 'orthodox' by others who say that their lawless 'Hyper' is rather one who preaches election and predestination as part of the gospel. Actually, as I have found out over the years, there is no single orthodox Christian doctrine which somebody does not think is Antinomian or Hyper-Calvinistic. This led Pastor Jim North to publicly appeal to readers of the *Evangelical Times*[31] to come forward with a definition of Hyperism which could have common approval from Reformed Christians. He also, rather daringly, asked for the names of those who teach these doctrines. The response shows that though readers seem to know what Calvinism is, they can neither define Hyper-Calvinism nor Antinomianism.

---

[31] September, 1996, p. 20.

The great Robert Traill sought in his century to gather up all the accusations of Antinomianism he could against the London clergy and found that not one of them fitted the categories defined and that all the allegations were groundless. Likewise, suggestions and insinuations in other magazines such as the *Banner of Truth, Foundations* and *Reformation Today* concerning Gill, Huntington, Brine and Romaine have revealed what an enormous ignorance of these men's works exist and how groundless such charges of Hyperism and Antinomianism can be. No definition has come from their pens since Iain Murray's abortive attempt in the July, 1988 issue of the *Banner of Truth* magazine when hundreds of perfectly orthodox subscribers and former article writers awoke to the 'fact' that they were considered Antinomians.

Is the *via negationis* the right way?
Because of the feelings involved in the modern Antinomian controversy, it has become almost impossible to judge justification Biblically and objectively. To be on the safe side and tread on no toes, Reformed theologians have become wary of bringing justification into contact with gospel doctrines at all and now tend to view the topic completely apart from the eternal will of God and the efficacious work of Christ. John Murray has some fine things to say about the blessings of justification but when it comes to definitions, Murray, in the second volume of his *Systematic Theology*, chooses to view justification not only apart from the work of salvation as a whole, but also views it merely as being accomplished in time with no reference to eternity at all. After quoting Buchanan, who obviously cannot view justification apart from God's entire plan of salvation, Murray says:

> Justification is not the eternal decree of God with respect to us, nor is it the finished work of Christ for us, when once-for-all he reconciled us to God by his death; nor is it the regenerative work of God in us, nor is it any activity on our part in response to and embrace of the gospel, but it is an act of God, accomplished in time wherein God passes judgment with respect to us as individuals.[32]

---

[32] Murray, op. cit. p. 203.

Obviously, Mr Murray is wishing to stress that justification is purely the will of God for His elect and we need ask for no other reason. Theoretically, this is no doubt true, but the Scriptures are always practical and never give us a dry, theoretical, legal verdict like this but they produce gospel evidence. Nor is this gospel evidence merely negative in the sense that it tells us what justification is not, rather than what it is. Indeed, whenever the Scriptures speak of justification, as will be seen, they speak of it being demonstrated to us by God's acts in eternity and by Christ's work on the cross. The story of justification, according to Scripture, cannot be separated from God's positively and actively willing it in eternity and providing the Sacrifice of Sacrifices to attain it in time. God obviously has sympathy with us men of little faith who cannot believe blindly and He gives us solid reasons for our being justified which are intrinsically bound up with His eternal work in salvation on which grounds He justifies us. Older writers from Calvin, through Gill to Berkhof, always anchored their teaching on justification in what God has worked out in order to declare His people righteous. To say that 'Justification is not the eternal decree of God with respect to us' makes no sense in view of all the many passages in the Bible which link our justification totally with those decrees and God's acts in eternity. To come down from the philosophical heights and speak in terms of common sense, we must ask, 'If our justification is not a matter of eternity, is not the only alternative a temporal and thus temporary justification which is no justification at all?'

Returning to the origins of justification for motivation to sanctification
To follow Scripture to the origin rather than the reception of justification is especially important today in preaching the full gospel of the doctrines of grace. Our once Reformed churches are now full of preaching which says God's provisions must be met by human agency. Thus what God does neither effects nor alters anything, but what man accepts effects and alters all. Furthermore, the idea is widespread in our churches that God decides to justify us on the grounds of what happens in time. This is Hyper-Arminianism but we read this in many once Reformed magazines.

There is a further danger. If we are to preach that believers are justified, irrespective of God's electing will and our union with Christ, what motivation for living a righteous life with our Saviour do we have? Are we then pronounced just by an arbitrary fiat and left on our own without knowing the origin, plan and purpose of it? Must not practical Antinomianism be the result of this? Where, too, is faith in relation to justification in this system of things?

Murray does try very hard to bring the gospel truths home to the justified in his commentary on his definition of justification but he always skirts the effecting and operating nature of justification and stresses merely its formal aspects. Indeed, he denies outright on several occasions that justification is anything but judicial. Now John Gill did not agree here. He believed that justification in its origin was primarily judicial as an act of grace but an activity was set in motion before the dawn of time to open the eyes of the believer to the righteousness he had in Christ and to the active holy life which this entails. He believed justification was a very practical judgment of God. It was not merely *pro-forma* and an entering of the name of a newly acquitted person into the Lamb's Book of Life when faith in God's justification was given. It was an active revelation of the inheritance eternally reserved for the elect. It was a spiritual coming of age so that the sinner could enter into the eternal joys of covenant blessings, reserved for him in timeless immanence with Christ and yet declare Christ's righteousness to the world of time. On the same page as his definition, Murray quotes Romans 3:24-26, which explains all, though Murray does not utilise this explanation: 'Whom God hath set forth to be a propitiation through faith in his blood, to declare his righteousness for the remission of sins that are past, through the forbearance of God; To declare, I say, at this time his righteousness: that he might be just, and the justifier of him which believeth in Jesus'. There we have it! Justification, is not a mere act of God in time with reference to an individual sinner but it is a great testimony to the wondrous works of God in Christ and to the justifying righteousness of His Son. That these works were enacted from eternity from whence the believer's union with Christ was effected is the clear teaching of Scripture, however time-bound our individual conceptions may be. Romans 3 also says, 'Let God's word be true but every man a liar; as it is written, That thou mightest be justified in thy sayings, and mightest overcome when thou art judged.' Justification has no locked door after it. It leads to faith, sanctification, a life of triumph and glorification.

Personal testimonies to the benefits of Gill's teaching, past and present

This introduction of the problems involved in defining justification leads me on to my last point and, again, a most personal testimony. Given the fact that we see through a glass darkly and none of us will ever have the privilege of full insight into this world marred by sin until we enter into our rest, I find in the vast and varied works of John Gill on justification a body of effective evidence which is as compelling as it is convincing. I believe also that its highly motivating power speaks to the present age with the same clarity and unction that it spoke to the world of two hundred and fifty years ago. Perhaps I can explain this by two examples, one from December 26, 1767 and one from October 21, 1996. The first quote is from Augustus M. Toplady's diary and reads:

> Gave Dr. Gill's tract on Justification another reading; not without much edification and comfort. I do think that this great man's arguments for the proper eternity of this blessing, *ex parte Dei*, are unanswerable. Glory be to thee, O Lord, for my sense of special interest in thy everlasting love! Were all the treasures of ten thousand worlds displayed to my view, the sight of them, the mere sight, would not make me the richer nor the happier; it is the knowledge of peculiar property in any blessing, that felicitates the soul. In this the comfort lies. And, thanks to divine grace, I can look upon all the unsearchable riches of Christ, as my own. Lord, increase my faith, and add to my thankfulness more and more.[33]

The following testimony was sent to me by a bright, young Christian via my e-mail address over the Internet whilst I was working on this introduction:

> I recall reading Gill's work on justification some years ago. It revolutionised my understanding of the grace of God and warmed my heart immensely to realise that the whole plan of salvation was so secure and unalterable. Those who believe that

---

[33] *Works*, p. 7. Sprinkle Publications, Harrisonburg, Virginia, 1987.

49

we are justified when we believe are hinging a change in God upon a change in man's will. It cannot be for we must at the very least be justified before God at our regeneration which must predate our conversion.

Viewing the criticisms of Gill's friends

I explained in the Introduction that I initially feared that some would take this book to be not only a *Festschrift* but a *Streitschrift* and further reasons for this anxiety which has been very much alleviated in recent months must now be given. Since writing my *John Gill and The Cause of God and Truth*, there has been some complaint from both friends and foes. The friends have tended to say, 'Why bother to defend Gill against the charges of Hyper-Calvinism and Antinomianism as it is clear to all that Gill's traducers are only striving to camouflage their own unorthodoxy by attacking Gill. Those who cry, "Antinomian" are so very obviously proved to be practical Antinomians themselves as they openly bear false witness.' Others say, 'If we take the arguments which are levelled at Gill concerning the doctrines of grace, it is obvious that Gill stood four-square in those doctrines, though called a Hyper-Calvinist. Thus let us accept the title as being a new name for orthodoxy as the Wesleyans took over the title "Methodists" with which they were mocked.' I have a good deal of sympathy with these arguments, which have also been raised in most generous reviews of my book, but I feel they do not apply to the real problem at hand. Many readers are not doctrinally aware of the issues at stake. When, for instance, the atonement, imputation, satisfaction, substitution, redemption and justification are virtually denied in that they are merely presented as forensic or even metaphorical conceptions with no actual basis in empirical fact, and such men of God as Gill and Huntington are called Antinomians because they accept God's testimony at its practical, experimental face value, it serves no one to allow the matter to pass without comment. The Christian faith consists in a change of heart and a renewed soul to be joined at the resurrection with a renewed body. It is a physical, mental, moral and spiritual change. It is not playing at make-believe to psychologically boost our ego or give us a new philosophy of life to ponder and soliloquise over, making us perhaps good, but, with reference to practical Christian work, good for nothing.

Gill was all too familiar with such an experience-denying philosophy of religion and took it to be an insult against the plan of God in His Word.

In his fine essay *On the Veracity of God*, he explains:

> The works of grace done by Him, His acts of grace, both in eternity and time; His choice of persons to eternal life, is true, firm, and real, the foundation of God, which stands sure; the covenant of grace, made in Christ, full of blessings and promises, faithfully performed; the mission of Christ into the world, and His incarnation, who was really made flesh, and dwelt among men; the truth of which the apostle confirms by the various senses of seeing, hearing, and handling, 1 John 1:1. Justification by His righteousness is really imputed to His people, and by which they truly become righteous; and not in a putative and imaginary sense; pardon by His blood, which is not merely typical, as by the blood of slain beasts, but real; atonement by the sacrifice of Himself, which He really and truly offered up to God; and sanctification by the Spirit, which is the new man, created in righteousness and true holiness; and not outward, typical, and ceremonial, nor feigned and hypocritical: and adoption, by which the saints are now really the sons of God; though it does not yet appear what they shall be; and to which the Spirit bears a true and real witness; and which is unto an inheritance, real, solid, and substantial.[34]

It was this conviction of realness and actuality that moved Traill to confess that the so-called Antinomians, 'of all men do most press on sinners to believe on Jesus Christ, and urge the damnation threatened in the gospel upon all unbelievers.'[35] When God has really and actually transformed a soul, it is automatic that the justified one wishes to pass on the good news of the gospel and warn men to flee from the wrath to come.

---

[34] Baptist Standard Bearer edition, Book I, Chap. XXII, pp. 112, 113.
[35] Op. cit., p. 318.

Looking at the criticisms of Gill's enemies
Unwary readers and hearers will accept modern teaching denying that an actual change takes place in a justified soul that is imputed with Christ's righteousness as fact when it comes from their trusted ministers. But they are receiving stones instead of bread. In defending Gill therefore against his traducers, I believe I am truly defending the cause of God and truth. Furthermore, Gill's critics not only empty his doctrines of their actuality and their basis in fact but they deceive the Christian public into believing that Gill's doctrines lead to lawlessness, an unwillingness to teach sinners, a lack of care and love for the unconverted, and even spread downright fables and myths about the person and history of Gill to boot. Again, such a perversion of truth and justice must be shown to be what it is, otherwise we shall educate our people to believe fables and withhold the gospel from them in doing so. Sadly, Evangelicalism has also its Jesuits.

Taking up Gill's mantle
In spite of a modern work which might suggest the contrary[36], Spurgeon professed to follow Gill's doctrines, putting him first in lists of those who had influenced him greatly for the good. The Prince of Preachers is ever full of praise for his predecessor in matters of faith but disagreed with him radically, and with a great deal of humour, on sermon construction. When referring to the Downgrade Controversy, however, he pointed out that he had not only inherited Gill's pulpit but also his mantle. It is my heart-felt conviction that Gill's works in the providence of God, have still their ancient power and will serve as a mighty bulwark against this terrible downgrading going on under the cloak of Antinomian-bashing. If my Christian readers would care to turn to Gill and are prepared to read him with an open mind and open heart, with a constant prayer that the Lord will open their eyes to all the blessings within it, but also help them recognise the dross, they will find a body of divinity second to none and a vindication of the Biblical doctrine of justification which will make them breathless in praise of what God has done for their souls.

---

[36] *Spurgeon v. Hyper-Calvinism*, The Banner of Truth Trust, 1996.

Chapter Two

The Eternal God Is Thy Refuge

Difficulties concerning Gill's doctrine

Writing to a friend on October 24, 1758, just two months before his death, James Hervey said, 'I have certainly a very great esteem for Dr Gill, yet I never could assent to his notion of eternal justification. I am very much obliged to you for pointing out to me the passage in *Theron and Aspasio* which seems to favour, or proceeds upon such a tenet. It shall be altered in the next edition.'[37] Hervey obviously did not make this statement lightly as he looked upon Gill as his mentor and Master in Israel and was usually full of praise for his Baptist brother and never forgot what he had learned from him when Gill visited him during his long convalescence at Miles Lane in London. Indeed, many sound men of unquestionable orthodoxy have affirmed with Hervey that Gill departed from true Biblical exposition when formulating his doctrine of justification. Yet, Hervey's statement is still surprising as his own doctrine of justification is as near Gill's as one might think made no difference and Gill certainly saw himself in agreement with the mainstream of past evangelical thinking. Furthermore, Hervey, in complete harmony with Gill, believed in God's eternal love for the elect as an essential aspect of God's unchanging character. Here we have two clues as to why Gill's doctrine of justification causes difficulties. Most theologians tend to systematise their doctrines analytically and

---

[37] *The Works of the Rev. James Hervey, A.M.*, one volume edition, 1837, pp. 916, 917.

53

independently and therefore view justification as a separate doctrine to that of God's unchanging love. Gill knew of no such distinction and certainly would not have accepted the modern teaching of a 'paradox' or 'tension' between God's love and His act of justifying the ungodly. Gill's aim in his *Body of Divinity* was to show how all true doctrine is 'fitly framed together'. It is also obvious that it is not so much Gill's doctrine of justification as his idea of eternity which caused Hervey and others problems of understanding.

False accusations based on unsound thinking
There is another reason, however, for rejecting Gill's doctrine which is purely hypothetical and reveals a most unnecessary fear in the minds of his critics. They claim to oppose Gill's doctrine of 'justification from eternity', which they re-name 'eternal justification', because they feel the doctrine automatically encourages the believer to think himself justified no matter how he behaves and that conversion and faith play no part in justification. Indeed, Gill's Latitudinarian and Grotian contemporaries openly called Gill an Antinomian because he taught the doctrine of justification from eternity. Taking up these heretics' faulty view of Gill's doctrine and its imagined consequences has moved the Banner of Truth to put this doctrine, held by a good number of men whose works they had formerly praised, at the head of their Five Points in the 'general creed of all theoretical Antinomians'.[38] This is the natural consequence of those who do not believe that God actually changes sinners when they become justified saints. How can they then bring forth fruits meet for repentance and sanctification? Gill, of course, taught that God has justified His elect from eternity so that they may eternally bear fruit to His glory. This listing of alleged Antinomian tenets by the Banner of Truth shows a great ignorance of the works of such men as Gill, Huntington and Romaine, who have come under their fire lately in their publications. One look at their fruits, especially in the form of their preaching and writing will show that their doctrines led them to denounce licentiousness and keep up a fine and godly witness. Gill's own testimony and teaching show clearly how unfounded such theorising is in comparison to the practical outworking of the Spirit's work in Gill's own life. As he was perhaps the greatest contender for

---

[38] *The Voice of Years*, ref. issue 298, July 1988, p. 8.

justification from eternity of his day, one would have expected—theoretically speaking—that he must have been the greatest Antinomian of his age. Nevertheless, Gill has left a well-documented testimony from his own pen and the pens of scores of others that he was a man of absolute integrity and, as John Rippon, his successor, affirmed, there was no one more eager than he was in combining faith with the duties of exercising it unto good works. Gill obviously lived out the truth of Paul's teaching in Romans 8 which states clearly that whom God called, He justified and put a Spirit of righteousness within them so that they might be conformed to the image of His Son.[39]

Much of the difficulty preventing a general acceptance of Gill's doctrine of justification amongst evangelicals is obviously based on nomenclature but also on prevailing schools of theology which have departed radically from the doctrines of the Reformation and the Puritans. Indeed, this misunderstanding of Gill coupled with a lack of sympathy with the doctrines of grace is even prevalent within schools of thought who nevertheless call themselves 'Reformed' for tradition's sake. Indeed, criticising Gill as an Antinomian and Hyper-Calvinist has become a slogan or rallying-point of what can only be called the Pseudo-Reformed. On scrutiny, we find, however, that they call Gill an Antinomian because he does not teach their brand of Neonomianism without the covenant of works, and the term 'Hyper-Calvinist' is used because Gill does not meet the requirements of what they call 'moderate Calvinism'. This belief reflects a Calvinism bereft of Particular Atonement (and often several other points) which is thus no Calvinism at all. There is also a good deal of unwillingness involved amongst Gill's critics to read his works so that the old taunt that Gill's doctrine of justification from eternity means justification irrespective of faith, is still raised against Gill, though his voluminous works do not separate justification from faith but see justifying faith as God's gift to His elect.

Justification and personal belief
One of the reasons for the modern unwillingness to examine Gill's doctrine of justification in the light of Scripture is that it has become 'sound' amongst evangelicals to view justification as occurring through believing, making personal belief the cause of justification. This was

---

[39] See especially vv. 10, 11; 28-30.

not the view of Hervey who quite agreed with Gill that righteousness, sanctification and justification were all in Christ and our being accepted in the Beloved.[40] Hervey, like Gill, thus looked upon justification as being determined by the mind and will of God in providing a Bride for His Son and thus justification, along with the whole of redemption both accomplished and applied, was a gift of God. This is exactly as Gill regarded the matter, but he used terminology to express it which had fallen into disuse and which had become questionable because the theology behind it was no longer representative of mainstream evangelical thought.

Gill himself was very aware of this difficulty yet refused to drop sound words because people were filling them with unsound contents. He believed it better to keep the old words and teach people their true Biblical meaning. Gill took up this point with his fellow Dissenter Samuel Chandler who so emphasised with the Latitudinarians the reasonableness of Christianity that he made Christianity subservient to his own view of reason or, as it was fashionable to describe reason at the time, 'the nature and fitness of things'. Gill saw that Chandler was denying the doctrine of justification as an act of God and making it an act of rational decision on the part of the one who allegedly grasped out in faith and believed and therefore was justified. Gill defended his position by saying:

> For my part, I have been traduced as an Antinomian, for innocently asserting, that the essence of justification lies in the eternal will of God; my meaning is, that God in his all-perfect and comprehensive mind, had from eternity, at once, a full view of all his elect; of all their sins and transgressions; of his holy and righteous law, as broken by them, and of the complete and perfect righteousness of his Son, who had engaged to be a surety for them; and in this view of things he willed them to be righteous, through the suretyship-righteousness of his Son, and accordingly esteemed, and accounted them so in him; in which will, esteem, and account their justification lies, as an immanent act in God. By this way of thinking and speaking I no ways set aside, nor in

---

[40] See Letter CLXII, *A Collection of Letters*, *The Works of The Rev. James Hervey, A. M.*, Thomas Nelson, 1837.

the least oppose the doctrine of justification by faith; I assert, that there is no knowledge of justification, no comfort from it, nor any claim of interest in it, until a man believes. I abhor the thoughts of setting the law of God aside as the rule of walk and conversation; and constantly affirm, that all that believe in Christ for righteousness, should be careful to maintain good works, for necessary uses. The cry of Antinomianism, upon such a principle as this, must be mere noise and stupidity.[41]

This argument alone ought to prove conclusive. Either justification is by the will of God who dwells in eternity, or it is by the will of man who dwells in time. Though modern 'Moderates' may rail against the above definition, one must admit that Gill is on the safer side. Who would like to build their eternal security on the fallen, corrupt will of a sinful creature? Yet these critics obviously denounce Gill because his theology of justification does not require man to do anything but work at it after it is once given him.

Justification and God's gracious love
Gill is quite certain where justification starts and where it does not start. Its origin is not to be found in the believer's reception or acceptance of the gospel but in the act of God which motivated that acceptance irrespective of time. Justification starts in the eternal love of God and its expression in His acts of grace. Writing on Romans 3:24 'Being justified freely by his grace', in his *Commentary*, Gill teaches:

The matter of justification is before expressed, and the persons that share in this blessing are described; here the several causes of it are mentioned. The moving cause of it is the free grace of God; for by '*the grace of God*' here, is not meant the Gospel, or what some men call the terms of the Gospel, and the constitution of it; nor the grace of God infused into the heart; but the free love and favour of God, as it is in his heart; which is wonderfully displayed in the business of a sinner's justification before him: it appears in his resolving upon the justification of

[41] The Moral Nature and Fitness of Things Considered, *Sermons and Tracts*, vol. iii, pp. 488, 489.

57

his chosen ones in Christ; in fixing on the method of doing it; in setting forth and pre-ordaining Christ to be the ransom; in calling Christ to engage herein; in Christ's engaging as a surety for his people, and in the father's sending him to bring in everlasting righteousness; in Christ's coming to do it, and in the gracious manner in which he wrought it out; in the father's gracious acceptation, imputation, and donation of it; in the free gift of the grace of faith, to apprehend and receive it; and in the persons that partake of it, who are of themselves sinners and ungodly. The meritorious cause of justification is, the redemption that is in Jesus Christ: redemption supposes a former state of captivity to sin, Satan, and the law, in which God's elect were by nature, and is a deliverance from it; it is of a spiritual nature, chiefly respects the soul, and is plenteous, complete, and eternal: this is in and by Christ; he was called unto it, was sent to effect it, had a right unto it, as being the near kinsman; and was every way fit for it, being both God and man; and has by his sufferings and death obtained it: now, as all the blessings of grace come through redemption by Christ, so does this of justification, and after this manner; Christ, as a Redeemer, had the sins of his people laid on him, and they were bore by him, and took away; the sentence of the law's condemnation was executed on him, as standing in their legal place and stead; and satisfaction was made by him for all offences committed by them, which was necessary, that God might appear to be just, in justifying all them that believe: nor is this any objection or contradiction to the free grace of God, in a sinner's justification; since it was grace in God to provide, send, and part with his son as a Redeemer, and to work out righteousness; it was grace in Christ, to come and give himself a sacrifice, and obtain salvation and righteousness, not for angels, but for men, and for some of them, and not all; and whatever this righteousness, salvation, and redemption cost Christ, they are all free to men.

Justification and Christ's sacrifice prepared before the foundation of the world

Bearing this in mind, it is obvious that whenever Gill broaches the subject of justification, he cannot possibly relate it to an act of human agency but sees such agency always on the receptive side, empowered by God's grace. Gill thinks wholly in terms of Romans 8:29, 30, 'For whom he did foreknow, he also did predestinate to be conformed to the image of his Son, that he might be the first born of many brethren. Moreover whom he did predestinate, them he also called: and whom he called, them he also *justified*'. Gill says of this passage in his *Commentary*, referring to the object of predestination:

> This predestination is of particular persons, who, in consequence of it, are called, justified, and glorified; it is the effect of divine grace, and entirely owing to it; it is the source of all the other blessings of grace, and is therefore placed at the head of them, and secures them all: them he also called; not to afflictions: many may be called to afflictions, and endure them, who are neither justified nor glorified; besides, the people of God, though they meet with many afflictions, between their call to eternal glory, and their enjoyment of it, yet they are not so much called to afflictions, as to patience under them: their call is of grace, by special grace, to peculiar blessings of grace, and to a kingdom and glory; and thus their calling is secured by predestination, and connected with glorification: and whom he called, them he also justified; the meaning of which is, not that he approved of them as sincere and faithful, on account of their faith and patience in sufferings; for neither of their sufferings, nor of their faith and patience in them, is there the least mention in the passage; nor can any instance be produced of the use of the word 'justified' in this epistle, or elsewhere in this sense: but the meaning is, that such persons whom God predestinates and calls, he makes righteous by the imputation of the righteousness of his son unto them; which is unto all, and upon all them that believe; by which they are justified before God, and in their own consciences, from all sin, and so secured from all wrath and condemnation; wherefore glorification stands inseparably connected with it: and whom he justified, them he also glorified;

which is not meant of being made glorious under sufferings; nor of being made glorious by the extraordinary gifts of the spirit; for the word is never used in this sense, nor is God ever said to glorify his people in this way; and the apostle is speaking of the saints in general, and not of particular ones: if this was the sense, none would be predestinated, called, and justified, but such who have the extraordinary gifts of the spirit; and none would have the extraordinary gifts of the spirit, but such persons; whereas many have had these, and yet no interest in the grace of God, and everlasting happiness: but eternal glory is here meant, which is what the apostle had been speaking of in the context; is what the elect are predestinated and called unto; and which their justification gives them a right and title to; and will consist in a likeness to Christ, in communion with him, in an everlasting vision of him, and in a freedom from all that is evil, and in an enjoyment of all that is good; and so the great end of predestinating grace will be answered in them mentioned in the foregoing verse: now this glorification may be said to be already done, with respect to that part of God's elect, who are in heaven, inheriting the promises; and is in some sense true also of that part of them which is on earth, who are called and justified; being made glorious within by the grace of Christ, and arrayed and adorned with the glorious robe of his righteousness; by the one they have a meetness, and by the other a right to eternal glory; of which this grace they have received is the beginning, pledge, and earnest: besides, they are already glorified in Christ, their head and representative, and in the view of God, and with respect to the certainty of it, it being prepared and made ready for them, is in the hands of Christ for them, and is insured to their faith and hope. It is an observation of a Jewish writer,[42] 'that a thing: "which is decreed to be", is spoken of in the past tense': this is the Scripture style concerning things decreed, and such is the glorification of all God's elect.

Paul emphasises this truth again in Romans 8:33, where the elect are represented as being justified by an act of God's sovereignty. In other

---

[42] Aben Ezra.

words, foreknowledge, predestination, election and justification are aspects of the redemption accomplished in Christ's redeeming act on the cross. Thus justification is not *accomplished* either actively or passively through the instrument of faith but through the act of redemption. Faith is not the *causa sine qua non* of justification but the gift which enables the ungodly to apprehend and appropriate it. Nor can it be maintained that Paul in Romans 8 is arguing from a this-happens-before-that sequence in time as redemption was wrought out in a point of time when the Old Testament saints were already counted justified, though time-wise, Christ had not yet died. This is a major point in Gill's argument for justification from eternity in *Truth Defended*. Similarly, New Testament saints still owe their justification to God's predestination in Christ though they were not born when redemption was accomplished. This was the unclear spot in Hervey's theology which did not allow him to accept Gill's doctrine of justification from eternity. Though Hervey argued that justification, like righteousness and sanctification were gifts of God, he did not knowingly place them in eternity or before the foundation of the world because he had no fixed doctrine of predestination. This is made clear when Wesley accused Hervey of teaching predestination in his *Theron and Aspasio*. Confiding this to Lady Francis Shirley on January 9, 1755, Hervey says:

> The person hinted at, is Mr John Wesley. He takes me very soundly to task, on the score of predestination. At which I am much surprised. Because a reader, ten times less penetrating than he is, may easily see, that this doctrine (be it true or false) makes no part of my scheme; never comes under consideration; is purposely and carefully avoided. I cannot but fear, he has some sinister design. Put the wolf's skin on the sheep, and the flock will shun him, the dogs will worry him.[43]

Wesley was skilled in picking out those who could not accept his own brand of Arminianism and believed that Antinomianism went hand in hand with a belief in the imputed righteousness of Christ and the doctrine of predestination. He felt Hervey was an Antinomian for preaching Christ's imputed righteousness and therefore labelled him a

---

[43] *Letters to Lady Francis Shirley*, p. 184.

predestinarian. Actually Wesley was quick to notice that the doctrines outlined in *Theron and Aspasio* stood or fell in association with the doctrines of predestination, election and particular atonement but Hervey was rather timid of naming these doctrines by name.[44] Gill had no such inhibitions as, along with other stalwarts such as Zanchius and Cotton Mather, he thought them the most comfortable doctrines of the gospel.

The danger of working things the wrong way round
Gill's critics are usually suspicious of his doctrine of justification, because their interpretations are far more narrow than Gill's and are not based on a similar mass of evidence. Plainly and simply, they have not done the same amount of work on the subject as Mr Voluminous.[45] In particular, these critics tend to isolate faith from the rest of Christ's redemptive work. Initially, Gill argues, it is not faith that saves us as faith is dependent on Christ's work on the cross. Redemption first makes faith possible. Things do not work the other way round. Faith is the seal and appropriation of justification but justification was wrought out on Calvary so that faith in that justification might become the believer's. Gill points out in Romans 5:9 of his *New Testament Commentary* that this was certainly Paul's view on writing, 'Much more then being now justified by his blood, we shall be saved from wrath through him.' Of this text, he says:

> The apostle here argues from justification by Christ to salvation by him, there being a certain and inseparable connection between these two; whoever is justified shall be saved; and speaks of justification 'as being now by his blood'. Justification in God's mind from eternity proceeded upon the suretyship engagements of Christ to be performed in time; the Old Testament saints were justified of God with a view to the blood of the Lamb which was to be shed; this blood was 'now' shed, and an application of justification by it was 'now' made to the persons spoken of; which is the reason of this way of

---

[44] See Letter CXCVI, p. 912, *A Collection of Letters*.
[45] Gill's nickname because of the great amount of scholarly research he did and books he produced.

speaking. The blood of Christ intends his death, as appears from the context, and shows it to be a violent death; death by the effusion of blood. There is an emphasis upon it, 'his blood'; not the blood of bulls and goats, nor of a mere innocent creature, but of Christ the son of God; which is therefore efficacious to all the purposes for which it was shed, and particularly justification. This being ascribed to it, shows the concern Christ had in it, his blood is here put for the whole matter of justification; the shedding of that being the finishing part of it; and that our justification before God proceeds upon the foot of a satisfaction made to the law and justice of God: hence such as are interested in it, shall be saved from wrath through him: not from wrath, as a corruption in their own hearts, which oftentimes breaks forth; nor as appearing among the people of God one towards another, which is sometimes very bitter; or as in their avowed enemies, the effects of which they often feel; nor from the wrath of devils, which is as the roaring of a lion; but from the wrath of God, from a sense and apprehension of it in their own consciences, which the law works; from which justification by the blood of Christ frees them; though under first awakenings they feel it, and sometimes, under afflictive dispensations of Providence, are ready to fear it: and also from the infliction of vindictive wrath or punishment for sin; for though they are as deserving of it as others, yet as they are not appointed to it, so they are entirely delivered from it, through Christ's sustaining it in their room and stead: wherefore they are secure from it both in this life, and in the world to come.

Here Gill has obviously put his finger on the great weakness of the modern discussion on justification by faith which is exercising the Reformed churches who have not lost their zeal for evangelism. Modern Arminian advertising and mass evangelism of the highly psychological type approved by Finney has sadly influenced Reformed views of evangelism. An emphasis on making a decision rather than studying the Word of Life, an emphasising of 'believing', rather than an explaining of what we are supposed to believe first, has so become the 'norm' of evangelism that one would almost think that the entire redemptive act of Christ on the Cross is a mere synonym for 'coming to faith'. Wesley and Fuller[46] used to argue that it is not necessary for a person coming to faith to know the deep 'secrets' of the atonement. This might be the case, but this does not mean that modern Reformed preachers to the unsaved and new converts should keep them in ignorance of these things as Fuller suggested.[47] According to the Bible, the very essence of evangelism is to take the 'secret' things of God and reveal them to the lost. Paul says in Romans 16:25, 'Now to him that is of power to establish you according to my gospel, and the preaching of Jesus Christ, according to the revelation of the mystery, which was kept secret since the world began.' Clearly, after what Paul has just said about justification in chapters 3, 4, 5 and 8 in his letter to the Romans, justification is certainly part of this mystery kept secret since the world began but revealed clearly in Christ.

Gill's systematic presentation of justification
Perhaps the most systematic presentation of Gill's doctrine of justification is to be found in his sermon entitled *The Doctrine of Justification by the Righteousness of Christ Stated and Maintained*[48] where Gill is preaching on Acts 13:39, 'And by him all that believe are justified from all things, from which ye could not be justified by the law of Moses.' In this sermon Gill tells his hearers:

1. What justification is not and what it is
Gill begins his sermon by defining what justification is not and then explaining what it is. Justification, he argues, is not the pardoning of sin though the two are so closely attached to each other that they cannot be separated. This is shown by the preceding verse to his text which states, before immediately going on to the subject of justification, 'Be it known unto you therefore, men and brethren, that through this man (Christ Jesus) is preached unto you the forgiveness of sins.'

Gill acknowledges that the bulk of theologians usually take justification to mean not only pardon of sin but also the imputation of righteousness because when God forgives sin, he pronounces the sinner

[46] See Wesley's *Letter to the Rev. James Hervey on Theron and Aspasio* and Fuller's *The Gospel Worthy of All Acceptation.*
[47] Fuller's *Works*, vol. ii, p. 374.
[48] *Sermons and Tracts*, vol. ii, p. 455ff.

righteous. Gill feels that this still does not adequately explain the full meaning of justification as, though pardon accompanies justification, it is to be distinguished from it.

Justification is a pronouncing a person righteous according to law as though he had never sinned. Pardon is quite different. Gill explains, 'It is one thing for a man to be tried by law, cast and condemned, and then receive the king's pardon; and another thing to be tried by the law, and by it, to be found and declared righteous, as though he had not sinned against it. Moreover, though pardon takes away sin, and therefore is expressed by God's casting of it behind his back, and into the depths of the sea, and by a removal of it from his people, as far as the east is from the west; yet it does not give a righteousness, as justification does; pardon of sin, indeed, takes away our filthy garments, but it is justification that clothes us with change of raiment. Besides, more is required, and was given for our justification, than for our pardon; the blood of Christ was sufficient to procure pardon; but, besides, his suffering of death, the holiness of his nature, and the perfect obedience of his life, must be imputed for justification. Again, though pardon frees from punishment, yet, strictly and properly speaking, it does not give a title to eternal life; that justification properly gives, and is one good reason why the apostle calls it *justification of life*.'[49]

Gill goes on to outline how justification is not a teaching programme to bring people to a knowledge of justification. When Christ, the righteous servant is said to justify many by his knowledge (Isaiah 53:11), it means that Christ imparts a spiritual knowledge of Himself to many, by way of faith. Nor is justification an infusion of righteousness into us. Justification is always to be seen in a forensic sense, though not merely so, but never in a physical sense and does not stand in opposition to unholiness but to a state of condemnation.

Justification to Gill is 'an act of God's grace, whereby he clears his people from sin, discharges them from condemnation, and reckons and accounts them righteous for the sake of Christ's righteousness, which he has accepted of, and imputes unto them.' This act on God's part can be viewed from three different angles. Considered *in foro Dei*, it is an eternal, immanent act in God. Considered in *foro conscientiae* it is a declarative act to and upon the conscience of the believer. Considered

---

[49] *Sermons and Tracts*, vol. ii, pp. 457, 458.

in foro mundi, it is an act that will be declared to men and angels at the last judgment.[50] In keeping with Witsius, Gill shows that God is virtually always justifying His elect.

2. The Author of justification

Now Gill goes on to examine the authorship of justification, maintaining that it is God alone that justifies. He sees this as a work of the Trinity with each Person playing His divine role in the process of justifying sinners. God the Father authored the scheme and worked through Christ, reconciling the world to Himself on the basis of His Son's ransom. Through this ransom which was paid in the fulness of time He 'finished transgressions, making an end of sin, making reconciliation for iniquity and bringing in an everlasting righteousness; which righteousness, being wrought out by Christ, God was well pleased with, because hereby his law was magnified and made honourable; and, having graciously accepted of it, he imputes it freely to all his people, and reckons them righteous on the account of it.'[51]

The co-efficient of the Father in forgiving sin, acquitting, discharging and justifying the sinner is God the Son who as our Mediator is our Head and Representative. He has answered the demands of the law on our behalf and is the Author and Finisher of our faith which 'looks unto, lays hold on, and apprehends that righteousness for justification.'[52]

Similarly, Gill sees the work of the Holy Spirit in justification as He convinces men of the insufficiency of their own state, sets before them the righteousness of Christ and works faith in them, intimating God's justifying sentence to their conscience, bearing witness to their spirit that they are the justified sons of God. Gill summarises the work of the Triune God by saying, 'the Father has contrived it, the Son has procured it, and the Spirit applies it.'[53]

---

[50] *Sermons and Tracts*, vol. ii, p. 459, 460.
[51] *Sermons and Tracts*, vol. ii, p. 461.
[52] *Sermons and Tracts*, vol. ii, p. 461.
[53] *Sermons and Tracts*, vol. ii, p. 462.

3. The matter of justification

Next, Gill considers, 'the matter of justification, or what that is for the sake of which God's elect are justified.' According to his usual pattern, Gill first deals with erroneous reasons given for God's justifying the ungodly before giving the true reason. Obviously, man's obedience to the law of works as the reason behind his justification can be ruled out straight away. Even if man could justify himself in this way, it would be justification by works and not grace. If righteousness could be gained by the law, Christ would have died in vain. Nor can the reason be man's obedience to the gospel as if it were a new and milder law. There is no easy way to salvation, however man is justified, he must be justified through a fulfilling of the whole law. Thus all the Neonomian preaching of a supposed new law of faith, repentance and sincere obedience is not preaching the gospel properly. It was far more easy for Adam to keep the whole law in a state of innocence than it is for a fallen man to repent and believe in Christ himself, yet Adam failed, so how can fallen man possibly succeed? God's judgment is according to His own truth and He will never call a pseudo-righteousness the real thing.[54]

Neither is a Christian profession and a form of godliness able to procure our justification. Sincerity is not enough as one can be seriously sincere in doing 'many things contrary to Jesus of Nazareth', as Paul found out when struck blind. That sincerity which is engendered by the Spirit of God is, indeed, a mark of grace but this belongs to the sanctification of the believer and is not part and parcel of his justification.

Even the act of believing is not imputed to us for our justification. The Arminians put forward Abraham as their prime example of a man justified by such an act, but the Scriptures teach that the same righteousness which Abraham received by imputation is imputed to all those who believe on Him, that raised up Jesus our Lord from the dead (Romans 4:22-24). Gill points out that Paul does not say Abraham's faith was accepted *instead* of righteousness (αντι δικαιοσυνης) but unto righteousness (εις δικαιοσυνην) as in 'with the heart man believes unto righteousness' (Romans 10:10). The object of faith shown

---

[54] The same can be said for the Baxterian and Fullerite theory that Christ did not place Himself under the law but was above the law. If Christ did not fulfil the law in the way mankind ought to fulfil it, then no justification is possible.

here is the righteousness of Christ which God imputes without any initiating act on the part of the sinner (Romans 4:6). Thus it was not Abraham's act of faith which persuaded God to justify him but the fact that he had been clothed with the righteousness of Another so that he might act in that way.[55] Gill argues that 'We are, indeed, said to be justified by faith (Romans 5:1), but not by faith, as an act of ours, for then we should be justified by works; nor by faith as a grace of the Spirit, for this would be to confound sanctification and justification; but we are justified by faith objectively, as it looks to, receives, apprehends, and embraces Christ's righteousness for justification.'[56]

Here Gill points out that he feels the common evangelical expression 'justifying faith' is misleading. No one speaks of an adopting faith or a pardoning faith on the part of the believer because this would indicate that the exercise of faith caused adoption and pardon. Faith is never said to adopt us or pardon us, nor does the Bible teach that it is our faith which justifies us. It is God who justifies us and we are justified for the sake of the Lord Jesus Christ who won this justification for us by conforming His life to the precepts of the law and His suffering and death to remove our penalties.

Gill also feels there is some confusion caused when dealing with Christ's righteous obedience by dividing it, for arguments sake, into its active and passive parts. Christ's obedience being described as active yet His suffering and death as passive. Gill feels such a distinction is merely academic and harmful experimentally, especially when it is used to claim that Christ's imputed righteousness merely refers to a passive 'as if' state of righteousness with no practical outworking of Christ's active obedience in us. Such a practical display of righteousness, they argue, is irrelevant to the Christian's position as Christ's own sufferings and death were sufficient for our justification. This is Antinomianism unmasked for Gill who argues:

> I firmly believe, that not only the active obedience of Christ, with his sufferings and death, but also that the holiness of his human nature is imputed to us for justification. The law requires

---

[55] This is made plain by Romans 5:1, 2 where it is emphasised that it is by Christ that we have access by faith into this grace wherein we stand (author's remark).
[56] *Sermons and Tracts*, vol. ii, p. 465.

an holy nature, and perfect obedience, and, in case of disobedience, enjoins punishment. Through sin, our nature is become unholy, our obedience imperfect, and so we are liable to punishment. Christ has assumed an holy human nature, and in it performed perfect obedience to the law, and suffered the penalty of it; all which he did not for himself, but for us; and unto us it is all imputed for our justification. He *is of God, made unto us*, that is, by imputation, *wisdom, righteousness, sanctification, and redemption* (1 Corinthians 1:30). *Wisdom* may stand in general for justification, because there is in it such a manifest display of the wisdom of God; and the other three may be considered as so many parts of it. *Sanctification* may intend the holiness of his human nature; which is that *law of the spirit of life in Christ Jesus, which frees from the law of sin and death. Righteousness* may signify his active obedience, *by which many are made righteous*; and *Redemption* may express his sufferings and death, whereby *sin was condemned in the flesh, and so the whole righteousness of the law is fulfilled in us*.[57]

Reasons for the imputation of Christ's active obedience

Gill, in arguing that not only Jesus' sufferings and death are imputed for justification but also His active obedience, maintains that:

a. Everything that the law requires must be imputed for our justification

Without the full demands of the law being met, there can be no satisfaction. The law demanded mere obedience of man before the fall but after the fall it demanded obedience and punishment. Jesus, as our surety made satisfaction for all that the law demanded of us in both these aspects. He obeyed all the precepts of the law on our behalf and suffered all its punishments on our behalf. Thus His full satisfaction is imputed to us for our justification.

---

[57] *Sermons and Tracts*, vol. ii, p. 468.

b. Christ's righteousness was shown in active obedience; in actively doing God's will

As we are justified by the righteousness of Christ imputed to us, we must be justified also by his active obedience and not merely sufferings and death.

c. The Scriptures teach that we are made righteous by the obedience of one (Romans 5:19), who is Christ

Here it is obvious that Christ's suffering and death are not meant as these were not His obedience but flowed from it. The text clearly shows that through one man's actual disobedience many were made sinners and by Christ's actual obedience many are made righteous.

d. The reward of life is attributed to active obedience of the law and not to suffering its penalties

The promise is 'Do this and live' and this reward of life is found solely in the One who actually did what was required and actually imputed that reward to His Bride, giving her justification of life.

e. Christ's active obedience was performed for us, in our room and in our stead

This must be imputed to us in order that we might be justified. He was not obliged to fulfil that law on His own account but obliged Himself to it on our account. If we say that Christ's passive obedience, shown through suffering and death, alone is imputed to us for justification, then we have only a suffering Christ and not an obeying one.

Does a belief in justification through Christ's active work promote Antinomianism?

Gill is obviously sensitive of criticism here as the doctrine of imputed righteousness was seen (and still is seen) by Amyraldians, Neonomians, Baxterians and Arminians as a letter of manumission, freeing a believer from the burden of living a moral life. As Wesley told Hervey, Arminians believed that this doctrine promoted lasciviousness. They have got it all wrong, explains Gill. Just as Christ's death does not free us from the death of the old man with its physical consequences, so Christ's obedience does not free us from the obedience which has been imputed to us. On the contrary, we are duty bound to live a holy life through Christ who strengthens us and meets all the duties of holiness for us. This is because we have not only the law as our example of holiness, given the fact that its curse has been lifted, but Christ's active obedience of it, a Christ who indwells us by His Spirit and testifies to our spirit how to live righteously. Furthermore, the standards of the law, now we are freed from its killing powers, provide us with a means of holy conduct 'by which we may glorify God, and express our thankfulness to him, for his abundant mercies.' This point is outlined in greater depth when Gill deals specifically with 'Righteousness' and 'Sanctification'.

4. The form of justification
The form justification takes is through imputation. As imputation is a major topic in itself, this will be dealt with under that general heading, hints being merely given here regarding its justifying aspects. Gill has five things to say about imputation in relation to justification:

a. As we are ungodly and God justifies the ungodly, we have no righteousness of our own
However, as righteousness is the qualification for justification, to be justified we must have another righteousness imputed to us which can only be the righteousness of Christ.

b. Justification must be either by inherent righteousness or imputed righteousness
We have no inherent righteousness but there is a righteousness 'unto all, and upon all them that believe' (Romans 3:22), which is the very imputed righteousness of Christ by which we are justified.

c. Paul tells us in Philippians 'That I might be found in Christ, not having mine own righteousness, which is of the law, but that which is through the faith of Christ.'
This makes Gill conclude that: 'Now the righteousness of another cannot be made ours, or we be justified by it, any other way than by imputation of it.'

d. Just as Adam's sin became ours by imputation, so Christ's righteousness became ours by imputation
In Adam we are sinners but in Christ we are made righteous.

71

e. In the same way that our sins became Christ's, by imputation only, so His righteousness becomes ours
'For he, who knew no sin, was made sin for us, that we might be made the righteousness of God in him' (2 Corinthians 5:21).[58]

5. The date of justification

Gill now devotes a very lengthy section to the dating of justification, very conscious that great minds certainly do not think alike on the topic. The Southwark pastor outlines a few of the many theories and part-truths that were current at the time regarding when God justifies the ungodly. We thus meet with the ideas that justification is accomplished on the day of judgment; at the time of believing; at Christ's resurrection; immediately after the fall and as the consequence of the covenant transactions between the Father and the Son, regarding Christ's suretyship engagements from eternity. Gill makes no bones about the fact that he holds to the latter view as the only possible position, bearing in mind all the Biblical evidence. He now proceeds to show that justification is antecedent to the act of believing and that justification upon believing is not true justification. He then takes up the arguments against his own position which will be taken up in a separate chapter.

Justification antecedent to belief
a. Faith is the fruit of justification

We have faith because we are justified, things do not happen in the reverse. The righteousness of Christ is given to us that faith and repentance might ensue. Justification is by (lit. *towards*) faith but justification is the cause and faith the effect. Effects follow causes, therefore justification must be before faith, the latter coming as the result of the former.

b. Justification is the object and faith the act which is conversant with it and depends on it

Faith is thus the evidence of justification, the evidence of things not seen. 'Faith is the hand which receives the blessing of justification from the Lord, and righteousness, by which the soul

---

[58] *Sermons and Tracts*, vol. ii, pp. 473-475.

is justified, from the God of its salvation.'[59] Here Gill takes up the argument that the object of faith is the righteousness of Christ and not justification and answers, 'Christ's righteousness justifying me, is my justification before God, and as such, my faith considers it, and says with the church, Surely, in the Lord have I righteousness and strength' (Isaiah 45:24).

c. The elect are justified whilst ungodly, which means, before belief

This view, which was the orthodox view of the Particular Baptists of Gill's day, was to be seriously challenged by later Fullerites who were nominally Calvinists but who held Wesley's view of justification i.e. through the act of believing. Andrew Fuller himself, argued that God would never justify unbelievers so the word 'ungodly' must refer to ungodly believers who are yet exercisers of faith.[60] Indeed, Fuller expounded this strange teaching from the very pulpit at Kettering from which Gill first started his orthodox ministry, believing he had found a new impetus for evangelism in it. Seemingly looking ahead to the deviations which were to come, Gill adequately refutes the Fullerite theory by quoting Romans 5:6 and Romans 4:5, 'While we were yet without strength, in due time Christ died for the ungodly.' and 'But to him that worketh not, but believeth on him that justifieth the ungodly, his faith is counted for righteousness.'[61]

d. Federal headship plays a part in justification

Gill teaches that all fallen men are represented in Adam, whereas all of those who are saved from fallen men are represented in Christ their Head of whom he says: 'The Lord Jesus Christ having, from eternity, engaged as a Surety for his people, all their sins were laid upon him, imputed to him, and placed to his account; for all which he was responsible to divine justice, and accordingly, in the fulness of time gave full satisfaction for them, by his sufferings and death; for, as he was put to death in the flesh, he was justified in the Spirit. Now as he

---

[59] *Sermons and Tracts*, vol. ii, p. 478.
[60] See 'Remarks on God's Justifying the Ungodly', *Works*, vol. iii, p. 714.
[61] *Sermons and Tracts*, vol. ii, p. 479.

suffered and died not as a private person, but as a public one, so he rose again, and was justified as such. Hence, when he was justified, all those for whom he made satisfaction, and brought in a righteousness, were justified in him; which seems to be the meaning of that scripture, Who was delivered for our offences, and was raised again for our justification' (Romans 4:25).[62]

e. No contradiction between justification from eternity and justification by faith

Here modern evangelicals have, at times, difficulty with Gill as he is now writing about a justification through the work of Christ on the cross and in His resurrection, rather than in a definite action before time which they understand by 'justification from eternity'. Such a thought does not trouble Gill at all as he sees no contradiction involved in what God determined before time and what Christ achieved in time. Following Dr Ames, Gill believes that the 'grand original sentence of justification' or the decree of God regarding justification is an eternal act of God's mind, as are all His acts. God is not a product of cause and effect change. He is constant and eternal in His will. Quoting Rutherford, he shows how all that passes in time, i.e. the whole *esse* of justification demonstrated and declared in time, is 'an eternal and immanent act of God, and not transient upon an external subject. Of which sort, adds he, are the acts of election and reprobation, which have their whole complete being before the persons elected, reprobated, or justified, either begin to be, live or believe, or do anything good or evil.'[63]

This passage is dealt with at length in Andrew Gunten Fuller's description of the progress of his father's mind on justification.[64]

---

[62] *Sermons and Tracts*, vol. ii, p. 479, 480.

[63] *Sermons and Tracts*, vol. ii, p. 483.

[64] Fuller's *Works*, vol. i, pp. 17, 18. See also Fuller's three articles, each entitled 'Justification', in vol. ii. It seems that Fuller fights shy of seeing justification as all of God. See also vol. ii, p. 338 where Fuller argues 'The gospel is a feast freely provided, and sinners of mankind are freely invited to partake of it. There is no mention of any gift, or grant, distinct from this but this is sufficient.' If Fuller is fearful that Gill, Hervey and others are emphasising God's sovereignty too much, it seems that he leaves himself

He quotes his father as writing that he once shared Gill's and Ames' view of justification through 'a purpose in the Divine mind' but went on to differ radically from their view, abstracting justification from the divine decrees and the realms of certainty and seeing it as a conditional and universal promise to whoever might partake of it. Justification, he argued, 'consists of the voice of God, in the gospel, declaring that whosoever believeth shall be saved'. Here, as so often, Fuller had misunderstood Gill's emphasis on God's sovereign will, feeling that this ignored personal belief and a holy walk or the *esse* of justification in the life of the believer. Rather than ignore these factors, Gill emphasised them but in their due order. First justification with its outcome in faith and then a walk in faith leading to the triumph of faith in the life of the justified.

Quoting Romans 8:33, Gill argues that none can lay anything to the charge of God's elect means that they can never do so because 'He hath chosen us in him before the foundation of the world' (Ephesians 1:4). This was clearly the occasion when God put us in Christ by means of His electing grace. Gill can thus conclude that, 'if there is an eternal election of persons in Christ, there must be an eternal acceptance and justification of them in him; since as he always was the beloved Son of his Father, in whom he is ever well pleased, so he always has graciously accepted of, and is well pleased with all his elect in him.'[65]

The eternal covenant with its Surety and its Mediator testifies to justification from eternity

Gill, now leaning on Thomas Goodwin (1600-1679), argues how the eternal covenant of salvation between Father and Son on account of the elect, testifies to justification from eternity. Goodwin's words sound rather archaic nowadays and may demand a little effort to read, but they are so succinctly Scriptural and clear on the subject that they are worth quoting at length. Goodwin says:

---

open, in the context, to emphasising the uncertain nature of justification and salvation resting on the choice of the sinner and his 'gratefully accepting it'.
[65] *Sermons and Tracts*, vol. ii, p. 485.

The first progress, or step, was at the first covenant-making and striking of the bargain from all eternity: we may say, of all spiritual blessings in Christ, what is said of Christ, that his goings forth are from everlasting. Justified then we were, when first elected, though not in our own persons, yet in our Head, as he had our persons then given him, and we came to have being and interest in him: You are in Christ, (saith the Apostle) and so we had the promise made of all spiritual blessings in him, and he took all the deeds of all in our name; so in Christ we were blessed with all spiritual blessings, Ephesians 1:3. As we were blessed with all other, and with this also, that we were justified then in Christ. To this purpose is that place, Romans 8:30 where he speaks of all those blessings which are applied to us after redemption, as calling, justification, glorification, as of things already past and done, even then when he did predestinate us: whom he hath predestinated, them he hath called, them he hath justified, them he hath glorified. He speaks it as in the time past; neither speaks he thus of these blessings as past simply in regard of that presence, in which all things stand before him in eternity; all things past, present and to come, being to him as present: nor doth he speak it only in regard of a resolution, or purpose, taken up to call and justify, he calling things that are not as though they were, Romans 4:17. For thus it may be said, of all his other works towards the creatures in common, that he hath created and preserved them from everlasting: but in a more special relation are these blessings decreed, said to have been bestowed, because, though they existed not in themselves, yet they existed really in a Head that represented them and us, who was by to answer for them, and to undertake for them, which other creatures could not do; and there was an actual donation and receiving of all these for us, (as truly as a feoffee in trust may take lands for one unborn) by virtue of a covenant made with Christ; whereby Christ had all our sins imputed to him, and so taken off from us, Christ having then covenanted to take all our sins upon him, when he took our person to be his; and God having covenanted not to impute sin unto us, but to look at him for the payment of all, and at us as discharged. Of this seems that place, 2

Corinthians 5:19 evidently to speak, as importing that everlasting transaction; God was in Christ, reconciling the world unto himself, not imputing their trespasses to them, that is, not imputing them then when he was reconciling us unto himself in Christ. So as then God told Christ, as it were, (for it was a real covenant) that he would look for his debt and satisfaction of him, and that he did let the sinners go free; and so they are, in this respect, justified from all eternity. And indeed, if the promise of life was then given us, (as the apostle Paul speaks, Titus 1:2) then also justification of life, without which we could not come to life. Yet this is but the inchoation, though it be an estating us into the whole tenure of life.[66]

Gill goes on to explain how Christ was set up from everlasting as the Mediator of this covenant. It was then that His suretyship was accepted and that 'as soon as any one becomes a surety for another, the other is immediately freed, if the surety is accepted;'[67] which Gill shows is the case at hand. As Christ is our surety, all the sins of those for whom He is a surety were reckoned and accounted to Him and laid to His charge. If there was such an imputation to Him, there was a non-imputation of them to the elect. This is what is meant by God was in Christ, i.e. from everlasting, reconciling the world unto Himself, not imputing their trespasses unto them (2 Corinthians 5:19). To back himself up in this reasoning, Gill quotes from Herman Witsius (1636-1708) who argues that as God has reconciled the whole world of the elect to Himself and has declared that He will not impute their sins to them because of the 'consummate satisfaction of Christ', this act of God may be called 'the general justification of the elect'.

God's immanent acts are from eternity
Gill's next point is that God willed from eternity to punish His elect's sin in His Son and not in the elect themselves. Christ was therefore made a propitiation for our sins. This intention, formed in the mind of God before time began, has been constantly revealed in Scripture. Now quoting William Twisse (1575-1646), the first moderator of the

---

[66] *Sermons and Tracts*, vol. ii, p. 485-487.
[67] Gill is quoting Maccovius.

Westminster Assembly, Gill shows how God's will not to punish is the essence of justification and 'as it is an immanent act in God, was from eternity.'[68]

The Old Testament saints, Gill adds, were justified by the same righteousness of Christ as the New Testament saints, that is, before the immanent act in God became an actual act in time. In this way, the shedding of Christ's blood was for sins that were past. These were saved on surety of what was to happen in time centuries later. This shows that the act of Christ's propitiation is to be seen from the aspect of God's will in eternity and Christ's eternal suretyship and not merely its fulfilment in time.

When arguing that faith is not the causal instrument of justification, Gill, surprisingly calls Richard Baxter (1615-1691) to his side, who affirms, 'if faith be the instrument of our justification, it is the instrument of either God or man. Not of man, for justification is God's act; he is the sole Justifier, Romans 3:26, man doth not justify himself: nor of God, for it is not God that believeth.'[69] Here Gill refers to the case of the elect who die in infancy who have not exercised the act of believing, yet are justified. Gill concludes:

> Faith is the sense, perception, and evidence of our justification. Christ's righteousness, as justifying, *is revealed from faith to faith*. It is that grace whereby the soul, in the light of the divine Spirit, beholds a complete righteousness in Christ, having seen its guilt, pollution, and misery; when it is enabled to renounce its own righteousness, and submit to the righteousness of Christ; which it puts on by faith, as its garment of justification: which it rejoices in, and gives him the glory of; the Spirit of God bearing witness with his Spirit, that he is a justified Person. And so he comes to be evidently and declaratively *justified in the name of the Lord Jesus, and by the Spirit of God.*[70]

---

[68] *Sermons and Tracts*, vol. ii, p. 489.
[69] *Sermons and Tracts*, vol. ii, p. 497.
[70] *Sermons and Tracts*, vol. ii, p. 492.

6. The objects of justification

Romans 8:33, 34 tells us that the objects of justification are the elect who stand delivered from all charges and condemnation in God's sight. For them Christ has died and equally, for them, He now bears them up through His intercessions. Gill looks in detail at the elect people of God.

a. Their number

Rather than emphasise 'the righteous few', Gill stresses their great number. Christ is the righteous servant who justifies *many*. He has borne the sins of *many* and *many* were ordained to eternal life so that *many* shall sit down with Abraham, Isaac, and Jacob, in the kingdom of heaven, that is, in the *many* mansions in their Father's house.[71] Accepting that few of the numbers who are called are chosen, they are still a number so extensive that no man can count them, thus magnifying the grace of God and the righteousness of His Son. This means that all mankind are not justified but only those who are justified by Christ's blood shall be saved from wrath by Him (Romans 5:9). These are the elect, who alone are justified.

b. Their state

Before conversion, the elect are described as the ungodly, yet after conversion as believers in Christ. Thus all that believe are justified, i.e. those whose hearts believe unto righteousness and whose faith works by love to Christ and to His people.

7. The general effects of justification

The justified are freed from all punitive, vindictive and wrathful treatment because of their sins, though God has still to chastise them in a fatherly way. They have peace with God but also peace of conscience which is one of the greatest blessings in life. They also have free access to God in Christ with boldness, through making mention of Christ's righteousness and great freedom in bringing their petitions to Him. They and their services are fully accepted by God for Christ's sake and they are now fully adopted as God's children, in fact the ancients called justification, the way to adoption (*via adoptionis*). A major effect of

---

[71] Isaiah 53:11, Romans 5:19, Matthew 20:28, Hebrews 9:28, Acts 13:48, Matthew 8:12 and John 14:2.

justification is sanctification, going hand in hand with faith for 'whom he justified, them he also glorified' (Romans 8:30).[72]

8. The properties of justification
a. Justification is an act of God's free grace
We are justified freely by His grace (Romans 3:24) as it was God's grace that fixed the method of justification, calling Christ to engage as our surety and sending Him in the fulness of time to work out a righteousness for His unrighteous Bride, imputing this to her and bestowing faith on her.

b. Justification is a universal and not partial act
All God's elect are justified fully from all their sins and are freed from all the punishments due to them. The whole righteousness of Christ is imputed to them and they are made complete in Christ.

c. Justification is an individual act
It is done at once. There are no degrees to justification. The elect's sins were removed at once on the cross. The satisfaction of Christ was at once successful. The *sense* of this justification may come by degrees, according to God's revelation from faith to faith, but justification is a once and for all matter. There are also fresh declarations or manifestations of justification revealed in Scripture, such as at the resurrection of Christ or at the final judgment but they all refer to the one divine act.

d. Justification is equal for all
No one is more justified than another. All are redeemed by the same price and all receive the same righteousness imputed. Though elect people may be weak or strong in faith, no one is weaker or stronger in justification.

e. Justification is irreversible
God's immutable decree cannot be frustrated because God's gifts are without repentance and His covenant of grace can never be broken. Once saved, always saved.

---

[72] Perhaps readers will wonder why Gill associates sanctification with glorification but the root meaning of δοξαζω is to invest with goodness, excellency, beauty and honour.

f. Justification does not take sin out of the believer

The justified are freed from their sins in that they are freed from the condemnation of their sins. They have been acquitted. Thus man's state in respect of providence (*in articulo providentiæ*) is sinful and God chastises those sins, however, in respect of justification (*in articulo justificationis*), God sees no sin in His elect.

g. Justification does not destroy the law

The elect are not discouraged in performing good works. The law is now really and truly established because the righteousness by which we are justified is equal to the law's demands which magnifies it and makes it honourable. The elect, therefore, are to deny ungodliness and worldly lusts and live soberly, righteously and godly, in this present world (Titus 2:11, 12).

Chapter Three

The Nature And Effects Of Faith

Gill's works describing faith, especially in its relationship to justification are numerous and lengthy. Critics who do not work systematically through his writings but merely browse through the titles in search of the word 'faith', confess that they find little on the subject apart from Chapter VI, Book I of Gill's third volume of his *Body of Divinity* entitled 'Of Faith in God and in Christ'. Actually there are over four hundred pages on the subject of faith in this volume alone but Gill has dealt with the topic of faith under such themes as the fear of God; trust and confidence in God; hope in God; the grace of love; spiritual joy in believing; of peace and tranquillity of mind; of spiritual contentment; of thankfulness to God; of zeal; of fortitude and many other fundamental aspects. Even a brief look at Gill's sermons will soon reveal that the doctrine of faith is returned to again and again. An outstanding example here is Gill's funeral sermon at the burial of Joshua Hayes, a member of Gill's church, entitled *A Knowledge of Christ, and of Interest in Him, the Support of a Believer in Life and in Death*. Indeed, it can be said with no exaggeration that Gill has written about faith more profusely than most other Christian writers and has delved into the furthest corners of faith where other writers have not been able to make the attempt. In this respect, it is often difficult to compare Gill's teaching with that of others as there is little basis for comparison on many issues connected with faith as the other writers have not outlined their views at all on the matter. It is, for instance, hardly profitable to compare Gill's close connection of faith with justification from eternity, as many who are praised above Gill by his critics have completely left out the relationship between God's decrees and faith from their system or even denied that there is a connection. We can therefore only compare Gill's findings with Scripture, a method which would have found Gill's complete agreement.

Gill's critics are without excuse for misrepresenting him

Gill's material on faith is enormous and easily come by as most of Gill's works are continually being published, so there is no excuse whatsoever for critics to condemn Gill's teaching without having given it wide and careful study. This is seldom the case. None of Gill's vast works, for instance, not even *Of Faith in God and in Christ*, managed to catch the eye of Peter Naylor when writing on the subject of Gill's doctrine of faith. Naylor composed his entire chapter entitled 'John Gill and Faith' in his book *Picking Up a Pin for the Lord* without one single reference to Gill's actual works on faith. Instead he merely quotes six passages from one single book, Gill's *Cause of God and Truth*, which is not a special treatise on faith but a defence of the Five Points of Calvinism against the criticisms of Dr Whitby, the Arminian-cum-Arian as recorded in his book *Discourse on the Five Points*. Furthermore, of these passages which Naylor quotes, one has to do with human responsibility, four with repentance and one is a criticism of half a sentence of Gill's in which he claimed that sinners are not initially condemned for not believing that Christ died for them as they are already condemned for their transgression of the law of God. This latter quote is the nearest Naylor ever gets to the subject in his chapter, but he only uses it as a basis to prove that Gill is 'off the track'![73] This is a most revealing strategy on Naylor's part as he opens his chapter on Gill's faith by saying, 'In point of fact, such is the vastness of Gill's writings that it is not always easy to pinpoint what Gill thought exactly about some matters.'[74] It seems that Naylor took the easiest way out.

---

[73] Naylor's own words.

[74] Op. cit. Naylor's Chapter IX on 'John Gill and Faith' is only 6 1/2 pages long whereas the preceding chapter on 'High Calvinism and the Particular Baptists' is 22 pages long, including a picture of Gill and a facsimile letter of his. This demonstrates clearly Naylor's polemic thrust at the cost of a fair documentation on Gill's doctrine of faith.

He pinpointed Gill's teaching in one book amidst the admitted vastness of Gill's writings and one that made no claims to being a treatise on the subject at hand. Actually, this should be seen as something of a compliment to Naylor. He has at least read one book, and he confesses to have read another on the subject of justification, but most of Gill's modern critics have obviously not read Gill at all, perhaps assuming that they have no need to read him in order to condemn him. It is not uncommon to meet ardent accusers of Gill who confess that they would be loath to think that anybody might discover they had actually read the works of such a heretic! In his excellent Foreword to my book *John Gill and The Cause of God and Truth*, Pastor Don Fortner relates:

> From the beginning, men who obviously never read Gill warned me of what they call his 'tendencies toward Hyper-Calvinism and Antinomianism'. Having read almost everything Gill wrote, I am still searching for even a hint of those 'tendencies'. Instead, I have found in all his writings the most faithful exposition of Holy Scripture, a consistent Christ-centred, Christ-exalting theology, and a constant, robust declaration of God's free and sovereign grace in Christ. Very few days have passed since my first introduction to Gill in which I have not read something from his pen. He is, by far, my favourite writer.

This is the testimony of a man who knows Gill and has learnt to love his message through taking the trouble to get to know him. Don Fortner is a good example of those who find that 'the proof of the pudding is in the eating'. The sad problem remains, however, that those who do not read Gill are his most ardent enemies, as the above example clearly shows. Sadder still is that these people write books to traduce a man's sound work. There is much need for God's grace and much educational work to be done in God's vineyard before even Christian writers are persuaded that honest personal testimony based on fact is what moves people and not blind prejudice which is sure to err. The following will prove beyond any doubt whatsoever that Naylor's accusations in his 'John Gill and Faith' that when Gill spoke of faith 'he theorised rather than expounded',[75] and 'In reality, his writings tended to redefine faith,

---

[75] Op. cit. p. 171.

and it is here that they seem to have departed from Scripture', are completely unfounded. Gill's argument below will also put to flight Naylor's strange idea that, in Gill's theology there is no coming to faith for the first time, but the sinner merely becomes aware of his blessed state. Is Naylor arguing that Gill does not believe in conversion and the new birth? It seems so. This ignores all that Gill has to say about God's implanting and ingenerating of faith in the sensible sinner[76] and the application of faith in the believer's life through the work of the Spirit. One wonders how Naylor interprets Gill's words concerning man's 'venturing act' and 'first acts of faith'. Gill is quite clear in his statement that when a person comes to faith 'eternal life is begun'. Also, too, Gill's argument below will show how unfounded are the many comments of Naylor implying that Gill believed faith was a mere 'notion'. Gill argues that knowledge is an essential element in faith but faith, which is essentially trust, love and dependence, is therefore far, far, more than 'a bare assent' to the facts of the gospel. This, however, is just the accusation that is levelled against Gill. Gill's complete essay *Of Faith* must be analysed as a whole below as I am rather sensitive of the quite groundless criticism that I present my subjects in their best light and leave out their 'warts'. As I explained in my biography of Huntington, what other people think are warts, I often think are characteristics which enhance the beauty of the individual's teaching. Beauty is indeed in the eye of the beholder. Again, the only yardstick possible to decide if the eye has captured a true picture is the Scriptures themselves which Gill applies with all the skill of a godly workman who needs not to be ashamed.

---

[76] It is usually argued by modern critics of Gill that the phrase 'sensible sinner' is an invention of the Antinomians. Both Bunyan and Hervey maintained that a sinner must first be made sensible by the Spirit before the truth could enter his soul as this was the widespread belief in that day. Modern evangelistic methods based on a belief that man is not fallen in his natural capacities, of course, must reject such a teaching. Also, as criticised in Naylor's chapter 'John Gill and Faith', Gill's distinction between evangelical and legal repentance is taken by his critics to be a sign of Hyper-Calvinism. It is interesting to note that Gill's doctrine was less 'Hyper' than Calvin's here (see Berkhof's criticism in Chapter One) and believers on both sides of the 'Modern Question' used the distinction, not least, Andrew Fuller himself.

Faith reflects inner experimental religion and godliness

Writing in *Of Faith in God and in Christ*,[77] Gill explains how faith reflects the work of God in the soul of man producing experimental religion and godliness and a longing to worship God so that 'with the heart man believeth unto righteousness'. There is no personal communication with God possible but that which faith affords. As the word 'faith' has many different meanings and is used differently in different contexts, Gill feels he must first explain the different uses and significances of the term. He starts with:

I. The different kinds of faith
1. The veracity and faithfulness of God
Romans 3:3, 4 teaches that it is the subjective faith of God that works in believers and it is the task of the justified believer to see that God is seen to be true, though every man a liar. This is in opposition to the faith and veracity of men in relation to the moral law (Matthew 23:23).
2. The word of faith
The term is often used for the doctrine of the gospel which is called the word of faith. This is the gospel preached (Galatians 1:23) which is the faith once delivered to the saints for which the Christian must earnestly contend and with which the Holy Spirit builds up the saints (Jude 3, 20). This faith exalts Christ ingenerating and increasing faith in men because faith comes by hearing and by the word of God (Romans 10:17).
3. The distinction between divine and human faith
1 John 5:9 tells us, 'If we receive the witness of men, the witness of God is greater: for this is the witness of God which he hath testified of his Son.' To believe this witness and receive it into one's own being is what is termed saving faith.
4. Faith in miracles
Here Gill refers to the miracles in the gospels where faith was given as the reason for their success. He also mentions Paul's words, 'Though I have all faith, so that I could remove mountains'. Gill divides this kind of faith into active, as in Luke 17:6, the grain of mustard seed, and passive as in the case of the lame man at Lystra. Gill shows that such

---

[77] This is found in Book I, Chapter VI, p. 730 ff. of the one-volume Baptist Standard Bearer edition, which is the one readily available today.

miracles at the time of the apostles occurred to both good and bad men and to believers and unbelievers alike.

5. Historical faith

This is credit given to the historicity of the Bible and even to the fact that it is of divine authority. Gill calls this a theoretical faith as it reduces everything to theory but nothing to practice. Even the devils have this faith.

6. Temporary faith

There are stony-ground hearers who believe for a while but fall away when temptation comes (Luke 8:13). This may be an assent to truth attended by joy and affection on hearing it as in the case of Herod who heard John gladly. Saving faith, however, is lasting.

7. Special faith

This is peculiar to God's elect and is otherwise called saving faith. Gill is not too fond of this term as many argue that salvation is in faith or in duty to faith or other graces. Salvation is only in Christ. He only is the author of eternal salvation. The end of this faith is the salvation of our souls (Mark 16:16; 1 Peter 1:9).

II. The objects of faith

Next, Gill goes on to consider the objects of faith and the acts of faith. The proper objects of faith is not what can be done by faith but whom our faith should be affixed upon. This can only be God in Christ who said, 'Ye believe in God, believe also in me' (John 14:1). This is not mere head knowledge or believing a mere notion but is 'to cleave to God, lean upon him, and acquiesce in him as our all-sufficient life and salvation' and to go forth in acts of faith motivated by Him. Concerning faith in the Triune God, we are to believe on Him as:

First: Faith in God the Father:

This is demonstrated by:

1. Faith in the Creator

It is an act of faith to believe in the Maker of heaven and earth, of things visible and invisible and of things past, present and future. This proves that God can support and supply us with all we need and therefore we commit our souls to Him in full assurance (Psalm 121:1, 2; 1 Peter 4:19; 1 Timothy 4:10).

2. Faith in God the Father who loves His people in Christ

This is because He has loved His people in Christ from eternity. He is 'God, even our Father, which hath loved us, and given us everlasting consolation' (2 Thessalonians 2:16). The believer can therefore say, 'nothing ... shall be able to separate us from the love of God, which is in Christ Jesus our Lord' (Romans 8:38, 39).

3. Faith in God the Father who chose us to grace and glory in Christ

Faith is in the effectual eternal calling of God and the fact that our names are written in the Lamb's *Book of Life* Ephesians 1:3, 4; 2 Thessalonians 2:13, 14: 1 Peter 1:2; Romans 8:30 and Acts 13:48, causes us all to rejoice in the faith that God has loved us from eternity and has prepared an inheritance for us.

4. Faith in the Covenant God of His people

In this covenant, made from eternity, the Father declares, 'I will be their God, and they shall be my people'. The believer can therefore say, 'Although my house be not so with God, yet he hath made with me an everlasting covenant, ordered in all things and sure' (2 Samuel 23:5).

5. Faith in God the Father of Christ but also of all who believe in Him

Christ ascended to His Father and our Father (John 20:17). Quoting 2 Corinthians 6:17, 18, Gill shows how God's command to us is to come out in faith and He shall become a Father to us and we shall be His sons and daughters. Here Gill has a bevy of Scripture verses at his disposal as he relates how God's love to His elect chooses them out to be the sons of God (1 John 3:1). This is a fitting reminder to those modern critics who proclaim that to believe that God loved His elect from eternity is a mark of Antinomianism. Gill was in good 'Antinomian' company with John! Another Scriptural teaching which contradicts Gill's modern critics who profess that God's election and the work of the Spirit is not made known to individuals is Romans 8:14-16, 'the Spirit itself beareth witness with our spirit, that we are the children of God.'

6. Faith in the God who forgives iniquity for Christ's sake

Christian faith is the confident trust that God has removed our sins and will remember them no more. Thus the believer can stand boldly before the Throne of Grace knowing that he stands fully acquitted before God.

7. Faith is in God as a justifier

Faith is exercised in the One who lays no charges to God's elect and by whom righteousness is imputed without works (Romans 8:33; 3:30; 4:5, 6; Isaiah 50:8). Who can contend against the Lord's people whom God has justified?

8. Faith in the God of all grace

He is the author and implanter of all grace and the believer can always apply to the Throne of Grace to obtain mercy and grace in time of need.

9. Faith in the God of promises

All God's promises are yea and amen in Christ and God who has promised is faithful and well able and willing to perform them. The object of faith is not the promises but the promising God.

Second: Faith in God the Son

This faith not only entails believing that Christ is the Son of the living God and the gates of hell shall not prevail against those who are found in Christ, it is also an entrance into a new life through His name (John 20:31). He who believes with saving faith on Christ also receives the witness of the Spirit in himself (1 John 3:23; 5:10). 'Believing in him is a going forth in acts of faith and confidence, and is called *faith towards our Lord Jesus Christ*', Acts 20:28.

A. Christ, the object of faith

Gill then shows how faith in Christ as the object of faith must be in Him as Mediator, Redeemer and Saviour. This faith includes:

1. Knowledge of Christ

Gill asks the New Testament's own question, 'How shall they believe in him whom they have not heard?' Before a sinner turns to Christ, he must know that there is a Christ to turn to and the awareness of his own need of Christ because of the sinfulness of his own sin and his lost condition. The remainder of this section and part of the following section must be given in full as Gill's words show how invalid are the numerous claims raised against Gill that faith is merely head knowledge. The sinner 'must be made acquainted with his impotency to save himself; that his own right-hand, his works and services, cannot save him; that if ever he is saved it must be by the grace of God, through the blood and righteousness of Christ, and not by them; he must have knowledge of the fulness and abilities of Christ as a Saviour; he must have seen him full of grace and truth, as having all the fulness of the blessings of grace in him suitable to his wants, whose redemption is plenteous, his salvation complete, he being made everything to his people they want, and able to save to the uttermost all that come unto God by him; and he being just such a Saviour they need, and his salvation so suitable to them, they that know his name, Jesus the Saviour, put their trust in him; and the more ready they are to do this, as they are fully convinced there is no other Saviour; that salvation is in him, and in none else; that it is in vain to expect it from any other quarter, from the works and services of the creature, and therefore determine upon it they shall not be their saviours; but say with Job, *Though he slay me yet will I trust him—he also shall be my salvation*! Psalm 9:10; Job 13:15, 16. Hence knowledge being so requisite to faith, and included in it, faith is sometimes expressed by it, Isaiah 53:11; John 17:3 both in spiritual knowledge and special faith, eternal life is begun, and with which it is connected; and so knowledge and faith are joined together as inseparable companions, and as expressive of the same thing; *And we have known and believed the love that God hath to us*, are firmly persuaded of it, 1 John 4:16 and some of the strongest acts of faith of the saints have been expressed by words of knowledge; 'I know that my Redeemer liveth, &c.' 'I know in whom I have believed, &c.' Job 19:25; 1 Timothy 1:12.[78]

2. An assent unto Christ as a Saviour

Here Gill speaks firmly against the idea that such an assent is 'a bare naked assent of the mind to the truth of the person and offices of Christ' etc., which, he adds, was the view of Simon Magus. Gill quotes John Owen's very strong language on this issue referring to the 'naked assent' view as pernicious and perverse poison. The fact that Jesus Christ is presented as the Saviour of the chief of sinners is a matter to be urgently experienced in one's own life than merely nodded to as an axiom to be intellectually accepted. 'Worthy of all acceptance' goes far deeper than the mind. We do not accept Christ as a saviour of sinners in general but as the suitable saviour of sinners in particular, among

---

[78] Op. cit. p. 735.

whom, we feel ourselves chief. We do not believe in the doctrine of Christ only but in Christ Himself.

3. Knowledge of Christ as Saviour worked by love

True faith provides the believer with a knowledge and realisation of Christ gained through experience which shows how precious Christ is. This has nothing to do with bare assent as when a sinner receives Christ, he receives the love of truth with him and is thus able to discern spiritual things withheld from others. This transforms the sinner into a saint.

4. True faith includes dependence, trust and confidence

Here Gill says: 'True, spiritual, special (i.e. saving) faith in Christ includes in it a dependence on him, trust and confidence in him alone for everlasting life and salvation; it is a soul's venturing on Christ, resolving if it perishes it will perish at his feet; it is a resignation of itself to Christ, a committing its soul, and the important welfare and salvation of it into Christ's hands, trusting him with all, looking to him, relying on him, and acquiescing in him as the alone Saviour.'[79]

B. Acts of faith as described in the Scriptures

1. Faith expressed in seeing the Son

This is one of the first acts of faith, reflecting the truth of Christ's words, 'This is the will of him that sent me, that every one which seeth the Son, and believeth on him, may have everlasting life' (John 6:40). To be enabled to look to Jesus, the author and finisher of our faith is a sure sign that faith is born. It is here that Gill blows away his accusers' myth that he refuses to preach to sinners but only to those who profess signs of being sensible to the working of the Spirit. Gill knew that his task, in the Spirit, was to break down the natural barriers of man through the preached word and make those sensible of their case whom the Spirit had chosen at that particular time. He thus continues:

Faith is a light struck into the heart of a sinner whose understanding was darkened, yea darkness itself, till God commanded light to shine in darkness; by which, though first but glimmering, he sees himself a sinner, miserable and undone, without a Saviour, when Christ is held forth in the gospel to be looked at by him; that as a glass in which he is to be beheld, and

---

[79] Op. cit. p. 736.

where he is evidently set forth crucified and slain for sinners; and so is the hope set before them, both to be looked at and to be laid hold on by them, who was typified by the brazen serpent set upon a pole by *Moses*, for the *Israelites* bitten by the serpents to look at and live, John 3:14, 15. And not only sensible sinners are directed to behold the Lamb of God which taketh away the sin of the world, as *John's* hearers were by him; and are encouraged by the ministers of the word, who shew unto men the way of salvation, to look to and believe on the Lord Jesus Christ and be saved; but they are encouraged by Christ himself; who says, *Behold me, behold me, to a nation not called by his name, look unto me and be ye saved all the ends of the earth, for I am God, and there is none else!* Isaiah 65:1 and 45:22 which sight of him fills their souls with love to him, signified by hungering and thirsting after his righteousness, and panting after his salvation. And this sight of Christ by faith is nigh, and not afar off; now, and not hereafter; and for a man's self, and not another; he looks to him not merely as a Saviour of others, but to him as a Saviour and Redeemer suitable for him.[80]

Rather than criticise Gill for allegedly not preaching to sinners, it ought to be acknowledged that few of the systematic works extant on doctrine, are so evangelical in their definitions of the outworking of faith.

2. Faith as a motion of the soul unto Christ

Having first seen Christ, the new believer feels drawn to him in joyful expectancy. He who believes on Christ shall never suffer spiritual want. Quite contrary to claims that Gill does not believe in invitations to Christ, he explains here how the gospel invitation is encouraged by the Spirit and the bride who say 'Come' and the gospel-trumpet which is blown with power with the message, 'Come unto me, all ye that labour and are heavy laden, and I will give you rest' (Matthew 11:28). Such souls come because they are effectively worked upon by the grace of God through the gospel invitation and Christ says, 'All that the Father giveth me shall come to me'. This coming to Christ is therefore because

---

[80] Op. cit. p. 736.

of the Father's teaching, instruction and drawing them with loving kindness and through the power of His grace.

3. Faith expressed in fleeing to Christ

This motion is the act of fleeing to Christ to escape the danger that one is in. This is an ever repeated theme in Gill's teaching that the gospel urges sinners to flee from the wrath to come. Strange it is that this is the very teaching that Gill's critics deny that he performs. Obviously this is only because they are fully ignorant of his works. Why God allows this blindness to thwart their usefulness as messengers of truth is unknown but well-known is the fact that things are so and reflect sadly on Gill's enemies as they hinder Gill's message of fleeing to Christ to reach needy souls. Of this fleeing Gill says:

> Fleeing supposes danger, and a sense of it; Christ is the city of refuge, the strong hold and tower, they are directed to; whither coming, they find shelter and safety from avenging justice and every enemy, a supply of wants, and ground of hope of eternal life and happiness.[81]

This fleeing in faith demonstrates that it is:

a. A venturing act

Gill explains how faith is at first a venture because the soul does not know how he will fare, it is rather a 'Peradventure he will save my life.' Such sinners come to Christ believing that if He saves them, it is well, but if not they will die as they would without Him.

b. A casting oneself into the arms of Christ

It is to go to Christ as a suckling to be nurtured in His arms. It is a casting of one's burdened self on His mercies.

c. A laying hold of Christ

It is experiencing that Christ is a tree of life to those who lay hold upon Him (Proverbs 3:18) and from this tree the new-born child finds fruit to succour him. It is a going to Christ, conscious of sin and guilt, pleading that God will be propitious and accept him.

---

[81] Op. cit. p. 737.

d. A retaining Christ

It is holding fast to Christ as Jacob would not let the angel go until he received a blessing. It is thus a continuous exercise of the grace of faith and a continuous being nourished by Christ. It is also a holding on to Him when it even seems that Christ has withdrawn Himself.

e. A leaning on Christ

It is a leaning on the Lord and a staying on Him as expressed in Isaiah 10:20 and 50:10. It is a wandering out of darkness into a marvellous light. Leaning on the Beloved is a sure mark of faith and a looking to Him for all supplies of grace and strength.

f. A receiving Christ

This is the grandest act of faith, 'As many as received him, even that believe on his name' (John 1:12) are the true faithful. Christ must not be received in the head alone but in the heart finding Christ altogether lovely. This is a receiving of Christ completely:

i. In all His offices

Here Gill outlines that Christ is Prophet, Priest and King and that it is in all these capacities that we must accept Him in faith. Just as the whole Pascal Lamb was for the faithful and had to be consumed in its entirety, so Christ is not divided and He must be received as all that He is in order to be Lord in our lives.

ii. In all the blessings of grace

Those who receive Christ receive the adoption so that they become the children of God. They receive a justifying righteousness which acquits them from all guilt and clothes them with a robe of righteousness and glory. By faith, the child of God receives the grace of forgiveness, the grace of atonement, indeed grace for grace and that in abundance. They also receive an inheritance among them which are sanctified by faith (Acts 26:18) and receive grace from God to make them meet for it; the Spirit being given them as the earnest of their inheritance until they take possession of it.

iii. As a free Gift

As a gift of God and expression of His love, Christ Himself is given to the faithful. Though unmerited, He is given freely.

iv. As the good part that will never be taken away

In receiving Christ, He is seen as being above all others in His multiple offices as Lord, Head, Mediator and Saviour, but not only this. He is seen as being above all things precious, more than any other ties a human being may have. The worst things that can happen to a Christian, be they imprisonment, afflictions or bonds for Christ's sake, are glorious experiences in comparison to the best that can be obtained outside of Christ.

Third: Faith in God the Holy Spirit

Though we read little of the Holy Spirit being the object of faith, He is such because of His co-equality with the Father and the Son. Faith must go out to Him in His being, perfections and offices as sanctifier and comforter and in His operations of grace on the soul. We are to be baptised in His Name and to Him we must pray and in Him we must trust for assistance and guidance in prayer. We are to trust in the Spirit to carry on and finish all the works of grace in our souls in the confidence that He who has begun a good work in us, will perform it until the day of Jesus Christ (Philippians 1:6). As, according to Galatians 5:22, faith is one of the fruits of the Spirit, it is obvious that the Spirit must be the object of our faith.[82]

III. The subjects of the grace of faith

Firstly: The subjects of faith are not good angels as these live by sight and not in faith to God and Christ as believers do. They are constantly in the presence of God and are ministering spirits to Christ.

Secondly: Men only are the subjects of the grace of faith but not all men (2 Thessalonians 3:2). Many have not even heard the gospel and many have rejected it. None but the elect of God can become subjects of faith. 'As many as were ordained unto eternal life believed' (Acts

---

[82] Gill mentions this in the following section but it may be added here.

13:48). Thus the faith of God's elect is given to those who are regenerated, called and sanctified, that is those who are said to be 'born of God' (John 1:12, 13; 1 John 5:1). Faith is also a fruit of the work of the Spirit in man, making him spiritually alive whilst others are dead in trespasses and sins.

Thirdly: Though this faith is common to all believers and like precious to all, it is different in them according to the degree and exercise of it.

1. In some it is great faith

We see this in the centurion and the woman of Canaan. Hebrews 11 lists individuals who have set a good example of great faith and power and efficacy in living according to it.

2. In some it is little faith

Matthew 6:30; 8:26 and 14:31 show that not all exercise the same faith and in some there is only a little of it in evidence.

3. In some it is least of all

Matthew 17:20; 13:32 show that there are those who have the least faith which is only the size of a mustard seed. Even where faith is so small, however, there is a sense of its smallness and a longing to be with God and a desire to see Jesus. Such people are Christ's little ones whom He carries in His arms like tiny lambs. They are people Christ does not despise.

4. In some, there seems to be none

At times some believers must be asked, 'Where is your faith?' as they have apparently none to show. Yet there is still a longing in such people's hearts for Jesus and a desire to be with Him. There is also a sadness because there is such a sense of the want of more faith. 'Lord I believe, help my unbelief' is the prayer of these people.

5. Faith can be weak and it can be strong

Abraham was strong in faith and did not stagger faced with the supposed impossible, but others are weak and always in danger of showing their weakness in doubtful disputations.

6. Faith as exercised is different in the same believer at different times

Abraham was the father of all who believe and mighty in faith but at times unbelief and distrust was his lot as in the case of David. This was not merely a feature of Old Testament believers as New Testament Peter boasted that if all men would forsake

Christ, he would not but when difficulties arose, we find him exercising no faith and denying Christ.

7. Faith in some is in full assurance

Hebrews 10:22 expresses this as does the testimony of Stephen at his death. There are times when certain believers can say, 'My beloved is mine and I am His' and here nothing can deter the exercise of full faith.

Fourthly: The seat of this grace

The seat of this grace, with reference to faith's subject, is the whole soul of man. It is with the heart that we believe unto righteousness and we are admonished to believe in the Lord with all our heart, as Philip said to the eunuch. All talk of whether the seat of faith is in the understanding or the will or in the affections misses the true point that faith must possess the whole soul and the whole soul must possess faith. Faith works in and through all our human faculties. We understand by faith (Hebrews 11:1-3); we trust by faith (Job 13:15, 16) and we love by faith (Galatians 5:6).

IV. The causes of faith

Firstly: The efficient cause

The efficient cause of faith is the work, operation and power of God (John 6:29; Colossians 2:12; 2 Thessalonians 1:11). The entire Trinity is at work in it.

1. God the Father

He is the God of all grace and no one comes to Christ without the wherewithal to do so given him by the Father (John 6:44, 45, 65).

2. The Lord Jesus Christ

Faith is prayed and wished for through Christ as the Father and the Scriptures teach that faith comes through the righteousness of God and our Saviour Jesus Christ. Furthermore, we are told that Christ is the Author and Finisher of our faith (Ephesians 6:23; 2 Peter 1:1; Hebrews 12:2).

3. The Holy Spirit

The Spirit is co-author of faith with the Father and the Son. The grace of faith is reckoned with the fruits of the Spirit and He is called the Spirit of faith. Faith is also called the gift of the Spirit and the operation of the Spirit (1 Corinthians 12:9; Galatians 5:22; 2 Corinthians 4:13).

Secondly: The moving cause

The moving cause of faith is the free grace of God which gives faith to the elect as a free gift and has nothing to do with the merits of the sinner. We believe through grace (Acts 18:27; 13:48; Matthew 11:25, 26).

Thirdly: The means and instruments

The Word of God and ministers of the gospel are the usual means and instruments of faith. The Word is written that men might believe that Jesus Christ is the Son of God. Faith comes by hearing the Word preached when it is attended with the power and Spirit of God (John 20:31; Romans 10:8, 17; Acts 17:4; 18:8; John 1:17, 20; 1 Corinthians 3:5; 1 Corinthians 2:4, 5).

V. The effects of faith

Firstly: Several blessings of grace are attributed to faith, through which access is made to them and enjoyment and comfort of them is obtained. These are:

1. Justification

Here Gill's argument will be given in full as it is so essential to the main subject matter of this book and *Of Faith in God and in Christ* is a work seldom turned to by critics of Gill's teaching on justification. Here Gill says:

> Justification; hence we read of *being justified by faith*, Romans 3:30; 5:1; Galatians 2:16; 3:8 not by it, or through it, as a work of righteousness done by men, for then they would be justified and saved by works, contrary to the Scriptures, Romans 4:2, 6; Titus 3:5. Nor as a grace of the Spirit of God wrought in men; for that is a part and branch of sanctification and would tend to confound justification and sanctification, which are two distinct things; the one an act of God's grace towards men, the other a work of his grace in them. Nor as a cause of it; for it is *God*, and not faith *that justifies*, Romans 8:33, for though men are said to be justified by faith, yet faith is never said to justify them. Nor as a condition of justification; for God *justifies*

the ungodly, Romans 4:5. Nor as a motive; for that is the free grace of God; *Being justified freely by his grace*, Romans 3:24. Nor as the matter of it; that is the righteousness of Christ: faith and righteousness are two different things, and are frequently distinguished; that by which men are justified are the obedience and blood of Christ, Romans 5:9, 19. But faith is neither of them; faith is a man's own, but justifying righteousness is another's; Not *having on mine own righteousness*, Philippians 3:9. Faith is imperfect; but the righteousness by which men are justified is perfect, or it cannot be reckoned righteousness, Deuteronomy 6:25, it is not the *credere*, or act of faith, but the object who, or what, is believed in, that is imputed for righteousness; it is Christ and his righteousness, the object of faith, by which men are justified; faith objectively, or the object of faith, Christ, who is sometimes called faith, Galatians 3:23, he is made righteousness unto them; faith only relatively considered, as it relates to Christ, receives the blessing of his justifying righteousness from him, being revealed from faith to faith, and given to it, and put into its hands; which faith puts on as a robe of righteousness, and rejoices and glories in it.[83]

2. Adoption
We are the children of God by faith in Christ Jesus (Galatians 3:26). Faith receives the adoption but does not make us the children of God but shows them to be such.
3. The remission of sins
God has set forth Christ to be a propitiation, through faith in his blood, for the remission of sins (Romans 3:25). This does not mean that faith has any merit or virtue in it to procure forgiveness but faith receives the remission of sin as flowing from the grace of God through the blood of Christ (Acts 10:43).
4. Sanctification and purification
These gifts are ascribed to faith. Whoever receives forgiveness of sins, receives an inheritance 'among them which

---

[83] Op. cit. p. 743.

are sanctified by faith that is in me,' that is, in Christ (Acts 26:18). Our hearts are said to be purified by faith (Acts 15:9).

5. Eternal life and salvation

Whoever believes in Christ has everlasting life. Not that faith procures everlasting life as 'eternal life is the gift of God through Jesus Christ our Lord', but faith looks to Christ for it (John 17:3; 6:47; Romans 6:23; Jude 21).

Secondly: By faith souls have communion with God, with Christ, and with His people in His Word and ordinances.

1. They have access to God at the Throne of Grace by faith in Christ, this faith giving them boldness (Ephesians 3:12).

2. Christ dwells in the hearts of believers through faith and believers dwell in Christ through faith (Ephesians 3:17; John 6:56).

3. Believers feed and live upon Christ by faith, 'The life which I now live in the flesh, I live by the faith of the Son of God' says Paul. The just live by faith but not upon faith but by faith in Christ (John 6:54, 57; Galatians 2:20; Romans 1:17).

4. Believers stand walk and go on by faith until faith's end, their eternal inheritance with Christ, is entered into (Romans 11:20; 2 Corinthians 1:24; 5:7; Colossians 2:6).

5. Faith makes Christ precious to souls, 'To them that believe he is precious.' Through faith He becomes the altogether Lovely One (1 Peter 2:7).

6. Faith works by love. The nearer the soul draws to Christ in faith, the more he learns to love Him. The more that the soul tastes and sees that the Lord is good, the more he desires Christ (Galatians 5:6).

7. Faith makes the Word useful and the ordinances pleasant and delightful, 'The word preached did not profit them, not being mixed with faith in them that heard it' (Hebrews 4:2).

Thirdly: There are other effects of faith such as:

1. Faith does not make the believer ashamed of his faith and hope in Christ. Nor of the reproaches and sufferings that might come his way because of his faith (Isaiah 28:16; Romans 9:33; 10:11; 1 Peter 2:6; Psalm 22:5).

2. Faith fills the soul with joy on hearing the Word of salvation preached. When Christ enters our lives we experience joy unspeakable and full of glory and continue to have joy and peace in believing (Acts 16:31-34; 1 Peter 1:8; Philippians 1:25; Romans 15:13).

3. Faith gains for the believer victory over Satan, the world and the enemies of truth. Faith holds up Christ our Shield and Defender and through faith, we can resist the devil so that he flees and can overcome the world in Christ (Ephesians 6:16; 1 Peter 5:9; 1 John 5:4, 5).

4. Faith keeps the saints along salvation's path. Salvation is the aim and end of faith and until we enter glory we are kept by the power of God through faith (1 Peter 1:5, 9; Ephesians 2:8, 9).

VI. The properties or adjuncts of faith
1. The first and principle grace
Without faith, it is impossible to please God. It starts off and sets at work all the other graces that enter the soul through its agency.
2. An exceedingly precious grace
The least degree of it in a believer can move mountains so that it is more precious than gold which perishes because it shows us how precious Christ is (2 Peter 1:1; 1 Peter 1:7; 2:7).
3. There is only one faith
There is only one doctrine of faith and it is that once delivered to the saints. Though there are divers kinds of faith, there is only one faith which is the faith of God's elect (Ephesians 4:5; 2 Peter 1:1).
4. Every man has his own faith
Though we speak of common faith, one man cannot have faith for another but each has his own faith. The Lord prayed for Peter so that Peter's faith would not fail. This makes Christ personally precious to us as He has given us a personal faith in Him (Habakkuk 2:4; James 2:18; Luke 22:32).
5. Saving faith is true, real and unfeigned
There is a hypocritical faith as in the case of Simon Magus but belief from the heart is put there by God (1 Timothy 1:5; 2 Timothy 1:5; Acts 8:13, 37; Romans 10:9, 10).
6. Faith cannot be lost
The believer's faith flows from, and is secured by, God's immutable will in election and it is a gift of God which is without repentance, that is, irreversible and irrevocable. This is confirmed by the intercession of Christ on our behalf in His office of Author and Finisher of our faith.

7. Our faith is imperfect

As we know only in part, our faith is only in part. We ought thus to pray that the Lord will increase our faith so that it might grow exceedingly according to Scriptural guidance (1 Thessalonians 3:10; 2 Thessalonians 1:3).

8. Faith is the substance of things hoped for

Faith is our earnest of what is to come. It gives substance to the as yet unseen and provides us with a glimpse into eternity and gives a certainty to things past, present and future, near and far.

Thus faith for Gill, far from being a mere 'notion' of a fact, is the life-blood of a Christian because it is in the blood of Christ and what this gains for us eternally that faith has its basis. It is the Father-given guarantee in the partaking of the faith and righteousness of the Son by the constant keeping of the Holy Spirit in our lives before we shall be like Christ in our resurrected bodies and see Him face to face. It is a glimpse of eternity before time is dissolved and thus what makes the believer eternal in himself. By faith, the eternal will of God for our very own entrance into eternity is made known to us.[84]

---

[84] It is recommended that the reader studies at least Gill's essay 'Of Trust and Confidence in God' but it would be better to read the entire Volume III of Gill's *Body of Divinity* as the above chapter in no way exhausts what Gill has to say on this grace of graces.

Chapter Four

The Relationship Between Pardon And Justification

Gill sees the doctrine of pardon as following systematically the doctrine of satisfaction as it is through the atonement that God is able to forgive sinners. The doctrine of pardon cannot be known through natural revelation, nor by the law as it is a pure doctrine of the gospel which Christ commissioned His apostles to preach. In his *Of the Pardon of Sin*[85], Gill lists seven points regarding the doctrine.

Firstly: That there is pardon of sin to be had

The blessing provided in the covenant of grace is that God says, 'I will be merciful to their unrighteousness, and their sins and their iniquities will I remember no more' (Hebrews 8:12). So closely is God connected with the promise of forgiveness that it has become part of His Name in Scripture (cf. Exodus 34:7). In the purposes of God, Christ was sent forth in the fulness of time to be a propitiation, through faith in His blood, which was shed for many for the remission of sins. Through Christ, we gain repentance and the forgiveness of sins (Acts 5:31). We are to pray for forgiveness and God would not encourage us to do so if He were not ready to forgive (Psalm 32:5; 51:1, 2, 7-9; Daniel 9:19; Matthew 6:12). Forgiveness of sins is part of the whole work of salvation which would be incomplete without it.

---

[85] *Body of Divinity*, Book VI, Chap. VII, p. 493ff.

Secondly: The way this pardon is ensured
1. Sin is lifted up and taken away
When the Psalmist says, 'Blessed is he whose transgression is forgiven' (Psalm 32:1), he uses a word to describe 'forgiven' which means 'to be taken off and carried away'. Sin lays on the sinner and is a great burden to him, laying upon him the obligation to punishment but God lifts this burden off the sinner and lays it on Christ who is willing and able to bear it. This sin is removed as far as the East is from the West and will never more be found.
2. Sin is covered and hid
The Psalmist also says in Psalm 32, 'Blessed is he whose sins are covered.' God hates to look on all that is impure and nauseating and goes to great lengths to have our sin buried. Our own efforts at doing good will never be able to cover our sin in God's sight nor remove the stench of it. This is why God covers us with the righteous robes of His Son. His work of atonement is described in the Scriptures as a covering. By His shed blood, our sins are completely smothered with His love.
3. Sin is not imputed
The Psalmist then tells us in Psalm 32, 'Blessed is the man to whom the Lord imputeth not iniquity.' This means that God refuses to take notice of it as a charge against us. He has acquitted His elect from it and imputed it to His Son who is willing to bear our punishments and thus the law is satisfied to our credit.
4. Sin is blotted out
Here, again, we can turn to David. He prayed, 'Blot out my transgressions—and blot out all mine iniquities' (Psalm 51:1, 9). The prophet Isaiah spoke of the God who blots out transgressions (Isaiah 43:25). One must think of an accounts book with the debts on one side and the credits on the other. Suddenly, by a gracious hand, the debts are all paid and the debt side crossed out. Christ has 'blotted out the handwriting of ordinances that was against us' (Colossians 2:14).
5. Sin is remembered no more
God is the gracious Non-Remembrancer. He has promised to remember our sins no more. They are not only blotted out of

existence, they are blotted out from God's own mind (Hebrews 8:12; Isaiah 43:25).

6. Filthy sinners become white as snow

David prays, 'Wash me, and I shall be whiter than snow' (Psalm 51:7). God answers such prayers and promises, 'Thy sins shall be as white as snow' (Isaiah 1:18) and even looks on His people as being purer than snow (Lamentations 4:7).

Thirdly: The quality and quantity of sins pardoned

1. The quality of sin is referred to in the Scriptures as 'trespasses'. Sin is entering forbidden territory and being where we have no business to be. The Bible sign here is certainly, 'Trespassers will be prosecuted!' Every sin is a sign of hostility against God, not recognising the boundaries He has given us in love for our own protection. Every trespass against the infinite God is an infinite sin. Any trespass against the law of God puts us under the infinite penalty of sin. This is why the Bible refers to sin also as debts which can never be paid off by sinners or a disease which is incurable. Thanks be to God that in spite of this seemingly hopeless situation for the sinner, there is One 'Who forgiveth all thine iniquities, who healeth all thy diseases' (Psalm 103:3; Isaiah 33:24; Malachi 4:2).

2. As to the quantity of sin, all sins of all kinds are forgiven us (Colossians 2:13; Psalm 103:3) whether they be original sin, which is the source and fountain of all sin, or the secret and open sins of our flesh. Whether they be our backslidings, revolts and attempts at apostasy. Whether they be sins of omission or commission. All our iniquities are laid on Christ and are forgiven for His sake (Isaiah 43:22-25; Jeremiah 3:12-14, 22; Hosea 14:4.)

Fourthly: The causes of the pardon of sin

1. The efficient cause is God

Neither men nor angels have a part in it.

a. A man can forgive a sin as committed against him but not one as committed against God. Only God, for Christ's sake can forgive such sin (Ephesians 4:32; Colossians 2:13). Here Gill expands what he is saying to criticise strongly the practice of absolution in various church bodies. He argues:

Ministers can remit sin ministerially and declaratively, but not authoritatively; no man that goes under the name of a priest, or a minister of the word, has a power of absolution, or has authority to absolve men from their sins: all that a true and faithful preacher of the gospel can do, is to preach remission of sins in the name of Christ; and to declare, that whosoever repent of their sins, and believe in Christ, shall receive the forgiveness of them; and which declaration of theirs God abides by and confirms; and whose sins, in this sense, they remit, they are remitted, John 20:23. To assume a power to forgive sin, and absolve from it, is the height of Antichristianism; it is, with respect to this, that antichrist is said to sit in the temple of God, *shewing himself that he is god*, by taking that to himself which belongs to God only; namely, to forgive sin; this is one of the blasphemies, and a principle one, which his mouth is opened to utter, to dispense with sin, grant indulgences of it, and pardon for it, 2 Thessalonians 2:4; Revelation 13:5, 6. The highest angel in heaven cannot forgive, nor procure the forgiveness, of one sin; they could not for those of their kind that sinned; nor can they for any of the sons of men.[86]

b. There is nothing a man can do of himself to pardon sin. It is also impossible for him to provide any service in return so that God might be moved to pardon the sinner from His side. The only way to be pardoned is by grace. There is a wrong belief that repentance earns pardon but repentance, as pardon are both gifts of God's grace and are entirely dependent on His will. Others say

---

[86] Op. cit. p. 496. Here, at home, the German Protestant churches have long been working towards unity with the Papists but this element of Roman Catholicism has, at last, broken their enthusiasm and caused them, for the first time in years, to openly criticise the people of the Pope. The criticism was sparked off by a German bishop, recently telling his flock that it is not a sin for the poor to steal. Here is a church dignitary who loses all Christian character by setting himself up as God, proclaiming what is sin and what is not sin, forgetting the Scriptures which clearly say, 'Let him that stole steal no more.' Gill's labelling this as 'Antichristianism' is in no way an exaggeration.

that faith secures pardon but this is also wrong. Faith cannot cause pardon by any virtue of its own as faith, too, as pardon, is only obtained by the blood of Christ and the satisfaction He makes on our behalf by His blood. Nor can submission for baptism pardon us. Baptism neither takes away original sin or any other sin. The Bible speaks of being baptised for the remission of sins but this means that by means of this ordinance, 'they might be led to the sufferings, death, and bloodshed of Christ, represented in it; for whose name's-sake remission of sins is granted, and whose blood was shed for it, and cleanses from it.'[87]

c. God alone can forgive sins and no other has this prerogative (Mark 2:7; Isaiah 43:25; Daniel 9:9). All sin is committed against God, so only God can ultimately forgive sin. Only the One who has made the laws can work out a method to appease their breakage (Micah 7:18; Psalm 51:1; Daniel 9:19; Matthew 6:9, 12; Acts 8:22).

d. All three Persons in the Trinity have a concern in forgiving sin. Gill's words here must be given in full as few can portray the work of the Godhead in salvation as he does. Gill is also so often criticised for leaving out the work of Christ and the Spirit in salvation seeing it as a mere declaration of the Father, irrespective of the work of the Son and the Spirit. This quote— as many others in this book—will put to flight such fancy. Indeed, Gill is always careful to point out the work of the entire Godhead in salvation and thus stands in stark contrast to most of his accusers who see the Godhead as three different modes in salvation, each doing His own job. Here, modern teaching regarding the Trinity is especially questionable. It views God as decreeing before time all that is to come and sees Christ as doing His part in His life of suffering and then leaving everything to the Holy Ghost to put all into practice in time as if neither the Father nor the Son were any longer active in His world. Gill's thoughts,

---

[87] Op. cit. p. 497. This definition of baptism is a further indication why Evangelical Anglicans found Gill close to their own conception of the gospel as reflected in baptism which eased their full fellowship with him.

when known, must be seen as far superior in their Biblical perspective:

God the Father made an early provision of this blessing of pardon in his heart, in his purpose, in his council and covenant; and sent his Son to be the propitiation for it, and for the remission of it, through faith in his blood; and does bestow it for his sake; in which he shews, not only his grace, but his justice and faithfulness; for upon the bloodshed of his Son for it, he is *just and faithful to forgive sin*; just, in that the blood of Christ is a sufficient atonement for it; and faithful to his counsels, covenant, and promises, concerning it.

Christ, as God, and the Son of God, has power to forgive sin, even as Immanuel, God with us, God in our nature, and when he was here on earth; of which he gave proof, by another act of his divine power, bidding a lame man take up his bed and walk, Matthew 9:2, 6. As God-man and Mediator, his blood was shed for the remission of sin; and by it, it was obtained; as the Advocate of his people, he calls for it, and demands and requires the application of it, when it is wanted; and as the exalted Saviour, he gives it, and in his name it is preached, according to his orders, by the ministers of the gospel.

The holy Spirit of God has also a concern in it: he convinces men of sin, and of their need of the pardon of it; he makes it manifest; he takes the blood of Christ, and applies it to the conscience, which speaks peace and pardon; he pronounces the sentence of it, in the conscience of a sinner; he is the holy Spirit of promise, and he seals up the pardon of sin with a promise; and witnesses to the spirits of God's people, that they are pardoned ones.[88]

---

[88] Op. cit. p. 497.

2. The moving cause is grace and mercy

Neither man's misery nor merits is the impulsive moving cause of pardon but alone the sovereign grace and mercy of God, through Christ (Ephesians 1:7; Psalm 51:1; Luke 1:77, 78).

3. The procuring, meritorious cause is the blood of Christ

Christ's blood has attained forgiveness for us as, because of it, God can forgive sin. This is because Christ's human nature is in union with the divine Person of the Son of God (Hebrews 9:14; 1 John 1:7).

Fifthly: The effects of pardon

The effects, once applied, are:

1. Peace of conscience

There is no peace of conscience until sin has been dealt with and pardoned. When there is a view of an interest in justification, through the righteousness of Christ and His shed blood, a peace that passes all understanding and which the world cannot give, enters the soul. This is better experienced than expressed.

2. Cheerfulness of spirit

Sin depresses the mind, leading often to despair, especially when accompanied with no hope of pardon. When the Lord's 'Be of good cheer, thy sins are forgiven thee' is heard, the bones that were broken, now rejoice.

3. Comfort of soul

When the anger of the Lord is turned away the soul is able to experience true comfort. It is the task of ministers to cry as Isaiah was told (40:1, 2), 'Speak comfortably to Jerusalem; cry unto her, that her iniquity is pardoned.'

4. Access to God with boldness and confidence

A soul burdened under guilt comes with bowed head to the Throne of Grace, pleading, 'God be merciful to me a sinner.' When he has a view of Christ's triumphant work on the cross for him and the burden of his sin is rolled away, he can come to the Throne of Grace with boldness and so enter into the Holiest of Holies with God.

5. Divine worship is attended with delight

When forgiveness is found in the Lord, the heart goes out in worship and the soul is eager to do service to the living God (Psalm 130:4; Hebrews 12:28; 9:14).

6. Love to God and Christ is raised

Love received from God produces love in its turn. Those who are forgiven much, love much (Luke 7:47).

7. The exercise of evangelical repentance is influenced by pardon being applied

Tears of repentance, shed on receipt of pardoning grace and from an assurance of it, occur when sin is seen at its worst and God's forgiving love at its height. This produces a frame of mind moved by godly sorrow and evangelical mourning. The more one is sensible to sin, the more one is sensible to pardon and the love, grace and mercy of God (Ezekiel 16:63; Zechariah 12:10).

8. Thankfulness of soul for such a mercy

What malefactor, pardoned on the brink of the scaffold would not thank his deliverer? How much more thankful will a soul be who has been rescued from the brink of hell and found a Saviour who forgives all iniquities eternally! (Psalm 103:2, 3).

Sixthly: The properties of pardon

1. It is an act of God's free grace

God has acted according to the multitudes of His tender mercies. It is an act of the Father's grace in finding a ransom for us to be the propitiation for our sins. It is an act of the Son's grace in shedding His blood for the remission of sin and it is an act of the Spirit's grace in leading a soul to the blood of Jesus which speaks peace and pardon to him. In this God is always sovereign, saying to the object of his love, 'I, even I, am he that blotteth out thy transgressions, for mine own sake!' (Ephesians 1:7; Psalm 51:1; Isaiah 43:25).

2. It is a point of justice

'If we confess our sins, he is faithful and just to forgive us our sins' (1 John 1:9). The counsel, covenant and promises of God are all satisfied because the blood of the covenant has been shed for the remission of sins. Christ as our Advocate now calls for and demands our pardon as a right of justice.

3. It is a complete act

All the sins and trespasses of God's people are forgiven together and at once, though its manifestation and application may be at different times. In the mind of God, this is passed at once for all sins past, present and to come which burden His people. The objection that sins cannot be forgiven before they are committed is invalid by virtue of Christ's suretyship-engagements and His performance of them.

4. It is an act which will never be repeated

Pardon is a gift of grace which is without repentance on God's part. Once sins are pardoned and blotted out, they cannot be found. God has put them away and they will never again see His countenance.

5. It is one of the chief articles and blessings of faith

When the Psalmist calls upon his soul to bless the Lord (Psalm 103:2, 3), he puts pardon first. Gill reckons that next to election it is one of the greatest spiritual blessings we are blessed with in Christ.

Seventhly: Further questions referring to pardon not answered above

1. Are there venial sins?

The Papist distinguishes between venial and mortal sins, arguing that the venial kind do not bring with them the penalty of eternal death as they are pardonable. There is no such distinction in reality as all sin leads to damnation but equally all sins, excepting the one against the Holy Ghost, can be pardoned. The Bible speaks of greater and lesser sins, sins committed in ignorance and those committed with knowledge (John 19:11; Luke 12:47, 48; Matthew 11:22, 24), yet every sin is mortal and deserving of death. He who offends in one point against the law is guilty of all. Every single sin must be accounted for on the Day of Judgment but all these sins are accounted for by Christ's vicarious life, suffering and death for His own people. His blood cleanses from all sin.

2. Will any sins be forgiven in the world to come?

Matthew 12:31, 32 tells us that the sin against the Holy Ghost will not be forgiven in this world, nor the world to come. This moves certain people to hope for a forgiveness in the world to come for other sins. The expression, however, merely refers to the certainty of this special sin not being forgiven. The Bible makes it plain that there will be no forgiveness in the world to come for any sin but that forgiveness in Christ is experienced now for both this world and the following. Their remission is perfect.

3. Will the sins of pardoned ones be made public on the day of judgment?

Gill cannot find definite teaching on this matter and, for once, he says what he thinks rather than what Scripture explicitly says. Even here, however, he is not without Scriptural backing. He believes that our personal sins will not be revealed to others as Matthew 25 teaches that only our good works will be noted. Pardon of sins means that they are blotted out so that it hardly seems likely that God, who tells us He will remember them no more, will change His mind on the Day of Judgment. Furthermore, Christ has gone to great pains to cleanse His church in order to present them spotless before God. Again, it cannot be thought that He will present us both spotless and filthy. The Church will be adorned as a Bride for the Bridegroom and presented in all her beauty for which Christ paid a great price. What earthly Bridegroom would spend his honeymoon in judgment over his bride? The marriage Supper of the Lamb will be a time of joyful deliverance from all worldly sorrows and a time of true love, resplendent with the 'Well done' of the Father!

4. Is it the duty of the saints to pray for pardon of sin?

It is a common belief amongst modern so-called Evangelical Calvinists that Antinomians, of whom they believe John Gill and William Huntington are chief, do not believe in praying for pardon of sin. I have dealt with William Huntington on prayer in two books elsewhere.[89] Now we must look closer at Gill's serious, sober and Scriptural thoughts on the matter.

---

[89] See my *William Huntington: Pastor of Providence* and references to him with regards to prayer in my *Law and Gospel in the Theology of Andrew Fuller.*

Prayer is a moral duty, incumbent on all, says Gill, but the moot question is ought we to pray for pardon of sin as Christians, knowing that our sins have been blotted out? Gill answers pastorally but not without urging the testimony of Scripture. If we are filled with a sense of pardon then, of course, here we ought to be thanking rather than praying for more pardon. It can be however, that the believer is still troubled by his sin and has no sense of pardon in particular matters. He ought to be praying, 'We have transgressed and rebelled, thou hast not pardoned,' (Lamentations 3:42) and recognising his duty, privilege and interest to pray for the manifestation and comfort of pardon. However, we also find saints sinning daily in thought, word and deed and Christ has specifically told us to not only pray for daily bread but to pray 'forgive us our sins' (Luke 11:3, 4.) This has been the practice of saints from all time. Moses, David and Daniel prayed in this way, proving to be examples for us. Gill refers particularly to David's prayer, 'I said, I will confess my transgressions unto the Lord', (Gill adds, 'and so he did!') 'and thou forgavest the iniquity of my sin; for this shall every one that is godly pray unto thee in a little time when thou mayest be found' (Psalm 32:5, 6). Here Gill emphasises again that David is praying for pardon for sins committed. Such prayers, Gill explains, are consistent with the nature of pardon as procured by Christ. Gill, however, stresses that he is not speaking of the Papist's need for Christ to be sacrificed again, nor that fresh pardons must be worked out in the mind of God for fresh sins. God has forgiven all trespasses through the blood of His Son, once and for all.

Of the relationship between pardon and justification

After giving his readers references where other questions on similar topics are answered in his works, Gill goes on in his next chapter to compare pardon with justification, of which he says:[90]

---

[90] Chapter VIII, 'On Justification', *Body of Divinity*, p. 507ff.

Pardon of sin, and justification from it, are very closely connected; the one follows upon the other; according to the position of them in some passages of scripture, pardon is first, and justification next; as in Acts 13:38, 39 and 26:18 though they are not, the one, in reality, prior to the other; they are both together in the divine mind, and in the application of them to the conscience of a sinner; indeed, according to the order of causes, justification by the righteousness of Christ, imputed, may be considered as before pardon; since God forgives sin for Christ's sake; that is, for the sake of his righteousness imputed. Now that for the sake of which a thing is, must be before that for which it is, as the cause is before the effect. Some take them to be the same, and that justification lies solely in the remission of sins; and others more rightly make the imputation of Christ's righteousness, and forgiveness of sins, the two parts of justification, distinct ones; whilst others think they are not two integral parts, really distinct, but only one act, respecting two terms, a *quo et ad quem*; just as by one and the same act darkness is expelled from the air, and light is introduced; so by one and the same act of justification, the sinner is absolved from guilt, and pronounced righteous; hence they suppose such express the whole of justification, who say, it consists in the remission of sins, and those that say it consists in the imputation of righteousness; because when God forgives men their sins, he pronounces them righteous, through the imputation of Christ's righteousness to them; and when he pronounces them righteous, by that he forgives them their sins; remission of sin supposes the imputation of Christ's righteousness; and the imputation of Christ's righteousness infers the remission of sin. But though these are not to be separated, yet they are to be distinguished; and I should choose to consider them, not as distinct parts of the same thing, but as distinct blessings of grace; for though pardon and justification agree in some things, in others they differ.[91]

---

[91] Op. cit. p. 502.

How pardon and justification can be said to be similar
1. In their efficient cause
Just as God alone can forgive sin (Mark 2:7), He alone can justify both Jew and Gentile who believe in Christ. Here Gill quotes Romans 3:30 'Seeing it is one God, which shall justify the circumcision by faith, and the uncircumcision through faith.' Gill adds here in his commentary that there is only one way of being justified, whether Jew or Gentile and that is through faith in Christ's righteousness (Romans 3:25). The different prepositions here, Gill explains mean one and the same thing.
2. In their moving cause
Pardon is by the free grace of God as is also justification (Ephesians 1:7; Psalm 51:1; Titus 3:7; Romans 3:24).
3. In their procuring cause
The blood of Christ was shed to procure forgiveness of sin and justification is by the same blood (Matthew 26:28; Romans 5:9).
4. In the objects of it
Those who are pardoned are also justified. To whomsoever God grants the imputed righteousness of Christ, He also grants remission of sin and justification (Romans 4:6-8).
5. In their commencement and completion
Colossians 2:13 and Acts 13:39 teach that pardon and justification commence together and are finished together.
6. In the manner of actually enjoying them
This is through faith. By faith one receives the forgiveness of sins, abundance of grace, and the gift of righteousness to justification of life (Acts 26:18; Romans 5:1, 17, 18).

How pardon and justification can be said to be different
1. Pardon is for sinners who remain such but justification is a pronouncing of people righteous as if they had never sinned. It is one thing for a man to be condemned at the bar and then pardoned but it is another thing to try a man by law and find him righteous as though he had not transgressed the law.

2. Pardon removes the sinner's sin but does not make him righteous. This happens when he is clothed in Christ's protecting righteousness (Zechariah 3:4).

3. Though pardon frees from punishment, it does not entitle to everlasting life and glory which justification does. If a king pardons a criminal, it does not mean he gives him a house and land to go with it. This would require quite a different favour. Justification, however, makes us heirs of an eternal inheritance (2 Samuel 12:13; Romans 5:18; Titus 3:7).

4. Though the blood of Christ was sufficient to procure our pardon, more is necessary for justification. The holiness of Christ's human nature, His perfect obedience and His sufferings and death must be imputed to the person pardoned for justification.

5. Men are justified by the righteousness of Christ which is the fulfilling of the law. Christ did this in the room of His Bride and He has become the fulfilment and end of the law to them for their righteousness. Pardon cannot fulfil the law, cannot give righteousness, does not reside in Christ as does His righteousness imputed to us (Romans 10:4; Isaiah 45:24).

6. Pardon is non-imputation, i.e. of sin; justification is imputation, i.e. of righteousness (Romans 4:6, 7).

7. Christ can be said to be justified in that, as the head and representative of His people, He had their sins laid on Him and imputed to Him and, having made satisfaction to the justice of God, was acquitted, discharged and justified. Christ was not pardoned as it is unwarrantable to speak of pardon where a Person is innocent. It is refreshing to read the great scholar's trust in the Word of God here. Gill says, 'We may truly say, Christ was justified, and that God justified him, because the scriptures say so.' The Scriptures were always Gill's measure of all things (Isaiah 50:8, 9; 1 Timothy 3:16).

8. An innocent person can be acquitted and discharged but we cannot here speak of pardon. We can however, speak of justification as Adam in his innocent state and the elect angels can be said to be justified. If we could perform the deeds of the law, we would be able to justify ourselves as Romans 2:13 and 10:5 tell us, but we cannot perform those deeds. We need therefore both to be pardoned and justified. One must distinguish between cause and effect, justification the cause and pardon the effect, which cannot be confused.

Gill concludes his two chapters on pardon and justification by saying:

> Through the act of justification, persons are freed from sin, and from obligation to punishment for it, sin is not thereby taken out of them. They are, indeed, so freed from it, that God sees no iniquity in them, to condemn them for it; he sees all the sins of his people in the article of providence, and chastises for them; but in the article of justification he sees none in them; they are acquitted, discharged, and justified from all; yet sin dwells in them, as it did in the apostle Paul, who, undoubtedly, was a justified person; yea, *There is not a just man upon earth*; one that is truly righteous, in an evangelical sense, *that doeth good and sinneth not*, Ecclesiastes 7:20.
>
> Through justification by the righteousness of Christ, neither the law is made void and of none effect, nor is the performance of good works discouraged. The law is not made void; *Do we make void the law through faith?* that is, through the doctrine of justification by faith in the righteousness of Christ; *God forbid! yea, we establish the law*; by presenting to it a righteousness every way commensurate to its demands, by which it is magnified and made honourable: nor does this doctrine discourage duty, but animates to it; and is to be constantly preached for this end, *That they which have believed in God, might be careful to maintain good works*, Titus 3:7, 8.[92]

---

[92] Op. cit. p. 518.

Chapter Five

Arguments Against Justification From Eternity Considered: 1. The Situation In Gill's Day

It is most surprising to find a writer who, after stating his own position with obvious firmness, goes on to attack the very position which he has just defended. Most teachers, after stating their case, live, speak and write as if they thought nobody could possibly disagree with them. Gill, however, was a scholar through and through and never tackled a problem from one side only but looked at it from all angles. We therefore find him on numerous occasions considering in great detail what ideas might be advanced against his doctrine of justification and how they might be met. Indeed, so thorough is Gill in his work of self-criticism that his opponents and traducers have really never come up with anything new against him, but have merely presented Gill's own arguments against himself as if they were their own without so much as a hint of an acknowledgement. Equally sadly, they have failed to acknowledge Gill's defence. There are two obvious reasons for this: the first is that most of Gill's modern critics, who believe that God's justifying attention is always motivated by the act of believing in time, have not the balance, poise and objectivity of the older scholars and divines. They appear to be religious controversialists, who tackle theology like politicians tackle the party programmes of their opponents before a General Election. Polemics and dialectics, they are assured, win more votes than scholarly argument and, furthermore, are easily mastered by the unscholarly. Secondly, this latter point, i.e. a lack of scholarship in the works of Gill's critics, is more than merely noticeable. Augustus Montague Toplady (1740-1778), the Anglican, looked up to Gill as his personal mentor in the faith, saying of him in his brief biographical sketch:

> If any one man can be supposed to have trod the *whole circle* of human learning, it was Dr Gill. His attainments, both in abstruse and polite literature, were (what is very uncommon) equally *extensive* and *profound*. Providence had, to this end, endued him with a firmness of constitution, and an unremitting vigour of mind, which rarely fall to the lot of the sedentary and learned. It would, perhaps, try the constitution of half the *literati* in England, only to read, with care and attention, the whole of what he *wrote*.
>
> The Doctor was not one who considered any subject superficially, and by halves. As deeply as human sagacity, enlightened by grace, could penetrate, he went to *the bottom* of everything he engaged in. With a solidity of judgment, and with an acuteness of discernment, peculiar to few, he *exhausted*, as it were, the very soul and substance of most arguments he undertook.—His style, too, resembles himself; it is manly, nervous, plain: conscious, if I may so speak, of the unutterable dignity, value, and importance of the freight it conveys; it drives, directly and perspicuously, to the point in view, regardless of affected cadence, and superior to the niceties of professed refinement.
>
> Perhaps, no man, since the days of St Austin, has written so largely, in defence of the system of Grace; and, certainly, no man has treated that momentous subject, in all its branches, more closely, judiciously, and successfully. What was said of Edward the Black Prince, that he never fought a battle, which he did not win; what has been remarked of the great Duke of Marlborough, that he never undertook a siege, which he did not carry; may be justly accommodated to our great Philosopher and Divine: who, so far as the distinguishing Doctrines of the Gospel are

concerned, never besieged an error, which he did not force from
its strongholds; nor ever encountered an adversary, whom he did
not baffle and subdue.

His learning and labours, if exceedable, were exceeded only
by the invariable *sanctity* of his *life* and *conversation*. From his
childhood, to his entrance on the ministry, to the moment of his
dissolution; not one of his most inveterate opposers was ever able
to charge him with the least shadow of immorality. Himself, no
less than his writings demonstrated, that the Doctrine of Grace
does not lead to licentiousness.[93]

Men like Ryland Sen., John Brine, Augustus Toplady and James
Hervey were no midget-scholars themselves but they were awed by the
profundity of Gill's learning and sanctity of his life. This alone, one
might think, would caution Gill's modern traducers against putting on
the whole rusty, dented, creaky armour of Fullerism and saddling up
like Don Quixote to go out and fight with giant windmills.

The following arguments against the doctrine of justification from
eternity are taken from Gill's sermon *The Doctrine of Justification by
the Righteousness of Christ Stated and Maintained*,[94] which is a heart
to heart talk to his people and 'Of Justification as an Immanent Act',
from Gill's famous *Body of Divinity*[95]. Arguments in the latter essay
were taken from the works of François Turretin (1623-87), the last
Reformed leader of Geneva. Turretin can be compared with Jonathan
Edwards. Both men, though orthodox in themselves, loved to express
that orthodoxy in analytical and philosophical language which was
open to various interpretations and strained at the boundaries of
Scripture. Both had sons who had not the intellectual stamina of their
fathers and who inherited their father's love of philosophy rather than
their love for Biblical truths. Turretin's son, Jean Alphonse (1674-
1737), came under the influence of Latitudinarian Anglicans and
developed what he called 'Moderate Calvinism'. Jonathan Edwards
Jun. (1745-1801) constructed his thinking along lines of the Cambridge
Platonists and Latitudinarians and gave birth to the development in New

---

[93] From Toplady's contribution to the 1772 biography, *Sermons and Tracts*, vol. i.

[94] *Sermons and Tracts*, vol. ii, p. 455 ff.

[95] Book II, Chap. V, p. 207ff.

England of the New Divinity School which was to build a whole theology on Edwards Sen.'s misleading philosophical distinction between moral and natural abilities. This philosophy reached England through the teaching of Bellamy and Hopkins and was also accepted as 'Moderate Calvinism'. It is this moderation of Calvinism which represents, to a great degree, the present day teaching of almost all opponents of John Gill. Here then, is Gill's self-criticism.

1. Men cannot be justified before they exist

It is objected that a person must bodily exist (*esse actu*) before he is declared justified. Gill begs to differ as the justified from eternity have a being in the mind of God (*esse cognitum*) as 'known unto God are all his works from eternity' (Acts 15:1). Furthermore, the justified have a representative being (*esse repræsentativum*) in Christ which means that they are 'blessed with all spiritual blessings in Christ, before the foundation of the world' (Ephesians 1:3) and had 'grace given them in Christ before the world began' (2 Timothy 1:9). This same argument could be raised against election as the elect have also a representative being in Christ and are chosen in Him and have grace given them in Him and abundant blessings in heavenly places and before the foundation of the world (Ephesians 1:3-5; 2 Timothy 1:9). Why then cannot one of these blessings be justification in Christ? Justification is a moral, declaratory act of God and does not need the physical presence of the subject to make it legitimate.

2. Men cannot be justified before they sin

It is further argued that if the elect were justified before their existence, they were justified before they had sinned which is a preposterous thought. This argument, Gill explains, would also deny that Christ atoned for our sins before they were committed and that our sins were imputed to Christ before they were committed. As those who argue in this way believe in the possibility of ransom before sins are committed, they must also accept the possibility of justification before sins are committed. Gill argues here that it is no more absurd to say that the elect are justified before they sin as to say that their sins were imputed to Christ and He died for them and made satisfaction for them before they were committed. Furthermore, Christ was chosen as a Surety and Bail for sinners before they ever sinned. This very fact shows that God made provisions to heal before the plague came.

3. The decree of justification is one thing, justification itself is another

Turretin held that just as the will to sanctify in God is one thing and the actual sanctification is another, so justification itself must be understood as separate from God's will to justify. Gill could not possibly agree. He explains how God's decree and will to elect certain men is the actual electing of them. Furthermore, His will not to impute sin to them is the non-imputation of sin in their case, just as His will to impute righteousness to them is the actual imputation of righteousness to them. Thus His decree and will to justify His people is their justification. God's will is consistent in itself and not conditioned by external circumstances. Sanctification, however, is a different matter as this is, in Gill's words, 'transient on an external subject, producing real, physical, inherent change'.[96] Gill means by this that justification is a procedure external to the believer, whereas sanctification is an internal, transforming procedure. Justification does not require the actual presence 'in court' of the one declared just but sanctification requires the existence of the sinner to be sanctified as this is a work of God wrought in man with an exercise of power and efficacious grace performed by God performed on them. Here Gill is distancing himself from the charge which leading 'evangelical Calvinistic' magazines are now levelling against their 'Antinomian' brethren, that justification is an infusion of inherent righteousness in men. If the decree of justification had to be followed by an infusion of righteousness in the believer, then Turretin's argument would stand. As justification has nothing whatsoever to do with the Papist dogma of infused righteousness, there is no force in Turretin's argument. The facts of the case are that the decree before the foundation of the world was to elect certain people to everlasting life and salvation and to justify these people which was settled there and then. God did not elect anyone theoretically but practically and as a matter of fact.

4. Romans 8:30 destroys the doctrine of justification from eternity

Turretin understands Paul as arguing that God justifies those who are called, therefore, because they are called in time, they must be justified in time, but after the experience of being called. This argument is rejected by Gill because Romans 8:30, 2 Peter 1:10 and 2 Timothy

---

[96] *Justification as an Immanent Act*, p. 207.

1:9 show clearly that there is no particular order in God's decrees. Paul in Romans 8 puts predestination first, then calling, then justification, then glorification. Peter puts calling even before election, a text on which Arminians build their doctrine of election on reception of Christ. When writing to Timothy, Paul says the entire work of salvation and the calling of the saints have been the believer's in Christ before the world began. Here, Paul puts salvation before calling. This is because there is no time-order in God's eternal decree of salvation for His own. Gill adds that when the Trinity is mentioned, at times the Father is put first, at times the Son and at times the Holy Spirit but these passages of Scripture cannot be used to work out an order of rank or order in time of the Trinity. This is, of course, begging the question that some modern evangelicals do place such an order and rank within the Trinity. However, this is not Gill's view and can hardly be argued from the texts which list the work of the Trinity in salvation. Gill accepts, however, that if these objectors mean by justification 'the declarative sentence of it upon the conscience, by the Spirit of God, and received by faith', he would have no quarrel with them.

5. If justification from eternity were true, faith could not be a prerequisite

Against this, Gill argues that justification by or through faith in no way contradicts justification from eternity. We must distinguish between the immanent, eternal acts of God and His transient acts in administrating His gifts in this world. We must distinguish between what happens in eternity and how this is manifested in time. An anonymous *Banner of Truth* editor strangely condemns this doctrine, arguing that to hold that, 'The elect are justified from all eternity, an act of which their justification in this world by faith is only a manifestation', is to believe 'the general creed of all theoretical Antinomians, more or less.'[97] The last three words are typical of the 'uncertain sound' coming from the 'Banner' headquarters in recent years. The editor[98] cannot make up his mind if a person is more than an Antinomian for believing as many an old Puritan and the old Particular

---

[97] *Banner of Truth*, July 1988, Issue 298, p. 8.
[98] Mr Iain Murray, who was editor at the time, took personal responsibility for this article without going into details as to authorship. It appears that one anonymous author wrote the body of the text whilst Mr Murray added editorial comments.

Baptists, or less than an Antinomian for doing so. The anonymous author's statement carries two nuances which must be looked at as they are misleading. Firstly, the word 'only' is quite out of place. It is used negatively and restrictively of the great acts of God in salvation. It befits a minister of the gospel to handle holy things with a holy care. Secondly, the critic is obviously using the word 'manifestation' incorrectly, that is, not in the meaning given it by such as Gill and Huntington. The *Banner of Truth* editor wishes to imply that here, to Huntington, justification was a mere projection or hologram of the real thing, a kind of reflection or phantasm. To Huntington, as Gill, a manifestation was a concrescence of God's effecting act in eternity and his operative act in time. This is Paul's use of the word in Romans 8:19. One cannot be more concrete than 1 John 3:8, 'For this purpose the Son of God was manifested, that he might destroy the works of the devil.' One would certainly have to be a Docetist to deny that! The editor, however, fails to provide us with an alternative Calvinistic view of how God's heavenly decrees are received on earth. One wonders also how the fact that God declares a person to be just by equipping him with justifying faith can possibly be a sign of Antinomianism as the Bible teaches clearly that whom God calls, he equips and that faith is a gift of God. Gill argues that faith can have no causal influence on justification, nor does it add anything to its being. Nor is it an ingredient of faith or the cause or matter of it. One should thus be careful about talking of human prerequisites for God's gifts as all that is required of us in matters of salvation is given us of God. Faith is, however, a prerequisite of justification in that it gives us a knowledge of justification and the comforts of justification, to a claim of interest in it and that no man is evidently and declaratively justified until he believes. In other words, faith receives the blessing of justification and the enjoyment of it. The only alternative seems to be that faith is not a manifestation on earth of what God has decreed in heaven but an activity of man which moves God to justify him.

6. Belief is the cause or prerequisite of justification, therefore there is no justification before the act of believing

This is a variant of the previous argument against which Gill maintains that if there were no justification before faith, there could be none by it without making the believer's faith the cause of justification.

The main text which is held to contradict Gill's doctrine is Galatians 2:16, 'Even we have believed in Jesus Christ, that we might be justified by the faith of Christ.' This does not ruffle Gill at all as he can argue quite consistently with his overall view of justification in its eternal and temporal aspects, 'Here the apostle is speaking of justification, as it terminates on the conscience of a believer; and this is readily granted to follow faith, and to be a consequent of it.'[99] Gill sees this as the work of the Spirit in the heart of the justified elect so that we 'expect justification alone by his (Christ's) righteousness, received by faith, and not by the works of the law'. In other words, such scriptures as Galatians 2:16 do not refer to the mind of God in election, nor to the elect being in Christ as our Head and representative, nor to the general pronouncement of justification before angels and men at the general judgment. It is merely a reference to faith awakening in the believer, so that he knows that he now stands guiltless before God and trusts in the Saviour who has made this possible.

Gill dismisses the objection rather too summarily here as he is dealing primarily with the half-quote which critics raise, irrespective of the rest of this verse. He is more specific in his *New Testament Commentary* on this passage. The full verse reads, 'Knowing that *a man is not justified by the works of the law, but by the faith of Jesus Christ,*[100] even we have believed in Jesus Christ, that we might be justified by the faith of Christ, and not by the works of the law: for by the works of the law shall no flesh be justified.' Perhaps it will be profitable to look at Gill's entire exegesis of this text, which is entirely in keeping with his views, as it is so often used as if it automatically refutes Gill's doctrine:

'Knowing that a man is not justified by the works of the law, &c.' That is, Peter, Paul, Barnabas, and other believing Jews knew this, and that from the law itself, which requires perfect and sinless obedience, and accuses, holds guilty, and adjudges to condemnation and death for the least failure, both as to matter or manner of duty; and from the prophets, which declare that by the deeds of the law no flesh can be justified in the sight of God, and who bear witness to the doctrines of remission of sin, and

---

[99] See *Sermons and Tracts* vol. ii, pp. 500, 501 and *Body of Divinity*, pp. 208, 209.
[100] My emphasis. Galatians 2:16. Gill's NT Commentary.

justification by the righteousness of Christ; and from the Gospel, in which this truth is most clearly revealed; and from the illumination of the blessed spirit, who led them into all truth; and from the revelation of Jesus Christ they were favoured with; and from their own experience, being fully convinced of the exceeding sinfulness of sin, the insufficiency of their own righteousness, and of the necessity, suitableness, and fulness of the righteousness of Christ. By 'the works of the law' are meant, not only obedience to the ceremonial law, though this is included, but also to the moral law; for it can hardly be thought, that the men the apostle opposes could ever dream of justification by their compliance with the rituals of the ceremonial law if they believed there could be no justification by their obedience to the moral law; for if there is no justification by the latter, there can be none by the former: the words are therefore to be taken in the largest sense, as rejecting all works of the law, of whatsoever kind, from justification in the sight of God; and such works are designed, as are performed by sinful men in and of themselves, otherwise men are justified by the works of the law as performed by Christ in their room and stead, but not by any as performed by themselves, for at best they are very imperfect, and so cannot justify; they are opposed to the grace of God, to which the justification of a sinner is always ascribed, and therefore cannot be by works; such a scheme would disannul the death of Christ, and promote boasting in men, and indeed is impracticable and impossible:

'but by the faith of Jesus Christ'; not by that faith, which Christ, as man, had in God, who promised him help, succour, and assistance, and for which he, as man, trusted in him, and exercised faith upon him; but that faith of which he is the object, author, and finisher; and not by that as a cause, for faith has no causal influence on the justification of a sinner; it is not the efficient cause, for it is God that justifies; nor the moving cause, or which induces God to justify any, for that is his own free grace and good will; nor the meritorious or procuring cause, for that is the obedience and bloodshed of Christ; nor is faith the matter of justification; it is not a justifying righteousness; it is a part of sanctification; it is imperfect; as an act it is a man's own, and will not continue for ever in its present form, nature, and use; and is always distinguished from the righteousness of God, by which we are justified, which is perfect, is another's, and will last for ever. Men are not justified by faith, either as an habit, or an act; not by it as an habit or principle, this would be to confound justification and sanctification; nor as an act, for as such it is a man's own, and then justification would be by a man's works, contrary to the Scripture: but faith is to be taken either objectively, as it relates to Christ, the object of it, and his justifying righteousness; or as it is a means of receiving and apprehending Christ's righteousness; the discovery of it is made to faith; that grace discerns the excellency and suitableness of it, approves of it, rejects a man's own, lays hold on this, and rejoices in it:

'even we have believed in Jesus Christ'; we who are Jews by nature, being fully apprized that there is no justification by the works of the law, but by the righteousness of Christ, received by faith, have quitted all confidence in our own works, and are come to Christ, and believe in him, not only as the Messiah, but as the Lord our righteousness:

'that we might be justified by the faith of Christ, and not by the works of the law'; not that faith, as before observed, has any causal influence on justification. These Jews did not believe in Christ, in order by their believing to procure their justification before God, and acceptance with him, but that they might receive, by faith, this blessing from the Lord in their own conscience, and enjoy the comfort of it, and all that spiritual peace which results from it, and which they could not find in the works of the law:

'for by the works of the law shall no flesh be justified'; reference seems to be had to Psalm 143:2 and contains a reason why these believing Jews relinquished Moses in his law, in whom they formerly trusted, and looked to, and depended on for their justification, 'because that by obedience to the law of works no sinful mortal man can be justified in the sight of God.'

Gill explains that justification by the works of the law, which is non-existent in the life of fallen man, is compared to that found through the faith of Christ which has, as its object, the justifying righteousness of

Christ. The words 'the faith of Christ', Gill argues, refer to the faith of which Christ is the Author and Finisher and with which He equips His Bride, the elect. Paul is here emphasising that we look to Christ and His work for justification and not to ourselves and our fallen nature, which, besides being a futile task, would be frustrating the grace of God (Galatians 2:21).

In Book III, Chapter XI of his *Institutes*, Calvin explains how it is wrong to believe that faith is the cause of justification rather than the instrument God uses to justify us. If our faith were the cause, Calvin argues, then we would have an imperfect justification because our faith is imperfect. The power of justification does not exist in faith considered in itself but in receiving Christ. He goes on to say, 'I say, therefore, that faith, which is only the instrument for receiving justification, is ignorantly confounded with Christ, who is the material cause, as well as the author and minister of this great blessing. This disposes of the difficulty—viz. how the term faith is to be understood when treating of justification.' Justification, according to Calvin, is synonymous with being accepted in the Beloved according to God's decrees (Ephesians 1:5, 6) and includes the forgiveness of sins (Romans 4:6-8).[101] Turretin might have disagreed with Calvin on this point but Gill certainly did not.

7. The unconverted elect are under condemnation and therefore cannot be justified

It is argued that justification begins when man believes and repents and therefore cannot be from eternity. If it were otherwise, such critics say, we must regard the elect before conversion as being at the same time justified and yet children of wrath, under the sentence of death. This argument is widely held, even today, by those who reject the two natures of the elect, i.e. being in Adam and being in Christ. In the present day opposition to the doctrines of grace this is the very doctrine, or rather un-biblical stand, that leads its adherents to argue for a justification through the act of believing. This act is seen as a response to one's natural duty to believe in Christ savingly which results in Christ's imputed righteousness being applied to the already-believer in an 'as if' form. Against the argument that a justified damned person would be a contradiction in terms Gill argues:

---

[101] Vol. ii, pp. 37-43.

Let it be observed, That God's elect may be considered under two different Heads, and as related to two different covenants at one and the same time. As they are the descendants of Adam, they are related to him, as a covenant-head, and as such, sinned in him; and, through his offence judgment came upon them all to condemnation; and so they are all, by nature, children of wrath, even as others. But then, as considered in Christ, they were loved with an everlasting love: God chose them in him before the foundation of the world; and always viewed and accounted them righteous in Christ, in whom they were eternally secured from eternal wrath and damnation. So that it is no contradiction to say, that the elect of God, as they are in Adam, and according to the covenant of works, are under the sentence of condemnation; and that as they are in Christ, and according to the covenant of grace, and the secret transactions thereof, they are justified and freed from all condemnation. This is no more a contradiction, than that they are loved with an everlasting love, and yet are children of wrath at one and the same time, as they certainly are. And again, this is no more a contradiction, than that Jesus Christ was the Object of the Father's love and wrath at one and the same time; sustaining two different capacities, and standing in two different relations when he suffered in the room and stead of his people.[102]

Gill works over and extends this argument when dealing with Turretin's argument in his *Institutes* that he who is not converted is in a state of damnation. The Carter Lane pastor says:

It is asserted that justification cannot be from eternity, but only in time, when a man actually believes and repents; otherwise it would follow, that he who is justified and consequently has passed from death to life, and is become a child of God, and an heir of eternal life, abides still in death, and is a child of wrath, because he who is not yet converted, and lies in sin, abides in death, 1 John 3:14, and is of the devil, 1 John 3:8, and in a state of damnation, Galatians 5:21, but this latter especially cannot be

---

[102] *Of Justification as an Immanent Act*, p. 208.

admitted of, with respect to God's elect, even while unconverted. And now, to remove this seeming difficulty, let it be observed that the elect of God may be considered under two different heads, Adam and Christ, and as related to two covenants at one and the same time; as they are the descendants of Adam, they are related to him as a covenant-head, and as such sinned in him, and judgment came upon them all to condemnation and death and so they are, by nature, children of wrath, even as others. But as considered in Christ, they are loved with an everlasting love, chosen in him before the world was, and always viewed and accounted righteous in him, and so secured from everlasting wrath and damnation; hence it is no contradiction to say, that the elect of God, as in Adam, and according to the covenant of works, are under the sentence of condemnation; and that as in Christ, and according to the covenant of grace, and the secret transactions thereof, they are justified, and saved from condemnation. This is no more a contradiction, than that they were loved with an everlasting love, and yet are children of wrath, at one and the same time, as they most certainly are; nor than that Jesus Christ was the object of his Father's love and wrath at the same time, he sustaining two different capacities and standing in two different relations, when suffered in the room and stead of his people; as the Son of God he was always the object of his love; as the Surety of his people, bearing their sins, and suffering for them, he was the object of his wrath, Psalm 89:38.[103]

8. Justification from eternity carries with it the belief that faith is a mere acceptance of facts

Gill takes up the objection that for him faith is isolated from justification and becomes a mere assurance of the nature of things, an acceptance of fact. He protests vigorously against such a view, arguing that the very devils, hypocrites and former professors have or had such head knowledge. Obviously faith, he argues has some relationship with assurance as Paul speaks of attaining the full assurance of faith (Hebrews 10:22), yet faith does not exclude doubts and fears. The faith by which a man is justified is by no means a mere persuasion that there

---

[103] Ibid., pp. 208, 209.

is justifying righteousness in Christ but 'that there is a justifying righteousness *for him*; and therefore he looks unto, leans, relies, and depends on, and pleads this righteousness for his justification: though this act of his may be attended with many doubts, fears, questionings and unbelief. And what is short of this I cannot apprehend to be true faith in Christ, as the Lord our righteousness.'[104]

It is here interesting to note that Gill's view of faith is far deeper and broader than that of his traditional opponents. To Gill faith declares to the believer that Christ has died, in particular, for him. Thus he can say with Paul in Galatians 2:20, 'I live by the faith of the Son of God who loved *me*, and gave himself for *me*.' Obviously here, the love of Christ for the sinner is eternal to the time process of the atonement. There was Christ's love for His people 'by individual name' before ever they were. This teaching, Fuller specifically denies in his essay *The Inward Witness of the Spirit*, arguing that the work of the Spirit in man comes only by inference based on hindsight and he is never personally addressed.

9. The faith of such as Gill has no purpose or function

Gill deals with the quite impractical objection that if justification is before faith then faith is quite superfluous. Again, Gill rejects this idea as absurd, arguing that faith apprehends and receives Christ's righteousness for salvation, bringing peace, joy and comfort to those who were in a state of bondage and under a sentence of condemnation. How could this be superfluous to the spiritual well-being of a child of God? The purpose of God's gift of faith by grace is to unfetter the mind and set a soul at liberty, showing how the whole of salvation is of grace and not of works.

10. 1 Corinthians 6:11 indicates that there is a time when the elect are not justified

Turretin believed that Paul's alleged words, 'Now ye are justified' in 1 Corinthians 6:11, were proof enough that before 'now' the Corinthians were not justified. Gill argues that Turretin's interpretation does not necessarily follow as we must distinguish between *in foro Dei* (in the court of God) and *in foro conscientiae* (in their own consciences). Between being in Christ our Head and Surety and what is

---

[104] The Doctrine of Justification Stated and Maintained, *Sermons and Tracts*, vol. ii, p. 502.

pronounced by the Spirit of God in the consciences of believers. Gill points out teasingly, however, that Turretin's 'now' is neither in the Greek text, nor in the Authorised Version, so the objection is irrelevant.

Gill ends this list of arguments with a twinkle in his eye, and takes up Dr John Owen's defence against Richard Baxter who accused him wrongly of believing in 'eternal justification'.[105] Owen replies 'I neither am, nor ever was of that judgment; though, as it may be explained, I know *better*, *wiser*, and more *learned* men than myself, that *have* been, and *are*.'[106]

Coping with the Sciolists and Liberals
Gill brought nothing new into the theology of his day. This is witnessed by the many authorities from previous centuries he quotes. He did, however, revive a theology which had been partly forgotten, partly discarded and partly suppressed. So great was Gill's authority in his day that he had few critics. Those who did take up their pens against him were either sciolists who thought they might earn laurels for themselves by contending with a master-theologian or they were educated men who had suddenly changed their more Bible-based views and decided to join the liberal minds of the age. It was obvious that Gill had little to fear in orthodox Calvinist ranks but that the Neonomians, Amyraldians, Baxterians and Arminians of the age would believe they had a cause for complaint. One of the most well-circulated criticisms of Gill's doctrine of justification came from the sciolists' corner. Job Burt, hiding within the cape of anonymity, attacked both Gill and his Particular Baptist denomination in a work entitled *Some Doctrines in the Supralapsarian Scheme impartially examined by the Word of God*. He accused the Particular Baptists of being Supralapsarians who believed that God chose both His elect and the reprobate irrespective of the fall and he especially linked Supralapsarianism with Gill's doctrine of justification from eternity, arguing that this was contrary to the rule and standards

---

[105] Gill uses 'eternal justification' when quoting what his critics call the doctrine. He believed in 'justification from eternity' which is not technically the same. Those who hold to 'justification from eternity' accept a threefold manifestation in justification *in foro Dei, in foro conscientiae* and *in foro mundi*. Those who use the term 'eternal justification' i.e. mostly Gill's opponents, usually either do not take note of these distinctions or deny them.
[106] Of Justification as an Immanent Act, *Body of Divinity*, p. 209.

laid down in the Word of God by which all doctrine should be measured. Gill responded with an essay entitled *Truth Defended*.[107]

On the Supralapsarian issue the Particular Baptists were not of one mind

In this work, Gill is quick to point out that his denomination was by no means of one mind concerning the supralapsarian-sublapsarian issue but this did not affect their united view of election in any way. He also explains that there was no unity of agreement on justification amongst professing Supralapsarians. He makes it clear that he himself finds the whole supralapsarian-sublapsarian debate a matter of metaphysical speculation and not doctrine. He finds himself now in agreement with the one side and now in agreement with the other, but on the point of justification from eternity he wishes to stand firm.

Burt was himself not at all clear as to what Supralapsarianism really was and how it differed from Sublapsarianism. He stressed, for instance, that God, according to the Supralapsarians, did not take the fallen nature of His creatures into consideration when deciding on election or reprobation. Gill takes the wind out of his sails at once and argues that anyone who believes that God justifies the ungodly, must believe that He justifies those who have yet no saving faith. This, he finds, if we are to split doctrine into Supralapsarian and Sublapsarian camps, is strictly a Sublapsarian doctrine based on the suretyship engagements of Christ.

Reconciling the elect

Gill's critic went on to accuse those who believe in justification from eternity of having a faulty view of reconciliation, or rather of having no view of reconciliation at all as he thought such as Gill denied the need for the reconciling work of Christ. He therefore wrongly concluded that his alleged Supralapsarians refused to pray for the pardon of sin and believed that God loves and delights in the sins and 'rebellion of his

---

[107] Its full title was 'Truth Defended: Being an Answer to an Anonymous Pamphlet, Intitled Some Doctrines in the Supralapsarian Scheme impartially examined by the Word of God'. 1736. *Sermons and Tracts*, vol. iii, p. 403ff.

elect, or loves and delights in them considered as sinners and rebellious persons.'[108]

In meeting Burt's arguments, Gill points out from 2 Corinthians 5:19 that God is not estranged from His elect and needs to reconcile Himself to them but His elect are estranged from Him and need the reconciling work of Christ in their lives so that their sins will not be imputed to them. Burt seemed to be arguing that the doctrine of justification from eternity denies that Christ dealt with the elect sinners' sins as such, because justification for them has no reference to the fall in any way. Burt could not have been more misinformed. Arguing contrary to such an idea, Gill states, 'surely reconciliation, atonement, or satisfaction for sin, which are synonymous terms, expressive of the same thing, must suppose persons sinners herein concerned.'[109] This reconciliation, however, Gill argues, in no way produced love for the elect on God's part as if He had hated the elect before their reconciliation to Him. The reconciliation the Bible speaks of is not to the love and affections of God as this was the reason for reconciliation being accomplished, 'but to the justice of God, which insisted upon a satisfaction to a broken law; which being given, both love and justice are reconciled together, righteousness and peace kiss each other, in the affair of their salvation.' He adds, 'Herein is love, not that we loved God, but that he loved us, and sent his Son to be the propitiation for our sins' (1 John 4:10).[110]

Taking sin seriously

Burt does not seem to have consulted Gill's 1729 *Declaration of Faith* on the subject as he would then not have thought that Gill's God did not take sin seriously. According to Gill it was the very fact that God did take sin seriously that moved Him to such great measures of grace to rescue His elect from it. Thus Article VII of the *Goat Yard Declaration* says: 'We believe that the justification of God's elect, is only by the

---

[108] Burt also accused such as Gill of holding a too literal view of imputation and union with Christ, which he found was a natural development of a faulty view of justification. Gill's views of imputation have been briefly discussed above but an analysis of his equally orthodox teaching on union with Christ would burst the boundaries of this study. Here it is sufficient to take up Burt's arguments concerning justification and its relationship to prayer and God's love.

[109] *Truth Defended*, p. 417.

[110] *Truth Defended*, p. 418.

righteousness of Christ imputed to them, without the consideration of any works of righteousness done by them; and that the full and free pardon of all their sins and transgressions, past, present, and to come, is only through the blood of Christ, according to the riches of grace.'[111] Thus, rather than Gill believing that God delighted in sin, he stressed that God made the greatest possible sacrifice to rid man of it.

Gill cannot help ask the rhetorical question whether Burt knows what he is talking about when he argues that those who believe in justification from eternity do not pray for the pardon of sin. Of course such believers have always done so, still do so and must continue to do so, he argues. He realises that Burt has an Arminian background which misleads him into believing that a sinner can be always falling in and out of grace according to the degree of prayer for pardon exercised by him. Gill, of course will have none of this supererogatory view of prayer nor of this weak view of God's pardon. He therefore argues, 'Now we apprehend, that when believers pray for the pardon of sin, that their sense and meaning is not, nor should it be, as if the blood of Christ should be shed again for the remission of sin, or as if complete pardon was not procured by it, or as though this was to be obtained by their praying, tears, humiliation and repentance, or that any new act of pardon should arise in the mind of God, and be afresh passed; but when they pray in this manner, their meaning is, either that God would, in a providential way, deliver them out of present distress, or avert those troubles and sorrows they might justly fear; or, that they might have the sense and manifestation of pardon to their souls, fresh sprinklings of the blood of Jesus, and renewed application of it to their consciences; and this, we believe, is their duty and interest to do daily, since they are daily sinning against God, grieving his Spirit, and wounding their own consciences.' Here Gill refers the reader to his *Discourse on Prayer* for a wider study of this topic.[112]

Gill was more than shocked at the very idea that God could find delight in anyone's sin and rebellion and protested that he abhorred such

---

[111] See these articles quoted and commented on in chapter 5 of my *John Gill and The Cause of God and Truth*, Go Publications.

[112] *Truth Defended*, pp. 421-423. See also *Body of Divinity*, Book III, Chap. v. p. 939ff. 'On Public Prayer', and *Sermons and Tracts*, vol. ii, 'A Discourse on Prayer', p. 536ff. More will be said on this subject in Chapter Seven of this book where pardon and justification are compared.

a thought as much as Burt, saying, 'what else can reflect dishonour on the Christian religion, or strike at the doctrine of God's holiness, or stand diametrically opposite to all practical godliness, or oppose those scriptures which speak of God as hating sin, and abhorring the workers of iniquity?' He, nevertheless, pointed out to Burt that God's viewing His elect in Christ was quite a different matter, arguing, 'We know that men in an unconverted state cannot please God, that is, do those things which are well-pleasing to him; and yet their persons may be acceptable in his sight, not as considered in themselves; for so they cannot be, even after conversion, notwithstanding all their humiliations, repentance, tears, prayers, and services; but as considered in Christ, in whom, and in whom alone, they are the objects of God's love and delight.'[113]

Writing against the errors of future generations
Hervey maintained that Gill wrote for the future and here he is obviously laying his finger on much of the weakness of modern, so-called Calvinism which neither identifies full reconciliation with Christ's atonement, nor full pardon through his vicarious death. If the elect are neither fully reconciled nor fully pardoned through Christ's work on the Cross, it stands to reason that there is no actual justification in Christ's being slain for our sakes before the foundation of the world.

There are two major figures of influence in today's Calvinism who do not take the 'It is finished' of Christ on the cross to mean 'all that secures salvation is accomplished'. We have become used to the so-called 'moderate' Calvinism of the Fullerites which is really more Arminian than the Arminians and argues that actual reconciliation takes place at the act of believing and not when Christ obtained satisfaction for our sins.[114] Yet even such a well-known and eagerly read Five-Point man as Arthur Pink goes out of his way to deny actual reconciliation in the atonement. Writing in his recently republished book *The Satisfaction of Christ*,[115] Pink throws all the orthodoxy expressed by

---

[113] *Truth Defended*, pp. 424.
[114] See my work *Law and Gospel in the Theology of Andrew Fuller*, Go publications, 1996 for an analysis of Fullerism.
[115] The practice of the Banner of Truth in editing Pink's works severely before publication has led to a controversy recently aired in Christian magazines in the English-speaking world. Particularly the removal of a chapter referring to the doctrine of reprobation in Pink's *Sovereignty of God* has been a matter of debate. Though this

Gill to the four winds and states dogmatically, 'A pertinent example of what we have just said is seen in the now almost current idea that the Atonement of Christ signifies 'at-one-ment', the bringing of God and the sinner together. But that is not the meaning of the term at all, either as used in Scripture or as employed in sound theology. Reconciliation is one of the many effects or fruits of Christ's Atonement, *but was not part of the work He did.*[116] Many others have failed to distinguish between what Christ did and that which has resulted therefrom.' Thus, for Pink—and he emphasises this on several occasions so that there is no chance of misunderstanding him—reconciliation has nothing to do

---

doctrine was one of the pillars of both the Established Church and Reformed Dissent as witnessed by older Articles of Faith, and is still held by many lovers of the truth, the Banner's action, wrong as it appears to be from a Reformed point of view, has highlighted a major problem in Pink's works. As Iain Murray has pointed out in his articles and book defending the Banner's action, Pink's works are of very mixed contents, a mixture which reflects Pink's own theological development and denominational allegiance at the time of writing. It has thus always been a practice of publishers to either edit Pink's works that they publish, or, as in The Baptist Standard Bearer's publication of Pink's book on Satisfaction, add an explanatory introduction. The present publishers of *The Satisfaction of Christ* (Truth for Today) ought to have followed one of these examples. Brilliantly sound, from this author's point of view, as many passages are in the book, Pink shows great weakness in demonstrating the finished work of Christ on the cross. Indeed, probably indicating Pink's development in the very early thirties, a number of passages are quite self-contradictory. His highly dogmatic interpretation of Biblical words to do with redemption shows a grave lack of understanding of their root meanings as he bases different theologies on different English words which have the same meaning in both Hebrew and English. This can only result in confusion, and indeed frustration for the readers. Much in this book would please the most staunch Calvinist but there is much in the book which would match Fullerism and Arminianism, particularly where the timing of the applications of grace is concerned and Pink's strange delayed-action theory of Christ's work. If ever a book needed to be wisely edited so as to feed the sheep correctly, this is such a book. It would have been far more useful to have cut out Pink's long philosophical speculations concerning the necessity or lack of necessity of God's actions as also his semantic speculations and allowed him to keep to the central subject of Christ's once-and-for-all-time Atonement. Then the book would have been more readable, its sound more certain and its message more effective. Cf. Iain Murray's, *The Life of Arthur W. Pink*, BOTT, 1981.

[116] My emphasis. See *The Satisfaction of Christ*, Truth for Today, p. 58. See my article 'The Atonement in Evangelical Thought: I-VIII' in the 1996-97 issues of *New Focus* magazine in which I argue that reconciliation, ransom and redemption are essential features of the atonement.

with what Christ actually did on Calvary but what eventually resulted from it. In his explanatory chapter 'The Atonement—Its Efficacy', Pink explains that *'The work of Christ, of itself, never did, never will, and never can, save a single soul.'*[117] This is a highly misleading statement couched in ill-chosen words, which actually challenges the Biblical teaching on atonement, ransom, redemption and reconciliation at its roots. It also directly challenges the work of the thrice holy God, Father, Son and Holy Ghost, in the atonement. Pink does not see salvation as an act of God in eternity but sees it as a sequence in time carried out by the Father, Son and Holy Spirit, each doing His individual task, the One after the Other. First Christ was called upon by the Father to perform the act of the atonement and then was required to hand over the remainder of the work, i.e. spreading the fruits of the atonement, to His Father who 'is in honour bound to bring to Heaven every one for whom Christ died'. The way God does this is by employing the Holy Spirit. Pink thus sees reconciliation as the work of the Spirit. Though Pink finds his explanation of reconciliation takes into account the whole work of the Trinity, he neither explains to his readers the purpose of Christ's act in performing a sacrifice which does not reconcile, nor does he adequately explain how the Holy Spirit can effect such a reconciliation of Himself. Furthermore, Pink's readers would hardly be guilty of wrong interpretation if they conclude that both Christ and the Holy Spirit are portrayed as instruments in the Father's hand and not co-equal in the Trinity. Thus whatever Christ's crucial words, 'It is finished', mean to Pink, they do not mean that reconciliation was accomplished. Nevertheless, Tindale, in coining the word 'atonement' believed, on the strongest linguistic and exegetical grounds, that reconciliation was meant. Pink never succeeds in tying up reconciliation with the atonement and explaining their exact relationship to each other.

Paradoxical tension theology

Robert Traill warned that once the doctrine of the sinner being made righteous by the righteousness of Another through His full obedience to the law and His total satisfaction paid is dropped, Arminianism would turn into Socinianism. This is, of course, happening in the

---

[117] My emphasis.

modern evangelical establishment in a form even more radical than Traill envisaged. The modern emphasis on alleged distinctions in the Trinity rather than their triune unity in salvation has led to the 'paradox' or 'tension' teaching of self-styled 'evangelical Calvinists' who stress the different functions of the Trinity and the alleged different wills within the Godhead. Indeed their view of God seems to reflect more the tensions between the gods of Greek mythology, rather than the unity of the Father, Son and Holy Spirit. The clearest display of this teaching can be found in David Gay's *Banner of Truth* articles in which he sees a clash between various passages in Scripture and a similar clash between the wills of the Father and the Son which must be accepted *because of* what Gay feels is their paradoxical nature.[118] Here, Jesus is presented as a hero who is fighting for man against the will of God. This view is more extreme than Socinianism as, though such heretics portray Christ as a mere hero or, in modern terms, a Probation Officer, pleading for man, the Socinian hero does not do so against the will of the Father. On the contrary, Gay's Jesus is the rebel child that dares to challenge his father. The necessity of believing in a Bible which contradicts itself is further propagated by Gay in his *Evangelical Times* review of Iain Murray's small book *Spurgeon v. Hyper-Calvinism*. Murray's booklet is an out and out attack on the theology which Gill represented, though Mr Murray has so misunderstood the facts that the highly edited snippets of quotes from Gill which he uses to back up his criticism, when completed in their context, prove conclusively the very opposite to Mr Murray's highly negative interpretation.[119] In his review, Gay again confesses that he finds the Scriptures irreconcilable within themselves and claims that the positive thing about Spurgeon in his attitude to the Bible was that 'Spurgeon did not attempt to reconcile the irreconcilable.'[120] Thus Spurgeon is being presented as a Liberal to save the face of a modern radical wolf in the sheep's clothing of the Reformed, evangelical faith. Again this view would seem too radical even for a Socinian as, though he emphasises that there are 'essential' and 'non-essential' elements in Scripture, he does not say they are

---

[118] See especially his 'Preaching the Gospel to Sinners: 2', Issue 371, 372.

[119] See my refutation of Mr Murray's handling of the facts in 'John Gill and his Successors', *Focus*, Spring, 1996.

[120] *Evangelical Times*, August, 1996, p. 19.

'irreconcilable'. There are sad signs that this pro-paradox group of critics are giving birth to another sect which presents a god who is willing to save all but is thwarted by his son's stubbornness in dying only for a chosen few.[121] Believing such a caricature of the Christian faith has caused many of these 'evangelical' or 'moderate' Calvinists to drop the Biblical and Reformed doctrine of particular atonement altogether and plead for an atonement that saves and reconciles nobody in particular. Thus the centre-piece of the gospel is robbed of its function. Tragically it is people within this group who are claiming that they are 'Strict Calvinists' and the only ones who are 'preaching the gospel properly'!

Making sinners righteous
Here, one can imagine how the modern 'Evangelical Calvinist', anti-Gill lobby will form their protest. 'Stop!' They will say, 'You have a wrong view of justification. The word does not mean "to make righteous" but merely to declare righteous, albeit when certain conditions, such as repentance and faith, are fulfilled.' This is the stance John Murray takes in his Banner of Truth publication 'Justification' in volume ii of his *Works*. Here we must retort that John Murray has said that justification does not mean to make righteous, but he has not shown this to be the Biblical position and has also shown that he is really very much in favour of such an interpretation although he rejects its formal wording. However, in the passage where he denies the factitive and operative function of justification, he draws a false parallel. He says, to prove his case, 'Condemnation is not to make wicked and justification no more means to make righteous than condemn means to make wicked.'[122] Obviously God, according to Scripture does not make men wicked in condemning them for the simple reason that they are wicked already. He pronounces condemnation on reprobate men because they are wicked. Likewise God pronounces His elect justified because He finds in them righteousness i.e. that righteousness which we have in being united with Christ in our eternal union with Him and being wedded to Christ as His Bride with all the following consequences and

---

[121] See the editorial entitled 'Tension Theology' in the August/September, 1996 edition of *New Focus* for a sober and analytical assessment of this teaching.
[122] Op. cit. p. 204.

outworkings. The results of such a union are highly factitive and operative. We are thus condemned for good reasons of justice and acquitted—a word Murray does not use in connection with justification—for good reasons of justice. Here, as the Puritans used to phrase it, justice kisses mercy. This does not mean, however, as Fuller teaches, that the soteriological deed was half justice and half mercy, but that God's justice is fully compatible with His mercy and that His justice is fully satisfied so that mercy may reign.

Taking Luther's lead

As Reformed men, we need not follow John Murray rather than the Reformers whom John Murray also looked to for theological and spiritual guidance. One of the fundamental questions of Luther which ushered in the Reformation was how can a sinner be made righteous before God. He experienced that grace was the justice of God with which he made us just by His gift of Christ's justifying righteousness. This message, Luther saw written in sun-beams throughout the entire Old and New Testaments. I had long argued against justification carrying the meaning to make just or righteous, believing what my modern tutors had told me concerning the term indicating a mere judicial manoeuvre or theoretical, non-operative formality. It was Luther's book on *The Seven Psalms of Repentance*,[123] usually translated *The Seven Penitential Psalms*, which opened my eyes. Here we see David begging the Lord to cause him to hear His loving kindness, to deliver him, to teach him, to quicken him in the ways of righteousness. He is continually praying, 'Father, being considered just merely theoretically, is not Thy way. Please make me really and truly just.' Luther sums up the whole of Psalm 143 in the words, 'Make me by thy grace truthful and righteous', explaining that David is not talking merely about the characteristics of God's grace which is according to truth and righteousness but he is speaking of, 'The grace by which, for Christ's sake, He makes us truthful and righteous.' Luther backs this interpretation up by referring to Romans chapters 1-3 and its teaching on justification, righteousness and truth. Were Luther contending against modern Liberals of the so-called 'Evangelical Calvinist' school who deny actual imputation as much as they deny actual justification

---

[123] *Die Sieben Bußpsalmen.*

from eternity, he would have possibly added 2 Corinthians 5:21, 'For he hath *made him* to be sin for us, who knew no sin; that *we might be made* the righteousness of God in him.' He might also have pointed out, like Calvin, that God has *made us* acceptable in the Beloved and *made known to us* the mystery of His will (Ephesians 1:6, 9). And then, of course, there is Colossians 1:12, 'Giving thanks unto the Father *which hath made us* meet to be partakers of the inheritance of the saints in light.'

Here we see how modern Reformed men are in danger of being enveloped by Arminianism and worse. Wesley maintained stubbornly that to believe that all the charges of the law are answered in Christ on our behalf was 'Antinomianism without a mask'. He hated the idea that Christ had done all that was necessary for our salvation because he felt that man must earn his heavenly reward. The teaching of the Bible and our Reformers, as Hervey pointed out to Wesley[124] was that God in His grace takes a sinner whilst still in his sins and makes him righteous by removing his sin and replacing it with the righteousness of Christ imputed to him. This is what justification entails.

It is difficult to know where the idea that God does not make us righteous in justification came from. The very root word itself, *justificare* is a compound of the two words 'just' and 'to make'. As the Germans, so also the Dutch and the Scandinavians, speak of justification in terms of being made righteous. In fact they use even stronger terms, expressing the making in the root noun and then using another form of 'doing' or 'making' to emphasise this. This gives us the Dutch *'rechtvaardigmaking'* and the Swedish *'rättfärdiggörelse'*. Obviously, these words are translations and, theoretically speaking, need not reflect the actual original Scriptural words. It is often difficult for scholars to access the exact meaning of Biblical words concerning important doctrines as they occur infrequently and their meaning must be obtained from very restrictive contents. No such embarrassment faces us, however, in determining the meaning of the Biblical words rendered by 'justify', 'justification' and 'make righteous' as they occur

---

[124] See Hervey's *Aspasio Vindicated.* I have gone into this debate between Arminianism and Fullerism on the one side and the Reformed doctrine of Christ fulfilling all righteousness as our Substitute in my *Law and Gospel in the Theology of Andrew Fuller* and *James Hervey: Preacher of Righteousness.*

many hundred-fold, showing what a dominant importance the doctrine is given by the divine Author. Writing in his book on Biblical key-words entitled *The Apostolic Preaching of the Cross*, Dr Leon Morris, admits that the word δικαιοω, 'I justify' is causative and one would expect it thus to mean 'I make just', yet he argues that we cannot accept it as such because it obviously means in context, 'to hold as right', 'to deem right' or 'to claim or demand as a right'.[125] One would have thought that here was no contradiction as obviously God deems us right because He makes us right; but this inference is denied. Morris' basic idea for not accepting a causative meaning is that the causative form is not used in extra Biblical literature. This is not always a good argument as God's Word often uses expressions common in pagan literature to mean special Christian things. This is clearly the case in the word used for baptism, for instance. Even John Murray cannot accept that there is no causative element in justification. In the article referred to above, he declares as Morris that justification is merely declarative and never factitive or operative and then he goes on to take this all back, arguing Biblically in the case of imputed righteousness as the constitutive element in justification:

> Now if there is an imputation of righteousness this is the clearest indication of that in which the constitutive act consists. That answers our question as to what the constitutive act is. If there is an imputation of righteousness, such righteousness meets the requirement of establishing a new relationship which not only warrants the declaration but elicits and demands it and ensures the acceptance of the person as righteous in God's sight.
>
> *Comprised in the Justifying Act.* In connection with the question: Is this constitutive act comprised in the act which is called justification or is it simply the presupposition of it? There is good reason for suspecting that it is conceived of as actually involved in the act of justification as it applies to the justifying of the ungodly. There are the following considerations which would favour this conclusion.
>
> (a) Presumptive argument. In some important instances of the use of the word *dikaioo* one may feel that the mere notion of,

---

[125] See Morris p. 225 but also his entire discussion of δικαιοω on p. 224ff.

'declaring righteous' is scarcely adequate. We may properly feel that it is not rich enough to express the thought. In Luke 18:14, referring to the publican, Jesus says, 'this one went down to his house justified' (*dedikaiõmenos*). Does it not mean that he went down to his house righteous, that is to say, righteous in the sense relevant to justification? If so, it means constituted righteous, in a righteous state established. Likewise in certain passages in Romans there is a paucity of conception which one feels if the bare notion of 'declaring righteous' is all that we have. In Romans 3:24, 'being justified freely by his grace through the redemption that is in Christ Jesus', we may properly sense a pregnancy of thought that can only be supplied by the idea of constituting righteous. Also in Romans 5:1, 'Therefore being justified by faith we have peace with God', the greater fulness supplied by the constitutive idea seems much more consonant with the thought. In a word, in all of these and such instances the thought is surely that of a relation established and the establishment of the relation is that which is expressed by the constitutive act.

(b) We should expect that the justification (*dikaioma*) of Romans 5:16 and the justification of life of Romans 5:18 (*dikaiosin zoes*), and receiving the free gift of righteousness of Romans 5:17, and the constituting righteous of Romans 5:19, are all variations of expression to denote the same unified action which is called justification, and the specific ideas expressed by some of the expressions are simply ways of unfolding the differing facets of the action which is most frequently expressed as justification.

(c) It is quite likely that the very term 'justify' or 'justification' when denoting an action of God in reference to the ungodly is charged with this creative or constitutive ingredient after the analogy of Scripture teaching elsewhere that the word of God and the call of God call into existence—'he calls the things that be not as though they were'—and that God speaks and it is done. The pronouncement, the judgment is not simply one which recognizes existence but causes it to be. His declarative word carries with it the effectuation of that which is declared.[126]

If Murray is arguing correctly here, and the Bible references he gives shows that he is, we see how the Banner of Truth's arguments elsewhere concerning imputation as being forensic only and never actual (to use their word) is a false antithesis.[127] Actually, when they argue that such as Gill and Huntington believed in actual imputation and not judicial, they are misrepresenting their supposed Antinomians. They were ardent in declaring that imputation and along with it justification, which was built on it, were both forensic *and* actual. God declares us just through the imputation of Christ's righteousness because He has an actual basis for doing so. We might ask why John Murray sways between the two interpretations, now looking at justification as if it were merely theoretical and now viewing it as factitive, operative and effecting a change. Perhaps Murray was somewhat bound by what has become the orthodox jargon of modern evangelicalism and when he put this aside and turned to the Scriptures and his own experience, he was able to release himself from his schoolmanship. My own opinion is that Murray was caught up in the theological changes in 'Banner' thinking which were taking place at the time and his works reflect this transition.

God was in Christ, reconciling the world to Himself
Contrary to modern views of a Trinity at loggerheads with itself, as if he foresaw them, Gill emphasises the work of the Trinity in unison at the Atonement. In Section XL of his *The Cause of God and Truth*, he takes up 2 Corinthians 5:19, 'To wit that God was in Christ, reconciling the world unto himself, not imputing their trespasses unto them.' Here Gill stresses that the Father was at work intentionally and actually in the process of reconciliation in His Son. He shows how the tenses used and the context show that this is not dating back to the time Paul's hearers believed but to Christ's atoning work on the Cross. Gill emphasises strongly that here a mere offer of reconciliation and justification in preaching to whoever will accept it is not meant. The

---

[126] *Collected Writings of John Murray*, vol. ii, pp. 208, 209.
[127] I am, of course, thinking of the new Banner teaching recorded in 'The Voice of Years', *Banner of Truth*, Issue 298, July, 1988, besides John Murray's article.

text refers to 'a proclamation or declaration of peace, made by the blood of Jesus, of reconciliation by the death of the Son of God.'[128] Gill also points out that this text does not refer to what God does subsequent to the death of His Son in the ministry of the apostles, 'but what he himself had been doing in his Son, and which was antecedent, and gave rise unto, and was the foundation of their ministry'. He goes on to say, 'There was a scheme of reconciliation drawn in God's counsels before the world began, and an *actual*[129] reconciliation by the death of Christ, which is published in the gospel.'

The atonement and the doctrine of imputation
In expounding 2 Corinthians 5:19, Gill points out that imputation is also a direct and immediate factor of the atonement. It was there and then that Christ removed all imputations of sin and applied all imputations of righteousness necessary for us to be declared new creatures by God. Expounding 1 Peter 1:2-4 in his *New Testament Commentary*, Gill shows how Peter in writing to, 'the elect according to the foreknowledge of God the Father, through sanctification of the Spirit, unto obedience and sprinkling of the blood of Jesus Christ', is portraying the whole gospel and the work of the Three Persons of the Trinity in the economy of salvation wrought out on Calvary. Here it is plain to see that the Father sets the operation of salvation in action, the Spirit separates the elect from the world and Christ provides not only the victim, His obedient self, but He is the Offerer, giving Himself for His Bride. The fact that the entire Trinity was at work in the plan of redemption is very relevant in combating modern views of the atonement which suggest that either God shows two conflicting wills, or Christ set His own will against His Father's in redeeming a people for Himself, or that Christ merely played the hero's part which was accepted with hindsight by God or that Christ was merely 'offered' by the Father as Abraham was prepared to offer Isaac. Pink believed that reconciliation was not the act of Christ in the atonement but the act of the Spirit in the believer's coming to faith. Gill saw coming to faith as an application of what had already been accomplished fully on the cross. Hervey supported Gill fully here and when combating similar

---

[128] *The* , Section XL, p. 43, 44.
[129] My emphasis.

views of Wesley's to Pink's, he argued in his *Aspasio Vindicated*, 'The work of the Spirit in the believer is not the cause of our acquittal and reconciliation but the privilege of those who are acquitted and reconciled.'

Pink's pardon by instalments

Arthur Pink's doctrine of pardon, which hinders the placing of justification in eternity, is also symptomatic of modern evangelical thought. Just as Pink believes that there is no actual and full reconciliation on the cross, so there is no full and complete pardon through purging to be found there. On page 182 of his *The Satisfaction of Christ*, Pink, quoting Manton's words, 'Sins to come cannot be properly said to be pardoned, for till they are committed we are not guilty of them', explains the words as if they mean the atonement brings pardon for all pre-conversion sins but not for those committed after conversion because there can be no pardon before sin is committed. Against such an odd idea, Gill argues in his book *The Doctrines of God's Everlasting Love to His Elect, and Their Eternal Union with Christ* [130] that Christ died for all the elect who were born before and after His death and died to pardon all their sins, though they were not yet committed and though many were not even born. This is an essential feature of Gill's doctrine of justification from eternity. God's pardon and the removal of guilt is that which justifies us and neither of these factors are conditional on the action of man, nor are they conditioned by time. Pink, however, argues that the atonement automatically pardons *pre-conversion sin only*.[131] Referring to 2 Peter 1:9, which surely has quite a different meaning to the one Pink gives it, he says, 'At conversion we receive the Divine forgiveness of all our *past*[132] sins but forgiveness of present sins must be sued daily.' Speaking of Christian virtues given by divine power, Peter, in the verse Pink quotes, is saying that, 'he that lacketh these things is blind, and cannot see afar off, and hath forgotten that he was purged of his old sins.' It is obvious

---

[130] See the chapter 'The Good News of God's Everlasting Love' in my *John Gill and The Cause of God and Truth*, Go Publications, 1995 for a detailed discussion of Gill's doctrine of eternal union with Christ.

[131] My emphasis. See *The Satisfaction of Christ*, pp. 182, 183.

[132] Pink's emphasis.

here that Peter is showing how ridiculous it is for a Christian to behave as if he were not one, forgetting that his sins had been purged and his old man crucified. Peter is not referring to new, unpurged sins, but the old ones which still plague us. Gill, doubting this man's state, says of him in his *Commentary*:

> he does not consider, nor think of it, that he was a sinner of old, a sinner in Adam, that he was conceived and shapen in sin, and went astray, and was called a transgressor from the womb; he does not think that he stands in any need of being purged from former sins; and is entirely unmindful of, and neglects, the purification of them by the blood of Christ.[133]

Gill, of course, is basing his words on the sound conclusion drawn from the entire testimony of the Scriptures that Jesus' blood cleanses from all sins, past present and future, and there is not a word in Scripture of the need for a repeated purging, though the believer knows that he ought to always bring his sins to the Lord in view of Christ's purging of them. To relate forgiveness timewise with conversion and to add that both only reflect past sins cannot be considered as truly representing the Bible's teaching on the satisfaction of Christ.

Pink however, maintains that if the believer sins, he only has personal pardon so far as he confesses every single sin, otherwise he will deserve death, if not die. To back up his theory, Pink tells the story of an heir who died before coming of age thus prematurely forfeiting his inheritance as his age was the condition of receiving it. This is a strange comparison indeed with an atoned-for soul who has not yet come to faith. Pink seems to be actually suggesting that God would allow a soul for whom Christ died to perish because he did not pray for pardon for every sin he committed. Indeed, Iain Murray argues in his well-written biography *The Life of Arthur W. Pink* that his subject refused to accept the 'once saved always saved' slogan.[134] Though Pink

---

[133] Gill's NT *Commentary* on 2 Peter 1:9, vol. ix, p. 589.
[134] This was obviously because Pink felt that such an idea led to Antinomianism. Elsewhere, as Murray points out, Pink held to the doctrines of election and perseverance. Obviously, Pink went to these extremes to emphasise human responsibility rather than deny God's sovereignty. Going to one extreme to attack another, however, provides no solid teaching for true, balanced faith.

uses very strong words against the Arminians in his book, Pink's is the very doctrine which Wesley levelled at Hervey who retorted in his *Aspasio Vindicated* by showing from such Scripture as Hebrews 10:14, Daniel 9:24 and Romans 5:10 that 'By this doing and suffering, believers are fully and perfectly reconciled; not for a day only, or for any particular time, but for ever. The pardon is irrevocable; the blessing inalienable.'[135]

In his biography of Pink, Iain Murray relates on several occasions how Pink was influenced by Fuller and shows his disagreement with Pink on Fuller's emphasis between moral and physical ability. Pink's view as illustrated in this comparatively early work (based on his 1930-31 *Studies in the Scriptures*) is basically that of Andrew Fuller who boasted that he was turning the Baptists away from the dunghill provided by Gill's theology. Fuller interpreted Romans 5:10 to refer to an actual reconciliation on reception through exercising duty faith.[136] He also maintained that God does not justify the ungodly,[137] i.e. unbelievers and enemies of Christ, arguing that Romans 4:5 does not refer to unbelievers but 'ungodly believers'!

Pardon is for keeps

Fuller rejects the Biblical teaching of the eternal love of Christ for His elect with the accompanying teaching of the eternal union of Christ with the elect and the doctrine of the Trinitarian covenant in eternity concerning the elect's salvation.[138] Judging by his sound teaching on the covenant and his belief in a union with Christ outlined in not only *The Satisfaction of Christ* but many other works, Pink fully accepts the doctrine of Christ's eternal love for His Bride. This doctrine and the doctrine of the eternal justification of the believer go hand in hand and one would think that to accept the one was to accede to the other.

---

[135] P. 531. Pink thinks of salvation in three stages i.e. as shed, as pleaded, as sprinkled. Christ's blood was shed at Calvary, its efficacy is pleaded in Heaven and then 'sprinkled' on the believer when reconciliation comes. I find Pink most unclear as to when the 'sprinkling' actually takes place. Clearly, according to Pink, it was not when Christ's blood was shed. See my discussion on this in my Hervey biography, p. 298.

[136] See Fuller's *Works*, vol. i, 'Conversation on Particular Redemption'.

[137] Ibid., vol. iii, '*Remarks on God's Justifying the Ungodly*'.

[138] See my book *Law and Gospel in the Theology of Andrew Fuller*, Go Publications, 1996 for a detailed analysis of Fuller's thought on these matters.

Furthermore as God is not a creature of time and dwells in eternity, one would think that all God's attributes and actions are products of eternity. Seen from this aspect, there ought to be no problem in believing that God personally pardons, reconciles and justifies His people from eternity.

Abraham Taylor and his 'ignorant enthusiasts'

One of Gill's most ardent critics on justification from eternity was the Independent pastor Abraham Taylor, whose verbal abuse of Gill for his doctrine of God's everlasting love for His elect is legend. Gill tackled his adversary in his jewel of a book *The Doctrines of God's Everlasting Love to His Elect*.[139] Leaving aside the foul remarks Taylor made against Gill, the latter concentrated his reply on charges which might have been in the realms of possibility. One of these charges was that only ignorant enthusiasts would believe in God's eternal love for His people. In his reply, Gill introduces to Taylor the learned Puritan Dr Thomas Goodwin (1600-1679), styled, since his rejection by Archbishop Laud, as the 'Patriarch and Atlas of Independency'. This learned Cambridge scholar, Gill shows at great length, believed in the Biblical truth of the everlasting love of God to His elect so how could people who accept such a doctrine be called 'ignorant'? Gill then goes on to outline the researches of Herman Witsius (1636-1708), one of the most learned men of his age.[140] Quoting profusely from Witsius, Gill shows how this great Christian scholar believed the very doctrines that Taylor thought were products of enthusiastic ignorance. Then Gill came up with an argument that must have shaken Taylor to the roots. His own learned father, Richard Taylor accepted the very doctrine that his son found ignorant and had recorded his views on these doctrines in a book that his son, Abraham, had edited. In his lengthy quotes from Richard Taylor, Gill shows how interwoven are the doctrines of God's eternal love and justification. On these doctrines he quotes Richard Taylor's words:

---

[139] This is available in a handy reprint from The Baptist Standard Bearer, 1987. Otherwise it is found in *Sermons and Tracts*, vol. iii, p. 1 ff.
[140] See my article 'Herman Witsius: Man of the Covenant' in *Evangelical Times*, October 1995.

It must, in deed be granted, that God, from eternity, decreed to justify elect sinners through Christ: and that as none but they are ever justified, so all that were decreed for justification are certainly justified. It must also be granted, that God, from eternity, entered into a covenant of grace with Christ, as the Head of elect sinners; wherein Christ as their surety, undertook for their justification.—It must likewise be granted, that there was a gift of all grace made to Christ for elect sinners, as he was their Head and Surety from eternity, 2 Timothy 1:9. It must be further granted, that all elect sinners had a *representative Union with Christ from eternity.* When Christ was chose as their Head, they were chose together with him, as his members.

In another page, he says: Believers may, with the greatest delight and comfort, take a survey of their justification, in the different gradations, or progressive steps of it. God decreed their justification, and they had a *representative union* with Christ, as their Head and *Surety, from eternity.* This lays such a sure foundation for their justification, as cannot be overturned by the joint power of men and devils.

Lastly, Gill says: 'For my own part, I should not greatly care to be reckoned ignorant, and especially enthusiastic, and yet think I may, in a safe and sound sense, insist upon the doctrine of eternal union.'[141]

Justification by the imputed righteousness of Christ
Realising how preachers, not grounded in the Word of God, were using the doctrines of grace to display them as signs of Antinomianism and not to promote good works, Gill took up the theme in his December 28, 1737 Great-Eastcheap lecture on 1 Timothy 6:3 ' ... and to the doctrine which is according to godliness.' Speaking under the title *The Doctrine of Grace Cleared from the Charge of Licentiousness,*[142] Gill takes up the doctrine of God's eternal love to His elect, the doctrine of particular redemption, the doctrine of satisfaction and Christ's fulfilling the law on our behalf. He then goes on to speak on justification through the imputed righteousness of Christ and says:

---

[141] Op. cit., p. 19.
[142] *Sermons and Tracts*, vol. i, p. 334 ff.

Arguments Against Justification From Eternity Considered:
1. The Situation In Gill's Day

The doctrine of justification by the imputed righteousness of Christ, is a doctrine according to godliness, however it may be traduced as a licentious one; It neither makes void the law: nor discourages the performance of good works; nor encourages in sin; it does not annul, or make the law useless: *Do we*, says the apostle, *make void the law through faith*, that is, by the doctrine of justification through the righteousness of Christ, received by faith? *God forbid: yea, we establish the law*; since we assert that men are justified by a perfect righteousness, which *is* every way agreeable to the demands of the law, and by which that is magnified and made honourable. Nor does it at all discountenance the discharge of duty, but is the greatest motive and inducement to it. Thus, the apostle, having observed that we are not saved by works of righteousness done by us, that we are justified by the grace of Christ, and are made heirs according to the hope of eternal life, adds, *This is a faithful saying; and these* things, that is, these doctrines, *I will that thou affirm constantly*; that thou assert them without any doubt or hesitation about them; and that thou dwell upon them in thy ministry, and frequently inculcate them; *that*, ινα, to this end and purpose, *they which have believed in God, might be careful to maintain good* works. Nothing like these doctrines will induce them thereunto. Nor does this doctrine give any countenance to sinful practices; for though God justifies the ungodly, yet he does not indulge them in ungodliness. Christ's righteousness justifies from all sin, but does not justify persons in a continuance in sin. *Besides, faith,* which *receives this blessing from the Lord, and righteousness from the God* of salvation, which is the reason why men are said to be justified by it, *works by love*; is an operative grace, is attended with the fruits of righteousness, is evinced by good works, made perfect by them, and is without them dead. Yet some will say, the doctrine of justification by faith is no licentious doctrine, but the doctrines of eternal justification and eternal union are. This comes from another quarter, from a set of men who should know better. What diabolical charm? what satanic influence can there possibly be in a *date*? If justification by the imputed righteousness of Christ alone, without the works of the creature, has no bad influence upon the life and conversation; the moving of the date of it higher than where it has been commonly put, can never be attended with any bad consequence that way; nor can any consequences arise from it, but what must also unavoidably follow upon eternal election: And as for eternal union with Christ, it is the foundation of all the good things Christ has done for his people, of all the good things the Spirit works in them, and of all the good works which are done by them; and therefore can never give birth and countenance to evil practices.[143]

Sending forth the Spirit into the hearts of sons

Gill again takes up the argument against the doctrine that union with Christ must come after belief and after the work of the Spirit in one's life. This is mixing up the divine economy, Gill argues, saying of believers, 'They do not first receive the Spirit of Christ, and then by the Spirit are united to him; but they are first united to him, and, by virtue of this union, receive the Spirit of him.'[144] He maintains that a person, to use the Bible term, is glued (κολλῶμενος), that is, closely united to Christ, and then becomes one spirit with Him (1 Corinthians 6:17). Christ is the One who has the Spirit without measure, the Head of the elect and the Mediator of the covenant. A believer, being one with Christ, receives the Spirit from Him, though in measure. 'They are first chosen in him, adopted through him, made one with him, become heirs of God, and joint-heirs with Christ; and then, as the apostle says, *Because ye are sons, God hath sent forth the Spirit of his Son into your hearts, crying, Abba, Father.* Besides, the Spirit of God, in his personal inhabitation in the saints, in the operations of his grace on their hearts, and in the influence of his power and love on their souls, is the evidence, and not the bond of their union to God or Christ, and of their communion with them: *For hereby we know*, says the apostle John, *that he abideth in us, by the Spirit which he hath given us.* And in another

---

[143] *Sermons and Tracts*, vol. i, pp. 350-357.
[144] *Sermons and Tracts*, vol. iii, p. 20.

place, *Hereby know we, that we dwell in him, and he in us, because he has given us his Spirit.*[145]

This highly Scriptural and personal theology was the faith of our fathers, but times change and obviously doctrines change with them as the Spirit blows where He will. In Robert Traill's excellent work *The Doctrine of Justification Vindicated from the Charge of Antinomianism*, written in 1692, Traill regards with amazement the fact that the doctrines shared by almost all the Puritans of twenty and thirty years previously were considered at the time of Traill's writing, to be Antinomian. As Traill himself had kept to the old paths, he too was considered an Antinomian by the Arminians of his time. Though in more recent years, Traill has stood in great standing amongst Reformed men, it has now become obvious that many of these men would now regard him as a fully-fledged Antinomian. This is because we have the same situation now as in Traill's day. The very doctrines which we learnt to love in the late fifties and early sixties and which rescued us from the miry pit of Arminianism and worse are now seen as Antinomian. A number of our teachers of those days who are still leaders, are the very ones that have made this U-turn and are criticising as Antinomians their former pupils, who refuse to put on the new doctrinal coat. Instead of repenting and being ashamed of their past, however, as one would expect of Christians who feel they have done wrong, they have no sense of sympathy with their old pupils and no remorse because it was they themselves who led their sheep astray. Indeed their attitude seems to be, 'More fool, them!'

It has suddenly become popular to preach a 'theologically correct' sermon that condemns no one, lays no excessive demands on any one but tells all that Jesus loves them and therefore they should love Him back. Oddly enough, what these people cannot stand is when an 'old school' preacher comes along and starts talking about man's total inability to do anything to change his plight, of God's wrath and the need for reconciliation and that a person might be a vessel of destruction. Apostasy from God and how God put this wrong right is not the theme of these men's preaching. The hearer is called to love God and forget his complex that he might, after all, be an apostate. 'Love Jesus', says modern Fullerism 'as if you had never apostatised.'

---

[145] *Sermons and Tracts*, vol. iii, p. 20.

It is now time to look at the works of a few representatives of the modern anti-Gill school and examine their arguments against Gill's doctrine of justification from eternity.

Chapter Six

Arguments Against Justification From Eternity Considered: 2. The Modern Situation

Chronological snobbery

One of the earliest of modern works reflecting an antagonistic attitude to the old orthodoxy and the modern sport of Hyper-Calvinist hunting was Peter Toon's book *The Emergence of Hyper-Calvinism in English Nonconformity 1689-1765*. This work was published in 1967 with—and this is really surprising—a foreword by none other than Dr J. I. Packer, then of Latimer House, Oxford. The surprise is that Jim Packer usually stands up for the old Puritans as witnessed by his first-class Introduction to *Witsius on the Covenants* republished in 1990 in the version that Gill introduced to English readers with John Brine. Packer recommends Toon's work which contains definitions of Hyper-Calvinists which would, however, make Witsius a Hyper of the Hypers. Toon's initial argument seems to have been that Calvin's successors got everything wrong but in the latter half of the twentieth century we are learning to understand Calvin aright. It is that kind of phenomenon which C. S. Lewis calls 'chronological snobbery', i.e. the fixed idea that the present generation always knows best. Naturally, with such a revolution going on, heads must fall. Thus we see Beza, Ames, Perkins, Maccovius, Hoornbeeck, Twisse, Crisp, Goodwin and Gill, to mention the most well-known stalwarts, all receiving punishment for their suddenly unacceptable theology, putting the theology of these

Calvinists down to, amongst worse things, 'Militant Lutherism'. Arguing that 'The most serious perversion of Puritan orthodoxy was doctrinal antinomianism',[146] Toon mentions John Saltmarsh, John Eaton, Tobias Crisp and Robert Lancaster and says of them:

> They explained the free grace of God to the elect in such a way as to neglect the Biblical teaching that a Christian has certain responsibilities to God such as daily humbling for sin, daily prayer, continual trust in God and continual love to men. One of their favourite doctrines was eternal justification, by which they meant that God not only elected the church to salvation but actually justified the elect before they were born. As a development of this they taught that justification in time was merely realisation that eternal justification was theirs already. Another favourite emphasis was the teaching that the only sure way for a Christian to know he was elect was the voice of the Spirit within his soul saying, 'You are elect'.[147]

Christian liberty is not licentiousness

Now, obviously, Toon has picked up an old hat, long discarded, and is wearing it as something which has become fashionable once more. The works of these men of outstanding holy lives and the comments on their lives by entirely orthodox men such as Twisse, Gill, John Brown of Whitburn and James Hervey, show that this concoction of truth and falsehood, originally designed by militant Amyraldians and Richard Baxter, is entirely misleading. Furthermore, in order to link Gill with Antinomianism, Toon states that in Gill's answer to Abraham Taylor who claimed that the doctrine of God's eternal love for His elect led to lasciviousness, he defended these men against Taylor. Toon has misread both Taylor and Gill. The latter corrected Taylor in showing that these men *did not teach* the eternal love of God for the elect, yet nevertheless, they were men of irreproachable moral lives.

As Toon returns to Crisp time and time again, judging him as a rebel against the law of God, it is astonishing that he has not bothered to

---

[146] Op. cit. p. 28.
[147] *Emergence of Hyper-Calvinism*, p. 28.

check his facts. On reading Toon's words, which completely contradicted my own reading of Crisp, I stretched out for my copy of Crisp's sermons and opened them at his 'Christian Liberty No Licentious Doctrine'. With Toon's words concerning the misuse of 'the free grace of God to the elect in such a way as to neglect the Biblical teaching that a Christian has certain responsibilities to God such as daily humbling for sin, daily prayer, continual trust in God and continual love to men',[148] in my mind, I turned over the pages. My eyes immediately fell on the words, 'Christ doth not give liberty unto licentiousness of life and conversation.' Soon, I was reading:

> We have our justification, our peace, our salvation, only by the righteousness Christ hath done for us: but this doth not take away our obedience, nor our services, in respect of those ends for which such are now required of believers. We have yet several ends for duties and obedience, namely, That they may glorify God, to make good what he hath promised. So far we are called out to service, and walking uprightly, sincerely, exactly, and strictly, according to the good pleasure of God; and, in regard of such ends, there is a gracious freedom that the free-men of Christ have by him; that is, so far forth as services and obediences are expected at the free-man's hand, for the ends that I have named, there is Christ, by his Spirit, present with those that are free men, to help them in all such kind of services, so that 'they become strong in the Lord, and in the power of his might', to do the will of God. Mark what the apostle speaks: 'I am able to do all things through Christ that strengthens me. Of myself (saith he) I am able to do nothing; but with Christ, and through him that strengthens me, I am able to do all things.' He that is Christ's free-man hath always the strength of Christ present, answerable to that weight and burden of employment God calls him forth unto. 'My grace (saith Christ) shall be sufficient for thee, and my strength shall be made perfect in weakness.' As you are free-men of Christ, you may confidently rest upon it, that he 'will never fail you, nor forsake you', when he calls you forth into employments. But you that are under the law, there is much required of you, and

---

[148] Op. cit. p. 28.

imposed upon you, but no help to be expected. You must do all by your own strength; the whole tale of brick shall be exacted of you, but no straw shall be given you. But you, that are free-men of Christ, he will help you: he will oil your wheels, fill your sails, and carry you upon eagles' wings, that you shall run and not be weary, walk and not faint. So, then, the free-men of Christ, having him and his Spirit for their life and strength, may go infinitely beyond the exactest legalist in the world, in more cheerful obedience than they can perform. He that walks in his own strength can never steer his business so well and so quickly, as he that hath the arms, the strength, and the principles of the great God of heaven and earth; as he that hath this great Supporter, this wise Director, this mighty Assister, to be continually by him. There is no burthen, you shall bear, but, by this freedom you have him to put his own shoulder to it to bear it up. [149]

Toon picks on the wrong people

Here, rather than promote lasciviousness, Crisp is showing how superior the good works of the soul saved by grace are, compared with the futile efforts of the legalist. Remarks of this kind in Crisp's works are legion[150] as Twisse, who made a special effort to study the reasons behind the vicious slander against Crisp, testifies. The only conclusion Twisse could come to was that Crisp's enemies were jealous because of the enormous success of Crisp's ministry. Furthermore, it is historically verifiable, as Toon also indirectly acknowledges several times in his book, that Crisp's critics (and this applies to those of the other 'Antinomians' Toon names), did not believe in the doctrine of imputation. Obviously, then, they did not believe that Crisp could do good works through faith in Christ's imputed righteousness which is true Biblical, justifying faith. Thus they concluded after their own unbiblical and faulty logic that Crisp was against doing good works. It

---

[149] Tobias Crisp Series, Issue 2, *The Sermons of Tobias Crisp*, with John Gill's notes, p. 74.
[150] See my *Law and Gospel in the Theology of Andrew Fuller* pp. 172-175 for further examples.

is also quite clear that Crisp's enemies were Amyraldians and Baxterians who had a far inferior view of the law than Crisp. Thus they were the Antinomians, not Crisp. Toon should have spent his time criticising the culprits and not their innocent victim! This reminds us of the present situation as many nowadays who criticise Crisp and Gill as Antinomians are themselves Amyraldians and are striving to instigate Moïse Amyraut, who was condemned as a heretic by contemporary Calvinists, as Calvin's true spokesman.

Toon's definition of an Antinomian as one who believes in justification from eternity, need not be commented on here as this is the theme of the whole book and Toon does not attempt to justify his statement. It is, however, important to examine his accusation that Antinomians believe that assurance comes from the voice of the Spirit which convinces the believer of election. Until Amyraldianism, Latitudinarianism and Fullerism came on the scene, the whole chapter of Romans 8, concerning the inner witness of the Spirit was considered orthodox Christian teaching. Now we are told by so-called 'Evangelical Calvinists' that this is Antinomianism unmasked because the Christian's assurance is based on inference, not inspiration. It is plain to see how our present day evangelicals have begun to reject the doctrine of the Holy Spirit's personal witness to the elect. The modern emphasis is on man's agency in conversion. It is man that grasps out and grips God. Thus if man is to seek assurance anywhere, it must be in his own decision-making and in his own abilities. To acknowledge that faith and assurance are divine gifts wrought out by the triune God is not flattering enough for the modern mind who likes to feel he is monarch of his own destiny.

Toon's own orthodoxy in doubt
In criticising such fine gospel preachers as Crisp and Richard Davis as being just the opposite to what they were, Toon obviously relies on their fiercest critics in the Baxterian-Amyraldian camp for 'evidence'. He lays great value on the 'anti-Antinomian' testimony of Daniel Williams although he admits that Williams was under suspicion of teaching salvation partly by works and even Socinianism. Williams, who believed that Hyper-Calvinists and Antinomians do not believe in evangelism was surprised to find that his arch-Antinomian Richard Davis had evangelised no less than thirteen counties. Instead of

accepting this as proof against his own theory, Williams took it as further evidence that Hyper-Calvinists were hyper-dangerous rather than exceptionally evangelistic.

Another, extremely questionable accusation of Toon's which reveals his own lack of orthodoxy is his argument that Antinomians reject the 'free offer' approach because they will not recognise that God has two wills; his secret will and his revealed will.[151] From the context, it appears that Toon means one will of God to save all and another will of God to save some as held in conventional Fullerism. This idea is not representative of Reformed Biblical thinking but is based on the old Latitudinarian conception of a God who reveals Himself in disguise, pandering to the weaknesses of humans, yet rewarding those who see through this well-meaning camouflage and are able to grasp how God really is. Here we have Fuller's dualistic conception of the arbitrary, temporal revelation of God who says a thing is right because He says so and the eternal truth which is correct as it displays 'the fitness of things', i.e. truth as it really is. Here David Gay's view of God the Father representing a different will than Jesus the Saviour is but one of the many variant forms this speculative theory takes. Of course, Toon's 'Antinomians' do not reject preaching the full gospel to the lost—Crisp was a great soul-winner—but they do object to what they called a 'universal offer' based on a universal atonement. If the atonement covers all men's sins, and all are thus made right with God, one wonders why these critics of the so-called Antinomians still talk about hell and perdition. Of course, the answer is that fewer and fewer of them do talk in such terms. The interesting thing about Toon's election of Crisp as a typical Hyper-Calvinist, is that Crisp nowhere conforms to Toon's Hyper-Calvinistic standards. Crisp even offered Christ to all to whom he was sent, seeing the word 'offer' as meaning 'presenting Christ' in the gospel.

Toon not only puts forward a two-willed God as the answer to his Hyper-Calvinists' trust in one God of one eternal will, but he criticises them for not believing that this two-willed God changes His mind concerning His elect and thus becomes a God of a changing will.[152] This

---

[151] *The Emergence of Hyper-Calvinism*, p. 130. See also the various writings of Dr Alan C. Clifford on this subject.

[152] Ibid., p. 124.

is because Toon views union with Christ also as a Hyper-Calvinist doctrine. He does not seem to be able to envisage Christ's choosing His Bride before the Bride was given faith to accept Christ. This entails a complete rejection of the believer being placed in Christ in eternity which is the clear teaching of Scripture. In conjunction with this, Toon states that his Hyper-Calvinists (Crisp, Gill, Brine and a few others) do not believe in a 'judicial declaration of acceptance by God' at conversion, which is not the case at all as clearly shown by the evidence produced in this book. In short, Toon's arguments are a mixture of Liberalism—illustrated further by his low view of the Scriptures which we cannot examine here[153]—and poor research.

Amid all this doctrinal confusion caused by Gill's critics, it is refreshing to return to Crisp and Gill's comments on his work. In Crisp's sermon on *The New Covenant of Free Grace*, the preacher expounds the words, 'To him that worketh not, but believeth on him who justifies the ungodly', arguing that it is Christ who justifies and not the act of believing. Faith is the evidence of things and not the being of things. Faith is the evidence of what Christ has done for the believer. When Gill republished these sermons, he provided them with copious notes. His comment on this passage of Crisp's was:

> Justification before faith, though cavilled at by many, is certain; since God justifies the ungodly, and since faith is the fruit and effect of justification, and the act which is conversant about it, and the object must be before the act; and besides justification took place at the resurrection of Christ; yea, from all eternity, as soon as he became the surety of his people; and which has been embraced, affirmed, and defended by Divines of the greatest note for orthodoxy and piety, as Twisse, Pemble, Parker, Goodwin. Ames, Witsius, Maccovius, and others. See my *Doctrine Of Justification*, p 36-38, 42-47, 50, 54.[154]

Gill goes on to explain how faith is the hand that receives the righteousness of Christ for justification. This was certainly the more or less generally accepted view of the Reformers and Puritans as Witsius

---

[153] See especially p. 116 where Toon tries to make a Barthian out of John Calvin.
[154] Op. cit., p. 40.

taught in his *Economy* and Traill argued in his excellent treatise *The Doctrine of Justification Vindicated from the Charge of Antinomianism.* Traill was more a Crispian than a Gillite in his timing of justification (i.e. not as specific as Gill) but he was in full unison with Gill when he said, 'The plain old Protestant doctrine is, That the place of faith in justification is only that of a hand or instrument, receiving the righteousness of Christ, for which only we are justified.'[155] Traill, with many others, believed in justification from eternity but did not divide justification into its active and passive elements but into its 'virtual' and 'actual' functions. 'Virtual' justification was a decree of God in eternity which is 'actualised' when the believer comes to faith. Gill did not quarrel with this interpretation at all but merely felt his was easier to understand. The word 'virtual' entails actual being and the word 'actual' entails the operative act, so that Traill and Gill were as near as makes no difference. This is perhaps why Toon also includes those who speak of 'virtual justification' before faith as Antinomians. This would certainly make Traill an Antinomian in Toon's eyes as well as the whole range of Particular Baptists before Fuller strove to reform them. In fact, before Toon is finished with his anti-Hyper-Calvinistic and anti-Antinomian campaign, one gains the impression that anyone remotely connected with Calvinist doctrines comes under his suspicion. Indeed, if we are to examine the lengthy list of doctrines that Toon presents under his main heading 'The Propagation of Hyper-Calvinism', then he must believe that Twisse, Chauncey, Rutherford, Spurgeon, Warfield, Berkhof, Lloyd-Jones and Jim Packer himself are all Hyper-Calvinists!

We must give Robert Traill the last word here. When Traill heard that those 'that say, that a sinner is actually justified before he be united to Christ', were accused of not pressing men to repent and believe, he answered:

> It is strange that such that are charged with this, *of all men do most press on sinners to believe on Jesus Christ,*[156] and urge the damnation threatened in the gospel upon all unbelievers. That there is a decreed justification from eternity, particular and fixed as to all the elect, and a virtual perfect justification of all the

---

[155] Traill's *Works*, vol. i, Glasgow, 1795, pp. 296-299.
[156] My emphasis.

redeemed, in and by the death and resurrection of Jesus Christ, Isaiah 53:11; Romans 4:25; Hebrews 9:26, 28 and 10:14, is not yet called in question by any among us; and more is not craved, but that a sinner, for his actual justification, must lay hold on and plead this redemption in Christ's blood by faith.

Picking up tiny pins and dropping huge clangers

Modern accusations of Gill being an Antinomian can be traced to a small, tight group of one-time Reformed evangelical leaders who are nevertheless still very influential in established Calvinist circles. Several of them have obviously changed their own theology radically in past years towards Liberalism, whereas others seem to have an axe to grind against Gill and Huntington (both names usually fall from their lips in the same breath) because of troubles they have had in their own ministries with so-called Gillites and Huntingtonians. Both Spurgeon and Philpot warned against this kind of behaviour as Gill and Huntington had their imitators who were very imperfect reflections of the real thing. Nowadays we have our Martyn Lloyd-Jones imitators in their hundreds but it would be folly to judge the 'Doctor' by these who ape him. One of the most radical and remarkable attacks on Gill's doctrine of justification from eternity in recent years has been Peter Naylor's chapters entitled, 'High Calvinism and the Particular Baptists', 'John Gill and Faith', 'John Gill and Eternal Justification', and 'John Gill and the Message of the Gospel' in his Grace Publications book *Picking up a Pin for the Lord.* As Naylor is the only one of this highly vocal group who has actually striven to criticise Gill on the basis of his works (or at least, so it is claimed) and not hearsay and personal prejudice, the reader is at last provided with concrete criticism of Gill which can be assessed, analysed and evaluated. If Naylor's arguments are found wanting, obviously the entire group of Gill critics must be put under the same suspicion as they have not come up with anything better. Rather than picking up a pin, Naylor, as spokesman against Gill, is certainly guilty of dropping a clanger as he seeks by devious means to destroy Gill's irreproachable testimony and reputation displaying his own theology as being far from the orthodox Calvinism he claims to represent. Naylor's general criticism of Gill has been dealt with elsewhere[157] but here, it will be instructive to look particularly at his arguments against the doctrine of justification from eternity, especially as they are almost identical with the arguments Gill himself uses to test the validity of his doctrine but claims they are wanting in force. These arguments, however, represent the entire programme of criticism used by the modern anti-Gill lobby, who are still arguing that their views as demonstrated by Naylor are still irrefutable. Nothing that Naylor lists against Gill's doctrine is new and not one argument is raised that Gill, one would think, has not applied in honest self-criticism to himself and found wanting. New is the disrespectful way in which Gill is criticised and the highly negative innuendoes made concerning Gill's abilities and methods of argument. The most surprising claim, however, that Naylor makes is that he believes, as Gill, in the eternal love of God for His people.[158] If God's love is eternally with His people as they stand in Christ, which Naylor appears to accept, one would think that God, who cannot look on sin, justifies this love in His people by seeing them as being in Christ rather than in Adam. This Naylor denies absolutely.

A basic but portentous misunderstanding

In his chapter 'John Gill and Faith', Naylor mistakenly works under the assumption that Gill sees faith as merely 'assent to the facts of the gospel'[159] which Gill utterly refutes in his copious writings on faith which Naylor leaves completely unexamined. Indeed, there is hardly anything of Gill's writings on faith referred to in the whole chapter and one wonders from which sources Naylor has obtained his view of Gill. Certainly not from Gill's own works. Thus when Naylor turns to attack Gill's doctrine of justification which is intrinsically connected to Gill's view of faith, Naylor is handicapped by cumbersome presuppositions, indeed, prejudice. In principle, he isolates Gill's doctrine of justification from the elements that are intrinsically bound up with it and then condemns Gill for not including them. Gill, possibly influenced by Witsius if not Calvin himself, believed that the doctrine of justification diffused itself throughout the whole body of divinity. Furthermore, Naylor is also obviously not aware of what constitutes acceptable

---

[157] See 'A Saint is Slandered', in my book *John Gill and The Cause of God and Truth*.
[158] Page 181 of Naylor's book.
[159] Ibid., p. 165.

orthodoxy. This is seen in Naylor's first point against Gill when he queries Gill's traditional Reformed distinction between active and passive justification. Calvin obviously views justification in its active and passive modes, just like Gill. Calvin emphasises that justification means that God embraces the sinner in whom he finds no cause for mercy, the cause for kindness being in Himself. The entire initiative is God's active will.[160] He sees the decreeing of the elect to justification as God's active work but the exercising of faith is 'only the instrument for receiving justification.'[161] He can thus conclude, 'For, in regard to justification, faith is merely passive, bringing nothing of our own to procure the favour of God, but receiving from Christ everything that we want.'[162] In Calvin's eyes this active justification is the status of those eternally elected by God.[163] He can thus argue that when Paul speaks of predestining the elect to the adoption of children by Jesus Christ, making them accepted in the Beloved, he is talking about being justified freely by His grace.[164]

Writing admittedly with his tongue in his cheek, Prof. David Engelsma explains in his book *Hyper-Calvinism and the Call of the Gospel*, that if we measure the Calvinism of many moderns alongside Calvin's own doctrines, Calvin himself will be seen to be a Hyper-Calvinist. Here, as so often, Naylor, in criticising Gill's supposed 'Hyper-Calvinism', is criticising Calvin, too. Few would imagine Calvin to be perfect and above criticism but it would appear ridiculous to accuse a person of Hyper-Calvinism who comes as near to Calvin as makes no difference. As shown in my opening chapter, Louis Berkhof presents active and passive justification as being the traditional and Biblical Reformed doctrine, worthy of all acceptance. Admittedly, in this connection, Berkhof does not expressively say that justification took place in the eternal counsel of God as other Calvinists teach, but he does say that it is God's declaration 'made in the tribunal of God', which would appear to be the same. However, writing on '*The Nature of the Divine Decrees*', Berkhof claims that justification *is* a decree of

---

[160] Institutes, Book III, Chap. XI, p. 53.
[161] Ibid., Chap. XI, p. 43.
[162] Ibid., Chap. XIV, p. 72.
[163] Ibid., Chap. XI, p. 42.
[164] Ibid., Chap. XI, pp. 39, 40.

God, thus reflecting, 'His eternal purpose according to the counsel of His will, whereby, for His own glory, He hath foreordained whatsoever comes to pass.'[165] In conjunction with this, he sees justification as (a) a decree that renders the act certain; and (b) the act itself. This is a little different from Gill's view as he sees no difference between God's decisions and their enacting from the point of view of eternity. When God declared John Gill to be one of the elect, John Gill became one of the elect as he was then placed in Christ. This even works from eternity to time. When God said, 'Let there be light', there was light. When writing on justification in his *Systematic Theology*, John Murray says expressively that 'Justification is not the eternal decree of God with respect to us.' Berkhof says it is. So we have one Banner of Truth publication contradicting another. Such disagreements amongst brethren, however, are no grounds for using what John Legg calls 'theological swearwords' against one another. Both John Murray and Berkhof believe in election and that the elect either are or will be certainly justified, so they may, in brotherly love, agree to disagree on minor points. John Gill also believed in election and also that all the elect are those who will be justified before angels and men on the Day of Judgment. It must therefore be deemed unwise and unbrotherly for the Banner of Truth to criticise Gill because he accepted the same practical outcome, though possibly on more demonstrable grounds.

Justified by the faith of Jesus Christ
Naylor cannot follow Gill's argument that what God decrees in eternity is the *causa sine qua non* of what happens in time. His problem seems to be a difficulty in conceiving that God can extend His being out of eternity and work out His eternal purpose within the confinements of time. Thus Naylor prefers to stick to time and says, 'Does not the Bible teach the child of God is justified before God only when he believes?' As evidence for his assertion he cites Galatians 2:16 but as with so many of Gill's critics he merely quotes the number of the chapter and verse as if this were a magical refutation in itself without either quoting the text nor expounding it. This text, 'Knowing that a man is not justified by the works of the law, but by the faith of Jesus Christ, even we have believed in Jesus Christ, that we might be justified by the faith of Christ,

---

[165] *Systematic Theology*, pp. 102, 103, 517.

and not by the works of the law' has been discussed at length in the previous chapter as it was used in Gill's days to refute his doctrine with as little force as it is used today. Now if any text could be thought to endorse Gill's belief in an active eternal justification and its passive manifestation in the believer, now activated justifyingly by his new faith, then this must be it. Here are the very two aspects of justification, seen from God's side and man's side or from the side of eternity and the side of time, which Gill is referring to. Justification is not a product of man in time but the product of the faith of the Eternal One and Holy One, Christ Jesus. This faith of Christ in reference to the elect, with whom He is in union, has been given them to share and with it all the blessings which come with that faith, including, as a most essential part, justification. This is also made very plain in Romans 8:30-35 where the emphasis is on God's decrees in eternity made available in time of which justification is highlighted. 'Who shall lay any thing to the charge of God's elect? It is God that justifieth.'

Refusing to consider the evidence
Naylor, sums up Ephesians 2:8 in the words 'saved by faith', and claims that Gill rejects this, the only possible meaning of the verse. Again, Naylor neither quotes not expounds the full text, 'For by grace are ye saved through faith; and that not of yourselves: it is the gift of God.' Happily Gill not only quotes the text in his *New Testament Commentary* in full but gives a detailed exposition of it, diligently exploring every single meaning that can be obtained. Gill looks at faith and salvation, (a) from the point of view of God in eternity, (b) from the point of view of God acting in time and (c) from the point of view of the believer himself both as a denizen of earth and the offspring of heaven. Naylor makes himself open to the charge that he is only interested in the first part of the latter aspect of the text and quite refuses to consider the other aspects. Thus he is not in a position to argue that what he refuses to consider is wrong. Gill explains:

> 'For by grace are ye saved etc.' This is to be understood, not
> of temporal salvation, nor of preservation in Christ, nor of
> providential salvation in order to vocation, and much less of
> being put in a way of salvation, or only in a salvable state; but of
> spiritual salvation, and that actual; for salvation was not only

resolved upon, contrived and secured in the covenant of grace, for the persons here spoken to, but it was actually obtained and wrought out for them by Christ, and was actually applied unto them by the Spirit; and even as to the full enjoyment of it, they had it in faith and hope; and because of the certainty of it, they are said to be already saved; and besides, were representatively possessed of it in Christ their head: those interested in this salvation, are not all mankind, but particular persons; and such who were by nature children of wrath, and sinners of the Gentiles; and it is a salvation from sin, Satan, the law, its curse and condemnation, and from eternal death, and wrath to come; and includes all the blessings of grace and glory; and is entirely owing to free grace: for by grace is not meant the Gospel, nor gifts of grace, nor grace infused; but the free favour of God, to which salvation in all its branches is ascribed; as election, redemption, justification, pardon, adoption, regeneration, and eternal glory: the Syriac, Arabic, and Ethiopic versions read, 'by his grace', and so some copies; and it may refer to the grace of all the three Persons; for men are saved by the grace of the Father, who drew the plan of salvation, appointed men to it, made a covenant with his Son, in which it is provided and secured, and sent him into the world to obtain it; and by the grace of the Son, who engaged as a surety to effect it, assumed human nature, obeyed and suffered in it for that purpose, and has procured it; and by the grace of the Spirit, who makes men sensible of their need of it, brings it near, sets it before them, and applies it to them, and gives them faith and hope in it: hence it follows, 'through faith, and that not of yourselves, it is the gift of God;' salvation is through faith, not as a cause or condition of salvation, or as what adds any thing to the blessing itself; but it is the way, or means, or instrument, which God has appointed, for the receiving and enjoying it, that so it might appear to be all of grace; and this faith is not the produce of man's free will and power, but it is the free gift of God; and therefore salvation through it is consistent with salvation by grace; since that itself is of grace, lies entirely in receiving grace and gives all the glory to the grace of God: the sense of this last clause may be, that salvation is not of ourselves; it is not of our desiring nor of our deserving, nor of our performing, but is of the free grace of God: though faith is elsewhere represented as the gift of God, (John 6:65; Philippians 1:29).[166]

Such teaching is a faithful warning to modern would-be exegetes that they expound the whole of a text and not base doctrines on their 'criticism with a penknife'.

The folly of basing an accusation on words removed from their sense context

Arguing that faith is quite superfluous in Gill's system, Naylor asks the rhetorical question, 'Would Paul, for instance, have told the Galatians that God's elect are justified "without" faith?' Naylor has found the preposition 'without' in a wider passage of Gill's where he is distinguishing between the *esse* of justification in eternity and the *bene esse* of faith in time. He is distinguishing between justification as an act of God and justification in its expression of faith. He is also referring to elect infants who die before coming to faith. This is highly differential work and Naylor ought to have explained this instead of taking the one word 'without' out of a lengthy treatise to prove that Gill's full teaching on justification *in foro Dei*, justification *in foro conscientiae* and justification *in foro mundi* has no reference to faith. It is obvious that Gill teaches that God's decrees are irrespective of the agency of man but God gives a justifying faith which activates man as a child of God so that justification seen as a declaration of God is without man's faith but justification seen as the status of the born again Christian is, of necessity, with faith. Yet, even then, elect children, dying in infancy cannot be supposed not to be justified and have union with Christ as they have not (as far as can be judged) come to faith. Berkhof certainly taught, as seen in Chapter One, that the elect who die in infancy are justified without faith. On the same page from which Naylor culls his hyper-truncated quotes of Gill, the pastor scholar expounds Galatians 3:22, 23, 'But the scriptures hath concluded all under sin, that the promise by faith of Jesus Christ might be given to them that believe. But before faith came, we were kept under the law, shut up unto the faith which should afterwards be revealed.' In expounding this text, Gill

---

[166] Op. cit., vol. ix, p. 73.

explains how Christ is the object of our faith and 'is the grace by which the soul lays hold on, apprehends, and embraces Christ's righteousness, as its justifying righteousness before God.' Faith is, of course, according to Gill, thus not the justification itself but the evidence of it. But faith must certainly be present in the believer otherwise there is no believer and no justification. The whole idea of a faithless, though justified believer which is thrust on Gill is quite ridiculous. Gill's critics must decide whether we are justified by the faith of Christ given to the believer by an act of grace or we are justified as a reward due to our own acts of believing. If they come down on the former side, they agree with Gill. If they come down on the latter side, then they must quickly drop all claims to be evangelical and Reformed.

Does God wait until faith comes before justifying?
Having said this, it is necessary to take another look at Naylor's question whether Paul would recommend justification without faith as it hides another fundamental error. Naylor's query is apparently a double one. He is, in fact, asking, 'Does God justify those who are still without faith or does He wait until faith is there?' The Scriptures answer the first part of the question with a firm and categorical 'Yes' and answer the second part with a firm 'No'. Romans 4:5, 'But to him that worketh not but believeth on him that justifieth the ungodly, his faith is counted for righteousness;' Romans 5:6, 'For when we were yet without strength, in due time Christ died for the ungodly;' Romans 5:10, 'For if, when we were enemies, we were reconciled to God by the death of his Son, much more, being reconciled, we shall be saved by his life.' These texts show that the benefits of salvation are irrespective of the status of the receiver, but respective of God's grace. Surprising for a professed Calvinist, Naylor departs radically from the teaching of the Reformer here. Calvin, however, argued that God chooses the ungodly for justification:

> The order of justification which it (God's mercy) sets before us is this: first, God of his mere gratuitous goodness is pleased to embrace the sinner, in whom he sees nothing that can move him to mercy but wretchedness, because he sees him altogether naked and destitute of good works. He, therefore, seeks the cause of kindness in himself, that thus he may affect the sinner by a sense

of his goodness, and induce him, in distrust of his own works, to cast himself entirely upon his mercy for salvation.[167]

Calvin, as Gill, thus maintained that faith was the manifestation and ratification of justification. No man was drawn to Christ because he was willing but the elect are drawn to Christ so that they might be made willing. No one can approach the Father unless he is drawn to the Father by the Father.[168] Robert Traill, a most balanced theologian, is in full agreement in accepting Romans 4:5 literally. God justifies the ungodly, he argues, 'neither by making him godly before he justified him, nor leaving him ungodly after he hath justified him.'[169]

What Paul would have written if he had followed Naylor's view of Gill

Now Naylor gets himself tangled in the snares of his own argument and speculates on what Paul would have written if he had followed Gill. He thus has Paul playfully contemplating that when elect sinners are led to renounce the 'works of the law', they will 'turn to Christ to experience for themselves the joy of a justification which has always been theirs; it was theirs even when they had been cursed by God for their sins. The unsophisticated student of John Gill might, perhaps, be forgiven if he asks how it is that any of the elect could be convinced that when unbelievers they had been cursed by the law yet were in a state of actual justification. The student might be forgiven, too, should he conclude that here Gill is difficult and, arguably, quite impossible.'[170]

Here, this writer, to use Naylor's phrase, might be forgiven for pointing out that Naylor is making a mockery of Gill's teaching, besides showing great indiscretion in so misusing Paul. Gill nowhere teaches that when faith comes to elect sinners, it is merely to tell them of a justification which they already possessed. On the contrary, they receive, according to Gill, a manifestation of justification which they did not possess i.e. justification *in foro conscientiae*. When faith comes,

---

[167] *Institutes*, Book III, Chap. XI, p. 53.
[168] See Calvin's argument in The Eternal Predestination of God, *Calvin's Calvinism*, p. 98
[169] *The Doctrine of Justification Vindicated*, p. 320.
[170] Op. cit. Chap. X, *John Gill and Eternal Justification*, p. 175.

according to Gill's teaching, it is Christ who brings it with Him and the elect sinner is enabled to receive Christ in faith. There is far more to being in Christ than having an assurance of justification. Being in Christ means that all the blessings of redemption, satisfaction, pardon, reconciliation and hope for the future are found in Christ. It means becoming the temple and dwelling place of the Holy Spirit. Furthermore, should a believer look back at the time before he was converted, he will realise that though he was condemned in Adam, he was justified in Christ, which will give him every reason to glory in Christ than question his justification from eternity. If the Holy Spirit has led him to read Gill and not allowed him to be led astray by Naylor, he will realise that his justification must have been in the eternal will of God because the wherewithal was never part of his earthly make-up. Justification is by grace and whom God elects, he justifies.

Gill accused of misquoting Paul to suit his exposition
Next, Naylor complains that 'it is just possible that Gill, an acute scholar who seldom missed much, misquoted Paul to suit his own exposition.'[171] To prove his case, Naylor presents us with a version of what Gill is supposed to have said, but erases over half of Gill's words from different places within the quote and adds to the insult above by arguing that he believes Gill was unsure of his exposition of Romans 8:1. What Gill actually says is:

> Justification is not only before faith, but it is from eternity, being an immanent act in the divine mind, and so an internal and external one; as may be concluded, 1. From eternal election: the objects of justification are God's elect; *Who shall lay anything to the charge of God's elect? it is God that justifies*; that is, the elect. Now if God's elect, as such, can have nothing laid to their charge; but are by God acquitted, discharged and justified; and if they bore this character of elect from eternity, or were chosen in Christ before the world began; then they must be acquitted, discharged and justified so early, so as nothing could be laid to their charge: besides, by electing grace men were put into Christ, and were considered as in him before the foundation of the world; and if

---
[171] Op. cit. pp. 175, 176.

they were considered in him, they must be considered as righteous or unrighteous, not surely as unrighteous, unjustified, and in a state of condemnation; *for there is no condemnation to them which are in Christ*, Romans 8:1 and therefore must be considered as righteous, and so justified: 'Justified then we were', says Dr Goodwin, 'when first elected, though not in our own persons, yet in our Head, as he had our persons then given him, and we came to have a being and an interest in him.'

What Naylor makes of this is:

Justification is not only before faith, but it is from eternity, being an immanent act in the divine mind and so an internal and eternal one: as may be concluded ... if they bore this character of elect from eternity, or were chosen in Christ before the world began; then they must be acquitted, discharged, and justified so early ... for there is no condemnation to them which are in Christ, Romans viii. 1; and therefore must be considered as righteous, and so justified.[172]

Naylor argues that because Gill has left out the word 'now' from Paul's words, 'There is therefore now no condemnation ...,' he is wilfully misleading his readers as the 'now' refers to when the hearers came to faith, implying that the text has thus nothing to do with the believer's eternal standing in Christ. 'Now', Naylor argues, can only mean 'when faith is born'. The word 'now' here merely strengthens the 'therefore' as being a logical conclusion from the aforesaid and Gill is embedding the words in a well-defined context. Paul is not referring to faith being born but to the point Gill is making i.e. being in Christ and being joint heirs with Christ and its consequences. Paul is showing that those in Christ cannot be considered as unrighteous and unjustified because God justifies those he predestinates. This leads him to ask rhetorically, 'Who shall lay anything to the charge of God's elect?'[173]

---

[172] Op. cit. p. 174. The full quote is found in *Body of Divinity*, vol. i, p. 334, 1769 edition and Book II, Chap. V. p. 205 in the Baptist Standard Bearer one volume edition. Naylor gives p. 296 for his edition.

[173] Romans 8:29-33.

It is thus most unfair of Naylor to charge Gill with misquoting Paul on purpose, especially as his own interpretation is wide off the mark.

Gill allegedly misunderstood the Old Testament saints
Naylor feels he has found 'an even more glaring weakness' than all the other presumed weaknesses in Gill's theology in Gill's remarks concerning the justification of elect sinners before the Atonement took place. This time, Gill is accused of not understanding Hebrews 1:1 and 11:4 referring to the faith of the Old Testament saints. Naylor quotes an extensive passage, this time without using his penknife, from Gill's *Of Justification as an Immanent Act* which is Gill's seventh and last point in his second main argument beginning with the point Naylor criticises above concerning the justification of the elect. It is a pity that Naylor has left out entirely Section I and arguments 2-6 in Section II in reference to point seven as these provide a background and logical build-up for it and answers many questions which could be raised by merely reading this last section. Naylor's quote from Gill reads:

> It deserves regard and attention, that the saints under the Old Testament, were justified by the same righteousness of Christ, as those under the New, and that before the sacrifice was offered up, the satisfaction given, and the everlasting righteousness brought in; for Christ's blood was shed for the remission of sins that were past, and his death was for the redemption of transgressions under the first Testament, Romans 3:25; Hebrews 9:15. Now if God could, and actually did, justify some, three or four thousand years before the righteousness of Christ was actually wrought out, taking his Son's word and bond as their Surety, and in a view of his future righteousness; why could he not, and why may it not be thought he did, justify all his elect from eternity, upon the word and bond of their Surety, and on the foot of his future righteousness; which he had engaged to work out, and which he full well knew he would most certainly work out? and if there is no difficulty in conceiving of the one, there can be none in conceiving of the other.[174]

---

[174] BSB edition, op. cit. Book II, Chap. V. p. 207.

Clearly, the point Gill is making here is that the work of Christ on the cross has not merely a forward looking aspect, as the Grotians affirm, but it has a past, present and future efficacy. Thus justification cannot possibly be limited to those who have received the remission of sins and Christ's righteousness *after* Christ's death. As justification is from eternity, there is no problem in accepting that the saints were justified irrespective of their position *in any time*. Christ's sacrifice was as efficacious in Abraham's case as it was in Paul's as it is in present day Christians.

Naylor attempts to refute Gill by completely side-stepping the issue. He points out that Gill does not take up the relationship between faith and justification here and thus presumes that Gill is failing to face up to facts. This is quite unfair because, section one of Gill's treatise on justification deals at great length with the relationship of faith to justification under no less than five heads on which Naylor hardly comments anywhere in his book. Yet Naylor overlooks this enormous amount of evidence and criticises Gill, who has gone on to write about the relationship of justification to the timing of the Atonement, for leaving faith out. Rather than Gill showing 'glaring weakness' here, Naylor's repeated method of isolating a topic from its context and then complaining that it is isolated is highly questionable and renders his own method of argumentation most unconvincing.

Further misrepresentation

Naylor has, however, yet another surprise up his sleeve. He feels free to read into the passage quoted that Gill views the Old Testament saints as being saved by a 'notional doctrine of eternal justification', apparently implying that Gill sees this doctrine as a substitute for faith. Needless to say, Gill taught no such thing—indeed, he taught the very opposite and saw no contradiction in the belief that the just shall live by faith and the fact that this faith is a gift of God according to God's eternal decree. Where Naylor obtained his notion that faith for Gill was a mere 'notion' is anyone's guess. Regarding faith, Gill says:

> Faith is the sense, perception, and evidence of our justification. Christ's righteousness, as justifying, is revealed from faith to faith. It is that grace whereby the soul, in the light of the divine Spirit, beholds a complete righteousness in Christ,

having seen its guilt, pollution, and misery; when it is enabled to renounce its own righteousness, and submit to the righteousness of Christ; which it puts on by faith, as its garment of justification: which it rejoices in, and gives him the glory of; the Spirit of God bearing witness with his Spirit, that he is a justified Person.[175]

Sadly, as shown in the cases of Toon and Fuller, Gill's modern critics cannot relate faith to the personal witness of the Spirit in the believer's life. They thus discard such 'Antinomian' teaching and then say that Gill has no doctrine of Biblical faith. Instead of criticising Gill on faith, they should come up with a better teaching; a step they seem reluctant to take. Again, we are reminded of party politics in which it is thought better to criticise the opposition than to present a better policy. To argue that Gill ought to have brought Hebrews 1:1 and 11:4 into his illustration of Romans 3:25 and Hebrews 9:15 and presenting this as a 'glaring weakness' on Gill's part is being hyper-critical. Gill has commented in detail and at length on both these verses in his sermons, writings and commentaries and Naylor could have found out how Gill views these verses there. It is most strange that Naylor feels that Gill is not being true to Hebrews 1:1, 'God, who at sundry times and in divers manners spake in time past unto the fathers by the prophets.' This verse does not deal with the question of justification by faith at all, nor with the idea that faith was indispensable to the fathers' salvation, though Naylor claims the verse does. When Gill expounds this verse in his commentary, he keeps to the subject, showing the various ways in which God has revealed Himself in Old Testament times, as he puts it, 'from the beginning to the end of it'. If Gill had added more, he would have had to bring in factors, like Naylor, which were not central to the topic. Given that Naylor has a different view of faith to Gill's and indeed, obviously does not understand Gill's doctrine, we need not take Naylor's criticism concerning missing Hebrews 11:4 too seriously. If Naylor wishes to find a sound exegesis from Gill's pen on 'the just shall live by faith', he could look up Gill's fine fifty-seven lined exposition of Hebrews 10:38 in his *New Testament Commentary* and his further exposition of the verse contra Dr Whitby's rough handling of that precious truth in Section LII of *The Cause of God and Truth*.

---

[175] See *Sermons and Tracts*, vol. ii, p. 492 and *Body of Divinity* pp. 332, 333.

Doubting the faithfulness of God to His people
Naylor again shows his skill at in-fighting when he criticises Gill's emphasis on a God who keeps to His covenant promises, a God who remains faithful, though we believe not. Naylor says this is yet another example of Gill's 'weakness' as he is here misusing Paul's words in 2 Timothy 2:13, though Gill was not referring directly to this passage. Naylor points out pedantically that Paul is referring to 'what will happen to spurious believers who deny the faith they once professed.' All that Gill is, however, saying in the context, using the language of Scripture, is that we can rely on the fact that God will keep His covenant promises, whatever human opposition—even from professing Christians, He receives. We have a God who keeps His word. Instead of saying 'Amen' to this fundamental truth of Scripture, Naylor says haughtily, 'We disagree',[176] and wishes to point out that Gill is misquoting Scripture. Naylor finds 'proof' for his disagreement in William Hendriksen's commentary on the text where he reads 'if Christ failed to remain faithful to his threat as well as to his promise, he would be denying himself.' This is, of course, a perfectly acceptable part-exposition of the text as it emphasises Paul's point and is in keeping with the rest of Scripture. A brief look into Gill's exposition of 2 Timothy 2:13 will reveal that this is the very line Gill takes. The difference is, however, that Naylor feels that anyone who is guilty of any form of unbelief is automatically a 'spurious believer'. Naylor has shown his Arminian-like aversion to 'covenant engagements', and appears now to be introducing an Arminian doctrine of Christian perfection. Naylor can hardly feel that Peter, who denied his Lord thrice is thus a reprobate and that the thankful father in Mark 9:24 proved himself to be a 'spurious believer' when he said, 'Lord, I believe; help thou my unbelief?' Though Gill is not using the words criticised in context but merely to assert God's faithfulness to His own Word, Paul is obviously using them in a way more open to Gill's usage than Naylor's. Paul is writing to Timothy, urging him not to be ashamed of the gospel. When Naylor says, 'We disagree', he is obviously referring to himself alone. When Paul says, If *we* suffer ..., If *we* deny ..., If *we* believe not ..., he is referring to himself and Timothy and obviously also

---

[176] Op. cit. p. 177.

to the 'faithful men' of Timothy's church. Paul is identifying himself with those who must be prepared to take the consequences of unbelief. He is not suggesting that he could be a 'spurious believer'. Matthew Henry speaks here of those who deny Christ 'out of fear or shame, or for the sake of some temporal advantage'. Sadly, many, if not most of us could be included here. Perhaps the best answer to Naylor's narrow analysis of words is Paul's next verse, 'Of these things put them in remembrance, charging them before the Lord that they strive not about words to no profit, but to the subverting of the hearers.' These are obviously words spoken for the benefit of the church and not merely a warning against 'spurious believers'.

If any reader who has the privilege of possessing an On-line Bible with its enormous compendium of first class commentaries, should type 2 Timothy 2:13 into any full text search programme, he will receive a summing up of the teaching of the text in the words, 'If we prove faithless, he will still be faithful to keep every promise he has made.' This refreshing interpretation and display of sympathy with struggling Christians is also to be found in Gill's exposition of the verse. The scholar-pastor says:

'If we believe not, yet he abideth faithful', &c. The Syriac and Ethiopic versions read, 'if we believe not him'. This may be understood, either of such who are altogether destitute of faith, who do not believe in Christ at all; and particularly do not believe what was just now said concerning his denying such that deny him, but mock and scoff at his coming, and at a future judgment: this unbelief of theirs will not make void his faith or faithfulness; see Romans 3:3, he will abide faithful to his word of threatening; and what he says in Mark 16:16 will be found to be an everlasting truth: or it may be understood of true believers, whose faith sometimes is very low, as to its exercise on Christ, and with reference to their future glory and happiness; but Christ is faithful to all his covenant engagements for them, to bring them to glory, and to every word of promise concerning their happiness, and to every branch of the faithful saying above mentioned; and he is ever the same in his love to them, and in the efficacy of his blood, righteousness, and sacrifice; and his salvation is an everlasting and unchangeable one; nor do the saints' interest in it, and security by it, depend upon their acts of believing, or their frames, but upon the firmness and unchangeableness of Christ, the object of faith. 'He cannot deny himself'; he cannot go contrary to his word; that would be to act contrary to his nature and perfections, and would be a denying of himself, which is not possible; wherefore his faithfulness will never fail, even though, the faith of his people does, as to the exercise of it.[177]

Gill's elect supposedly suffer from 'an unenlightened fiction of the imagination'

Naylor now accuses Gill of teaching that sinners are not expected to show godly sorrow before coming to faith. Gill has likened justification to the lot of an imprisoned man who fears his punishment, knowing that it is just, but suddenly experiences the joy of receiving the King's pardon. Naylor thinks Gill is here purposefully avoiding teaching the need for true evangelical repentance, but Gill's arch-critic is merely reading this into Gill's words. What Gill says can be compared to Louis Berkhof's statement which is even briefer, i.e. 'The granting of a pardon would mean nothing to a prisoner, unless the glad tidings were communicated to him and the doors of the prison were opened.' Calvin also uses an almost identical illustration, likewise not mentioning 'godly sorrow' or repentance in any way in the context. Calvin concludes this by saying, 'Thus we simply interpret justification as the acceptance with which God receives us into his favour as if we were righteous; and we say that this justification consists in the forgiveness of sins and the imputation of the righteousness of Christ.'[178] Are we now to use such statements against Berkhof and Calvin to prove that they neither believed in true repentance nor faith because they do not mention them in a very limited context? This is how Naylor attacks Gill. Gill, too, merely relates the brief story to show how the King had pardoned the soldier before he received news of it. Additional to Berkhof's and Calvin's stories, however, Gill stresses that this man knew he was justly guilty and expressed thankful 'joy unspeakable and full of glory' at his release. Needless to say, Gill, Calvin and Berkhof

---

[177] *Commentary*, vol. ix, p. 327.
[178] *Institutes*, vol. ii, Book III, Chap. XI, p. 38.

all stress the need for repentance and faith in other parts of their works. Naylor, in an argument that makes the reader wonder where on earth he gets his ideas from, transfers this story into the realms of his own hyper-critical imagination and his low view of Gill's doctrines and argues that this proves that Gill believed that elect sinners before coming to faith were suffering under 'an unenlightened fiction of the imagination'. This delusion of Naylor's own imagination is pasted on to Gill and declared to be 'questionable' and 'inadequate'. This is primitive polemics at their worst and shows a completely unbrotherly unwillingness to ever allow Gill the benefit of the doubt or even allow Gill to express his mind at all on the topic. The words 'questionable' and 'inadequate' cannot fully describe this most unfair treatment.

Being in Adam and being in Christ
One feature of Naylor's criticism here, however, that of the state of the elect before and after conversion is worthy of note as it provides the basis for Naylor's final criticism concerning Gill's method of viewing man as an offspring of Adam or in his union with Christ. Here, Naylor, as in most of his criticisms is merely repeating what Gill has already advanced as a possible argument in his *The Doctrine of Justification Stated and Maintained*, already dealt with above. As usual, Naylor maintains that Gill is 'confused', this time in his doctrine of the two natures of the Christian. What upsets Naylor is again the Biblical doctrine of God's justifying His enemies, that is, the ungodly. It is impossible, Naylor says, to be in a state of condemnation (in Adam) and also be in a state of justification (in Christ). Again it is Gill's doctrine of the covenant of works and the covenant of grace that puzzles Naylor. Gill teaches that the unsaved are under the covenant of works but the covenant of grace releases the elect at conversion from the covenant of works so that grace might reign in the believer's life. Apart from being a fully Scriptural position, this is the stand of our Reformers. Naylor, however, is a self-confessed Fullerite and not a Reformed man. Therefore he hides behind Andrew Fuller in his criticism of Gill, maintaining that the requirements of the covenant of works has been done away with as a means of satisfying God. Fullerites argue in this way because they do not accept that our salvation relies on Christ's fully satisfying the covenant of works i.e. the law on our behalf so that God can freely justify us. Here Grotians, Fullerites and Socinians join hands

but Gill keeps his clean from such pollution. Man is in Adam and as such is required to keep the law and live. This he cannot do. Christ has kept the law for those who are in Him. Obviously believers are, according to God's word, chosen in Christ from eternity but all mankind are under Adam their federal head until released from this status by God's intervention. The 'body of flesh' or 'the man of sin' which we have inherited from Adam is robbed of its power to have us condemned but must stay with us till the grave when all that remains of being in Adam shall cease. Actually and Biblically speaking, these two natures are still with us as Christ indwells our mortal bodies. In Christ we are new creatures but in our flesh, as Paul said, though he had walked with Christ many years, dwells no good thing. This denial of a most fundamental doctrine provides modern critics of Gill with their ammunition. As this denial, as taught, for instance, by the Banner of Truth, is based on a departure from the Authorised Version, and a re-translation of the salient passages based on unwarranted theories of tense construction. This quite technical subject will be dealt with in chapter seven.

Wrangling with words
Now, finally, Naylor refers to Keach, Crosby, Witsius, Fuller, Ivimey and Watts, to show up 'the radicalism of Gill's theology'. This wrangling of words shows nothing of the kind and merely underlines that Naylor has his own preferences which, however, he displays partly in acts of prejudice and partly with faulty argument. It also shows that Naylor's confession that the bulk of his knowledge of Gill has been gained from but one of Gill's works on justification has not paid off. If Naylor is looking for 'radical theology', he will find it in the writings of Crosby, Fuller and Watts far easier than in Gill's works. As pointed out in my Gill biography, Naylor has presented us with a thoroughly unbalanced picture of Ivimey in his *Picking Up a Pin*. But we must now examine Naylor's evidence in detail.

Keach contra Gill?
Naylor quotes Keach's definition of justification as:

Justification is an act of God's rich Grace, through the Redemption which is in Christ, wherein he freely pardoneth and acquitteth us of all our sins, and accepteth us as righteous, only for the sake of Christ and his righteousness, which is imputed to us.[179]

Gill, of course, would have said 'Amen' to this as the previous chapters have shown. So what is Naylor's point? Obviously, Keach has not said the last word on justification as there is much to be added. Naylor argues that Keach did not add the ideas which would have, presumably, spoken against Gill because he was 'probing a sensitive issue'. Now though I have read *The Child's Delight,* from which this quote is taken, I was not aware that Keach was covering up on anything. I feel he was, though faced with a threat of annoying the authorities, pouring out his honest heart. What Naylor feels Keach was not wishing to underline, in order not to unnecessarily offend, was his view that 'Fundamental and Virtual Justification in Christ, as our Head and Representative, and our actual and Personal Justification when we are united to him' is a distinction which must be made. Naylor interprets this as an effort on Keach's part to back away from the doctrine of justification from eternity but doing it in a most confusing way. The confusion, however is perhaps in Naylor's mind alone. Naylor feels Keach's version is an improvement on Gill's way of dividing justification into active and passive[180] or into an *actus immanens* and *actus transiens.* To an unprejudiced reader, it may appear, however, that there is no essential difference to find here but that Gill's presentation of the two aspects of justification are more simply put and easier to understand. Keach is merely arguing that we must distinguish between justification as a fundamental and virtual truth based on union with Christ and its outworking in the faith and life of the believer. Gill said no less, though he said much more, as did also Keach. It would seem that Naylor believes that 'virtual' means 'not yet real' and 'actual' means, 'it was not there before acquired by faith'. Keach, in keeping with the language of his day, certainly believed that virtual justification

---

[179] Op. cit. p. 182.
[180] Of course, Keach strongly believed in justification by Christ's active and passive obedience, a further point Naylor seemed to have missed. See Keach's *A postscript containing a few reflections upon some passages in Mr. Clark's new book entitled Scriptural Justification at the end of Betwixt Two Extremes.*

was real justification and that this was activated, actualised and operated via union with Christ. Here Gill and Keach are far nearer each other than they are to Naylor. It must also be pointed out that both the old Puritan doctrine of virtual justification and the Reformed doctrine of actual justification are rejected by Toon (the former) and the Banner of Truth (the latter) as being Hyper-Calvinistic and Antinomian.

Furthermore, in Keach's thirty-five paged tract *A medium Betwixt and Between Two Extremes* which is the second work Naylor quotes, though Keach disagrees with the 'gracious person' Naylor mentions who believes in a rather extreme form of justification from eternity, he, nevertheless defends her against the charge of Antinomianism and himself against the charge of Arminianism for disagreeing with her on the point that the elect are not under God's wrath before calling. Here Gill agreed fully with Keach. In this work, Keach emphasises that justification is before faith but faith is the hand which receives and apprehends Christ and therefore the justification which Christ brings. Again, Gill was fully one with his predecessor.

The difference between Keach and Gill on justification is that the former emphasises that he is not primarily considering 'what a sight God might have of men, or how he sees, of how things are before him; before whom, or in whose sight the world was from eternity', but the execution of it in the faith of the believer. Keach is more interested in what happens to justification in its outworking in the life of the believer, i.e. justification in time. Though Gill does not neglect this latter factor, his covenant theology compels him to stress more the side which Keach tended not to emphasise. However, when Keach comes to speak of justification as a decree of God, as being in 'federal union with Christ, as our surety and blessed sponsor, from eternity' and a covenantal act of the Godhead, he says, completely in unison with Gill, that justification was made sure before the world began. As evidence of this he quotes 2 Timothy 1:9 and Titus 1:2, i.e. the very texts that Gill uses in this connection.

Naylor's last point concerning Keach's supposed superiority over Gill is only valid if we believe that Keach was three or four generations before his time. Naylor affirms that he believed in an offer of Christ to all men. Keach used the term 'offer' in the sense of Dort, that is, 'presenting'. This was the legitimate use of the word at the time. Fifty and more years later, however, the word 'universal' was being put before the word 'offer' to indicate that the preacher could warrant i.e. guarantee, every sinner that Christ wanted to save him and had provided for that salvation. If ever a contemporary Particular Baptist believed that in Keach's day, history appears to have forgotten him. This was certainly not Keach's theology. This is why Richard Davis stopped using the term 'offer' fairly late in life, because he could not accept the new meaning. Gill explains carefully in several of his works, listed by Naylor, how this change of meaning occurred and why he personally refused to use the word 'offer' in its altered meaning. Naylor is always suspicious of Gill's motives. Perhaps we ought to seriously ask Naylor if he is suppressing such information to make a weak case more presentable.

Lastly, two points must be stressed that Naylor has obviously overlooked in setting up Keach against Gill. In *Betwixt Two Extremes*, Keach sandwiches his words on justification between two clear statements that even a rather extreme form of justification from eternity and his own position seem to be merely a matter of words. Oddly enough, Naylor does not deal with Keach's second extreme which is the very doctrine of justification taught nowadays by modern Baxterians, Amyraldians and Fullerites. Here Gill and Keach agree heartily against much that Naylor argues in his book.

Crosby contra Gill?

Naylor now quotes a few words of Thomas Crosby[181] concerning Edward Wallin, a friend of Gill's whom Crosby says:

> ... did not run into those flights of justification before faith ... but with the English Baptists in general held, That none can be said to be actually reconciled, justified, or adopted, until they are really implanted into Jesus by faith.[182]

Naylor remarks that these words were a 'barely concealed criticism of Gill'. Actually, they were part of a very marked, intentional and open criticism of Gill. Crosby, a Maths teacher, was smarting under the

---

[181] Crosby's *The History of the English Baptists*, vol. iv, pp. 393, 394.
[182] Naylor has omitted, 'and of good works, in no sense, being necessary to salvation'. op. cit. p. 182.

shame of being excommunicated from Gill's Particular Baptist church and about to be excommunicated from another. Crosby was an opponent of the 'Particular' in Particular Baptists and sought to present General and Particular Baptists as one denomination which he called *English* Baptists, or simply 'Baptists in general', as in the above quote, though the churches with which he was in and out of fellowship had called themselves 'Particular' since at least 1717 when the Particular Baptist Fund came into being. Ivimey's words of protest at the cavalier manner in which Crosby recorded his findings as if there were no difference between the two denominations and their theologies have been recorded in his subsequent history of the Baptists. Ivimey also specifically records in that history Gill's fine comments on Wallin's character, testimony and learning which runs into several pages. When Gill died, it was Wallin's son who preached at Gill's funeral as Gill had preached at his father's. Crosby's history, very much of which he took over from Benjamin Stinton, is marked by theological unawareness and a tolerance of other views which did not stop at Arianism. He is thus a very odd person to be chosen as one who could teach Gill a thing or two theologically speaking. Having said this, however, it is noticeable that Crosby (or Naylor in selecting his quotes) has misunderstood Gill. Gill speaks of justification from eternity. Justification before faith is only a part of this referring to that justification with which God accepts sinners whilst they are still ungodly. It would be difficult to find a Reformer, Puritan, Evangelical or old Particular Baptist who did not believe this truth, so plainly taught in Scripture. Nor does this doctrine contradict in any way the fact that *actual* reconciliation, justification and adoption are the lot of those who are 'implanted into Jesus by faith', as Crosby seems to think. It is interesting also to note that even Crosby believed in actual justification, a doctrine many 'Moderate Calvinists' when linked with actual imputation, regard as Antinomian.

Witsius contra Gill?
Naylor now gives two quotes from Witsius, 'the satisfaction of Christ being supposed, and apprehended by faith, by which the whole righteousness of the law is fulfilled, the man is then justified', and, with reference to Galatians 2:16, 'the MEANS by which we receive the righteousness of Christ, and justification depending thereon, is FAITH,

and that ONLY',[183] and argues that the word 'then' in the first quote and the word 'depending' in the second quote show that 'Witsius was nearer the mark than Gill'.

Now again, Naylor bases his idea that Gill would think differently to Witsius, and therefore wrongly (?), on his own interpretation of Galatians 2:16 which actually is neither Gill's nor Witsius' interpretation. Nevertheless, if Naylor would accept Gill's (and Calvin's) term 'instrument' rather than 'means', he would find Gill quite in agreement with Witsius' words, as far as their interpretation of Galatians 2:16 went. It is, however, most strange that Naylor takes his very short quotes from Section's XLV and XLVII of Witsius' book, where this great writer is discussing the generalities of justification without saying when, where and how they occur. This he does in Sections LVII to LXIII where he outlines the seven periods or stages, or 'articles' of justification in relation to time instrumental to the elective decree of God outside of time. Now the question is, where did Witsius place the sentiments Naylor quotes? A studious examination of Witsius' eight stages will show that Naylor's quotes must be seen parallel to the first five periods which take us from God's sentence of absolution for his elect as soon as Adam fell to the sinner entering into 'familiar converse with God' which process, Witsius calls being *actively* and *passively* justified. Now, had Naylor gone to the right sources, he would have found a teaching which he can as little stomach as Gill's. Naylor argues at great length to show how he does not think that Gill's doctrine of active and passive justification is Biblical but here is Witsius asserting it as strongly as Gill!

Actually, if Naylor had studied Gill's doctrine of *in foro conscientiae*, he might have found new dimensions in Gill's doctrine which he would see are quite in keeping with Scripture. It would be difficult to find fault with Gill's explanation of the relationship of faith to justification, Gill outlines in the very sermon that Naylor says he has used as the basis of his views on Gill's doctrine of justification. 'Faith is the sense, perception, and evidence of our justification. Christ's righteousness, as justifying, *is revealed from faith to faith*. It is this

---

[183] Naylor's ref. *Economy of the Covenants*, 1775, vol. ii (three-volumed edition), p. 120 f. In the 1822 two-volumed edition the first quote is in vol. i, Book iii, Chap. vii, Section XLV, p. 408 and the second quote is in Section XLVII on the following page.

grace whereby the soul, in the light of the divine Spirit, beholds a complete righteousness in Christ, having seen its guilt, pollution, and misery; when it is enabled to renounce its own righteousness, and submit to the righteousness of Christ; which it puts on by faith, as its garment of justification: which it rejoices in, and gives him the glory of; the Spirit of God bearing witness with his Spirit, that he is a justified Person. And so he comes to be evidently and declaratively *justified in the name of the Lord Jesus, and by the Spirit of God.*'[184]

Perhaps Naylor has not quite understood Witsius in the brief quotes he gives. The Dutch divine is not arguing that faith is the *cause* or the *condition* of justification, nor even a *pre-requisite* as Naylor seems to suppose. He is showing that it is God's *means* of bringing home to the elect person his state in Christ. It is the method used whereby God communicates with His elect so that they can apprehend and trust in the righteousness of Christ for their justification. This is stressed time and time again by Gill but the one thing that is made clear in Naylor's chapter on 'John Gill and Faith' is that he has completely failed to grasp, outline and come to terms with Gill's teaching.

Fuller contra Gill?
Naylor's way of putting Gill in Fuller's shadow is very revealing. Naylor explains that Fuller was formerly a member of a High-Calvinist church but changed his views before taking over the church in which Gill was formerly a co-pastor. Perhaps Naylor is wanting to show that Fuller once pastored a church holding Gill-like views but then saw the folly of his ways. Fuller's Soham church, however, had a policy of faith and duty radically different from Gill's. Fuller, as his former pastor John Eve, was 'much entangled', to use his own words, in Johnsonism, which Gill never was, and the teaching in his church tended towards Arianism. It was, indeed, Gill and especially John Brine whose views Naylor finds identical with Gill's, who pointed out to the churches the folly of Johnson's ways. Also, it must be noted that both pastor and people of the Soham church disbelieved in preaching the gospel to sinners. The result was that there was not a single conversion during all the time Fuller was a member of that church. One only has to read

---

[184] *Sermons and Tracts*, vol. ii, The Doctrine of Justification Stated and Maintained, p. 492. Gill has a great deal more to say about faith in this sermon.

Rippon's glowing testimony to the way Gill filled his church and read the Goat Yard church books to see how often souls were converted and new members added to the church. Anyone reading Gill's long series of sermons on the Song of Solomon alone cannot but be impressed by his evangelistic fervour. It is just not true to say that when Fuller left Soham to take over Gill's first joint pastorate at Kettering, he was a changed man. Johnsonism stuck to him in various forms as long as he lived and he never dropped the quite un-Christian belief that the full gospel was for believers only, as can be clearly read in Fuller's attack on evangelical-minded Dan Taylor in his *Reply to Philanthropos*. Nevertheless, Naylor takes Fuller's theology as his standard and quotes from a paper found amongst his belongings after his death which gives a most refreshing testimony as compared with that found in works published in his lifetime. Fuller says:

> Before our believing in Christ, we are considered and treated by God, as a lawgiver, as under condemnation; but having fled to him for refuge, the law, as to its condemning power, hath no more dominion over us, but we are treated, even by God the judge, as in a state of justification.[185]

One wonders, what Naylor is seeking to prove here and what the force of Naylor's argument is supposed to be. There is nothing whatsoever here that Gill does not also state. Article IV of Gill's *Goat Yard Declaration of Faith* says as much, though using even stronger language concerning the state of the fallen until Christ enters their lives. Gill's words in Romans 3:24, when commenting on 'Being justified freely by his grace', show how the unconverted elect are under condemnation in Adam for breaking the law, and that Christ took this condemnation on Himself for their sakes. Christ did not die to remove condemnation from the non-elect but the elect.

Watts contra Gill?
Naylor's misuse of a quote from Watts reveals the full depths of Naylor's truly obnoxious criticism of Gill as this modern Baptist pastor throws all Christian decorum to the four winds and becomes plainly and

---

[185] Taken from Ryland's *Memoirs of Mr. Fuller*, p. 68.

simply nasty. Shortly before Gill was called home, a visitor asked him how he was feeling. Gill answered that he had nothing to make him uneasy and could say with the hymn-writer:

> He raised me from the deeps of sin,
> The gates of gaping hell,
> And fix'd my standing more secure
> Than 'twas before I fell.

Now no one could possibly find that there is any touch of Antinomianism or Hyper-Calvinism in these words. Yet Naylor is not prepared to accept that these words were Gill's honest, dying conviction. He suggests that Gill ought to have said:

> And fix'd my standing most secure
> In Christ before I fell.

Naylor then asks, 'In other words, if the elect were actually justified in Christ before they fell, when they were, allegedly, 'most secure', how was it that they fell at all? Does the Bible ever teach that there can be justification without sanctification?'[186] This final stab at Gill is symptomatic of not only Naylor's method of argumentation but that of other critics such as Robert Oliver, Michael Haykin, Erroll Hulse and especially Iain Murray. They put up arguments that do not represent Gill in any way and refute them to their own satisfaction and then retire with a new feather in their cap to crow over their success. The whole verbal exercise has no purpose but to reveal to men, to use a favourite saying of Iain Murray's, that 'the best of men are but men at best', these good men being Gill's accusers themselves.

The answer to Naylor's question is fourfold. As the words quoted were never spoken by Gill, Naylor should keep his false logic based on false premises for his own personal use and not display himself in such a negative way like a cheeky fresher trying to portray his professor for a laugh—behind the latter's back, of course. This fresher's cheek is all the more blameworthy when that professor is actually on his death bed. Secondly, Naylor must be familiar with the first three chapters of

---

[186] Op. cit. p. 184.

Genesis which informs us about man made the crowning glory and Chief Steward of Creation but become worse than the meanest member of that creation, dragging all that he had formerly commanded down with him to his doom. If Naylor wants to ask that doubting question of 'Why hast thou made me thus?', I am sure that Gill could give Naylor a good answer but the correct addressee of that question is the Lord of Creation. Thirdly, Gill confessed in his dying breath that he knew he had fallen and he knew Christ had saved him. These things Mr Naylor seems unable to understand. It seems that Naylor is striving to rob Gill posthumously of a glorious and triumphant testimony by pretending that it was not genuine. Is Naylor really of the opinion that Gill's public testimony during over fifty years in the ministry was so bad that he could not have had such a peaceful home-call? Naylor leaves us puzzled as to his Christian motives.

Lastly, Naylor has consulted few of Gill's works, and these only to cull out quotes with which he chooses to disagree as far as he has understood them. Gill, however, speaks often of sanctification and Naylor has read enough of Gill to know that he teaches that the man who scorns sanctification, scorns Christ and that the process of sanctification, to Gill, was a lifelong process. This view alone might not be acceptable to many but it can hardly be taken as proof that Gill was a 'Hyper'.

Chapter Seven

God's Love For His Elect In Their Natural State

From the days of Abraham Taylor to Peter Naylor, Gill's traducers have ridiculed his thoroughly Biblical belief in a Triune God who loves the people of His choice so that whilst they were yet sinners, Christ died because of that love for them. Taylor rejects any idea of God's loving his elect before justification so he is quite consistent with himself when he argues that a sinner cannot be under God's love and the covenant of works at the same time. Naylor, however, professes to believe in the eternal love of God for His people but argues that God's wrath cannot be on them if they are considered justified. As God's wrath is on the unsaved elect, he argues, they cannot logically be justified. But, here, Naylor is not only side-stepping the doctrine of the two natures of man, but he is also side-stepping his own doctrine of the eternal love of God for His elect. He is also arguing that Gill does not believe that the elect before conversion are in any way under wrath, forgetting he has quoted Gill as saying they are. For Gill, there is no contradiction at all in viewing man as fallen in Adam and under God's wrath and man as accepted in union with Christ and an object of His eternal love. This is evident in his teaching on the difference between pardon and justification. God's pardoning a sinner does not mean that the sinner sins no more even on becoming a Christian as he is still in Adam. God's justifying that sinner, however, means He views that sinner as if he had never sinned. These two ways of viewing elect man by God are simultaneous. God will always frown on the sin of those He has justified until their old man is done away with in the renewal that death and resurrection brings. This is why Gill was particular in pointing out that justification had past, present and future aspects, seen from the point of view of time, though it is one in eternity. The fact is, God does not merely love the elect eternally with a view to their being planted in Christ but He loves them in time, during their fallen, unconverted natural state. If eternal love means anything, it must mean for all time and all eternity. If God loves His elect eternally, surely it must be because He sees them as eternally justified and loves them in union with His Son.

Abraham Taylor, argued, as so many scoffers after him, that the doctrine of God's eternal love for the elect, even in their fallen state, encouraged and vouchsafed Antinomianism. It seems that Scriptural passages such as John 3:16 are unknown to such critics, not to mention those glorious words in Romans 5:6 ff.,

> For when we were yet without strength, in due time Christ died for the ungodly. For scarcely for a righteous man will one die: yet peradventure for a good man some would even dare to die. But God commendeth his love toward us, in that, while we were yet sinners, Christ died for us. Much more then, being now justified by his blood, we shall be saved from wrath through him. For if, when we were enemies, we were reconciled to God by the death of his Son, much more, being reconciled, we shall be saved by his life.

Here, of course, all Taylor's and Naylor's problems are solved. Paul is talking about God's weak, ungodly, sinful enemies who are under His wrath. Does He cast them into hell where they belong? No! Believe it or not, He actually loves them, agrees to His Son dying for them, justifies them, saves them from wrath and reconciles them—whilst they are at enmity with Him. Here, not a word is spoken about believers, but the whole context has to do with God's eternal, justifying, saving, reconciling love for His elect, *whilst they are in their natural, fallen state!*

Taking up Taylor's criticisms of the eternal love of God in his two talks on *Of the Insufficiency of Natural Religion*, Gill is careful to turn Taylor's gaze back to revealed religion. He tells him that if he regards

God's eternal love for His elect as a fancy, he must admit that it is a Scriptural fancy. Gill finds it not a fancy, though it is written with sunbeams throughout the whole of the Bible. Gill points out:

1. God's love to his elect is not of yesterday; it does not begin with their love to him, *We love him, because he first loved* us, It was bore in his heart towards them long before they *were delivered from the power of darkness, and translated into the kingdom of his dear Son.* It does not commence in time, but bears date from eternity, and is the ground and foundation of the elect's being called in time out of darkness into marvellous light: *I have loved thee*, says the Lord to the church, *with an everlasting love; therefore with loving-kindness have I drawn thee*, that is in effectual vocation. Many are the instances which might be given in proof of the antiquity of God's love to his elect, and as it is antecedent to their being brought out of a state of nature. God's choosing them in Christ before the foundation of the world, was an act of his love towards them, the fruit and effect of it; for election presupposes love. His making an everlasting covenant with his Son, ordered in all things, and sure, on account of those he chose in him; his setting him up as the Mediator of the covenant from everlasting; his donation of grace to them in him before the world began; his putting their persons into his hands, and so making them his care and charge, are so many demonstrative proofs of his early love to them; for can it ever be imagined that there should be a choice of persons made, a covenant of grace so well formed and stored, a promise of life granted, and a security made, both of persons and grace, and yet no love all this while?

2. The love of God to his elect is unchangeable and unalterable; it is as invariable as his own nature and being; yea, *God is love, and he that dwelleth in love, dwelleth in God, and God in him.* Hence it is that the blessings of his grace are irreversible, because they are gifts of him, who is *the Father of lights, with whom there is no variableness, nor shadow of turning.* Hence also it is that the salvation of God's elect does not stand upon a precarious foundation, as it would, if his love changed as theirs does; but *he is the Lord, who changes not, and*

therefore the sons of Jacob are not consumed. The several changes the elect of God pass under, through the fall of *Adam*, and their own actual transgressions make no change or alteration in the love of God. The love of God makes a change in them when he converts them, but no change or alteration is made in God's love; that does not admit of more or less; it cannot be said to be more ardent and intense at one time, than at another, it is always invariably the Same in his heart. Love produced a wonderful and surprising change in him, who was afterwards the great apostle of the Gentiles, and of a blaspheming, persecuting, and injurious *Saul*, made a believer in Christ, and a preacher of the everlasting gospel: but then this produced no change in God, nor in his love. God sometimes changes the dispensations of his providence to his people, but he never changes his love; he sometimes hides his face from them, and chides them in a fatherly manner; but at all times he loves them: he loves when he rebukes and chastens, and though *he hides his face for a moment* from them *yet with everlasting kindness will he have mercy on them*; for he has said, *The mountains shall depart, and the hills be removed; but my kindness shall not depart from thee, neither shall the covenant of my peace be removed.* There is, indeed, no sensible manifestation of God's love to his elect before conversion, or while they are in a state of nature; and it must be allowed, that the manifestations of it to their souls after conversion, are not always alike; and that God's love appears more evident in some instances and acts of it, than in others; yet still this love as in his own heart, is unchangeably and invariably the same, as it needs must be, if he is God. Since then God's love to his elect is from everlasting, and never changes upon any consideration whatever, why should God's love to his elect, while in a state of nature, be accounted a fancy, and those who maintain it, be represented as amusing themselves with a fancy?

3. There are instances to be given of God's love to his elect, while they are in a state of nature: I have already observed some instances of it to his elect, from eternity. I will just mention one or two instances of it to them in time, and which respect them, while in a state of nature. Christ's coming into this world, and dying in the room and stead of the elect, are, at once, proofs, both

of his own and his Father's love to them; God so loved them, as to give his only begotten Son; and Christ so loved them as to give himself for them, in a way of offering and sacrifice for their sins; at which time they were considered as ungodly, as being yet sinners, as enemies in their minds, by wicked works, and without love to God: for the apostle says, *When we were yet without strength, in due time Christ died for the ungodly. God commendeth his love towards us, in that while we were yet sinners, Christ died for us; for if when we were enemies we were reconciled to God by the death of his Son, much more being reconciled, we shall be saved by his life.* Now certainly these persons were in a state of nature, who are said to be 'without strength', to be ungodly, sinners, 'and enemies'; and yet God commended his love towards them, when and while they were such, in a matchless instance of it: and so the apostle John makes use of this circumstance, respecting the state of God's elect, to magnify, to set off, and illustrate the greatness of God's love: *Herein is love, says he, not that we loved God, but that he loved us, and sent his Son to be the propitiation for our sins.* From whence it may strongly be concluded that God loved his people while in a state of nature, when enemies to him, destitute of all grace, without a principle of love to him, or faith in him. Again, the quickening of God's elect, when dead in trespasses and sins, the drawing of them to Christ with the cords of powerful and efficacious grace in effectual vocation, are instances of his special grace and favour, and fruits and effects of his everlasting love to them, *God who is rich in mercy, for the great love wherewith he loved us, even when we were dead in sins, hath quickened us together with Christ.* The time of the effectual vocation of God's people being come, fixed in his everlasting counsels and covenant, it is a time of open love to their souls, and that time becomes a time of life; for seeing them wallowing in their blood, in all the impurities of their nature, fulfilling the desires of the flesh, and of the mind, *he says unto them, when in their blood, live; yea, when in their blood he says unto them, live.* The Spirit of God, as an instance of God's love, is sent down into their hearts in order to begin, carry on, and finish a work of grace, when he finds them in a state of nature, dead in sin, devoid of all

199

grace, impotent to all that is spiritually good: *We ourselves also,* says the apostle, *were sometimes foolish, disobedient, deceived, serving divers lusts and pleasures, living in malice and envy, hateful and hating one another,* οτε, *when the kindness and love of God our Saviour toward man appeared; not by works of righteousness which we have done, but according to his mercy he saved us, by the washing of regeneration, and renewing of the Holy Ghost, which he shed on us abundantly, through Jesus Christ our Saviour.* If God did not love his elect, while in a state of nature, they must for ever remain in that state, since they are unable to help themselves out of it; and it is only the love, grace and mercy of God, which engage his almighty power to deliver them from thence. There are three gifts and instances of God's love to his people before conversion, which are not to be matched by any instance or instances of love after conversion; the one is the gift of God himself to them in the everlasting covenant; which covenant runs thus: *I will be their God, and they shall be my people*: The other is the gift of his Son, to suffer and die in their room and stead, and so obtain eternal redemption for them: the third is the gift of his Spirit to them, to convince them of sin, of righteousness, and of judgment. And now what greater instance is there of God's love to his people after conversion? If the heavenly glory, with all the entertaining joys of that delightful state, should be fixed upon, I deny it to be a greater instance of God's love, than the gift of himself, his Son, and Spirit; and, indeed, all that God does in time, or will do to all eternity, is only telling his people how much he loved them from everlasting; all is but as it were, a comment upon, and an opening of that ancient act of his; nor has this doctrine any tendency to licentiousness, or to discourage the performance of good works. The consideration of this, that God loved me before I loved him, nay, when I was an enemy to him: that his thoughts were employed about my salvation, when I had no thoughts of him, nor concern for myself, lays me under ten thousand times greater obligations, to fear, serve and glorify him; than such a consideration as this, that he began to love me when I loved him, or because I have loved him, can possibly do. Why then should this doctrine be accounted a mere fancy, which has so good a foundation, both in the word of

God, and in the experience of his people; and the maintainers of it traduced as amusers of themselves with fancies?[187]

Sanctified from the womb

When speaking of the origin of election, Gill always traces it back to the love of God, in fact, one could say that his personal motto was *electio praesupponit dilectionem* as he often quoted this to emphasise that 'election presupposes love'. In his *Of Election* he emphasises in the words of 2 Thessalonians 2:13 that God chose those whom He loved from the beginning for 'salvation through sanctification of the Spirit and belief of the truth'. Here, it is obvious that God's love did not rest in the Thessalonians merely after belief but belonged to them from eternity. Even our sanctification, in the sense of being set apart by God, is obviously eternal, Gill argues in the same work, quoting Jeremiah 1:5, 'Before I formed thee in the belly I knew thee, and before thou camest forth out of the womb, I sanctified thee, and I ordained thee a prophet unto the nations.' Nobody ought to have difficulty with the doctrine of justification from eternity after reading that! Gill points out that all God's characteristics are eternal, including His love. Just as God has loved His Son from eternity, so He has loved His people. This must be seen as the clear teaching of John 17:23, 24.

The first step in election for Gill is a step in love, demonstrated by His putting the elect whom He loves in union with His Son whom He loves. After laying the foundation of the Biblical doctrine of union with Christ from eternity, Gill sums up his essay *Of the Eternal Union of the Elect of God unto Him*, by saying:

> In a word, union to Christ is the first thing, the first blessing of grace flowing from love and effected by it; and hence is the application of all others; of him are ye in Christ Jesus, first loved and united to Christ, and then it follows, who of God is made unto us wisdom and righteousness, sanctification, and redemption, 1 Corinthians 1:30. So Dr Goodwin observes, that 'union with Christ is the first fundamental thing of justification and sanctification and all: Christ first takes us, and then sends his

---

[187] *The Doctrines of God's Everlasting Love*, op. cit. pp. 30-35. Both editions.

Spirit; he apprehends us first; it is not my being regenerate that puts me into a right of all these privileges; but it is Christ takes me, and then gives me his Spirit, faith, holiness, etc. ...'.[188]

The two natures doctrine ignored
Such arguments from Scripture on Gill's part must make it obvious that the quarrel men have with God's love in that they deny He can both love the elect in Christ whilst still in their sin under Adam, is completely without foundation, whether in sense or Scripture. In Grotianism and Cambridge-Platonism, which lies at the roots of modern Fullerism and much Neonomian thinking, there is a fundamental lack of teaching concerning union with Christ through election, an election of love and the practical outworking of the indwelling of Christ in the believer. This is because it neither holds to the doctrine of man being fallen in the first Adam nor the doctrine of man's becoming a new creature in the second Adam, Christ. Man is ever in an in-between state of neither being in Adam nor in Christ. He is not in Adam because his natural abilities are not fallen, nor is he strictly speaking in Christ as Christ's influence is not exercised through indwelling him but by providing an external moral deterrent to frighten him into God's arms. There is thus no two-natures doctrine in Governmentalism whereby the Old Man remains in conflict with the New Man until death frees the believer from the relics of sin which have burdened him all his life and are part of his lot for being in Adam and inheriting a corrupt nature.

Robert Traill, writing in his *The Doctrine of Justification Vindicated from the Charge of Antinomianism*, pointed out that it was the Arminians, Governmentalists and Neonomians who were in fact raising the cry of Antinomianism against orthodox Christians. He also complained that instead of believing in a justification due to Christ's perfect obedience imputed to the elect, 'we are now to be justified by our own evangelical righteousness, made up of faith, repentance and sincere obedience.'[189] This alarming state of affairs describes once again, or, perhaps it is better to say, still describes, the low standards of belief within modern evangelistic circles. We have not learned from

---

[188] BSB edition, Book III, Chap. V, p. 201.
[189] Op. cit. pp. 326, 327. See also pp. 298, 307 and 313, 314.

history. Though Arminians[190] are less vocal nowadays in denouncing their Calvinist brethren as Antinomians, Governmentalists and Neonomians, who have a far lower view of the law than Arminians, they are more enthusiastic than ever in denouncing as Antinomian those who do not follow their own lax law. They are also more vigorous than ever in maintaining that atonement and reconciliation come through repentance and belief shown in sincere obedience. There is a difference, however. Modern Neonomians have kept the old terms of the doctrines of grace such as atonement, reconciliation, satisfaction, propitiation and election but they envisage these as all coming into being on the obedient response of the sinner to the gospel. Much emphasis is hereby made on the work of the Spirit in the believer but the work of Christ on the cross, which alone makes faith possible, is quite neglected. The cross, we are told, displays merely God's provisions which are only effectual when taken via man's agency. This is why these pseudo-evangelicals can speak of salvation being a work entirely of God but also entirely of man. Traill told these Antinomian-hunters that they should clean up their own house before attacking an Antinomianism that hardly existed. Their own lack of sound doctrine, however, was widespread and for all to see. Traill put his finger on the weak spot of those who hid their own lack of orthodoxy behind their Antinomian protests by pointing to their unbiblical doctrine of the two Adams. Because they have a wrong view of being in Adam and being in Christ they have also a wrong view of the relationship of faith to justification and a wrong view of Christ's righteousness imputed to the believer and apprehended by faith which is the basis for justification. Traill goes on to argue:

We seem to misunderstand one another about the two Adams, and especially the latter. See Romans 5:12 to the end. In that excellent scripture a comparison is instituted, which if we did duly understand, and agree in, we should not readily differ in the main things of the gospel. The apostle there tells us, that the first Adam stood in the room of all his natural posterity. He had their

---

[190] This author believes that Arminianism is a perversion of the true gospel but must accept the fact that traditional Arminians have a higher view of the fall, the law and the atonement than many present day writers who claim to be Reformed and combat Arminians for not being 'Reformed' as they understand the word.

stock in his hand. While he stood, they stood in him; when he
fell, they fell with him. By his fall he derived sin and death to all
them that spring from him by natural generation. This is the sad
side. But he tells us in opposition thereto, and in comparing
therewith, that Christ, the second man, is the new head of the
redeemed world. He stands in their room: his obedience is theirs;
and he communicates to his spiritual offspring, the just, contrary
to what the first sinful Adam doth to his natural offspring;
righteousness instead of guilt and sin, life instead of death,
justification instead of condemnation, and eternal life instead of
hell deserved. So that I think the third, fourth, and fifth chapters
of the epistle to the Romans, for the mystery of justification; and
the sixth, seventh and eighth, for the mystery of sanctification,
deserve our deep study. But what say others about Christ being
the second Adam? We find them unwilling to speak of it; and
when they do, it is quite alien from the scope of the apostle in
that chapter. Thus to us they seem to say, 'That God as a rector,
ruler, governor, hath resolved to save men by Jesus Christ: That
the rule of this government is the gospel, as a new law of grace:
That Jesus Christ is set at the head of his rectoral government:
That in that state he sits in glory, ready and able, out of his
purchase and merits, to give justification and eternal life to all
that bring good evidence of their having complied with the terms
and conditions of the law of grace.' Thus they antedate the last
day, and hold forth Christ as a judge, rather than a Saviour.
Luther was wont to warn people of this distinction, frequently in
his comment on the epistle to the Galatians. And no other
headship to Christ do we find some willing to admit, but what
belongs to his kingly office. As for his suretyship, and being the
second Adam, and a public person, some treat it with contempt[191]
... Now though we maintain steadfastly this headship of Jesus
Christ, yet we say not, that there is an actual partaking of his
fulness of grace, till we be in him by faith; tho' this *faith* is also
given us on Christ's behalf, Philippians 1:29 and *we believe
through grace*, Acts 18:27. And we know no grace, but what

---

[191] Omitted is a reference to Sibbes' assistance to Goodwin on this point.

comes from his head, the Saviour of the body. But so much shall serve to point forth the main things of difference and mistakes.

It is not a little provoking, that some are so captious, that no minister can preach in the hearing of some, of the freedom of God's grace; of the imputation of Christ's righteousness; of sole and single believing on him for righteousness and eternal life; of the impossibility of a natural man's doing any good work before he be in Christ; of the impossibility of the mixing of man's righteousness and works, with Christ's righteousness, in the business of justification; and several other points, but he is immediately called, or suspected to be an *Antinomian*. If we say, that faith in Jesus Christ is neither work, nor condition, nor qualification, in justification; but is a mere instrument, receiving (as an empty hand receiveth the freely-given alms) the righteousness of Christ; and that, in its very act, it is a renouncing of all things but the gift of grace; the fire is kindled. So that it is come to that, as Mr Christopher Fowler said, 'That he that will not be *Antichristian*, must be called an *Antinomian*.'[192]

Once the Pauline doctrine of the two natures of man (which is intrinsically connected to the doctrine of the two natures in Christ) is abandoned, it is far easier for Grotianism to find refuge in human rationalism and metaphorical views of salvation. This is why Pauline theology is considered too 'Hyper' by many modern Governmentalists and Fullerites who tend to adhere to the kind of Liberalism made popular by the Tübingen School in seeing several strands of gospel in the New Testament. Baur saw the Pauline and the Petrine strands whereas Fullerites see a Jamesian, Johannine and Petrine teaching with the victory being given James. Pauline teaching is tacitly ignored.[193] It is, however, by the grace of God, that the Pauline epistles, comprising a large section of the New Testament, contain the doctrines of Grace taught also in other parts of Scripture but perhaps nowhere else so succinctly put. If we dismiss one part of Scripture, however, no matter how large or small, there will be a great deficiency left in our doctrines.

---

[192] Op. cit. pp. 299-301.
[193] See Alderson's *No Holiness No Heaven*, pp. 100, 101.

As Traill so clearly shows, if we fail to understand, or ignore, Paul's teaching on justification in chapters three to five of Romans, we shall also fail to understand Paul's teaching in the following chapters on the struggle for sanctification hindered by our Adamic nature. Governmentalists and Neonomians have long preached that the old man is no longer present in the believer but now this doctrine which shuts its eyes to the man of flesh still present in the believer until its transformation in glory has been adopted by so-called and self-styled 'Moderate' and 'Evangelical' Calvinists. The doctrine of the total annihilation of the old man at conversion appeared in the pages of the *Banner of Truth* magazine as early as Issue 92.[194] This gave worried friends the fear that the writing on the wall spelt I-C-H-A-B-O-D and this could be the first step in a down-hill trend from the promising start the Banner of Truth made. In this article by Donald MacLeod entitled *'Paul's Use of the Term "The Old Man"'*, it is argued that the putting away of the old man means that the old man is completely extinct. In what follows, there will be a few references to the basic grammar of the Greek language which readers may skip should their interest wane. The fact is that modern critics of the Reformed faith invariably make their own private translations the basis of their rejection of traditional Reformed doctrines. In my book *John Gill and The Cause of God and Truth,* I pointed out how this is the method those adopt who wish to promote an indiscriminate 'free offer' of Christ on the basis of an indefinite atonement. The grounds for this re-interpreting of Scripture is usually put at the feet of the Authorised Version and its language which is not that of the modern mass media. The linguistic uniqueness of the Authorised Version is acknowledged but who wants a Bible reduced to a language of those who do not know God? Whatever the new version, it is a version with more rather than fewer defects in comparison to the Authorised Version. Nowadays, with the Babel of new versions on the market, each with its own mistakes, it is obvious that human nature is absorbing the sum total of these mistakes and is being trained to believe in the fallibility of the Word of God. When professing Reformed evangelicals such as Donald MacLeod and John Murray then come up with their own private interpretation, who can blame the world for re-interpreting 2 Peter 1:20 to mean 'Knowing this

---

[194] May, 1971, pp. 13-19.

first, that all prophecy of the scripture is of private interpretation'? It is symptomatic of this modern revival of Babelism that those publishing houses who are attacking the orthodox faith are doing so with an increasing bevy of different translations, using the one that suits their position as 'authorised' for the occasion.

Donald MacLeod and the decease of the old man
Criticising James Frazer of Alness who believed with Paul that 'the old man, sin, and lusts thereof do remain in the believer'.[195] MacLeod, with true disdain for Reformed standards, tells us that what has been 'for long dominant in Reformed circles' as an orthodox doctrine has proved to be of 'extremely doubtful' origin. With Wesleyan perfectionist enthusiasm, he argues that the doctrine cannot command acceptance as the old man has been put off once and for all, is dead and therefore non-existent. Everything appertaining to the old man is a thing of the past. MacLeod bases his reasoning on Colossians 3:9 'Lie not one to another, seeing that ye have put off the old man with his deeds.' He gets off to a bad start, however, by arguing that the verb 'to put off', in the original, refers to a finished action in the past with its effects still present. He can thus conclude that putting off the old man is 'not a gradual process but a definite and decisive act.'[196] This once and for all decisive act in which the old man was put away was in the past, and thus the old man is with us no more. Thus, right from the start, Professor MacLeod leaves his credentials on the table. He tells us that we should not base our ideas of the conflict between the two natures on our Christian experience but on Scripture. He then goes on to re-translate Scripture to prove that his new notion is valid.

Actually the word in Greek is not a verbal tense at all but an aorist participle with the root meaning 'to put off' in the sense of 'renounce'. Christians have renounced the old man but this does not mean he has been annihilated, just as they have renounced their own sin, which is still sadly present. Any conscientious Christian will realise that the old man and his deeds make their presence all too obvious! Furthermore, an aorist is a non-tense carrier, usually indicating unlimited time. In this instance, the idea is strengthened by the participle form. Paul is

---

[195] Op. cit. p. 13.
[196] Op. cit. p. 13.

exhorting believers to renounce the old man continually for very obvious reasons. MacLeod, however, feels he is driving his point home by referring to verse 3, 'For ye are dead, and your life is hid with Christ in God'. Here, however, Paul is obviously comparing the lot of the pre-converted man with being in Christ. He is certainly not saying that all believers are no longer alive as humans but literally dead human corpses although he says, 'For ye are dead'. It is equally obvious that Paul is not arguing that the old man in the believer is no more as he goes on to say in verse 5, 'Mortify your members which are upon the earth'. One cannot mortify that which one no longer has; and surely MacLeod does not think this is a reference to the new man![197]

The need to quote full Bible passages in context
It is strange that MacLeod does not quote the full passage referring to putting off the old man and his deeds. This would have helped his exegesis. The passage actually reads, 'But now ye also put off all these: anger, wrath, malice, blasphemy, filthy communication out of your mouth. Lie not one to another, seeing that ye have put off the old man with his deeds'. Paul is making it quite obvious that anger, wrath, malice etc. are deeds of the old man. If MacLeod argues that the old nature no longer exists, then it ought to be obvious that his attributes no longer exist. These attributes are sadly very much alive even in born again Christians and a denial of the old man's presence in this way would show an adherence to a view of Christian sinlessness which is quite foreign to the Bible. Paul is obviously exhorting Christians to keep from the ways of the old man and thus keep from sinning.

John Gill, in his *New Testament Commentary*, says of the exhortation in verse 8:

> 'But now you also put off all these, &c.' Intimating, that now since they were converted and delivered out of the former state in which they were once, and professed not to walk and live in sin, it became them to separate, remove, and put at a distance from them all sins, and every vice, to lay them aside as dead

---

[197] Actually, and surprisingly, he does!

weights upon them, and put them off as filthy garments; for such sins are never to be put on, and cleaved to again as formerly.[198]

MacLeod claims repeatedly that the Bible is wrongly translated
Gill's interpretation takes in all the circumstances of the context and is realistic in its view of converted man. Still content to differ radically from this traditional view, however, MacLeod moves on to Romans 6:6, 'Knowing this, that our old man is crucified with him, that the body of sin might be destroyed, that henceforth we should not serve sin.' In his well-meant efforts to rid us of our sinful old self, MacLeod tells us that the verse is wrongly translated. It should read, 'our old man *was* crucified with him,' and not, as the Authorised Version says, 'our old man *is* crucified with him.' This is enough to frustrate any pupil of the Greek language. MacLeod moves the word for crucify back a tense, insisting that it has an imperfect meaning although it, too, is an aorist as is also the word translated 'destroyed'. In maintaining that aorists are in fact exact imperfect tenses,[199] MacLeod is defeating his own argument. The imperfect tense in Greek does not refer to a finished action in the past but to a continuous action in past time or an action which has often been repeated in the past. If MacLeod would have us continually being crucified with Christ in the past, he would have us continually, or repeatedly, putting on the new man in the past—with no guarantee that we are doing so today. If MacLeod is merely arguing for the English imperfect tense (as opposed to the Greek), this would still contradict his argument. That tense refers to a fixed action in the past with no reference to what is happening today. MacLeod speaks, however, of an action in the past which has present consequences. This would give us a present perfect tense and would give us, 'Your old man has been crucified with Christ' which is not the translation for which MacLeod is arguing in this passage. Actually, he is arguing for translating the aorist here with a different tense to the aorist in Colossians 3:9 which seems very much like a case of keeping one's cake and eating it.

---

[198] Vol. ix, p. 199.
[199] It is accepted that aorists sometimes may be translated by the imperfect tense given the right context and within the correct restrictions.

Usually, in the case of a Greek aorist, one looks to the context to determine the tense. In this case, however, the only other verb 'to serve' is in the *present* infinitive, indicating purpose. This, however, obviously gave the Authorised Version translators their major cue. The whole gist of the sentence is that our present state (not a gone-by state as MacLeod's ideas would presume) should dictate our continuous action. The fact that the aorist translated 'might be destroyed' is in the subjunctive, expressing a thought or wish, strengthens the case. Again, MacLeod says Romans 6:6 refers 'not to a process but to an accomplished fact', which has 'radically altered his relation to sin'. This is coming very near to the Governmental and Fullerite doctrine that conversion means Adamic restoration, i.e. a making good of what was lost in Adam so that Christians are restored Adams. They are like Adam in his innocence. If this were true, Christians would not experience the marks of the fall. If the old man i.e. fallen Adam in them, were truly abolished, the born-again believer would not experience all the moral and physical signs of the fall, including infirmity, old age and death.

John Gill gives a definitive exposition
Again, it will be profitable to turn to John Gill's exegesis of the text in view of modern Neo-Evangelical criticism that he is a Hyper-Calvinist and Antinomian which merely indicates that he is neither a Governmentalist nor a Neonomian. The faithful Particular Baptist pastor says:

> By the old man is meant the corruption of nature; called a man, because natural to men; it lives and dwells in them; it has spread itself over the whole man; it rules and governs in men; and consists of various parts and members, as a man does: it is called 'old', because it is the poison of the old serpent, with which man was infected by him from the beginning; it is derived from the first man that ever was; it is as old as the man is, in whom it is, and is likewise called so, with respect to its duration and continuance; and in opposition to, and contradistinction from, the new man, or principle of grace: it is called 'ours', because continual to us; it is in our nature, it cleaves to us, and abides in us ... Now this is said to be 'crucified with him'; that is, with Christ, when he was crucified: the Jews have a notion that

the evil imagination, or corruption of nature, will not be made to cease, or be abolished out of the world, till the King Messiah comes, and by him it is abolished: this is so crucified by the death, and at the cross of Christ, as that it cannot exert its damning power over believers; and is so crucified by the spirit and grace of Christ in them, as that it cannot reign over them, or exercise its domineering power over them; wherefore they are dead unto it, and that to them, and therefore cannot live in it; which is done, 'that the body of sin might be destroyed': by 'the body of sin' is meant sin itself, which consists, as a body does, of various members; and also the power and strength of it, which the Jews call, 'the power of the evil imagination'; this is crucified with Christ, and nailed to his cross by his sacrifice and satisfaction, that its damning power might be destroyed, abolished, and done away: and it is crucified by the spirit and grace of Christ, that its governing power might be took away, and that itself be subdued, weakened, and laid under restraints, and its members and deeds mortified: 'that henceforth we should not serve sin'; not that it should not be in us, for as yet, neither by virtue of the sacrifice of Christ, nor by the power of his grace, is sin as to its being removed from the people of God: but that we should not serve it, make provision for it, indulge it and obey it, in the lusts thereof.[200]

Separating the old man from his deeds

MacLeod believes he can refute such a traditional Reformed view by nicely distinguishing between the old man and his deeds. He now turns to Ephesians 4:22-24, 'That ye put off concerning the former conversation the old man, which is corrupt according to the deceitful lusts; and be renewed in the spirit of your mind; and that you put on the new man, which after God is created in righteousness and true holiness.' Again, MacLeod is dealing with aorists and again MacLeod calls for a new translation, claiming that, 'there is, to say the least, no compelling reason to translate this passage as a command or exhortation as this

---

[200] Vol. viii, p. 460.

would contradict other passages of Scripture.'[201] What MacLeod is really saying is that the Authorised Version and the Revised Standard Version always contradict *his* translations. They contradict other passages of Scripture after he has retranslated them. This reasoning leads MacLeod to argue that it would be 'hazardous to impose' another meaning on the Greek words as that given by him and concludes, 'It is incorrect, therefore, to speak of the old man as remaining in the believer. The old man *has been put off*, crucified, destroyed.' MacLeod now reveals the besetting mistake in his argumentation. He says that he has shown how the old man is not to be equated with besetting sin. *The old man is gone but his deeds remain.*[202] This is strange exegesis indeed as Paul tells his readers to put off the old man *with* his deeds. The one belongs to the other. If the old man is annihilated, so are his deeds. If his deeds remain, the old man must be there, too, though his power to keep a soul from Christ has been removed. This is made clear in the passage in Colossians 3:8 which MacLeod has so unskilfully circumnavigated with no little damage to his argument. MacLeod, in fact, is now presenting us with a Christian who has rid himself of the old man but the new man in Christ Jesus has kept the old man's sins. This seems to be very much an out of the frying pan into the fire experience for the poor sinner. MacLeod seems to be conscious of this quite novel position, but argues, quite illogically, that if we disagree with him, we make room for Antinomianism! This is the old cry of our new would-be reformers. One might argue on firmer evidence, that MacLeod is the Antinomian as he thinks he has rid himself of the old sinful culprit! This method is very much part of Fullerite utilitarianism. One method, no matter how bad, may be used if it avoids a worse.[203] He is, of course, making things too simplistic. He removes Authorised Version and Revised Standard Version opposition by saying they translate hazardously and he thrusts aside those who cannot accept his novel theology by calling them lawless. We need better arguments

---

[201] Op. cit. p. 15.
[202] My emphasis.
[203] Cf. Oliver's A 'Highly Biased' Biography, *B.O.T.*, issue 376, pp. 9-27 where he confesses that he is not 'happy'(!) with Fuller's heretical doctrine of imputation but is willing to accept it as it prevents one believing in 'imputed holiness', which he feels would be a worse heresy. As Oliver does not explain what he means by 'imputed holiness', it is very difficult to grasp his point.

before giving up Biblical doctrines that are so true to experience and, we might add, in spite of MacLeod's private theory, so true to the Scriptures.

What ever happened to the Christian's sin?
Once MacLeod has rid himself of the doctrine of the old man, he turns to his new man who has, strangely enough, all the characteristics of the old man. But suddenly his tone changes. There is no more talk of sin's presence in the believer in his life of holiness and sanctification. This new man, MacLeod argues, correctly enough, has been transformed by Christ, is hidden with Christ in God and lives a life of elevation, purity and power. It is the life of God in the soul of man, 'It is the river of His irresistible grace coursing in sovereign and efficacious majesty through the Christian heart and making glad the city of God.' He then goes on to talk almost lyrically and most beautifully about union in Christ which means Christ indwelling the believer. In other words, MacLeod, after telling us that the new man has taken over the sins of the old man, now portrays this new man, quite contrarily, as a man who must be fully sanctified as his soul contains the life of God and his life is also Christ's dwelling place, full of irresistible grace in its efficacious majesty. This is truly an excellent description of the new man. But where is here the sinful self in this spotless saint?

Truly sinful and truly sanctified though there are no two natures
The reader now wonders how MacLeod will go on to explain how man can be both truly sinful and truly sanctified at the same time in spite of not having two natures, not being in Adam and in Christ at the same time until death rids us of this mortal body. This explanation is never given as MacLeod now quite forgets his topic! He forgets the sin that he has placed in the new man. He argues that the first theological implication of Paul's teaching is that the Christian lives a life of '*definitive sanctification*'[204]. This entails being justified, having our condemnation lifted, being separated from the dominion of sin and being consecrated in Jehovah. MacLeod continues, 'The consecration implicit in effectual calling constitutes a radical and irreversible breach

---

[204] Issue 92, p. 18, MacLeod's emphasis.

with sin; and it is from this base of *definitive sanctification* that we advance to work out our own salvation with fear and trembling'.[205]

This may be all very well, but still the presence of sin in the saint is not explained. We have grown wary by now and are not a little suspicious of MacLeod's doctrine of sanctification. The latter half-quote seems to indicate that all MacLeod is saying is that God has done His bit, so we must now do ours. The important key to the text is the part left out, 'For it is God which worketh in you both to will and to do of his good pleasure, (Philippians 2:13). Here we see that God is sovereign in the life of the new man whom he activates savingly but we still do not see what role sin could possibly play here. Is MacLeod actually saying that the conditions of salvation are conversion first and sincere obedience ever afterwards in keeping with Neonomian terms? It seems so.

MacLeod does not answer the questions raised by his theory
MacLeod, however, sees no need for an explanation. He ends his article by arguing that Paul taught not only *definite sanctification* but also a life of *efficacious* or *irresistible sanctification*. God not only calls the saints but he also justifies and glorifies them. MacLeod touches on one of the most beautiful truths here in the Bible but in spite of his finishing his article on this note of triumph, we cannot so very well join in his jubilation as he has left us in the lurch. He has told us that the old nature has gone but the old sin remains in the new man but he develops the doctrine of the new man by ignoring the sin that he believes so obviously still besets him. At least he must admit that the two natures teaching of traditional Christianity has the advantage of explaining the presence of the old and new man, the old Adam and new Adam, the sinful flesh and the sinless spirit in the saved sinner, 'which after God is created in righteousness and true holiness'. MacLeod must also see that if he rejects one doctrine and does not replace it with another, or at least shows how his new doctrine meets the old problems better, he owes his readers an explanation before they can begin to take him seriously. We agree with MacLeod concerning the glories of the risen Christ in the believer but we Christians want to know how to deal with the sin that wars in our mortal body. This is where the practical,

---

[205] Op. cit., p. 18. my emphasis here.

experimental religion of the Bible triumphs over dry, philosophical, speculative argumentation. Knowing one's sinful self rather than pretending it is not there is the first step in practical holiness.

If we follow MacLeod's re-interpretation, we do not have the Old Adam versus the New, the sinful self in conflict with the risen Lord indwelling us and representing us as spotless before God. Instead we have the Governmentalist idea of an Adam restored, of a new Old Man placed back in Adam before he broke his probation. Christ however, does not make probationers of us but new creatures. God is so holy that He cannot accept a patched up old man, He accepts us in the Beloved as sinless because Christ has carried our sins and guilt away. We hear so often that the so-called Antinomians have no active, practical sense of holiness, believing that even holiness is merely 'imputed', in their empty sense of the word 'imputed'. MacLeod's view of sanctification, however is completely and utterly *theoretical*, though it comes from the anti-Antinomian camp. God, according to MacLeod, has pronounced His people justified and now they must work out their own salvation. It is all *de jure* and not *de facto*. There is no actuality or practicability about it, which MacLeod labours to emphasise by showing that in ridding himself of the old man, the new man has kept his sins, which, apparently, can be ignored.

Released from prison but still behind bars!

Now MacLeod does express a belief in the indwelling Christ but where does he place Him in the believer? He places Him in the man of sin. He puts Him in the place where sin is still practised. This is a quite revolutionary idea as traditionally Christians have, with Paul, placed the deeds of the old man with the old man and have believed that Christ reigns supreme in the new man who is a completely new creature. Thus this new eternal man, sanctified by Christ and indwelt by the Spirit can say, 'I live, yet not I, but Christ liveth in me.' Yet MacLeod places Christ in an actively sinning new man who is supposed to be a new creation (2 Corinthians 5:17), a member of the body of Christ (Ephesians 2:13-22), recreated in the image of God (Colossians 3:10). This is a most unorthodox thought, if not a blasphemous one. In thrusting out the old man, MacLeod has been of no use to anyone as the problems involved in his new theory must force those who accept it to take a completely *de jure*, *pro-forma* view of Christ's indwelling the sinner as the *de facto*, practical outworking of Christ makes Him a co-worker with our sinful self, our body of death—an impossible thought for a Christian and quite contradictory to God's Word. At best MacLeod can only interpret 'Christ lives in me' as, 'Christ has shown me the way, I will try to walk in it'. The Banner criticises orthodoxy for viewing sanctification passively. Happier the saint who is 'passively' taken over by our sovereign God and used to live a life of witness and great benefit to others as Paul, Hervey, Romaine, Gill, Huntington and Whitefield, than the poor soul who merely believes that he is *de jure* released from prison but it is up to him to saw through the bars!

A more valid approach

The Word of God, however, shows that MacLeod's attempt to reconstruct the facts cannot possibly be valid. The whole of Romans chapters seven and eight portrays the great difference in justified man between the two natures and the enormous every day struggle, chastening and suffering that goes on in the life of a Christian. There is what Paul here calls his flesh (7:18) or the body of death (7:24) in which no good thing dwells and there is his inner man (7:22) which loves to do good. The body of death, alias the flesh, alias the natural body, alias the bondage of corruption (8:21) is condemned and the believer is longing for the time when it will be put off for ever when he receives the spiritual resurrection body (1 Corinthians 15:44). Until that time, man has two natures, the spirit of death and the spirit of life in him (Romans 8:9-11). Until then, the Christian is to await patiently for the redemption of the body (8:23). All this throws no shadow on the new birth itself. MacLeod, by changing his imperatives, aorists, infinitives, subjunctives and participles into his own pet, personal grammar, is denying the actuality of the old man and the struggles of the new man with him. He equates the supposed disappearance of the old man, with the once-and-for-all-time new birth of the elect. Renouncing the old man, however, is plainly the believer's call until the resurrection morning. The new birth, however, is described in the very tense that MacLeod will have for the renouncing of the old man—the perfect. This emphasis on the definite act of regeneration with its permanent consequences is a speciality of John as witnessed by John 3:6, 8; 1 John 2:29; 3:9; 4:7; 5:1, 4, 18. Comparing Scripture with Scripture is the best

216

way to find out God's truth rather than striving to confound Scripture with private interpretations of Scripture.

MacLeod has paid little attention to the distinction between being in the flesh and being in the Spirit. Robert Hawker, that great preacher of righteousness, explains this factor which is necessary to the teaching of the two natures and the two Adams:

And do thou dearest Lord, say—Is not the new birth at regeneration wholly spiritual? Yea, did not Jesus himself teach as much, when in that gracious scripture of his, the Lord said, 'that which is born of the flesh is flesh: and that which is born of the Spirit is spirit,' John 3:6. Are not thy people to apprehend by this plain and familiar illustration, that when, by the quickening influence of God the Holy Ghost at the new birth, the Spirit is brought forth into a new and spiritual life; the body remains unrenewed, and, as much as before, the object and subject of sin and death? And doth not God the Holy Ghost most plainly testify the same, when telling the church—'If Christ be in you, the body is dead, because of sin; but the Spirit is life, because of righteousness,' Romans 8:10. Can a body, dead because of sin, perform one act of spiritual life; much less while unrenewed, be going on in a state of progressive sanctification? A child of God may, and through grace will, sometimes restrain the swellings of sin from breaking out into deeds of actual transgression; for so the Holy Ghost saith,—'If ye, through the Spirit, do mortify the deeds of the body, ye shall live,' Romans 8:13. But if the body, as it is said, 'be dead because of sin', how is it possible to do a single act of righteousness?

Anticipating his own bodily subdual and renewal on the resurrection morn, Hawker says:

Yes, yes! thou precious Lord Jesus! when thou shalt take home my spirit, to join the assembly of 'the spirits of just men made perfect' before thy throne, then will 'my flesh rest in hope', until that joyful morning when 'this corruptible shall put on incorruption; and this mortal shall put on immortality.' And then, that which is sown in weakness, will be raised in power; and that which is sown a natural body, will be raised a spiritual body. Yes! for my God, my Saviour Jesus himself, shall descend from heaven with a shout, with the voice of the archangel, and with the trump of God. And then will my Lord 'change my vile body, that it may be fashioned like unto his glorious body, according to the working whereby he is able to subdue all things unto himself.'[206]

Death in Adam and life in Christ

Similarly, MacLeod has neglected to bring his teaching concerning the old and new man in line with the Biblical teaching concerning the Old and New Adams. All men are seminally in Adam as his natural descendants and all men die in Adam. Believers who are therefore in Christ, as Gill so clearly teaches, are also in Adam until their deaths. Though Christ is both man and God, He is not man in the sense that He is a partaker of Adam's fall, and so Adam is not Christ's head and representative as he is man's. Adam failed his probation and those who are in Adam—all mankind—are partakers of his failure. The Second Adam kept Adam's probation in order to redeem us and His triumphs are imputed to all those for whom He suffered, died and lived a life of full obedience to God's law. Christ, as the New Adam, has virtually created a new kind of man who is not of old Adam's line. Christ takes up His abode in this new spiritual man whom He has made righteous and justified. This new man does not sin and He is not part and parcel of our sinful body of flesh. This has very much to do with the doctrine of justification through Christ's actual imputed righteousness and Christ's active obedience. The Socinians, followed by many Neo-Evangelicals, deny that Christ's righteous, obedience to the whole law can be actually imputed to us as they falsely argue that Christ, being in Adam, was Himself subject to the law and any obedience to the law was for His own sake and therefore could not be for ours. Christ, however, had no necessity to become a man and to place Himself under the law for His own sake. He is the Lord of the law and His divine character needs no justifying. The only reason Christ put Himself under the Law was as the representative of His people so that as man's sin was imputed to Christ, so Christ's fulfilment of the law could be put to our reckoning.

---

[206] Tract XV, *On the Subject of Sanctification*, Church Bookshop reprint, pp. 16, 19.

As in Adam all die, so in Christ shall all be made alive. Alive, that is, *de jure* and *de facto*. Fuller's half-way salvation does not satisfy the Bible believer because this practical outworking of Christ in the new man does not come into consideration. He sees Christ's death as pardon and forgiveness only. But pardon and forgiveness do not transform men. Salvation is not merely non-imputation of sin. Christ would never have gained our salvation if He had merely taken on Himself our punishment. It is Christ's blood *and* righteousness which saves. It is this that justifies God's justifying us. Christ's obedience to the law in every respect was just as essential as His sacrificial death. In this way Christ could not only remove our past guilt, He could also remove our inability to carry on living a guiltless life by placing us under His own life of full obedience and righteousness. Our old man arises from Adam in us and thus we have become partakers of his nature. Our new man arises from what Christ is in us and He makes us partakers of His Divine nature. The old Adamic nature, however, will perish in the dust with our sin and shame when Christ, who has already clothed us in righteousness, clothes us in our new spiritual body. Only then will our old man, whom we have already renounced, be exterminated.

Chapter Eight

Spanning Eternity

The subject of eternity and its characteristics was briefly touched upon in Chapter One where we found Witsius rather astonished at his British brethren's conception of eternity and time and the acts of God within these spheres. Indeed, Gill's own understanding of eternity can be traced to Dutch sources as it is also obvious that Gill's theology was at times, more in tune with international Puritan thought than it was with the rather insular-minded British theology of the day which, too, was being influenced by the Dutch, but those of another calibre. British ideas concerning the Biblical doctrine of eternity and the infinity of God, were coming under the strong influence of rationalism, bringing with it new conceptions of God's actions in time and ruling out all that was not empirically verifiable in time through man's reason. The rationalists (including the Deists and Latitudinarians) did not rule out the acts of God in revelation but claimed that they were acceptable in as far as reason made them such. This seriously affected the time-thinking of man in terms of the Christian faith. Christianity was as old as creation, they taught, meaning that true religion was in the reason of man and thus can only exist in that reason.

The fear of a God from outside of the human mind
Hugo de Groot (1583-1645, otherwise called Grotius) was of special influence here with his speculation concerning Natural Law and its

objective place in the mind of man. So great was the fear of allowing anything 'from outside' to meddle with the thoughts of man, many Christians' concepts of God were determined by the thought of a God who had created a world which he had then left alone to be ruled by the dictates of man's reason. These pseudo-Christian rationalists had little time for revealed religion and the idea of absolute decrees and acts of God. They looked on atonement in the sense of propitiation and penal substitution as the last vestiges of the old superstitions of the Jews. The Jews, they argued, relied on mysterious laws for their morals but the Church lived in the enlightened times of direct insight into what they called 'the nature and fitness of things'. In the seventeenth and eighteenth centuries, though there was a great movement of the Spirit leading eventually to a true Awakening, the churches remained suspicious of anything to do with a God beyond time and the sacrifice of His Son which mysteriously was said to pacify God's wrath and reconcile people to God. Since those days, it appears that the problem of eternity has been quite taken out of the hands of British Christian conception and has been placed in the hands of Continental philosophers such as Spinoza, Kant, Bergson and Hegel. Whether the above brief survey can be accepted or not, the truth is that very many of our leading evangelical and reformed preachers and theologians today reject outright any doctrine based on an immutable act of God, and plead for the sole existence of transient acts. This, though the Bible sounds out from almost every book the infinity, eternity, immutability and immanency of God in all that He does.

Gill and his infinite God
In his *Of the Infinity of God, his Omnipresence and Eternity*, Gill begins by arguing from Isaiah 43:10 and 44:6 that there was no God before our God, nor will there ever be a God after Him as He is the First and the Last. All creatures have their being in Him, yet He has His being only in His eternal self. This self is immutable as He is the same yesterday, today and forever and He never changes. As He is immutable, He was never in non-being and will never become non-being. Gill discovers also, that these eternal, immutable aspects belong also to Christ and the Holy Spirit who are one with the Father. Our God is infinite in all His characteristics, whether it be in His infinite understanding (Isaiah 40:28), wisdom and knowledge (Romans 11:33; 1 Samuel 2:3), power

(Romans 1:20; Hebrews 1:3), goodness (Psalm 16:2), purity, holiness, justice and love (Job 4:17, 18; Isaiah 6:2, 3; Ephesians 3:17-19), so that His ways for us are past finding out because of His infinite perfections.

According to Scripture, even the heaven of heavens cannot contain God who is omnipresent in space and time, upholding all that is in existence (Acts 17:27, 28). There is no being that does not owe its existence to God whether in time or eternity. For God, there is no spatial or temporal distinction. God is plainly and simply everywhere. His governing knowledge spans entire eternity but He also governs time from the beginning to the end, seeing all and everything at once.

Eternity is where God is

Gill points out that an old Jewish word for God is מקום, which means 'place' because nothing has a place but what He gives and nothing takes place outside of His control.[207] Thus the Psalmist can say:

> Whither shall I go from thy spirit? or whither shall I flee from thy presence? If I ascend up into heaven, thou art there: if I make my bed in hell, behold, thou art there. If I take the wings of the morning, and dwell in the utmost parts of the sea; Even there shall thy hand lead me, and thy right hand shall hold me. If I say, Surely the darkness shall cover me; even the night shall be light unto me. Yea, the darkness hideth not from thee but the night shineth as the day: the darkness and the light are both alike to thee.[208]

Here, we have a vivid portrayal of all the aspects of time, space and eternity in which it is not possible to flee from the love or wrath of God. In quoting this passage and also Isaiah 66:1, 'Thus saith the Lord, the heaven is my throne, and the earth is my footstool', Gill shows us that the God of the Bible is not the Deists' and rationalists' God who has left man to get on with the job He started. God interacts in all that there is. Just as light and darkness are no hindrance to Him, neither is being in time and eternity at once. He is the God who is at hand and the God who is afar off (Jeremiah 23:23, 24).

---

[207] Joseph Albo in *Sepher Ikkarim*.
[208] Psalm 139:7-13.

God is thus not only immutable and omnipresent, with especial respect to time from a human point of view, but He is eternal from His own nature's point of view. He is the everlasting God and King eternal. (Deuteronomy 33:27; Isaiah 40:28; Jeremiah 10:10; Romans 16:28; 1 Timothy 1:17). Indeed, the Scriptures say that God is eternity and inhabits eternity (Isaiah 57:15). Thus the Psalmist can also say, 'Before the mountains were brought forth, or ever thou hadst formed the earth and the world, from everlasting to everlasting, thou art God' (Psalm 90:2). This leads Gill on to argue that it can be proved from Scripture that God is eternal because of His very nature and being, because of His attributes, because of His purposes, because of the covenant of grace which is an everlasting covenant and because of God's works in time.

Looking through dark glass

We all see through a glass darkly and the tragedy of Christendom is that the number of 'theologies' held by Christians is even greater than the number of denominations and sects. Scripturally speaking, however, Gill's arguments for justification from eternity are backed with a good deal of sound evidence that cannot easily be rejected. Whatever one might think of Gill's views, it cannot be said that they are argued badly and it most certainly cannot be said that they are doctrines which promote Antinomianism. Nor can they be called Hyper-Calvinist because Gill clearly departed from Calvin where he thought he was too forensic and less theological. Gill's view of Scripture teaching is that the grace which saves us is eternal to us, as is also our election in Christ. Those who are in Christ have everlasting life by that virtue alone and it is also plain Scriptural teaching that when God loves, He loves with an everlasting love and therefore draws His own to Him (Jeremiah 31:3). Now there can be no eternal saving grace, no eternal election in Christ, no experience of God's eternal love where a soul is not justified. These aspects belong together as integral parts.

The clarity with which Gill saw things

It is made quite clear in Gill's theology when and where God's plan of salvation began. Article III of the *Goat Yard Confession of Faith* declares:

We believe, That before the world began God did elect[209] a certain number of men unto everlasting salvation; whom he did predestinate to the adoption of children by Jesus Christ of his own free grace, and according to the good pleasure of his will; and that in pursuance of this gracious design, he did contrive and make a covenant of grace and peace with his son Jesus Christ, on the behalf of those persons; wherein a Saviour was appointed, and all spiritual blessings provided for them; as also their persons, with all their grace and glory, were put into the hands of Christ, and made his care and charge.[210]

When Gill tackled the subject of eternity in his *Body of Divinity*, he argued that the purposes, counsels and decrees of God was one of the five methods of deducing that God is eternal along with the arguments from God's nature and being, from His attributes, from His covenant of grace and from all the works of God in time. Whatever the blessings are that man finds in Christ, they stem from God's decisions in eternity. Concerning God's eternity as reflected by His eternal decrees, Gill argues:

That God is Eternal, may be argued from his purposes, counsels, and decrees; which are said to be *of old*, that is, from everlasting, Isaiah 25:1, this is true of them in general; for no new purposes and resolutions rise up, or are framed by him in his mind; for then there would be something in him which was not before; which would imply mutability. Besides, they are expressly said to be *eternal*, Ephesians 3:11, and if they are eternal, then God, in whom they are, and by whom they are formed, must be eternal also. In particular, the purpose of God, according to election, or his choice of men to everlasting life, is eternal; not only was before men had done any good or evil, Romans 9:11, but they were chosen by him *from the beginning*, 2 Thessalonians 2:13, not from the beginning of the gospel

---

[209] Ephesians 1:4; 1 Thessalonians 1:4; 5:9; 2 Thessalonians 2:13; Romans 8:30; Ephesians 1:5; 1 John 3:1; Galatians 4:4, 5; John 1:12.
[210] See *Sermons and Tracts*, vol. iii, p. 559 and also my *John Gill and The Cause of God and Truth*, pp. 75, 76.

coming to them, nor of their faith and conversion by it; but from the beginning of time, and before time, even *before the foundation of the world*, as is in so many words expressed, Ephesians 1:4, wherefore God, that chose them to salvation, must be eternal. Christ is eminently called the elect of God, being as Man and Mediator, chosen out from among the people, Isaiah 42:1; Psalm 89:19, and the appointment of him, to be the Redeemer and Saviour of men, or the preordination of him to be the Lamb slain for the redemption of his people, was before the foundation of the world, 1 Peter 1:20, and therefore God, that foreordained him there unto, must be as early.[211]

The two factors of time
There are two factors to time. The physical and the spiritual. The physical is that the earth turns on its axis and day and night occur. We have God's promise in Genesis 9:22, *While the earth remaineth, seedtime and harvest, and cold and heat, and day and night shall not cease.* Time, physically speaking in the purpose of God, is a continual renewal and restitution until the elect are gathered in. What God has created, can go on unchanging until He tells it to stop because He has eternal powers and can stretch a day into a thousand years or reduce a thousand years to a day at will. He can even remove time altogether as He has promised to do. It can be demonstrated in the life of Adam. Had he not sinned, he would have lived for ever, never growing old. He was born in eternity or aeviternity, as Gill describes human immortality and would have remained there. This, at least, is Gill's argument in such essays as *Of the Creation of Man*[212] where he is at his most lyrical describing Adam's Edenic state:

Man was made last of all the creatures, being the chief and master-piece of the whole creation on earth, whom God had principally and first in view in making the world, and all things in it; according to that known rule that which is first in attention, is last in execution; God proceeding in his works as artificers in

---

[211] Vol. i, Book I, Chap. VI, p. 95.
[212] See especially, p. 274.

theirs from a less perfect, to a more perfect work, till they come to what they have chiefly in view, a finished piece of work, in which they employ all their skill; and which, coming after the rest, appears to greater advantage. Man is a compendium of the creation, and therefore is sometimes called a microcosm, a little world, the world in miniature; something of the vegetable, animal and rational world meet in him; spiritual and corporal substance, or spirit and matter are joined together in him; yea, heaven and earth centre in him, he is the bond that connects them both together; all creatures were made for his sake, to possess, enjoy, and have the dominion over, and therefore he was made last of all: and herein appear the wisdom and goodness of God to him, that all accommodations were ready provided for him when made; the earth for his inhabitation, all creatures for his use; the fruits of the earth for his profit and pleasure; light, heat, and air for his delight, comfort, and refreshment; with every thing that could be wished for and desired to make his life happy.[213]

Gill goes on to argue that Man is made up of body and soul; the first being formed out of the dust of creation and the second being breathed into him. Thus Man was given the capacity to carry this dual nature into eternity as Adam's body was endued with immortality by its very nature. This does not mean that it was immortal of itself, independent of its Creator. It means that had Adam remained true to his Creator, His creator would have supported him and his offspring in body and soul without let or hindrance for ever in the state he was when first created.[214] Adam's eventual physical death did not arise from a necessity of nature but as the consequences of sin which broke the threads of holiness which had bound Adam to God's eternal will. Incidentally, Gill, a professed Sublapsarian, argues against the Supralapsarian view that God gave Adam a body that was prone to fall, explaining that this would have made the Incarnation impossible:[215]

---

[213] *Body of Divinity*, Of the Creation of Man, Book III, Chap. III, pp. 268, 269.
[214] *Of the Creation of Man*, Book III, Chap. III, p. 271.
[215] See op. cit. p. 271.

... for as that is defiled, since the fall with the corruption of nature; so before, it was pure and holy; as when sanctified by the Spirit of God, it became a temple, in which he dwells; and particularly at the resurrection, when it is raised a powerful, incorruptible, spiritual and glorious body, saints will then awake in the likeness of God, and appear to bear the image of the heavenly One, as in soul so in body; and whereas another branch of this image lies in dominion over the creatures, that is chiefly exercised by the organs of the body. To say no more, I see no difficulty in admitting it: that whereas all the members of Christ's human body were written and delineated in the book of God's eternal purposes and decrees, before they were fashioned, or were in actual being; and God prepared a body for him in covenant, agreeable thereunto; or it was concluded in it, he should assume such a body in the fulness of time, Psalms 139:16; Hebrews 10:5. I say, I see no difficulty in admitting that the body of Adam was formed according to the idea of the body of Christ in the divine mind; and which may be the reason, at least in part, of that expression; Behold, the man is, or rather was, as one of us; and so as Eve was flesh of Adam's flesh, and bone of his bone, the members of Christ are also flesh of his flesh, and bone of his bone, Genesis 3:22; Genesis 2:23; Ephesians 5:30.[216]

Thus, although Gill argued that sinners whom God passed by were ordained to condemnation, he did not believe that Adam was ordained to fall but could have remained standing. God, however, told Adam that the day he was disobedient, he would die—and Adam was disobedient, following his wife who followed Satan, and Adam had to die. It was then that the clock of this world started to tick in a new way, now indicating a new aspect to time as that which brings decay and death to sinful man. Time became the indicator to tell man of his doom. Time began to take its toll. That which ages man and ages the whole groaning creation, is the sin of man. Time as we know it, time proper, came for us sinners, came into the world with our sin. There was no time in this sense before sin as all was ageless. When sin entered the world, we find the Bible telling us that ageing and decay—the products of time—came

---

[216] Op. cit. p. 275.

into the world. The whole creation was marred and if God's restraining hand had not been there, the flood would have brought on the wages of sin which is death to the whole world but God used His restraining Hand because of a higher plan for a people in Christ. Nevertheless, Gill tells us in *Of the Creation of Man*, 'The soul is a created substance with a subsistence of itself. It is thus not merely an accident or quality of man. Man was created as a spiritual being in the image of God who is Spirit. As man's soul was breathed directly from the Spirit, it is a spirit, though a created one. Though, after the fall, the body of sin returns to dust, his soul returns to God to be treated as God wills.'

Gill emphasises that Adam's former will to believe was not natural or even personal to him in any way. He did not believe because he willed to believe, he believed because he had acquired belief from God. Though he was able to reject God's gift, he was by no means able to will it back as there was nothing in him to associate with God's gift. When a man bores out his own God-given eyes, no amount of willing will make him see! But man's pathetic, tragic, fallen fate is far worse. Even the will itself has gone.

Man received a life span and that was counted in time from birth to death. Thus time is obviously a different factor to eternity and is a factor into which we cannot possibly force God's ways as God is not a product of time and not affected in time. God never ages. Time as a recorder of decay is the product of sin. Many theologians speak and write of Christ being made sin for us as if this all started on the Cross in Christ's substitutionary death. Gill argues that Christ's becoming sin for us is an act of God's immanent will in conceiving and putting into practice the incarnation to save His people from their sins and their fallen time-bound nature. Christ took upon himself our sin-marred flesh and subjected Himself to the growth and ageing process of sin's natural development in time. Adam was burdened with no infirmities, yet he sinned. Christ was burdened with all our infirmities but he proved obedient for our sakes, fulfilling the law and our penalty for breaking it for us. He thus showed himself greater than Adam and wrought out for us a greater righteousness than Adam possessed as a probationer.

This shows that seeing eternal things, such as God's attributes and actions in respect of time is merely our spiritual and physical incapacity to see them otherwise. It is our fallen way of fitting all things into the logic of our fallen mind. We have difficulty in grasping the fact that

God's actions in view of our redemption are outside of the ageing before-and-after process. God always acts immediately and directly from eternity. The fact that we cannot grasp this makes it difficult for us to conceive of justification from eternity as we bind God into our fallen understanding of time. We tend to regard eternity, indeed, as time. Twisse, in his *Vindiciis Gratiae* saw eternity as past time. Modern writers such as Curt Daniel in his *Biblical Calvinism* apply time concepts to eternity and view God's decrees as being thought out in 'eternity past'.[217] which is isolated by thousands of years from a presumably 'eternity present'. Thus Daniel can argue that God 'did not make them (His elect) saved'[218] when He decreed them to be saved. Apparently this wrong view of eternity and the immediacy of God's actions in eternity lead him also to separate the scope and extent of the atonement from the people who benefit by it, arguing merely that 'by His death on the Cross, He removed all legal barriers in case any man believes.'[219] This is why Daniel can also view the atonement as not being an exact satisfaction for the sins of God's elect but a 'super-abundant' source of salvation which each and every man jack could partake of 'in case' they believed. In this sense, the atonement was not a once-and-for-all-time division of the wall of partition between the elect and their salvation but an act merely thought out by the Father in the distant past, set into motion by the Son, and completed by the Spirit at faith's birth. Only then is the atonement valid and activated as a saving act. Whatever this is, it is not Biblical Calvinism which teaches an atonement for and limited to the elect. This is, of course, in its saving sense. As Daniel also rightly teaches, the life, testimony and death of Christ has also a wider significance for the world until Christ returns. It is interesting to note that when Fuller gave up his belief in justification from eternity, which he says he once held, he gave up his orthodox belief in the atonement. Two days before writing these words, an interesting encounter via the Internet occurred. A very irate Dutchman wrote me a most critical e-mail letter, warning me that I was throwing away my Christian witness because of attacking Fuller whom he felt was orthodox in all respects. Or, at least, so he had been told. I wrote

---

[217] *Biblical Calvinism*, p. 5.
[218] Op. cit. p. 6.
[219] Op. cit. p. 6.

back immediately quoting Fuller on the main doctrines of the Bible, informing the young man where to read on. The student of theology replied the following day in much milder tones. He felt, he said, that if what I said about Fuller's rejection of justification from eternity were true, he could not call himself a Fullerite as that doctrine was so precious to one who believes in the doctrines of grace. They go together. This is exactly what Gill taught.

Though fallen in time, we may gain insight into God's eternal mind
God, however, has provided us with insight into His eternal mind. The Scriptures have not been polluted by sin and are not temporals. The Scriptures' reveal to us the eternal mind of God. This has been challenged by Grotians, Latitudinarians, Neo-Platonists, Chandlerism, the New Divinity School and Fullerism since the Reformation but the only way in which they can take up their case is to deny the validity of the Scriptures' testimony and thus put themselves outside of Bible-believing Christianity. Either we have a Bible and believe it, or we reject the Bible and believe anything else but the Bible. The latter way may seem reasonable to some but when that same reason convinces them that they are still Christians and 'Strict Calvinists' at that, we can only say that these people have departed from what the Scriptures have taught them. They have departed also from plain common sense. Our message to them is, 'But ye have not so learned Christ. If so be that ye have heard him, and have been taught by him, as the truth is in Jesus: That ye put off concerning the former conversation the old man, which is corrupt according to the deceitful lusts; and be renewed in the spirit of your mind.'

As man is the fallen victim of time, it is no wonder that he misunderstands eternity. It appears that this is one of the most difficult doctrines of the Bible to understand and numerous and various are its interpretations. We thus find Gill's critics holding to a completely different view of eternity and a different view of the outworking of eternity in time according to the Scriptures. Understanding Gill's opponents' view of eternity is like attempting to comprehend the incomprehensible or systematise chaos. They appear, however, to make three basic mistakes in formulating their philosophy of time, the first being with reference to the decrees of God.

Viewing eternity as time past
Firstly, they view eternity as a stage in past time. They cannot think outside of time categories, even though the Bible tells them that God dwells in eternity. Some of them, indeed, even translate eternity as meaning 'ages'. This was Twisse's difficulty as Witsius saw when he moderated between the British Antinomians and Arminians. What happened before the world was formed, happened for them so many days, months, years or ages previous to that event. As sinners were not around at that time to have anything happen to them—nothing did! This, rather naive concept of eternity is evident even in the writings of learned theologians such as Turretin and Berkhof, which has made its acceptance in certain circles all the more sure. Both these theologians believe that God's decrees were first worked out in some pre-historical time and eventually, after aeons had gone by, turned into acts. Berkhof, as shown in the first chapter, distinguishes between the thought in God's mind to justify the elect and the actual deed of justification. All God's decrees are seen as being followed by a delayed action. It is true that Gill uses such prepositions as 'before' and 'at the beginning' to describe when God's decrees were enacted but he did not expect anyone to view this via the movement of a clock's hands. Speaking of this problem in *Of the Eternity of God*, he says:

> The Eternity of God, or his being from everlasting to everlasting, is without succession, or any distinctions of time succeeding one another, as moments, minutes, hours, days, months, and years: the reasons are, because he existed before such were in being; *Before the day was, I am he*, Isaiah 43:13, before there was a day, before the first day of the creation, before there were any days, consisting of so many hours, and these of so many minutes; and if his eternity past, may it be so called, was without successive duration, or without succeeding moments, and other distinctions of time, why not his duration through time, and to all eternity, in the same manner? Should it be said, that days and years are ascribed to God; it is true, they are; but it is in accommodation and condescension to our weak minds, which are not capable of conceiving of duration but as successive: and besides, those days and years ascribed to God are expressly said not to be as ours, Job 10:5. He is, indeed, called, *The Ancient of*

Days, Daniel 7:13, not ancient *in* days, or *through* them, as aged persons are said to be in years, and well stricken in them; not so God: the meaning is, that he is more ancient than days; he was before all days, and his duration is not to be measured by them. And it may be observed, that the differences and distinctions of time are together ascribed to God, and not as succeeding one another; *he is the same yesterday, to day, and for ever*; these are all at once, and together with him; he is he which is, and was, and is to come, Hebrews 13:8; Revelation 1:4, these meet together in his name, Jehovah;[220] and so in his nature; he co-exists, with all the points of time, in time; but is unmoved and unaffected with any, as a rock in the rolling waves of the sea, or a tower in a torrent of gliding water; or as the gnomon or stile of a sundial, which has all the hours of the day surrounding it, and the sun, by it casts a shade upon them, points at and distinguishes them, but the stile stands firm and unmoved, and not affected thereby: *hence it is that one day is with the Lord as a thousand years; and a thousand years as one day*, 2 Peter 3:8. But if his duration was successive, or proceeded by succeeding moments, days, and years; one day would be but one day with him, and not a thousand; and a thousand days would answer to a thousand days, and not be as one only. Besides, if his duration was measured by a succession of moments, &c. then he would not be immense, immutable, and perfect, as he is: not immense, or unmeasurable, if to be measured by minutes, hours, days, months, and years; whereas, as he is not to be measured by space, so not by time: nor immutable; since he would be one minute what he was not before, even older, which cannot be said of God; for as a Jewish writer[221] well observes, it cannot be said of him, that he is older now than he was in the days of David, or when the world was created; for he is always, both before the world was made, and after it will cease to be; times make no change in him. Nor

---

[220] It was thought that the word Jehovah was built up of three tenses of the verb to be, past, present and future. The matter is complicated as this is one of the special Hebrew words which is to be read other than written and examining this problem would result in too wide a digression.

[221] Joseph Albo in *Sepher Ikkarim.*

perfect; for if his duration was successive, there would be every moment something past and gone, lost and irrecoverable; and something to come not yet arrived to and obtained; and in other respects he must be imperfect: the *knowledge* of God proves him without successive duration. God knows all things, past, present, and to come, that is, which are so to us; not that they are so to him; these he knows at once, and all together, not one thing after another, as they successively come into being; all things are open and manifest to him at once and together, not only what are past and present, but he calls things that are not yet, as though they were; he sees and knows all in one view, in his all-comprehending mind: and as his knowledge is not successive, so not his duration. Moreover, in successive duration, there is an order of former and latter; there must be a beginning from whence every flux of time, every distinction proceeds; every moment and minute has a beginning, from whence it is reckoned, so every hour, day, month, and year: but as it is said of Christ, with respect to his divine nature, so it is true of God, essentially considered, that he has *neither beginning of days, nor end of life*, Hebrews 7:3. In short, God is Eternity itself, and inhabits eternity; so he did before time, and without succession; so he does throughout time; and so he will to all eternity.[222]

It cannot then be illogical to conclude that just as God is not a day older today than He was in King David's day, because neither God nor His attributes, nor His will change, neither is His decree to act in justification to be separated from its happening in time. God is immutable and does all things in eternity, however they might appear to us to be grounded in time. When God says 'Let him be justified' in eternity, He applies it in time seeing the whole process of time as a single unit before His eyes and addressing Himself to it. Perhaps, though only perhaps, one might compare God's view of time from the aspect of eternity as our viewing a metre rule. The ruler is marked from zero to one hundred but we are not compelled to always survey the ruler by progressing all the notches from start to finish. We can see the whole device at once and all its measurements from beginning to end.

---

[222] Ibid., pp. 97, 98. BSB edition, Book I, Chap. VII, pp. 48, 49.

Viewing time as a continuation of eternity

Another view held by Gill's critics sees time variously as a continuation of or part of eternity. It is as if eternity starts somewhere, then time takes over. Eternity is thus a process antecedent to time and time is, as it were, the heir of eternity, carrying it along until this dispensation ends. These critics are thus able, or rather, they think themselves able, to understand all the Bible's expressions concerning eternity in terms of the time which they are now experiencing. Election, atonement, sanctification, reconciliation and justification are all worked out in time at the act of believing through the active reception of the believer. Thus we find modern Calvinists professing to believe in the Five Points but these Five Points have nothing to do with 'the mind of God' for particular individuals outside of time but are an expression of 'whosoever will may believe'. God is doing nothing more in salvation than making the offer, the result of which will determine His mind. He has His Lamb's Book of Life in His hand and, though He is technically in eternity, He is writing down the names of the 'whosoevers' with a view to saving them. One Dutch professing Calvinist, and successful evangelist is at present shocking his colleagues in the ministry by urging his hearers to 'get their names written in the Book!' So many of his hearers take up the offer that he is convinced he has hit upon the correct method of evangelism. Privately, this is a 'Five Point' man!

Repentance, faith, atonement, election, reconciliation and justification are viewed as being worked out by the believer's grasping out and taking them from a general feast spread before all by the Father. Thus repentance, atonement, election, reconciliation and justification, though provided by God in a way that is never explained to us, they come into being during the 'now' of reception. Such receivers are, in fact, creating eternity out of their actions in time by entering into and partaking of a change of life which will go on for ever. In this way, the historical work of Christ in the atonement is quite superfluous, as is also the question of God's decrees. Indeed, many Fullerites, following their master, see the atonement as one big figure of speech, to be interpreted by those who understand 'the nature and fitness of things' who can thus separate 'spirit' from 'letter' and get behind the picture of the atonement to find the realities which it disguises. Though they deny that justification is in, what they call 'the mind of God', they, nevertheless, feel that the atoning truth is in 'the nature and fitness of things' and thus in the mind of the sinner disposed to holiness. Thus the whole idea of our reconciliation with God being worked out in eternity as an act of Christ being slain before the foundation of the world, which impinged on time at the sacrificial termination of His earthly life is now looked on by many as a myth to be demythologised or a metaphor to be demetaphorised. These anti-atonement enthusiasts are the first to proclaim that they are the only ones who truly understand the atonement. Whether they understand what they profess or not is perhaps open to question but, as far as a Biblical, experimental faith is concerned, one cannot have an atonement which does not hide the sinner's sins with the righteousness of Christ imputed to them, which is their justification; nor can one have an atonement which does not reconcile the sinner to God. The covering, reconciling, justifying work of Christ in the atonement, is however, for many modern evangelicals, Reformed or otherwise, an antiquated view.

There are various theories in vogue as to how the atonement is circumnavigated in order that reconciliation might be accomplished. These vary from a go-it-alone work of the Holy Spirit to the natural results of the natural abilities and good works of good men, but they all fall terribly short of the Scriptural norm. We are used to Fullerites telling us that the only actual reconciliation which ever happens is when the believer turns to God in love and, metaphorically speaking, puts his hand in God's hand in the act of believing. We know that Fuller sees the work of the Holy Spirit as an encouragement to keep the law, the end of which is salvation through duty faith.[223] Surprising, however, is

---

[223] It is accepted that modern Fullerites deny that their master ever taught such nonsense. In the past, all, with perhaps one exception, who have approached me on the subject—and many have done so—had never read Fuller himself on that subject. Most professing Fullerites have not the foggiest idea what Fuller taught. Indeed, it is only because of the present widespread criticism of Fuller that dyed-in-the-wool Fullerites are now happily turning to the works of their master. The same can be said of Huntington's and Gill's critics. I have corresponded with three magazine editors who fiercely oppose these men but at the date of their published opposition, the first was only very vaguely familiar with their works; the second was completely ignorant, and the third made a pretence at knowledge which contradicted the known facts but for which he refused to disclose his sources. Again, these men are now happily turning to Huntington's and Gill's works. It is to be hoped that this will improve and objectify criticism of Huntington and Gill in future issues of these magazines. I have given detailed evidence for my above assertion

that more recent writers who have made a name for themselves as the heirs of the Reformation and the Puritans are following in this wake. Arthur Pink's book *The Satisfaction of Christ,* first written in 1930-31 as a number of magazine articles has now been reprinted in book form and, as shown above, completely denies that reconciliation is a work of Christ in the atonement. Correspondence with the new publishers, known for being rather 'high' in their Calvinism, has revealed that they back Pink up on this teaching, arguing that reconciliation is the Spirit's work in time.

Eternity as the continuation of time

Other critics tend to see eternity manifesting itself at the end of time as the continuation of time in the form of time without end. Thus, for them, all the saving eternals of the Bible have no eternity before creation and the signal for time to start but go on for time everlasting after this world ceases to function. Thus all that is wrought out, supplied, applied, activated and received concerning the gospel in time, has from then on, perpetual consequences. This view, too, holds that, for the Christian, this means that eternity starts the moment he believes.

Not everything is to be rejected concerning these views. In one way, when thinking of our entering into faith, the third view above, for instance, approaches very near to the truth. He who believes on Christ is changed from a being who remains within the corruptibility of sin and time and after death, eternally under the wrath of God, to becoming an everlasting creature of abundant life, entering into Christ's resurrection and continuing for ever in that state. This is, however, only part of the truth. Gill explains:

> Some creatures and things are said to be everlasting, and even eternal, which have a beginning, though they have no end: and this is what the schools call aeviternity, as distinct from eternity: thus angels, and the souls of men, being creatures of God, have a beginning; though, being immaterial and immortal, shall never die. The happiness of the saints is called eternal glory, 'an eternal weight of glory; eternal life; an eternal inheritance; an house

---

concerning Fuller's view of the gospel in my book *Law and Gospel in the Theology of Andrew Fuller* and my various articles on Fuller. See bibliography.

eternal in the heavens', 1 Peter 5:10; Titus 1:2; 2 Corinthians 4:17; 5:1; Hebrews 9:15. And the misery of the wicked is signified by suffering the vengeance of eternal fire, by everlasting fire, and everlasting punishment, Jude 7; Matthew 25:41, 46, yet these have a beginning, though they will have no end; and so are improperly called eternal.[224]

This is, however, not the whole story for Gill who is careful to point out that though one can think of the birth and death of man as an entrance into eternity, in another sense, the elect are eternal. He argues this in *The Doctrine of God's Everlasting Love to His Elect*, which was written against Abraham Taylor's breaking away from his father's orthodoxy and denying the doctrine as being Antinomian. Against Taylor's view of a change in God motivated by a change in man, Gill argues that in Christ, though not eternal as a created being, the elect have a legal, federal, natural and representative union with the eternal Son which covers time and eternity. He therefore argues:

There is an eternal legal union with Christ

There is a legal union between Christ and the elect from everlasting: they are one in a law-sense, as surety and debtor are one; the bond of this union is Christ's suretyship, which is from everlasting, and in which Christ engaged, as a proof of his strong love and affections to his people. He is the surety of the better Testament, the εγγυος, that drew near to God the Father in the name of the elect, substituted himself in their place and stead, and laid himself under obligation to pay their debts, satisfy for their sins, and procure for them all the blessings of grace and glory. This being accepted of by God, Christ and the elect were looked upon, in the eye of the law, as one person, even as the bondsman and the debtor, among men, are one, in a legal sense; so that if one pays the debt, it is the same as if the other did it. This legal union arising from Christ's suretyship engagements, is the foundation of the imputation of our sins to Christ, and of his satisfaction for them, and also of the imputation of Christ's

---

[224] Vol. i, *Of the Eternity of God*, pp. 92, 93. Also BSB edition, Book I, Chap. VI, pp. 45.

righteousness to us, and of our justification by it. Christ and his people being one, in a law sense, their sins become his, and his righteousness becomes theirs.

There is an eternal federal union with Christ

There is a federal union between Christ and the elect from everlasting. As they were considered as one, he as head, and they as members, in election; they are likewise considered after the same manner in the covenant of grace. Christ has a very great concern in the covenant; he is given for a covenant to the people; he is the Mediator, Surety, and Messenger of it. It is made with him, not as a single person, but as a common head, representing all the elect, who are given to him, in a federal way, as his seed and posterity. What he promised in the covenant, he promised for them, and on their account; and what he received, he received for them, and on their account. Hence grace is said to be given to them in him before the world began;[225] and they are said to be blessed with *all spiritual blessings in heavenly places in Christ*.[226]

There is a natural union with Christ fulfilled in time

There is a natural union between Christ and his people; for *both he that sanctifieth, and they who are sanctified, are all of one*; that is, of one nature; *for which cause he is not ashamed to call them brethren*.[227] This is an union in time, but is the effect of Christ's love before time; *Forasmuch then as the children are partakers of flesh and blood, he also himself likewise took part of the same*.[228] The nature he assumed is the same with that of all mankind, but was taken to him with a peculiar regard to the elect, the children, the spiritual seed of *Abraham*, who are *members of his body, of his flesh, and of his bones*. Now this natural union, which is the fruit of Christ's everlasting love, is antecedent to the faith of New Testament saints.

---

[225] 2 Timothy 1:9.
[226] Ephesians 1:3.
[227] Hebrews 2:11.
[228] Hebrews 2:14.

There is a representative union with Christ, eternal and temporal

It is sufficiently evident, that there is a representative union between Christ and the elect, both from everlasting and in time, which is independent of, and prior to their believing in him. He represented them as their head in election, and in the covenant of grace, as has been already observed; and so he did, when upon the cross, and in the grave, when he rose from the dead, *entered into heaven, and sat down at the right hand of God*. Hence they are said to be crucified with him, dead with him, buried with him, risen with him, yea, to be made *to sit together in heavenly places in Christ Jesus*.

This union eternal and temporal stems from the eternal love of God for His people

Now all these several unions take their rise from, and have their foundation in, the everlasting love of Christ to his people; which is the grand original, strong and firm bond of union between him and them, and is the spring of all that fellowship and communion they have with him in time, and shall have to all eternity. It is from hence that the Spirit of God is sent down into our hearts to regenerate and renew us, and faith is wrought in our souls by the Spirit. Faith does not give us a being in Christ, or unite us to him; it is the fruit, effect, and evidence of our being in Christ and union to him.

Viewing time from the correct perspective

The concept under which such time-bound views as Turretin's are formed, logical as they may appear, do not work on the Biblical principle that as far as God in eternity is concerned, the beginning and end of all time-activities are ever present before His sovereign mind. Indeed, such logic as Turretin's is highly questionable. Philosophically speaking, God is outside of time, viewing time's limitations from the outside though He is able according to His ubiquitous nature to interact in time as He is in space, which is a platform where time and eternity meet. Indeed, if one wishes to demonstrate the relationship between time and eternity in a philosophical way which comes nearest Scripture, it may help to see eternity in terms of the attributes of space rather than the variants of time. Space, as far as we know, is endless, and, according to our conceptions, eternal. Eternity is God's basic attribute. When one looks into the sky, there are no conceivable boundaries where the sky stops. It goes on for ever. Yet our understanding of endless space does not annul our knowledge of the temporal limits of the time dispensation into which we are born and in which we shall die should the Lord not come beforehand. Whatever happens in time, be it 1066, 1939 or 2000, we may logically deduce, it happens in the same space.[229] The Bible clearly teaches, through the many passages Gill gives to show God at work in eternity, that whatever happens in time, God is in control of it from eternity. Thus, in eternity, there is no yesterday, today and tomorrow, but when Christ enters our lives in time as the great Always-the-Same, He is telling us that we are children of eternity in conceptions which enable us to see that there is no beginning and no end to God's love for His Son and those who are chosen in Him. The Bible message that we are one with the One who calls Himself the Alpha and the Omega is God's way in time of showing us that we are one with Christ in eternity.

Time can only inherit from eternity
Those critics of Gill who see time as a continuation of the first stage in eternity are, in reality, making eternity a product of time or back-projecting time onto eternity thus rejecting fully Scriptural concepts which spread eternity before our mortal eyes and show eternity as being there when time is not. It is impossible for time to produce anything savingly of itself as time, in the physical sense, along with the revolving world which marks that time, is a creation of Christ's whereas His love for His Bride and His unity with her is His act in eternity. Thus time can produce nothing to save a soul apart from that which it inherits, to use a Biblical term, from eternity. All that entails our eternal salvation is reserved in heaven for us, whose true citizens we are. Needless to say, heaven is not a product of time. This is vouchsafed by Scripture in those

---

[229] Still keeping to our philosophic effort to comprehend these incomprehensible things. Of course, space is a creation of God but it still gives us some idea of the eternity in which God dwells.

time-exploding words of Peter's first chapter, informing us of our election secured through the work of the Father, Son and Holy Ghost. We notice that election is secured, not on believing but 'through the foreknowledge of God, demonstrated by the sanctification of the Spirit unto obedience and sprinkling of the blood of Jesus Christ.' Now, though others may interpret this verse figuratively and say that the sprinkling is post-atonement work connected with the independent work of the Holy Spirit at the time of reconciliation via belief, the whole context here refers to what Christ did when the eternal mind of God manifested itself in time to secure our salvation by the God-Man who fulfilled all that is necessary for our justification at the atonement. That justification is also included here is obvious by the mention of our sanctification and Christ's obedience. It is Christ's righteous obedience, imputed to us which is the grounds for our justification. That this justification is for eternal creatures, justified from eternity is plain from the fact that we are elected in eternity to an eternal, incorruptible and undefiled inheritance in heaven. Only those found clothed in the righteousness of Christ and declared justified could feel at home in such a home.

The world as God's pulpit for declaring eternal salvation
The idea that time is the starting place for eternity and the salvation which we have gained in this life provides us with a key to sail away into new endless dimensions, is a romantic idea that would have done honour to Darwin and modern science-fiction authors. God never designed earth as a launching ramp for the conquest of the universe but as the place where His strength could be made perfect in our weakness and His abundant grace overcome our unbounded sin. The Bible clearly teaches that our salvation is neither a product of this life nor of the times we live in but a product of the will of God that was there when time was not and will be there when time is no more. There is nothing, just nothing, that has happened to us which was not wrought out in eternity, secured for us in that single element of time named 'the fulness' which displayed the whole purpose of time, past, present and future, so that in that blessed moment when Christ was nailed to His pulpit-cross that He might announce to His Church, 'It is finished', their eternal salvation was declared and vouchsafed to all witnesses, whether human, angelic or demonic.

The logic of eternity impinging on time

Nevertheless, time is still a crucial element in the salvation of God's people and there is a clear logic in the fact that eternity impinged on time two thousand years ago. The Incarnation had its eternal purpose linking time with eternity through that act so that Christ could prove His love to the elect by becoming one with them not only in their eternal designation of heaven-dwellers but in their misery and sin as earth-inhabitants. As the God-Man, He not only fulfilled for us the law that we were unable to keep, but He took upon Himself the punishment that we were unable to bear and live on because the wages of sin is death. He did this for us, because we were His very own. In this way, Christ demonstrated in time what God had ordained in eternity, namely, that His elect, though human and born in time, are children of God and joint heirs with Christ of His eternal glory.

Chapter Nine

Removing The Last Objections

Before closing this book on Gill's well-argued doctrine of justification from eternity, there are still a few matters to be cleared up. Though the main prejudices and counter-arguments have been dealt with, a number of factors, mostly of the hypothetical kind, remain which seem to frighten Reformed and evangelical Christians from turning to Gill for solid gospel teaching. These must now be closely scrutinised to reveal how incredibly weak they are.

The doctrine leads to licentiousness

This is still the main prejudice, as it can hardly be called an argument, of present day critics against the doctrine of the eternal love of God for His elect and the accompanying doctrine of justification from eternity, both held by Gill. These are old hats that one would think Gill has adequately rebutted and shown to be completely erroneous but as few of Gill's critics read Gill, they are ignorant of the fact that their criticism has no basis. Both accusations were taken up by Gill in his Great Eastcheap lecture on *The Doctrine of Grace Cleared from the Charge of Licentiousness* given on December 28, 1737, so were refuted comparatively early in his preaching career. It is quite incredible to what unscriptural, illogical and even licentious length those who reject Gill's doctrine, dating from his contemporary Abraham Taylor to modern traducers, are prepared to go in denouncing God's eternal love for His people. Surely the very fact that God has His eye on His own would be something of a guarantee that He will keep them from falling? This is Gill's honest opinion, backed by Scripture as he argues concerning:

The doctrine of God's everlasting and unchangeable love to his elect, in every state and condition and circumstance of life into which they come. This is no ways contrary to the purity and holiness of the divine nature; for though he loves the persons of his people, and in them as considered in Christ, he takes no delight in their sins; sin is the abominable thing he hates; he is of purer eyes than to behold it with approbation and delight; *he is not a God that hath pleasure in wickedness, nor shall evil dwell with him*: nor does he encourage them in sin; or connive at it, but rebukes and chastises them for it in a fatherly way; though at the same time he does not take away his loving-kindness from them; for he takes pleasure in their persons, though he bears a displicency to their sins; nor does this doctrine in the least lead men to sin, but on the contrary, most strongly engages to the love of God, and a cheerful obedience to him: his love to them indeed does not arise from their love to him, it being prior to theirs; *but then they love him because he first loved them*, and this love in them to him, constrains them to a willing obedience; when their hearts are *enlarged* with it, then do they *run* with alacrity *the ways of his commandments*; when this loving-kindness of God in choosing them in Christ, redeeming them by his blood, and calling them by his grace is before their eyes, and they have a sense of it upon their hearts, they *walk in his truth*; in the truth of his gospel, and have their conversations as become it. This love, according as it is shed abroad in their hearts, *casts out fear*, and influences them to *serve* the Lord *without fear, in righteousness and holiness all the days of their lives*. What can lay a man under a greater obligation to love the Lord, fear and obey him, than this consideration, that he loved him when he had no love in his heart to him, nay was an enemy to him; and that his thoughts were concerned about his everlasting salvation, when he had no thoughts of God, nor any for himself? Such a consideration as this, must work much more powerfully upon him, as it must upon any ingenuous mind, than such a one as this; that the Lord began to love him and continued to do so, because he loved him and was obedient to him; and would continue to do so as long, and no longer. That is the purest obedience that is influenced by love; it is the obedience of a child, and not of a slave; and must be the most acceptable unto God; nay, there is no other service that is acceptable to him, but what springs from love influenced by his own.[230]

What makes this argument against Gill so thread-bare is that the very people who are denying God's eternal saving love to the elect are openly propagating God's universal saving love to *all* sinners. One would think that a universal love cannot be a temporary love, nor can it be a changing love and must also embrace all sorts and conditions of men whatever their relationship to God. If this is the case, and this is argued by Gill's critics, it is difficult to understand why such critics are prepared to believe that God loves all the unconverted savingly with the exception of His yet unconverted elect!

God's timing upsets contenders for man's agency in justification
It is, of course, the dating of justification which really annoys those who are quick to call others licentious. They wish to see man's agency in salvation emphasised and believe unbiblically and illogically that where man is not allowed to grasp out and take justification on his own morally sound initiative, justification will be given to a man still in his sins and therefore still practising them as if nothing had happened to change him. Change must therefore, they argue, come before justification. Gill saw through this false logic early in his ministry and put it down to a false view of man's righteousness and a false view of Christ's righteousness imputed to the believer. Gill therefore connects objections to the doctrine of justification from eternity closely with objections against the Reformed doctrine of justification by the imputed righteousness of Christ. This is still the case today where modern traducers of Gill have been quick to deny the Biblical doctrine of imputed righteousness, retaining the term *pro-forma* but rejecting its basic meaning of crossing out our debts and balancing our books. The

---

[230] *Sermons and Tracts*, vol. i, pp. 344, 345.

argument seems to be that if we are justified by the righteousness of another, then we have no need to practice a righteous life ourselves. This displays a purely legal sense of imputed righteousness, quite contrary to Gill's view. Indeed, it is interesting to note that one of the older claims against so-called Antinomians was that they merely believed in a legal 'as if' status in imputation[231] which in no way changed the life of the one to whom Christ's righteousness was figuratively imputed. What has happened today, however, is that those who cry 'Antinomian' the loudest, are arguing the old Hyper-Calvinist case that justification is merely forensic and has no actual outworking in the life of the believer. They argue that the believer is merely formally justified but must earn actual justification by keeping the law. Gill, of course, taught that those who were justified were fitted out to do righteous acts by the Lord who had taken possession of their lives. This is the difference between having a law written on tablets of stone and having one written on the heart. Gill goes a long way to clearing up this problem by writing:

> The doctrine of justification by the imputed righteousness of Christ, is a doctrine according to godliness, however it may be traduced as a licentious one; It neither makes void the law: nor discourages the performance of good works; nor encourages in sin; it does not annul, or make the law useless: *Do we*, says the apostle, *make void the law through faith*, that is, by the doctrine of justification through the righteousness of Christ, received by faith? *God forbid: yea, we establish the law*; since we assert that men are justified by a perfect righteousness, which is every way agreeable to the demands of the law, and by which that is magnified and made honourable.
> Nor does it at all discountenance the discharge of duty, but is the greatest motive and inducement to it. Thus the apostle, having observed that we are not saved by works of righteousness done

---

[231] Toon, in his *The Emergence of Hyper-Calvinism*, p. 61, seems to be implying that this is solely the view of High-Calvinists though he argues that the High-Calvinist position is similar to the Antinomian position but the former were able to explain their position 'more carefully'! Writers such as Naylor and Hoad do not distinguish between Hyper-Calvinists and High-Calvinists.

by us, that we are justified by the grace of Christ, and are made heirs according to the hope of eternal life, adds, *This is a faithful saying*; and *these* things, that is, these doctrines, *I will that thou affirm constantly*; that thou assert them without any doubt or hesitation about them; and that thou dwell upon them in thy ministry, and frequently inculcate them; *that*, ινα, to this end and purpose, *they which have believed in God, might be careful to maintain good works*. Nothing like these doctrines will induce them thereunto.

Nor does this doctrine give any countenance to sinful practices; for though God justifies the ungodly, yet he does not indulge them in ungodliness. Christ's righteousness justifies from all sin, but does not justify persons in a continuance in sin. Besides, faith, which *receives this blessing from the Lord, and righteousness from the God of salvation*, which is the reason why men are said to be justified by it, *works by love*; is an operative grace, is attended with the fruits of righteousness, is evinced by good works, made perfect by them, and is without them dead.

Yet some will say, the doctrine of justification by faith is no licentious doctrine, but the doctrines of eternal justification and eternal union are. This comes from another quarter, from a set of men who should know better. What diabolical charm? What satanic influence can there possibly be in a *date*? If justification by the imputed righteousness of Christ alone, without the works of the creature, has no bad influence upon the life and conversation; the moving of the date of it higher than where it has been commonly put, can never be attended with any bad consequence that way; nor can any consequences arise from it, but what must also unavoidably follow upon eternal election: And as for eternal union with Christ, it is the foundation of all the good things Christ has done for his people, of all the good things the Spirit works in them, and of all the good works which arc done by them; and therefore can never give birth and countenance to evil practices.[232]

---

[232] *Sermons and Tracts*, vol. i. pp. 350, 351.

One need not read a great deal of Gill before finding a quote from Thomas Goodwin in whose writings it is no exaggeration to say Gill was steeped. This fine Puritan writer combined sound theology with a style that is lyrical and elevating as he clearly showed how all God's mercies are eternal to Him and an essential part of His infinite nature. Though Goodwin has also been criticised as a Hyper-Calvinist in recent years, we must be thankful to the Banner of Truth for republishing Goodwin's works in 1985. In his volume entitled *Of the Object and Acts of Justifying Faith,* Goodwin defines justification in complete harmony with Gill, stressing both the forensic and experimental natures of the act of God. Arguing that all God's acts of mercy are both *external*, that is, declarations of His will to his people, and also *internal* in that God provides the graces to live according to the status given. Goodwin therefore continues:

It is thus also in justification. It is but calling us from what we are not, yea, from the contrary, to be righteous in his righteousness, by the power and dominion of him that is Jehovah, the fountain of being, who says to an ungodly person, 'Thou art righteous', and in saying it makes him such: Romans 5:19, 'By the obedience of one many shall be made (or constituted) righteous.' This is a matter of the greatest reality, and hath the firmest being in it, and yet is but an act external upon us; the soul in itself hath no being as to this righteousness, for God justifies it as ungodly; it hath no such being, but God gives it, and gives it by an act that is external to us, answering to that forensical act of pronouncing a man innocent at the bar.

The second sort of beings or blessings of grace are such as do impress something upon us, and their beings consist wholly in such an impression. As when God comes to a soul that is nothing but sin, and gives it a new heart, and a new spirit, and it becomes a workmanship created to good works, this he does by working this new creature in it, by internal changing our corrupt hearts, as one day he will do our vile bodies. These, and all such effects, are but the fruits of Jehovah merciful.[233]

---

[233] Vol. viii, Book I, Chap. VI, p. 36.

Justification from eternity allegedly denies human responsibility
Not only do modern critics of Gill join hands to 'prove' that his
doctrines automatically bring in licentiousness but they also, in the face
of overwhelming evidence to the contrary, argue that Gill does not
believe in human responsibility at all, whether from the point of view
of the sinner or the saint. This is indeed a strange development in
modern theological thinking as Gill's contemporaries on all sides were
unanimous in their decision that Gill did believe in human
accountability and responsibility. Those who agreed with his doctrines
obviously believed so, but those who did not, such as Andrew Fuller,
felt that Gill's belief in human responsibility was plain for all to see but,
he thought, it contradicted his other doctrines. This gives us a clue as to
why modern critics accuse Gill of rejecting human responsibility. They
feel it is a logical conclusion from their belief that Gill is an Antinomian
through and through. They will not even accept that Gill contradicted
himself! Thus one false belief is piled up on another. Once a dog has a
bad name ... .

Interesting, too, in this modern development is the fact that opposite
ends in the Calvinist party are meeting over their criticism of Gill
regarding human responsibility. Thus we read both in the writings of
'low' Calvinist Iain Murray and 'high' Calvinist Prof. David Engelsma
the very same criticism. Actually, this criticism coming from two
extreme corners can only lead readers to believe that Gill must stand in
a balanced position in the middle, which, of course, he does.

The *Banner of Truth* Magazine for November, 1995 published an
article from the pen of Iain Murray under the title 'John Gill and
Spurgeon' which was eventually extended to a small book entitled
Spurgeon v. Hyper-Calvinism: The Battle for Gospel Preaching. In this
article, Mr Murray strove to show how Gill refused to accept human
responsibility in matters of accepting or rejecting the gospel. Instead of
attempting to prove his case from Gill's works and the Scriptures,
Murray introduces Spurgeon, Gill's successor to show how he felt that
Gill was guilty of Hyper-Calvinism. Murray's speculative remarks are
the very epitome of what is known as 'special pleading'. In an effort to
prove that Spurgeon believed Gill did not accept human responsibility,
Murray quotes words from *The Sword and the Trowel*, without giving

the year, issue and page, stating that certain Baptists with a tendency to Antinomianism, 'ate out the life of the churches' because 'Divine sovereignty was maintained and taught, not only in exaggerated proportions, but to the practical exclusion of moral responsibility: the obligation of sinners to "repent and believe the gospel" was ignored, and even denied, and all gospel invitations and pleadings were restricted to those who were supposed to give evidence of a gracious state.'[234]

Now, although this statement names no names, Murray makes it obvious to whom he thinks it applies and argues this by making three statements. He says firstly that it was not written by Spurgeon; secondly that 'it is clear that it represents his (Spurgeon's) general views', and thirdly that Spurgeon would have linked these views with Gill. Now this is a most daring piece of argument. As Spurgeon did not write what Murray quotes, and Murray nowhere shows that Spurgeon linked those views with Gill, and Spurgeon nowhere claims that Gill rejected human responsibility, we read on, trusting that Murray will get down to some basic evidence for his seemingly wild presuppositions. Murray goes on to quote Spurgeon without giving the source, taking words from a criticism of those who misused and misapplied Gill and assumes that Spurgeon would have included Gill though Spurgeon is obviously stating quite the opposite. Feeling that he has perhaps left the question open, Murray goes on to argue that Spurgeon was 'over-generous' in his view of Gill. In other words, Murray is misusing the good name of Spurgeon to back up his own far-fetched criticism of Gill's supposed low view of human responsibility, in order to give Gill a bad name. Furthermore, he scolds Spurgeon for not denouncing Gill as Murray feels he ought. We are used to this kind of thing in the scandal-mongering of the tabloid press but to see it in a respectable Christian magazine is a surprise indeed, if not to say a shock. The truth is that Murray has not the shade of a shadow of evidence that Spurgeon taught that his predecessor rejected human responsibility, so we wonder why Mr Murray is making such a threadbare effort to prove this. Furthermore, even if Spurgeon thought Gill were a Hyper of Hypers, this would not indicate evidence against Gill unless Scripture proof were provided.

---

[234] *Banner of Truth*, Issue 386, p. 17.

Quoting piecemeal from Gill's work *The Cause of God and Truth* which is a treatise against the anti-Calvinistic teaching of Arminian-Arian Dr Daniel Whitby (1638-1726) and a rejection of the universal atonement theory, Mr Murray, picks out the words 'coming to him, or believing in him to the saving of their souls' and 'without the special grace of God', which convey little meaning as they stand, and, without giving us the sources or context of his bits and bats, fits them into an argument of his own making to 'prove' that Gill did not believe in human responsibility. The whole reconstruction is presented as Gill's express argument, even though moderate Rippon argues at length from this very book to prove beyond any shadow of a doubt that Gill emphasised human responsibility.[235] But Mr Murray claims that Rippon has been too 'peace loving' and 'moderate' in defending Gill. Mr Murray's method is reminiscent of the mock-scientific work of the palaeontologists who discover part of a tooth and reconstruct a skeleton from it, claiming that it is the real thing and calling other people 'unscientific' who object.

Judging by the fractions of quotes Mr Murray gives, he appears, though it is difficult to check such meagre 'evidence', to be referring to Gill's exposition of John 5:40 where Christ says, 'And ye will not come to me, that ye might have life.' This is a decisive text in separating false Calvinists of the Fullerite school from the genuine Reformed Faith as Gill argued that the words must be taken literally, whereas Fuller argued that its doctrine, as that of sin, the atonement, imputed righteousness, satisfaction and substitution were to be understood figuratively according to what he termed 'the nature and fitness of things'.[236] Andrew Fuller, however, on viewing this text, admitted that Gill clearly taught human responsibility in expounding it![237]

When Gill takes up this text in Part I, Section XXX of *The Cause of God and Truth*, he is arguing completely contrary to the way Mr Murray presents his views. Furthermore, John Rippon's account of Gill's teaching on the subject is taken verbatim from this passage and in no way implies an up-valuing of it. After explaining the disabilities that

---

[235] *Life and Writings of Rev. John Gill*, pp. 43-51.
[236] See Fuller's *Passages Apparently Contradictory, Principles of Church Discipline* and *On Moral and Positive Obedience*.
[237] *Works*, vol. ii, p. 356.

sinners lie under in not coming to Christ, Rippon quotes Gill correctly as saying:

> Though man lies under such a disability and has neither power[238] nor will of himself to come to Christ for life; yet his not coming to Christ, when revealed in the external ministry of the Gospel, as God's way of salvation, is criminal and blameworthy; since the disability and perverseness of his will are not owing to any decree of God, but to the corruption and vitiosity of his nature through sin. And therefore, since this vitiosity of nature is blameworthy, that which follows upon it, and is the effect of it must be so too.[239]

How Mr Murray can possibly interpret this central doctrine of Gill's which he anchored in the 1729 Declaration of Faith as being the very opposite of what Gill actually affirmed shows either acute negative prejudice or a total neglect of sources.

Mr Murray produces a red herring in his references to the *1689 Particular Baptist Declaration of Faith*. He infers that Rippon's 1790 reprint implies a rejection of Gill's (and Rippon's church's) 1729 statement of faith. He omits to add that Rippon reprinted Gill's confession in 1800! Rippon was a historian and theologian of note and rescued many a worthy Particular Baptist document from oblivion. This does not mean that he rejected his own church's creed every time he printed another. Contrary to what Murray postulates, Rippon was still using Gill's declaration of faith in his own church well into the nineteenth century.[240] Writing in 1800, Rippon states that his new members were only accepted into fellowship on giving their full assent to the 1729 declaration. Indeed, the *1729 Goat Yard Declaration of Faith* became the standard orthodox confession of many Particular Baptist churches for over a hundred years and it is still used almost verbatim by a good number of Baptist churches of various associations

---

[238] Fuller argues that fallen man still possesses this power. See *Works*, vol. ii, pp. 546, 547.

[239] *Life and Writings of the Rev. John Gill, DD*, Gano Books, 1992, pp. 46, 47 and *The Cause of God and Truth*, Baker, 1980, p. 33.

[240] See Rippon's biography of Gill, p. 14.

in Britain and the USA. Rippon stresses that Gill's Declaration is a positive testimony of how he united faith with practice. This statement by Rippon is of great importance in the face of modern Fullerite criticism that Gill's theology taught passive rather than active faith. Rippon thus affirms, 'few are the formulas which have at any time been more closely united with duty. The term and the thing are remarkable, in this confession—and no man was more fond of either in their proper place, and fairly understood.'[241]

Mr Murray gives the impression that the old Particular Baptist confessions contained articles on a universal offer of salvation. This would, of course, mean that they believed as Fuller later argued, that there is a universal offer of salvation based on a universally applicable atonement which warrants, i.e. guarantees, salvation to those who are prepared, in Fullerite terminology, to partake of the feast freely provided.[242] He even states that Gill drew up his own declaration of faith in order to provide a creed without such a 'free offer' article. This is a great distortion of the facts. There are no such articles in the great eighteenth century Particular Baptist declarations of faith including the two major London confessions.[243] Furthermore there are no such articles even in the bulk of Arminian Baptist creeds, the *Orthodox Creed* of 1679 being no exception. Here Article XXI speaks of a vocational and effectual calling, a distinction Gill himself makes in Part I, Article X of *The Cause of God and Truth* and in his *Doctrine of Predestination Stated and Set in the Scriptural Light* which he wrote against Wesley's *Predestination Calmly Considered*. Gill shows here that the gospel must be preached to all as the Spirit leads but it comes as a savour of life unto life to some and a savour of death unto death to others. The former is the effectual call, outlined carefully in the old Baptist creeds, which is the 'powerful operation of the Spirit of God on the soul'[244] which cannot be resisted and the latter is the external call by the ministry of the Word which puts a man under his obligations but 'may be resisted, rejected, and despised, and become useless.'[245] This

---

[241] Ibid., p. 20.
[242] *Works*, vol. ii, p. 338.
[243] See my discussion of 'the offer' in the creeds in Chapter One.
[244] Op. cit. p. 15.
[245] *The Cause of God and Truth*, sect. X., p. 15.

teaching echoes that of Calvin's in his *Institutes*, Book III, chapter 21 where he explains that it is God's good pleasure that the gospel does not come equally to all and receives the same reception and 'it is plain how greatly ignorance of this principle detracts from the glory of God, and impairs true humility.' Anyone taking care to compare the *1729 Goat Yard Declaration of Faith* with its forerunners, good as they are, will notice that the confession stresses the sinner's responsibility before God and Christian duties to uphold and spread the Faith. This causes Timothy George to argue that Spurgeon himself would have fully accepted Gill's confession.[246]

In mentioning that the Puritan creeds included a free offer clause, Mr Murray is no doubt thinking of the Council of Dort and the *Westminster Confession*. These understood the free offer to mean Christ should be preached to all as the Spirit leads. The novelty which Alvery Jackson brought into Particular Baptist church history in 1752 and which influenced Fuller so much was to change the meaning of the free offer of grace to a universal offer of salvation wrought out in the teamwork of God's purpose and human agency. This is not a Puritan doctrine. It is not even an Arminian doctrine as, though it is based on a legal view of grace which would please many an Arminian, it also shows a disbelief in the total depravity of man, a doctrine which Arminian leaders such as Wesley held dear. As the 'free offer' is used to mean a universal atonement by the modern evangelical Establishment, it is best avoided, especially as it is not a Scriptural term. Mr Murray shows on which side of the Puritans he stands by attaching a eulogy of Fuller to his denunciation of Gill. He also fails to see how much the *Goat Yard Declaration* was a product of the whole church membership. The church book states that it was the members who asked Gill to draw up the confession and Rippon tells us explicitly how 'cordially one' they were with their pastor.[247]

Charles Haddon Spurgeon is glowing in his praise of Gill. Of his ordination, Spurgeon says, 'Little did the friends dream what sort of man they had thus chosen to be their teacher; but had they known it they would have rejoiced that a man of such vast erudition, such indefatigable industry, such sound judgment, and such sterling honesty,

---

[246] *Baptist Theologians*, p. 9.
[247] *Life and writings of the Rev. John Gill*, p. 20.

had come among them.'[248] Spurgeon loved reading Gill's sermons and wrote, for instance in his copy of Gill's preaching on the Song of Solomon, 'This priceless work of my learned predecessor has always been helpful to me.' In his *Commenting and Commentaries*, he says of this work, 'Those who despise it, have never read it, or are incapable of elevated spiritual feelings.'[249] This sums up much of present day second-hand criticism of Gill which is rarely based on a first-hand knowledge of his works. Gill's commentaries, which were merely his sermons in writing, were regularly and eagerly consulted by the Prince of Preachers who marked them all with three stars which was Spurgeon's way of saying, 'The very best!'. In 1886 he jotted in his copy of *Ezekiel to Malachi* the words, 'Many sneer at Gill, but he is not to be dispensed with. In some respects, he has no superior. He is always well worth consulting.'[250] In a letter dated February 1855, Spurgeon pays tribute to Gill's influence on him by stating 'My position, as Pastor of one of the most influential churches, enables me to make myself heard and my daily labour is to revive the old doctrines of Gill, Owen, Calvin, Augustine and Christ.'[251] It would seem here that Spurgeon was so taken up by the testimony of Gill that he mixed up his priorities and put Gill first and Christ last.

It is such utterances as Spurgeon's exuberant praise of Gill that have obviously coloured Mr Murray's views of the scholar-pastor. So great was Gill's influence throughout the eighteenth and nineteenth centuries that thousands of would-be preachers aped him. This was rightly deplored by Gill's successors in his pastorate. This led John Fawcett, for instance, whilst considering a call to Carter Lane, to make his own position clear concerning the man he admired:

> To be brief, my dear friends, you may say what you will,
> I'll ne'er be confined to read nothing but Gill.

---

[248] *The Metropolitan Tabernacle: Its History and Work*, p. 40.
[249] Op. cit. p. 104.
[250] C. H. Spurgeon's *Autobiography*, vol. i, p. 220.
[251] Iain Murray, *The Forgotten Spurgeon*, p. 58.

If anyone can be viewed as a spiritual successor of John Gill, it must be J. C. Philpot who nevertheless wrote concerning his contemporaries' tendency to imitate great men:

> Unless a man comes nowadays with a Shibboleth, he is almost set aside as a man of truth. He must use certain words, whether Scripture or not, must preach in a prescribed manner, as well as with prescribed matter. He must not vary from a certain mould, and if he dares to use his own way of setting forth truth, in his own simple language, and as he simply feels and has felt, many can hardly tell whether he is right or wrong, and the majority perhaps set him down as wrong altogether. I dislike, amazingly, the artificial mode of setting forth truth by which, when you hear a text given out, you know all the divisions and mode of handling it before they are mentioned, and can tell the end of every sentence nearly as soon as you hear the beginning. It smells too strongly of Dr Gill and premeditation to suit me, but some cannot eat the dish unless served up every day in a plate of the same pattern; and, like children, when a different shaped or different painted cup comes on the table, cannot drink, as being so occupied with the novelty. But God will bless His own truth and His own servants, and when He thrusts forth His own stewards, will not send them forth as apes and imitators either of Huntington, Gadsby, or Warburton. They shall have their own line of truth and their own method of setting it forth, and they shall be commended, sooner or later, to spiritual consciences as men taught of Him.[252]

Such words, of course, ought never to be so construed that they are taken for a criticism of Gill himself. Elsewhere, Philpot says of the pastor who under God influenced his own denomination so much:

> For a sound, consistent, scriptural exposition of the word of God, no commentary, we believe, in any language can be compared with Dr Gill's. There may be commentaries on individual books of Scripture, such as Vitringa on Isaiah,

---

[252] *The Seceders*, vol. ii, pp. 207, 208 (letter to Fanny Philpot).

Venema on the Psalms, Alting on Jeremiah, Caryll on Job, Lampe on John, Luther on the Galatians, Owen on the Hebrews, Mede on the Revelation, which may surpass Dr Gill's in depth of research and fulness of exposition; and the great work from which Poole compiled his Synopsis may be more suitable to scholars and divines, as bringing together into one focus all the learning of those eminent men who in the sixteenth century devoted days and nights to the study and interpretation of the word of God. But for English readers there is no commentary equal to Dr Gill's. His alone of all we have seen is based upon consistent, harmonious views of divine truth, without turning aside to the right hand or the left. It is said of the late Mr Simeon, of Cambridge, that his plan of preaching was, if he had what is called an Arminian text, to preach from it Arminianism, and if he took a Calvinistic text, to preach from it Calvinism. Not so Dr Gill. He knew nothing about Arminian texts, or Arminian interpretations. He believed that the Scriptures, as an inspired revelation from God, must be harmonious and consistent with itself, and that no two passages could so contradict each other as the doctrines of free-will contradict the doctrines of grace. The exhortation of the Apostle is, 'Having then gifts differing according to the grace that is given to us whether prophecy, let us prophesy according to the proportion of faith' (Romans 12:6). This apostolic rule was followed closely by Dr Gill. 'The proportion', or as the word literally means, 'analogy of faith', was his rule and guide in interpreting the Scripture; and therefore, as all his explanations were modelled according to the beautiful proportions of divine truth as received by faith, so every view disproportionate to the same harmonious plan was rejected by him as God-dishonouring, inconsistent, and contradictory. It is this sound, consistent, harmonious interpretation of divine truth which has stamped a peculiar weight and value on Dr Gill's *Commentary*, such as no other exposition of the whole Scripture possesses.[253]

---

[253] *Reviews*, vol. ii, pp. 299, 300.

In a similar way to Philpot, Spurgeon warned continually against those who imitated Gill but he always emphasised that he did not include Gill in his criticism of those who claimed to be Gill's followers. Thus Mr Murray is being unfair to both Spurgeon and Gill when he allows Spurgeon's words concerning Gill's imitators to cast a shadow over Gill himself.[254] Murray's own quotes from Spurgeon confute him, however such as when he quotes Spurgeon as saying, 'Gill is the Coryphaeus of Hyper-Calvinism, but if his followers never went beyond their master, the would not go very far astray.' Here in *Commentating and Commentaries*,[255] Spurgeon is not criticising Gill's theology but his way of sermon construction and systematising doctrine. Here, again, Spurgeon refers to Gill's imitators but stresses that if they really stuck to Gill's teaching, even 'they would not go very far astray.' Murray claims that this is 'over generous', but this is Spurgeon's honest opinion which obviously differs from Mr Murray's.

Finally a word must be said concerning Murray's claim that churches of Gill's Biblical persuasions died and Fuller's brand of so-called 'Evangelical Calvinism' flourished. Gill had about the largest Baptist churches in Britain for almost half a century. This was at a time when the duty-faith, free-offer Modern Question theology was being preached by Jackson, Taylor and Stennett. The churches of these men never rivalled Gill's in any way. When Gill died, there was no rapid growth of Fullerite churches. In spite of the Northampton Association Baptist churches (i.e. those who came most under Fuller's influence) receiving thousands of converts through Hervey's and Maddox's preaching, after these two Anglican stalwarts died, the churches in the central area of what Murray calls 'the Evangelical Revival on Nonconformist churches' averaged around fifty baptised adults although there had been a general growth in Baptist numbers since the 1750s. Seen on a wider basis, successful Particular Baptist preachers such as Ryland Sen., Rippon, Beddome, Kinghorn, Button and Booth refused to be tainted by Fuller's figurative interpretations of Scripture. Booth, indeed, said Fuller was lost. Many of these churches refused to accept Fuller's view of para-church missionary work and fund-raising. Fuller admitted in his old age that his cause was waning but that of the

---

[254] 'John Gill and C. H. Spurgeon', *Banner of Truth*, Issue 386, p. 17.
[255] *Commenting and Commentaries*, p. 16.

Evangelicals in the Church of England was growing.[256] Meanwhile preachers of righteousness such as William Huntington were pastoring thousands. These were followed by such men as William Gadsby who founded some forty to fifty churches in a matter of no time and filled them with converts through his own ministry. They were treading in the footsteps of Richard Davis who evangelised the eighty miles radius around his Rothwell church and instructed some hundreds of evangelists to go out into the highways and byways in Christ's name. All these, according to modern Fullerites are Hyper-Calvinists who do not believe in preaching to sinners. How ridiculous can such criticism get?

Rather than reject Gill's teaching concerning the pastorate and practical divinity, Spurgeon testified regularly to having not only inherited Gill's pulpit but also his mantle. He and Rippon knew that Gill's value as a preacher was because those under his ministry knew he was a man who practised what he preached. His hearers trusted him with full and thankful hearts, knowing that his great aim was to lead his flock into green pastures and protect them from the snares and wolves of the world. Referring to the fact that all who knew him from his childhood on were deeply impressed by the sanctity of Gill's life, Rippon says:

> Those who had the honour and happiness of being admitted into the number of his friends can go still further in their testimony. They know, that his moral demeanour was more than blameless: it was, from first to last, consistently exemplary. And, indeed, an undeviating consistency, both in his views of evangelical truths, and in his obedience, as a servant of God, was one of those qualities, by which his cast of character was eminently marked. He was, in every respect, a burning and a shining light—Burning with love to God, to Truth, and to Souls—Shining, as 'an ensample to believers, in word, in faith, in purity;' a pattern of good works, and a model of all holy conversation and godliness.[257]

---

[256] *Works*, vol. iii, pp. 481-489.
[257] From the short biography appended to Rippon's *Life and Writings of Rev. John Gill*, pp. 138, 139.

Almost thirty years after Gill died, John Rippon recorded that such were the number of remembrance sermons preached and published at his death that never before and never since had such a lamentation gone up in the English speaking world because a great man had fallen in Israel. Both Rippon and Spurgeon would have been deeply saddened if any contemporary of theirs, in leading evangelical positions, would have refused to join in this lamentation and bemoan the fact that such a saint was with them no more. They would have thought that such a refusal to honour Gill's name and testimony was to dishonour the Gospel for which Gill stood. It was in conjunction with the down-grade controversy that Spurgeon affirmed he had taken up Gill's mantle. He wished to be for his age what Gill had been in the century before. Mr Murray has other wishes and he is respectfully entitled to them. He has no business, however, to denigrate the memory of a true saint and replace it with his own brand of negative 'special pleading' that serves no gospel purpose.

Professor David Engelsma, writing in the *Standard Bearer* for April, 1996 under the title 'John Gill: Hyper-Calvinist?'[258] has the following to say about Gill and human responsibility:

> The basic mistake of Gill and his present-day disciples is their failure to recognize that total depravity, or inability, does not rule out full responsibility.
>
> To put it as sharply as possible: The gospel commands the unregenerated and totally depraved sinner to do what he cannot do, and his punishment will one day be the greater for his refusal. The reason why he is accountable to do what he cannot do is that the fault for his inability is his own, not God's. Besides, when the sinner rejects the gospel in unbelief, he does so willingly.
>
> If Gill hesitated to affirm the serious external call to all hearers because he feared that this was the Arminian offer, his error lay in not distinguishing between the Arminian offer and

---

[258] This was a 'well-meant' review of my book *John Gill and the Cause of God and Truth*. See also the Standard Bearer for June and August 1996 and also the Presbyterian Reformed Theological Journal (PRTJ) November 1997, pp. 65-69, which continues the debate.

the Reformed external call. The Arminian offer consists of a gracious attempt by God to save all who hear, dependent upon their supposed free will. The Reformed call consists of a summons to all, setting forth their duty and making plain the one way of salvation, which summons God makes effectual by His particular grace in the hearts of the elect in the audience.

Engelsma holds that Gill cannot possibly believe in human responsibility as he maintains that man is so fallen that it would be wrong of God to expect him to bear any responsibility whatsoever for what he could not possibly do because of the state he is in. We notice that this is merely Engelsma's argument concerning what he thinks Gill's position is, but we must ask what proof he has for such an inference. An inference it must remain until Engelsma backs his accusation with evidence. Such evidence is not given in the article in question but rather Engelsma merely deduces his opinion of Gill from a further inference, namely:

> ... in addition to the Reformed charge that Gill as a Baptist seriously erred in denying God's covenantal work of grace in the infants of believers, it must be noted that Gill did, in fact, deny that the call, or summons, of the gospel comes to all who hear. This denial is real, and serious, Hyper-Calvinism.

Engelsma's logic runs on the following lines. Gill, he presumes, does not believe that what Engelsma calls an 'external call' may be addressed to sinners in preaching the gospel. The Professor asks himself why this should be the case and, placing himself in Gill's supposed shoes, answers himself with the reply that sinners are not responsible for their situation, so it would be pointless preaching to them. Now this is a very nice piece of dog-catching-its-tail reasoning. It reminds one of the argument of Andrew Fuller in his *The Gospel Worthy of All Acceptation*, which runs 'Or if the inability of sinners to believe in Christ were of the same nature as that of a dead body in a grave to rise up and walk, it were absurd to suppose that they would on this account fall under the Divine censure. No man is reproved for not doing that which is naturally impossible.'[259] Needless to say, Gill argued that though man was incapable of pleasing God, it was most certainly his own fault.

Now this is all very interesting, coming from Engelsma's pen as he is, judging by his book *Hyper-Calvinism and the Call of the Gospel*, one of those hyper-high Calvinists who believe that Adam was not placed on probation as a perfect man who fell of his own accord from his position as an eternal being. He was rather placed in Eden as a clockwork toy of God's which was wound up so that it would run down in time.[260] In other words, man did not really fall as he could never have remained standing. He fell when the grace given him to remain standing was purposefully withdrawn. Worse, he fell because he was not fitted out to be perfect. Now this view really does remove all claims for man's responsibility from him. Yet this was not Gill's view at all and he took human responsibility seriously as made clear in his *1729 Declaration of Faith*:

> Article IV. We believe, That God created the first man; Adam, after his image, and in his likeness, an upright, holy, and innocent creature, capable of serving and glorifying him:[261] but he sinning, all his posterity sinned in him, and came short of the glory of God;[262] the guilt of whose sin is imputed;[263] and a corrupt nature derived to all his offspring descending from him by ordinary and natural generation:[264] that they are by their first birth carnal and unclean; averse to all that is good, incapable of doing any, and prone to every[265] sin: and are also by nature children or wrath, and under a sentence of condemnation;[266] and so are subject, not

---

[259] *Works*, vol. ii, p. 355.

[260] See *Hyper-Calvinism and the Call of the Gospel*, passim but especially pp. 40, 41 where the fall is said to have been ordained by God. Throughout the book, Engelsma adopts a severe supralapsarian position and repeatedly points out that those whom he most respects such as Hoeksema held that position. Gill was ardently sublapsarian on this issue as seen in his debate with Wesley.

[261] Genesis 1:26, 27; Ecclesiastes 7:29; Psalm 8:5.

[262] Romans 5:12; 3:23.

[263] Romans 5:12, 14, 18, 19; 1 Corinthians 15:22; Ephesians 2:3.

[264] Job 14:4; Psalm 51:5; John 3:6; Ezekiel 16:4-6.

[265] Romans 8:7, 8; 3:10-12; Genesis 6:5.

[266] Ephesians 2:3; Romans 5:12, 18.

only to a corporal death,[267] and involved in a moral one, commonly called spiritual;[268] but are also liable to an eternal death,[269] as considered in the first Adam, fallen and sinners; from all which there is no deliverance, but by Christ, the second Adam.[270]

For Gill, Adam was a perfect probationer who used his perfections to revolt against God and thus lost those perfections. Since then man is doubly responsible for his state. He is responsible for his sin federally in Adam and he is responsible for committing sin after the similitude of Adam's transgression.

However, having not yet produced any evidence for his surmise, Engelsma further argues:

> But it becomes clear that Gill did not think that God and the preacher of the gospel command every hearer, unregenerate as well as regenerate, reprobate as well as elect, to repent of his sins with true, heartfelt repentance and to believe on the Saviour from the heart with a genuine faith. The reason given was that the unregenerate is incapable of true repentance and faith by virtue of his total depravity,

and continues,[271]

> That Gill denied what Reformed theology teaches as the 'external call of the gospel' is plain enough from his handling of the call in his dogmatics. The only command that is given to the unregenerate in the audience of the preacher is that he does what lies in his natural powers: 'perform the natural duties of religion'; exercise a 'natural faith'; 'believe the external report of the

---

[267] Genesis 2:17; Romans 5:12, 14; Hebrews 9:27.

[268] Matthew 8:22; Luke 15:24, 32; John 5:25; Ephesians 2:1.

[269] Romans 5:18; 6:23; Ephesians 2:3.

[270] Romans 6:23; 7:24, 25; 8:2; 2 Timothy 1:10; 1 Corinthians 15:45, 47. *Sermons and Tracts*, vol. iii, p. 560. *John Gill and the Cause of God and Truth*, p. 76.

[271] A large quote from my book *John Gill and the Cause of God and Truth* is placed between these two passages, so that no part of Prof. Engelsma's argument has been removed here. *Standard Bearer*, April 15, 1996, p. 332.

gospel'; and the like (see Gill's *Body of Divinity*, vol. ii, Baker, repr. 1978, pp. 122-125).

During his article, Engelsma criticised Gill's use of the words 'legal repentance' and 'evangelical repentance', obviously believing that such a distinction was a sign of Hyper-Calvinism. Actually, Gill does not divide repentance into merely two parts, which was the common way of looking at repentance in his day but sees both the legal and evangelical aspects of repentance as being mere parts in a much wider whole.[272]

As Professor Engelsma's otherwise most positive assessment of Gill contained two fundamental errors concerning Gill's alleged rejection of human responsibility and the call of the gospel to sinners, I wrote a defence of Gill on these two positions which Professor Engelsma kindly published in full in the *Standard Bearer*[273] with his lengthy comments on what I had to say. Referring in particular to Engelsma's arguments quoted above, I argued with reference to the chapter entitled 'A Saint is Slandered' in my Gill biography:

Though you write 'That Gill denied what Reformed theology teaches as the "external call" of the gospel is plain enough ... ,' I show in the above mentioned chapter, quoting extensively and verbatim from Gill's works, that Gill distinguished between an external and an internal call and believed firmly that both were part of gospel preaching. See also *The Cause of God and Truth*, Section X. Gill also believed that even the elect could reject the external call until God put a new spirit in them in His own good time.

Where the completely erroneous idea that Gill rejected 'full responsibility', as you term it, came from, I cannot imagine. Certainly there is no basis whatsoever for this presumption in Gill's works. Even Andrew Fuller came admirably to Gill's rescue here, pointing out in his *Gospel Worthy of All Acceptation* that Gill 'established the principle' of man's responsibility when he says that the 'perverseness of their wills was blameworthy,

---

[272] See Gill's *Of the Gospel*, and *Of Repentance towards God.*
[273] June 1, 1996.

being owing to the corruption and vitiosity of their nature; which being blameworthy in them, that which follows upon it must be so too.' Fuller does not give the reference but it is from *The Cause of God and Truth*, Section XXX, point 3. John Rippon, Gill's successor, in his *Life and Writings of Rev. John Gill*, speaks of the former pastor of his church with great enthusiasm, stressing his preaching, soul-winning and evangelistic capacities. He defends Gill at length against charges of Hyper-Calvinism and Antinomianism, arguing in particular, that Gill stressed man's responsibility regarding both law and gospel. Though Rippon seems to have accepted Fuller's Grotian view of sin, and strives to thrust it on Gill, he yet claims correctly that Gill's exposition of John 5:40 clearly teaches human responsibility and furthermore, he refers to Gill's distinction between the external and internal ministry of the gospel.

I sympathise with your strictures concerning the expressions 'legal repentance' and 'evangelical repentance' though they are hardly helpful here as this was a common semantic distinction of the time, used by Christians on both sides of the duty-faith/free-offer debate. Remember that Fuller says that 'the former leads to rebellious despair and the latter leads to a holy submission to God.' Here Fuller is in complete agreement with both Gill and Huntington![274]

In his lengthy response to my letter in the June, 1996 issue of *Standard Bearer*, Engelsma explains that though he admitted that Gill taught *an* external call, it was not *the* external call. Readers will no doubt have taken this remark to indicate that Engelsma has shifted his position. Of interest here is that Engelsma quoted a passage to prove his case which one would have thought would convince any reader that Engelsma had no case at all! This passage is taken from Gill's lengthy

---

[274] *Standard Bearer*, June 1, 1996, p. 398. Calvin, in his *Institutes*, Book III, Chap. III, §6, recognises the two distinctions, giving examples of each from Scripture but prefers not to use the terms. Nevertheless, he, himself, divides repentance into two parts, one a turning to God and the other a sincere fear of God, both obtained by union with Christ. Nowhere does Calvin condemn the legal/evangelical division as being extreme in any way. Calvin rejects 'legal repentance' as having any saving value which is exactly as Gill sees the matter.

eleven page definition of the effectual call of which three pages refer to the external call and where Gill explains the difference but shows how the one is caught up in the other. This one article by Gill, however, displays only a fraction of his entire teaching on the subject but even so, Engelsma has been rather too narrowly selective in choosing his material from this single source.

First, Gill argues here, that there is the universal call which comes to all through nature and the outworking of Providence, declaring the wonderful works of God. This call is God's witness to Himself as the only God worthy of worship. Then there is a particular call which Gill subdivides into two parts. First, there is the external call which comes through the ministry of the word, starting with God's witness in the Old Testament, through the prophets, John the Baptist, Christ Incarnate, the apostles and all subsequent ambassadors for Christ. Then there is the internal call which is 'by the Spirit and grace of God to the hearts and consciences of men.' Gill explains that the two calls sometimes go together but at other times do not. The external call, which Gill equates with the gospel ministry, he explains, comes alike to saints and sinners. It builds up the saints in the faith, providing them with all the blessings and graces of the gospel. Gill then deals with the same external call to the unconverted in general, saying that 'this external call may be considered, as a call of sinners in a state of nature and unregeneracy', and goes on to say that,

> They may, and should be called upon to attend the outward means of grace, and to make use of them; to read the holy Scriptures, which have been the means of the conversion of some; to hear the word, and wait on the ministry of it, which may be blessed unto them, for the effectual calling of them.[275] And it is part of the ministry of the word to lay before men their fallen, miserable, lost, and undone estate by nature; to open to them the nature of sin, its pollution and guilt, and the sad consequences of it; to inform them of their incapacity to make atonement for it; and of their impotence and inability to do what is spiritually good; and of the insufficiency of their own righteousness to justify them in the sight of God: and they are to be made

---

[275] Engelsma ends his quote here.

acquainted, that salvation is alone by Christ, and not otherways; and the fulness, freeness, and suitableness of this salvation, are to be preached before them; and the whole to be left to the Spirit of God, to make application of it as he shall think fit.[276]

It needs to be emphasised here that Gill is writing of an 'external call to sinners in a state of nature and unregeneracy' which has, as its divine aim, the conversion of some. Surprisingly Engelsma argues immediately after this quote, obviously basing his findings on it, 'It is the doctrine of John Gill that there may be no "external call" to "sinners in a state of unregeneracy".', and emphasises again that Gill 'rules out an external call'.[277] At first glance, it seems that either Engelsma has misread Gill or he refuses to believe that Gill actually means what he says. It soon becomes clear that Engelsma is denying that when Gill stresses the need to preach the gospel of salvation to both saint and sinner alike, he is referring to what Engelsma believes is the external call. He is saying, 'Gill believes in an external call, but not the right one.' Engelsma explains what he means by saying that Gill has not stressed the need to preach repentance and faith to sinners, therefore, he does not really believe in an external call. This is a most unfair criticism because Engelsma has cut off the bit from his quote where Gill stresses that sinners must be shown the folly of their ways and the need to get right with God. Furthermore, Engelsma has merely quoted from Gill's definition of the effectual call and not from his works dealing with repentance and faith. Gill is highly analytical in what Engelsma calls his 'Dogmatics' and deals in detail with each gospel feature separately. Engelsma claims from the evidence he gives that it shows that Gill only teaches that already-believers can be urged to repent, proving that Gill is a Hyper-Calvinist. This is an inference of Engelsma's which is not stated in the work to which Engelsma refers. Gill speaks in detail here as little on repentance and faith with reference to saints as he does sinners. It is just not his topic. For Gill's teaching on repentance and faith, though, as seen from the above quote, such a need for a demonstration of turning to God is strongly implied, we must be prepared to look at the relevant sections.

---

[276] *A Body of Doctrinal Divinity*, vol. ii, Book III, Chap. XII, pp. 852, 853.
[277] Op. cit. p. 399.

Turning to Gill's entry in the same *Body of Divinity* on 'Of the Gospel', Gill takes up the subject of repentance, showing how Peter says in Acts 2:37, 38, 'Repent and be baptised, every one of you, for the remission of sins.' Gill goes on to say:

> And this is also clear from the ministry of Christ himself; who came, not to call the righteous, but sinners to repentance; which was not a legal, but *evangelical*[278] repentance (Engelsma maintains that Gill only taught the need for sinners to repent legally). He began his ministry thus; Repent, and believe the gospel; see Matthew 9:13; Mark 1:15. With which agrees the ministry of the apostles in general; who, by the direction of Christ, preached repentance and remission of sins in his name; which was most certainly the gospel; the one, as well as the other, a doctrine of the gospel, Luke 24:47. And the apostle Paul, who was a most evangelical preacher, divides his whole ministry into these two parts; Repentance towards God, and faith towards our Lord Jesus Christ, Acts 20:21.[279]

So great was Gill's emphasis on preaching repentance and faith as being identical with the gospel for all, when Rippon came to sum up Gill's entire ministry, he quoted Paul here, with reference to Gill. This was also emphasised by Ivimey in his *History of the English Baptists*. It is thus a far cry from reality to argue that Gill would not preach repentance and faith to sinners.

In his long and carefully argued treatise *Of Repentance Towards God*, Gill provides Engelsma with all that he misses in other works on other subjects. Referring to the word preached which brings with it God's call, Gill points out how it is intrinsically a call to repentance. Of this he says:

> The usual means and instrument of repentance are the word, and the ministers of it, as faith, so repentance, comes by hearing the word; the three thousand were pricked to their heart, and were brought to repentance, through the ministry of the apostle Peter;

---

[278] My emphasis.
[279] Baptist Standard Bearer edition, Book IV, Chap. VII, pp. 376, 377.

and as all the apostles were ordered by Christ to preach repentance in his name among all nations, so they went forth everywhere, and God in and by their ministry commanded all men everywhere to repent; and when and where the command was attended with power it produced the effect; and so the apostle Paul declared to Jews and Gentiles, that *they should repent and turn to God, and do works meet for repentance*; and the hand of the Lord being with him, great numbers everywhere believed and turned to the Lord, Luke 24:47; Acts 17:30; 26:20.[280]

It would have assisted Engelsma's cause greatly if he had brought in these considerations from the appropriate places instead of condemning Gill for not saying everything where he believed it did not belong. As a result, Engelsma insists on believing, 'For Gill, the Calvinist doctrine of total depravity rules out the external call of the gospel. Only those are to be summoned to genuine repentance and true faith who are already born again.'[281] That these findings are in no way in agreement with Gill's sources will be clear from the above and following quotes.

Nevertheless, Engelsma is not yet done with his misinterpretation of Gill. There is still the matter of human responsibility. Basing his further comments on the false foundation he has built up, Engelsma now argues:

In this line, Gill is guilty of the Hyper-Calvinist error: The sinner is not required to exercise faith because he lacks the ability. The truth is that the totally unable sinner is required to believe on Jesus Christ presented in the gospel. He knows it. If the external call is not accompanied by the internal call— particular grace in the preaching!—he willingly refuses to do what he knows he ought to do. He will one day be damned into deeper hell for disobeying the gospel call.[282]

It always pays to read an opponent in context, which Engelsma has obviously failed to do. Before the quote Engelsma gives, Gill had

---

[280] B.S.B. edition, Book I, Chap. IV, p. 721.
[281] Op. cit. June 1, 1996, p. 399.
[282] Op. cit. p. 399.

reasoned that the external call must be accompanied with the internal call to make it effective and after the quote, he goes on to argue that a rejection of the external call makes the sinner all the more damnable. If Engelsma had only turned over the page after his quote, he would have also read:

> All things are for the elect's sake, and particularly the ministrations of the gospel, which to them is the savour of life unto life; as it is the will of God that his chosen people, and others, should promiscuously dwell together, so he sends his gospel to them in general, and by it takes out a people for his name; calls them by his grace effectually, out of the world, and separates them from the men of it, to be a peculiar people unto himself; and *the rest are thereby left inexcusable*; for if the light of nature leaves men so, much more the light of the gospel; *the condemnation of men is aggravated by it; inasmuch as though they are surrounded with light, they love darkness rather than light*.[283]

Gill then concludes this definition of the external call by saying:

> Wherefore, when the ministry of the word is slighted, and the gospel-call rejected, it is most righteously resented by the Lord; see Proverbs 1:24-28, and such are justly punished with everlasting destruction by him, 1 Peter 4:17; 2 Thessalonians 1:8, 9.[284]

In *The Cause of God*, Section X, p. 15, Gill teaches how the Gospel is to be preached to all, as the Spirit leads. It does not therefore come 'equally to all'. It comes as 'a savour of death unto death' for some and 'a savour of life unto life' for others.[285] Gill speaks positively of 'calls, invitations, and messages of God to men by his ministers'[286] but explains that such are 'not sufficient in themselves, without powerful

---

[283] *Of Effectual Calling*, p. 854. B.S.B. edition, p. 540. My emphasis.
[284] Ibid.
[285] *The Cause of God and Truth*, Baker Bookhouse Reprint, 1980, Section X, p. 15.
[286] Ibid.

grace, to produce true faith in Christ, evangelical repentance towards God, and new spiritual obedience, in life and conversation.' Gill points out that there is a two-fold call in evangelism. First there is the internal effectual call which is the 'powerful operation of the Spirit of God on the soul' which cannot be resisted, then there is the external call by the ministry of the Word which, 'may be resisted, rejected, and despised, and become useless.'[287]

In the August issue of the *Standard Bearer* without dealing with my contrary evidence, which he had, however, kindly quoted, Engelsma reiterated his points and added a good deal of material that had to do with modern Baptist thinking but not John Gill. He had confessed to be 'almost persuaded' but wanted more solid evidence concerning Gill on responsibility and preaching repentance and faith. He therefore gave me a challenge in print to produce such information and sent me a copy of this printed challenge accompanied by a personal letter. I had, however, already sent him the detailed information which has been recorded in the last few pages. My surprise and dismay were great when Prof. Engelsma replied to say that he would not publish my reply as it was too long and he had closed the debate. This answer was very disappointing as the length of my reply was quite within the usual limits set by the Standard Bearer and determined largely by the evidence from Gill's works which Engelsma had overlooked and whose existence he had doubted, yet which he had asked me to produce. Also, I had expressly told the professor that he could edit my letter as he wished. Engelsma's argument that the debate was closed is not backed by the fact that he himself carried the debate into the end of the following year. My surprise grew as I heard a rumour from friends that Prof. Engelsma was denying that I had responded to his challenge. Then my surprise and dismay were complete when I read in the November 1997 edition of the *Presbyterian Reformed Theological Journal* (PRTJ), the organ of the Protestant Reformed Seminary, that Professor Engelsma was continuing the debate with me and complaining that I had not replied to his challenge. In a context using the strongest hypercritical language and polemic, Engelsma writes:

---

[287] Ibid.

But the final flaw is unpardonable: Ella will not address the issue in the controversy of the eighteenth and nineteenth centuries that he is covering. He will not address this issue head on, clearly, and thoroughly. He will not address this issue in its bearing on the current debate. This issue is whether God in the gospel seriously, earnestly calls, or commands, every hearer, unconverted as well as converted, to repent of his sins (with heartfelt sorrow toward God) and to believe in Jesus Christ (with true faith).

In an earlier exchange with Dr Ella in the Standard Bearer, I put this issue to him as a pointed question, asking for a 'yes' or 'no' answer (*Standard Bearer*, August 1, 1996, p. 443). No such answer has been forthcoming.

On reading these surprising words I wrote respectfully to Prof. Engelsma, reminding him that I had not only answered him at length but we had discussed my answer in personal correspondence. I then wrote a letter to the editor of the *PRTJ* correcting the mistake and giving some insight into the material I had produced. The *PRTJ* told me that they could not publish my letter but had sent it on to Prof. Engelsma for attention. No reply from Prof. Engelsma has been forthcoming. This is not the way to carry out theological debate.

As emphasised in the previous chapters, Gill believed in bringing the gospel call or invitation to all men, everywhere as the Spirit led. If this call is rejected, his teaching is clear; those who slight it are responsible for doing so. Such teaching fully knocks the bottom out of the modern Murray-Engelsma opposition from two extremes of Calvinism and proves beyond any shadow of a doubt that Gill must be vindicated from the evil report given him.[288]

Trying to prove the rule by listing the exceptions

Obviously another main difficulty in accepting the fact that God directly justifies fallen people who are bound by the laws of time and accepts them in union with His son before belief is the fact that He justifies them when they have no faith to deserve it. In view of the teaching of Scripture that God justifies the ungodly and saves us while

---

[288] *Banner of Truth*, 1986, p. 127.

we are yet sinners and even enemies of God, one would think the argument is conclusive. Few of those who argue for faith before justification follow their own precepts thoroughly.

Children are alleged exceptions

A point in question is infants who die before a fixed age, this age of faithlessness varying from birth to five years of age and more, according to the views of the protagonist. We even find Berkhof, after much consideration and a making of uncertain sounds, coming down on the side of those who say no justification from eternity and no justification without faith, saying 'except in the case of children'. If we look a little closer at this 'except in the case of children' group, we find nothing that might indicate that their views of justification come any where near the standard of John Gill. Some believe that all children are automatically in a justified state whatever might happen to them later. Others belief as W. G. T. Shedd who says in his *Calvinism Pure & Mixed*[289] that 'The Protestant Church understands the Bible to declare that all who die in infancy die regenerate'. We would then presume that Shedd believes that they all die justified. Others believe that only the children of covenant members are justified. Others say that this exception applies only to elect children. Yet others argue that this anomaly only refers to children who have not yet reached 'the age of understanding'. This latter argument is strange indeed as what human, young or old, understands the ways of God, especially considering his fallen state?

The mentally retarded are allegedly exceptions

Others who deny Gill's doctrine argue that not only children are exempt from their ruling but all adults who are mentally ill or educationally subnormal. Again, the difficulty is to define what 'mentally ill' or 'educationally subnormal' is or if the terms have any absolute meaning at all. Once more, this is indicating that it is our understanding that deprives us of God's justification. Furthermore, the same problems attached to children's salvation without faith apply to mentally retarded adults. Are all justified? Are only those within covenant families justified or merely the elect who are handicapped in this way?

---

[289] Op. cit. p. 127.

Heathens with a good conscience are allegedly exceptions
Others, such as W. G. T. Shedd, go a step further and declare that all
the heathen who have 'the law written in their hearts' which he
associates with a good conscience, will be saved, i.e. justified. Shedd
seems to be arguing that such people will far outnumber those who have
come to faith through the preaching of the gospel of Jesus Christ. He
calls this mass conversion of those who have never heard of Christ, the
'Larger Hope'.

Making exceptions the norm
As most of Gill's critics believe in one or all of these exceptions or
anomalies, which in terms of number would appear to outnumber those
saved by the usual Biblical pattern of preaching Christ, one wonders
why they find Gill's doctrine of God justifying the ungodly from
eternity 'un-Biblical'. Furthermore, if these people are prepared to
believe that God's saving love extends to all the immature, ignorant,
mentally sick and great masses of heathens, why exclude those who Gill
argues on strong Scriptural grounds are justified from eternity? After
all, God must justify us from somewhere, otherwise we must postulate
that God is nowhere, and as God dwells in eternity, that is the place
where we would expect Him to justify us. Speaking of God the Father
and the Son who are both designated Alpha and Omega because they
are both from eternity and both One, Goodwin relates how all matters
of grace, salvation and our peace relate comprehensively to the eternity
of God and that:

> Thus God is the immediate forger of every link of that golden
> chain, whereof the first is riveted in His own heart, and the last
> ends in Him also. Thus it is in His loving us, and thus it is in His
> saving us; He is the first and the last in both.[290]

Taken to its logical conclusion, however, the argument that rejects
justification from eternity as dogmatically as it allows for many and

---

[290] *Of the Object and Acts of Justifying Faith*, p. 39.

massive exceptions, would prove so much that it would disprove itself and present us with universal salvation. Shedd believes that the salvation of all dying infants amounts to 'one half of the human family' alone. If the too young, the ignorant, the undeveloped, the simple and the seriously mentally ill are exempt from being justified after faith, what about those who are dead in trespasses and sin and are really disabled and completely lack any mental, physical or moral power to reach an 'age of understanding' where they can not only comprehend but choose God so that they might be justified? Ought not then those who plead for exceptions exempt all from the need to display faith before they are justified? This is not the way God has chosen, but He has chosen a way that nevertheless recognises that all men are equally unsaveable. The Father's love for His Son and Christ's love for His Bride and the Spirit's love of illuminating the darkened fallen soul, have in their own good counsel, chosen from eternity to elect the, naturally speaking, unelectable and save a Bride who has, naturally speaking, no love for her Husband until that Husband displays His justifying and redeeming love to her.

Being merciful by fits
This was the phrase the Puritans used for those of their critics who argued against the immutability of God and who put forward the theory that Christ did not love His Bride from eternity but began to love her when she was loveable, i.e. after she had shown faith in believing. This is one of the main arguments today constantly levelled against Gill and the whole doctrine of God's covenant love for His people. God cannot love elect sinners because His wrath lies on them. These critics are obviously far less gracious than God. Thomas Goodwin used to ask such critics whether they thought God was a mere man who became merciful merely when the good humour came upon Him and something titillated Him into action. He used to tell such doubters that God is 'my strong habitation whereunto I may continually resort: thou hast given commandment to save me; for thou art my rock and my fortress' (Psalm 71:3). Believing strongly that God's mercies are coeval with His graces and that all election blessings have their eternal place in God's will, Goodwin argued:

Now, as his (God's) being, so these his mercies are from everlasting; for both Jehovah and merciful are still correspondent: Psalm 25:6, 'Remember, O Lord, thy tender mercies, and thy loving-kindnesses; for they have been ever of old.' They are mercies as to time past, which the word 'remember' insinuates; and they are his special mercies to his elect, which with difference he styleth his, 'tender mercies'; and they are his, loving-kindnesses, which word imports his entirest love, as Psalm 18:2. The same word signifies to love heartily in the midst of the bowels. And these have been, ever of old; and that not only as of a time of an old date, and so the word is elsewhere used, but these have been for ever of old; it is that oldness of eternity. They are as old as Jehovah himself, the 'Ancient of days', is. And why? Because they are the mercies of him that is Jehovah. And thus we find his everlasting love stated in difference from what is of old: Jeremiah 31:3, the Lord hath 'appeared to me of old'. This the church says, that is, in ancient times, in former times; ah, but appears not new to me. In answer thereto says God, Dost thou speak of times of old? Yea, 'I have loved thee with an everlasting love,' &c., and so of an elder date than that old time thou speakest of, in which I should have appeared to thee. And thus here our translators have emphatically translated the words, for ever of old.

But what, are they everlasting only from time past? No; but as Jehovah imports his being to everlasting also, so his mercies are: Psalm 100:5, 'The Lord is good, his mercy is everlasting, and his truth endureth to all generations.' And the eternity in this place is that part of it for time to come, for it is from generation to generation. And as we find the everlastingness of them either way thus singly and apart set out in these Psalms mentioned, so we find them in Psalm 103:17 to be conjoined, 'The mercy of the Lord is from everlasting to everlasting upon them that fear him.'

So, then, Jehovah that was, that is, and that is to come, is merciful and gracious.

And this speaks more than what is in the former assertion; for by this he is not simply the first in grace, and so in mercy to us: that might have been, though he had begun to have loved but then when he first wrought on us, or as having purposed it from some very ancient date; but this imports his having ever loved us since he was God, and had being, or shall have being, both his own nature inclining him, together with his purposes of mercy taken up by his own will towards us. For he would have his mercies unto his children to bear the resemblance of his very being Jehovah, and so answer to his name in being as eternal as himself: Isaiah 54: 7, 8, 10, 'For a small moment have I forsaken thee; but with great mercies will I gather thee. In a little wrath I hid my face from thee for a moment; but with everlasting kindness will I have mercy on thee, saith the Lord thy Redeemer. For the mountains shall depart, and the hills be removed; but my kindness shall not depart from thee, neither shall the covenant of my peace be removed, saith the Lord that hath mercy on thee.'[291]

The teaching here is plain. God loves His people from eternity but He has a short period when He hides His face because of their sin until the time when His great mercies in Christ pour into their lives in the fulfilling of His covenant plan of salvation. Actually, the fact of God's loving the elect in union with Christ as their Father but still condemning them in Adam as their offended Judge, pervades all the doctrines of salvation, whatever they are and is in no way merely existent in justification. Those who have such problems with justification will have them with all aspects of the atonement and with Christ's purpose in dying for His elect. They will have them with man before conversion and with man after conversion. Referring to the great chapter on reconciliation, Romans 5, Smeaton, pointing out that reconciliation was worked out in the atonement and not on the basis of a moral change in man, deals with the very same problem i.e. that critics argue that God cannot love the elect and be wrathful at the same time. Of course He can, says Smeaton:

To this, however, it is urged as an objection, that such a mode of viewing reconciliation makes us at once enemies and friends: and it is said, Can we regard God as both hating and loving us: as evincing displeasure, and concerting the means of taking us into favour? This difficulty vanishes when we come to see that

---

[291] *Of the Object and Acts of Justifying Faith*, pp. 40, 41.

love and wrath well enough consist together, because men are presented to His view both as the creatures of His hand, and as sinners, yet the objects of His grace. He had wrath and enmity against their sin, according to His holy nature and the inalienable claims of justice; but He had love to His creatures, and a disposition to do them good. And the atonement, as an arrangement interposed between divine wrath on the one hand, and the sinful human race on the other, was the removal of all the impediments that stood in the way of the divine love. The text shows that free love provided the atonement, but that men were actually taken into favour on the ground of satisfaction.[292]

A changeless God is out of fashion
Although viewing God as unchanging in His attributes, and eternal in His saving love, has become unpopular amongst so-called 'evangelical Calvinists' in recent years, it does not take a great deal of detective work to discover that the strongest influence on these people comes from extra-Calvinist sources and is based on an ancient heresy and secular thinking as hinted above. The view of Hugo Grotius that all God's revelation is a mere product of time and shows God's arbitrary will in time which does not, of necessity, show what is permanent Natural Law or even the character of God Himself, has entered modern Reformed evangelical teaching via the seventeenth century Latitudinarians, the so-called New Philosophy and New Divinity Schools and Fullerism. These all teach a Scriptural revelation that is temporary and does not reflect the true mind of God but is a kind of theological allegory, metaphor or figure of speech which assists man to come to a knowledge of the 'nature and fitness of things' by separating the 'spiritual' from the 'letter'. This tendency is also clearly seen in Pink's book *The Satisfaction of Christ*, written in his less mature days, in which he spends the opening chapters speculating on the alternative ways God could have saved sinners. His extremely strong language against those with whom he disagrees on such a speculative and metaphysical subject is quite astonishing. He terms it 'nigh unto blasphemy', for instance, for anyone to suggest that God used the 'only way' possible to save

---

[292] *Atonement According to Christ and His Apostles*, Smeaton, p. 73 Second Part.

sinners.[293] It is obvious that Pink does not share the Grotian view that the atonement was a mere sham to act as a moral deterrent but his teaching does leave the reader wondering if Pink is suggesting that God unnecessarily sacrificed His Son as He could have provided a different, if not easier, way. Pink's assurance that there is a philosophical difference between 'necessity' and 'absolute necessity' does not help the reader find a Biblical basis for his wild speculation as to what God could have done but did not do in his chapter 'The Atonement. Its Necessity.' Like the views of Grotius, however, Pink's speculations empty Mrs Alexander's well-known hymn *There is a Green Hill Far Away*, of all its Scriptural doctrine concerning the uniqueness of Christ:

> There was no other good enough
> To pay the price of sin.
> He only could unlock the gate
> Of Heaven and let us in.

The whole exercise reminds us of Fuller's attempts to defend his 'positive' view of revelation based on the idea that God's revelation is not 'absolute' but merely an arbitrary method of influencing His creatures for the best. Furthermore, the fact that nearly all of the influential handful of Gill and Huntington's harsh, modern critics profess to following Fuller as a 'theological genius' and 'the greatest theologian of the century' and are willing to excuse all Fuller's many departures from Scriptural truths by saying he wishes to 'guard against' their abuse, speaks volumes. As yet, such writers have not come up with an alternative view of justification which would appeal to traditional Calvinists who believe in:

a. The true fall of man from a perfect, eternal Adam to a sinful, mortal creature as opposed to the doctrine of an imperfect and sin-prone progenitor created to fall.

b. A total fall as opposed to a partial fall as, for instance, taught by Fuller in his doctrine of man's 'inclinations'.

c. The elects' eternal union with Christ as opposed to a union wrought in time.

---

[293] *The Satisfaction of Christ*, p. 33.

d. The eternal love of God for His people as opposed to a common saving love for all without distinction which comes to naught in the case of many.

e. Actual atonement as opposed to hypothetical universalism which destroys the Biblical doctrine of salvation.

f. A particular and limited atonement as opposed to the modern 'evangelical Calvinist' idea of an atonement only rendered effective on application or by the already-believer's reception. Here again, Fullerites take the lead in this downgrading of doctrine by following the teaching of *The Gospel Worthy of All Acceptation*, and refusing to preach particular atonement as it is not part of the gospel rule.[294]

g. Actual justification, and actual imputation as opposed to figurative justification and imputation where the sinner is merely pardoned but left in his guilt and sin so that neither justification nor imputation has really taken place.

h. Penal substitution as opposed to a token substitution in which Christ was neither called upon to fulfil the law on our behalf, nor was He truly punished on our behalf.

i. Actual ransom as opposed to a token ransom in which Christ paid a full, equivalent compensation in order to free us from the bondage of sin.

j. The doctrine that God's revelation actually reveals what is permanently His character and will.

k. The doctrine of the Oneness of wills in the Trinity as opposed to the Banner of Truth's recent allegations that the Father and the Son have conflicting wills.

l. The unity of the Scriptures as opposed to the Banner of Truth's and David Gay's recent claims that Scripture is not only paradoxical but irreconcilable with itself.

m. The comforting doctrines of predestination and election as opposed to refusing to preach on them because of a false notion that they are not part of God's word and ought to remain the 'secret things of God'.[295]

---

[294] See Fuller's *Works*, vol. ii, p. 374.

[295] Ibid. p. 374 where Fuller speaks of sinners as having 'no natural impossibility as to a compliance' with the gospel and therefore particular redemption and election should

These great doctrines were all taught by our fathers in Christ, including Gill, but where is their like today amongst those who profess to be leaders in Israel? It is as if the cream has been taken away from the Church in order to prevent the whole from going rancid.

Where is a better teaching than those who took the old paths?
Nor have these 'Moderate Calvinists', to use another self-imposed name, come up with a teaching on righteousness, holiness and sanctification which betters that of such writers as Crisp, Perkins, Sibbes, Chauncey, Ames, Hoornbeeck, Witsius, Bunyan, Goodwin, Twisse, Traill, Davis, Alting, Maccovius, Pemble, Gill, Toplady, Hervey, Ryland Sen., Brine, Romaine, Huntington, Hawker, Gadsby, Tiptaft and Philpot, writers and preachers they are constantly criticising. Nor by their repeated denunciations of godly, Bible-believing men of a holy walk by labelling them 'Antinomians' and 'Hyper-Calvinist' have they impressed others concerning their own resolution to keep the law and not bear false-witness and live holy, blameless lives. The extreme one-sidedness of these modern critics of phantom-Antinomianism and make-believe Hyper-Calvinism is apparent from the way they are attacking the memory of Gill and Brine. These men were peace-makers to a high degree, intervening wherever strife arose so that the brethren could live in harmony with one another. John Ryland Sen. testified that the one big reason why the Particular Baptists did not fall apart as some other denominations was the uniting agency of John Gill. The facts also show that Gill and Brine were honoured, indeed, treasured, amongst other denominations as Masters in Israel, the Evangelicals of the Church of England, in particular, paying them high tribute. There was never such a man of peace as Anglican James Hervey but he looked to both Gill and Brine as his mentors. Anyone reading Anglican Erasmus Middleton's fine biography of Gill in his *Biographia Evangelica* will soon find out how free Gill was from the all too usual denominational narrow-mindedness. When that great scourge the 'Modern Question', hit the churches, removing particular atonement out of their polite vocabulary and splitting them down the middle with the new Liberalism

---

be dropped from preaching. It seems that such doctrines would convince the sinner that his natural abilities were not so natural and not so able, after all!

which came with it, it was Brine of all people who stood in the middle of the parties, urging them to put Christ first and rejoice in that union rather than quarrel with the brethren over definitions of faith which were becoming more and more legal, metaphysical and un-experimental as the debate went on. Then came Andrew Fuller who saw nothing of a Christian nature in those who took the so-called High Side of the Modern Question debate and thus quarrelled not only with the memory of Gill, Brine and Hervey but with those living members of Christ, with whom he should have been rejoicing in such blessed unity, such as Booth, Button, Kinghorn, Beddome, John Martin, Dan Taylor and a host of other men made known to readers through Fuller's controversial works. Now, it seems that modern Fullerites are pointing a finger at the very peace-makers themselves and saying sanctimoniously, 'Depart from me, for I never knew thee.' One hopes and prays that those they oppose will not forget their Christian witness and responsible duties to these 'exclusive' brethren and react as they have done.

Looking for a Biblical pattern worth adopting
This author must confess that due to such worldly behaviour from those who are so quick to cry 'Antinomian!' he has been driven to delve deeper into the works of Gill because there he finds standards of doctrine that Gill's critics lack to a severe degree. Gill also presents a pattern of righteousness, and lived it out in his own life, which can only be highly recommended—especially to his critics. Gill's works reveal a sure and certain call to preach the Word to the conversion and edification of souls, rightly dividing the Word concerning the whole law and the whole gospel as a workman who need not be ashamed. He is a vowed opponent of the Latitudinarianism, Neo-Platonism, Neonomianism, Socinianism and Fullerism which are striving to flood into modern evangelicalism thus stifling its gospel-nature. Such preaching as Gill's is coupled with a sturdy assurance that it is the sure way God has chosen to call out His elect from the world. This is quite absent from Gill's modern opponents who base their theory of Christian ministry on the view that preaching the gospel is telling sinners that they ought to love God as if they had never apostatised and exercise a saving faith which they have either not yet been given or may never

receive.[296] The following tiny section of general evangelical articles from Gill's pen, may suffice to prompt readers to find new treasures based on the old doctrines of salvation and to turn the gaze of many a doubting Thomas to the refreshing gospel truths contained in Gill's preaching. It is to be hoped that this will encourage the reader to dig deeper into the many great works which gave John Gill the name Mr Voluminous.

---

[296] See Fuller's *Works*, vol. ii., The Gospel Worthy of All Acceptation, an appeal for the exercise of 'legal faith,' especially pp. 375, 376.

Appendix I

A Sermon Sample:
On The Knowledge Of Faith Which Justifies

SERMON XXV.
A KNOWLEDGE OF CHRIST,
AND OF INTEREST IN HIM,

THE SUPPORT OF A BELIEVER
IN LIFE AND IN DEATH.

A Discourse occasioned by the Death of Mr Joshua Hayes.

2 TIMOTHY 1:12

I know whom I have believed, and am persuaded that he is able to keep that which I have committed unto him against that day.

The occasion of my reading these words, at this time is the decease of Mr Joshua Hayes, late member of this church of Christ: who frequently made use of them, and expressed his faith in a living Redeemer by them. It was therefore thought, by his friends, that they would be very suitable for the subject of a Funeral Discourse; in compliance with whose request, I have read them unto you.

In the 9th and 10th verses of this chapter, we have the sum and substance of the everlasting gospel; which lies in salvation by the free grace of God (in distinction from the works of men), according to the eternal purpose of God, and the wise scheme of things formed in the divine mind from everlasting: where it was a secret and hidden thing, but now made manifest by the appearance of our Lord Jesus Christ in our nature; who by his obedience, sufferings, and death, hath abolished death, and brought life and immortality to light through the gospel. All this you will see in the verses I have referred to, which run thus: *Who hath saved us, and called us with an holy calling, not according to our works, but according to his own purpose and grace, which was given us in Christ Jesus, before the world began; but is now made manifest by the appearing of our Saviour Jesus Christ, who hath abolished death, and hath brought life and immortality to light, through the gospel.* Which exactly agrees with what the apostle elsewhere affirms, that we are saved *by grace not by works, lest any man should boast.*[297] And that those, who are the chosen of God are *blessed with all spiritual blessings in heavenly things in Christ Jesus; according as he hath chosen us in him, before the foundation of the world.*[298] Christ incarnate is become the High Priest of these great things laid up in the everlasting purpose, covenant, and promise of God: and has abolished death, even corporal death, as a penal evil, and destroyed the second death, so that it shall have no power over those whom he has redeemed by his precious blood: and by his obedience, sufferings and death, hath opened a way for them to enjoy eternal life. He came that we might have life, and that we might have it more abundantly.[299] This is a compendium of the grace of the gospel; of that gospel, of which the apostle says he was appointed a preacher. And a gospel preacher indeed he was. Never was the gospel more freely, fully, faithfully, and powerfully or constantly preached, than it was by him. He was appointed to this work from all eternity. He was a chosen vessel of salvation (as the Lord himself says) to bear his

---

[297] Ephesians 2:9.
[298] Ephesians 1:3, 4.
[299] John 10:10.

name among the Gentiles.[300] He was also appointed by a gospel church at Antioch: for, said the Spirit of God in the prophets there, *Separate me Barnabas and Saul for the work whereunto I have called them.*[301] He was an apostle of Jesus Christ, and had all the signs of apostleship in him. *An apostle, not of men, neither by man, but by Jesus Christ:*[302] sent forth, commissioned and qualified by him for the important work of preaching the everlasting gospel. And particularly he was, as he said, a teacher of the Gentiles: for though all the apostles and ministers of the word were included in the same commission, and commanded to go into all nations, teaching and baptizing them in the name of the Father, and of the Son, and of the Holy Ghost; yet our apostle had a special and particular commission to preach the gospel among the Gentiles. As the gospel of the circumcision was committed to Peter (for he was the person more particularly pitched upon to preach the gospel to the circumcised Jews), so Paul was particularly pitched upon to preach among the Gentiles the unsearchable riches of Christ. And it is not easy to say, to how many nations he was sent, and among whom he preached the gospel, and among whom he was made successful in founding and raising churches for the honour and glory of God.

Now, on the account of this his office, and the faithful execution of it, he met with much persecution. *For the which cause* (says he), *I also suffer these things;*[303] for he was at this time a prisoner at Rome. Again, he says, *I suffer trouble as an evil doer, even unto bonds; but the word of God is not bound. Therefore I endure all things for the elects' sake, that they may also obtain the salvation which is in Christ Jesus, with eternal glory.* And this was no other than what he always expected wherever he came. He knew, from the nature of things, and from divine appointment, that bonds and afflictions awaited him wherever he went; and he cheerfully endured them for the good of souls, and the glory of the divine name. *For the which cause, I also suffer these things*, verse 12; that is, for being a preacher of the gospel, an apostle of Christ: he was hated by Jews and Gentiles on this account: of the Jews, partly because he preached the gospel, and partly because he preached it to the

---

[300] Acts 9:15.
[301] Acts 13:2.
[302] Galatians 1:1.
[303] 2 Timothy 1:12.

Gentiles, that they might be saved; than which nothing more provoking to them. Hated by the Gentiles, because they thought he introduced a new religion among them, and that he was a setter up of strange Gods, because he preached unto them Jesus and the resurrection;[304] because his ministry tended to the demolishing of idolatry and superstition amongst them. Wherefore he was hated by them, and endured the things he did; to all which he was appointed, as well as to be a preacher of the gospel. *Nevertheless*, (he adds) *I am not ashamed*. Not ashamed of the sufferings I endure in a righteous cause: not ashamed of the gospel, for which I suffer these things, which is the power of God unto salvation. Nor am I ashamed of Christ, the sum and substance of this gospel; not ashamed of my faith in him, nor of my hope of eternal life and salvation by him; for hope makes not ashamed.[305] Now the ground of all this, lies in the words I have read: *For I know whom I have believed; and I am persuaded that he is able to keep that which I have committed unto him, against that day.* This was the foundation of the apostle's joy and comfort, of the satisfaction of soul, and serenity of mind, which he enjoyed amidst all the sufferings he endured for the sake of the gospel. He had believed in the Lord Jesus Christ. He knew the object in whom he had believed. He knew him at first conversion; and had, throughout the whole of his ministrations, committed his natural life, and the preservation of it, into the hands of a good God, and a blessed Redeemer. He was therefore easy, come what would. Whatever suffering he endured, he knew all was safe. *I know whom I have believed.* I know he will never leave me, nor forsake me; he will preserve and bring me safe to his everlasting kingdom and glory, where I shall enjoy the crown of righteousness, which the Lord, the righteous Judge, shall give me at that day.[306]

And that which was the ground and support of him, under all his trials and exercises, may be, and often is, the support of the people of God under all their trials and exercises; or what gives them relief under their present troubles, and in the view of an eternal world. This will better appear, and we shall have a clearer understanding thereof, by enquiring into, and observing the following things.

---

[304] Acts 17:18.
[305] Romans 5:5.
[306] 2 Timothy 4:8.

I. Who the object of the apostle's faith was, or who it was he believed and trusted his all with; *I know whom I have believed, or trusted.*
II. The knowledge he had of this object of Faith whom he believed and trusted. *I know*, &c.
III. The persuasion he had of the ability of this person he had believed in, to keep what he had committed to him against a certain day.
IV. The support this was to him in his present circumstances, and in the view of death and eternity, which he saw was near at hand; for he says in a following passage, *I am now ready to be offered, and the time of my departure is at hand.*[307]

I. Let us consider who it was that was the object of the apostle's faith, and is the object of the faith of every true believer. Now this can be no other than our Lord Jesus Christ. How often do we hear him speak of his faith in our Lord Jesus Christ! This was the constant course of his spiritual life. This he assures us himself. *I am crucified with Christ, nevertheless I live: yet not I, but Christ liveth in me: and the life which I now live in the flesh I live by the faith of the Son of God, who loved me, and gave himself for me.*[308] From hence it is clear, that the object he believed in, or trusted, was the Son of God: the Messiah: the Lord Jesus Christ. And he is the object of every true believer's faith, and ought to be so. Our Lord himself directs unto it when he says to his disciples, *Ye believe in God, believe also in me.*[309] There is the same reason to believe in Christ as in God the Father because he is equally God with him; so is as proper an object of faith as the first person in the blessed Trinity. And it is unto him that souls, made sensible of their lost state and condition by nature, are encouraged to look, to believe in, and exercise faith upon, as you will observe in the instance of the Jailor. When he came in trembling and said, 'Sirs, what shall I do to be saved?' they answer at once, *'Believe on the Lord Jesus Christ, and thou shalt be saved.'*[310]

---

[307] 2 Timothy 4:6.
[308] Galatians 2:20.
[309] John 14:1.
[310] Acts 16:31.

Christ is the object of a sensible sinner's trust: the object of a true believer's faith in the business of salvation. But then let us enquire a little into the nature of this faith he exercises upon him. It is not to be considered as a mere *historical* faith: a bare assent to a set of propositions concerning Christ, his person, offices, and the like; no, the devils have a faith; they have a creed, and in many respects a more orthodox one too than some that call themselves Christians. The devils believe that there is a God, and that there is one God; though they tremble at it. They know and believe, that Jesus Christ is the Holy One of God; yea, that he is the Son of God, and that he is the Christ, the Anointed of the Lord, sent into the world to be the Saviour of men. All this they believe, and a great deal more that they are obliged to believe, and cannot help it, concerning the Son of God; but this is not the faith of God's Elect. There are some weak people in our days that talk of a bare belief of the simple truth, and call this, faith in Christ Jesus; but it falls greatly short of it. For a man may have all faith of this kind, may believe every thing that is proposed and revealed in the word of God, and yet not have that faith which is of the operation of God.

Special faith is a spiritual thing. It is a spiritual sight of Christ. Yea, faith is the eye of the soul, the enlightened eye of the soul, opened by the Spirit of God, to see the glory, the excellency, there is in our Lord Jesus Christ: to see his glory as the glory of the only begotten of the Father full of grace and truth: to see him as the able, willing, all-sufficient, and most suitable Saviour. Faith is said to be the evidence of things not seen. It has a sight of unseen things, as of the unseen Saviour; and in its continual and constant actings is a looking unto Jesus. Looking off from every other object (a man's own righteousness, and every thing else) unto Jesus Christ the Lord our righteousness, as the living Redeemer, the only and all-sufficient Saviour. It is no other than a soul's going out of itself to Christ, to lay hold upon him, and trust in him for everlasting life and happiness. Expressed often by a coming to him, influenced by his Spirit and grace, and the declarations of grace he makes, saying, *Come unto me all ye that labour and are heavy laden, and I will give you rest.*[311] And *all that the Father giveth me shall come to me; and him that cometh to me I will in no wise cast out.*[312] A poor

---

[311] Matthew 11:28.
[312] John 6:37.

sinner, sensible of his wretched lost state by nature, and of what he deserves, is encouraged to go out of himself to lay hold on Christ, who is the tree of life to them that lay hold upon him. It is, I say, a going forth and laying hold of Christ, under a sight of sin and a sense of danger, of ruin and destruction without him. Some people in our days talk of faith as a very easy thing—only believe—only believe, say they; but it is to be feared these persons that talk in this manner, and make such an easy thing of believing in Christ, never saw their lost state by nature, the sinfulness of sin, and the ruin and destruction that it brings: never saw themselves upon the precipice of hell, dropping as it were into everlasting damnation. Let a person be in these circumstances, and then let him tell me, whether it is an easy thing for him to believe in Christ for life and salvation: and yet this is done, and herein lies the trial of faith. This shews the genuineness of it, when a soul under a sense of all its iniquities, with all their aggravating circumstances, demerits and deserts, can venture his soul upon Christ. Give me this man. It is he that knows what it is to believe in the Lord Jesus Christ. But he finds a great many discouragements, doubts, and fears; a thousand objections before he can do this. He does not find it a very easy thing: it is a work of almighty power and efficacious grace.

It was under such a sense of sin as I have mentioned, that the apostle trusted in Christ; and he considers that grace as *exceeding abundant* which communicated faith and love to his soul who had been before a blasphemer, a persecutor, and injurious, 1 Timothy 1:13, 14. And his faith arose to a full assurance, as the words of our text expresses; and elsewhere he says, *The life I live in the flesh is by the faith of the Son of God, who loved me and gave himself for me.*[313] He had a firm belief of interest in Christ: an assurance of faith in Christ. And it is what the Lord is pleased to grant unto some of his children that have not that share of grace and gifts as that great man had; *Let us* (he says) *draw near with a true heart.*[314] He does not mean himself only, and his fellow apostles, or men of the highest gifts and character in the church; but the children of God in general; believers in common: *Let* us, all of us, draw near to God *with a true heart, in a full assurance of faith*. In full assurance of the object of faith prayed unto; that he is, and that he is a rewarder of

---

[313] Galatians 2:20.
[314] Hebrews 10:22.

them that diligently seek him. In full assurance of having those petitions put up unto him that are agreeable to his will answered; in full assurance of a Mediator between God and man, and of an interest in his prevailing mediation and intercession; 'Let us draw near with true hearts in full assurance of faith', by the blood of Jesus. For that is the ground and foundation of all assurance: even the precious blood of Jesus, shed for many for the remission of sins.

Now this faith, whether in a higher or in a lower degree, as to the principle of it, is of *God*. It is not of a man's self; no, it is by the *grace* of God, and the *power* of God, that it is wrought. *All men have not faith*:[315] no, far from it. The greater part appear to have none, no true faith; and it is to be feared, that many that talk of it, are destitute of it, and know not what the thing is. And they that have it, have it not of themselves: *By grace are ye saved, through faith; and that not of yourselves, it is the gift of God*.[316] Hence our Lord says, *No man can come unto me*, (that is, believe in me) *except it be given unto him of my Father*.[317] Special faith is a gift of God's grace; and it is of the operation of the Spirit of God in the soul. He works it there. It is he that gives this spiritual eye, the eye of faith; which communicates light to the understanding, and enables the soul to go out of itself to Christ, and venture upon him for life and salvation. It is the fruit and effect of electing grace; and therefore it is sometimes called *the faith of God's elect*.[318] It is an exceeding precious grace in all, it is *like precious faith*;[319] for those that have the least degree of it, obtain the same precious faith as the greatest and strongest believer. It is precious faith, it can never be lost; it is more precious than gold which perisheth. Gold is a very durable metal, but it perishes; but faith never does. Christ, who is the object and the author of it, he is the finisher of it; and he prays for his people, as he did for Peter, that their faith fail not. That same Spirit of grace that works faith in the soul, performs the work of faith with power upon the soul. Those that truly believe in Christ, shall most certainly receive the end of their faith, even the salvation of their souls.

---

[315] 2 Thessalonians 3:2.

[316] Ephesians 2:8.

[317] John 6:65.

[318] Titus 1:1.

[319] 2 Peter 1:1.

So much for the first thing, the object of faith; and the exercise of faith upon the object. *I know whom I have believed.*

II. I am to consider the knowledge the apostle had of the object of his faith; and which every true believer also has. *I know* whom I have believed.

Faith in Christ, is not a blind and implicit thing, a faith in an object unknown; no, it is in a known object. Faith and knowledge go together! where the one is, the other is also. Though there may be, and is, faith in an unseen Christ, that is, who is not seen with the bodily eyes; *whom having not seen, ye love; in whom, though now ye see him not, yet believing, ye rejoice with joy unspeakable, and full of glory:*[320] yet an unknown Christ can never be the object of faith. He must be known, or he can never be believed in. Our Lord said to the blind man, whom he had cured, *Dost thou believe on the Son of God?*[321] The poor man made answer, and very wisely, *Who is he, Lord, that I might believe on him?* Suggesting, that he must know him, before he could believe in him. *He* knew there was such *a* person as the Messiah, that was to come into the world as the Saviour of Sinners; but as yet he did not know him, and therefore says, *Who is he?*

There is an external knowledge and hearing that is necessary, even to a bare assent, before any can know or believe in him; *For how shall they believe in him of whom they have not heard?*[322] so there is a special knowledge necessary to special faith. And as a man's knowledge is, so is his faith: if he has only an historical knowledge of Christ, he has only an historical faith: if he has a special knowledge of Christ, he has a special faith. And as his knowledge increases, so does his faith. They that know the Lord, follow on to know him; and as they know more of him, faith grows stronger and stronger in him. *They that know thy name, will put their trust in thee.*[323] And the more a soul knows of Christ, the more will he trust him; the stronger will his faith be in him. As it is among men, the more we know a man, a friend, the greater confidence we put in him; so the more we know of Christ, and of *God* in Christ, the

---

[320] 1 Peter 1:8.
[321] John 9:35.
[322] Romans 10:14.
[323] Psalm 9:10.

stronger will our faith be in him. But then, this knowledge is not to be understood of a speculative knowledge: it is not a mere notional knowledge of Christ, of his person, his nature, and his offices: or, as he is revealed in the sacred Scriptures, as the Saviour of men; it is a more spiritual knowledge than this. Men may have a great deal of knowledge of Christ, and of things relative to him, and yet have no spiritual knowledge. They may have that kind of knowledge that may enable them to preach him to others, and plead in the great day, 'Have we not prophesied in thy name? and in thy name have cast out devils: and in thy name done many wonderful works?'[324] To whom Christ will say, 'Depart from me, I never knew you.'[325] And therefore you may depend upon it, they never knew him, notwithstanding all the knowledge they may pretend to have had; or otherwise, he would not thus address them. *Spiritual knowledge* of Christ is joined with spiritual affection to him. It is a knowledge of approbation: a knowledge of his person, as the chiefest among ten thousand. It is a knowledge of Christ as a Saviour, altogether suitable and all-sufficient; and which determines a soul at once to look to no other but him, and to say, *He also shall be my salvation.*[326] He first knows him, then believes in him, and commits his all unto him. And this is an *experimental* knowledge of Christ, which is expressed by the various senses; for there is that in the new man which answers to all the senses of the outward man. It is a *seeing* the Son, and believing on him.[327] It is a *hearing* his voice, so as to distinguish it from that of a stranger.[328] It is a *tasting* that the Lord is gracious.[329] A *handling* the word of life;[330] and a *savouring* the things of God, and not of man; *smelling* a sweet smell in Christ's garments, which smelt of myrrh, aloes, and cassia.[331] These expressions set forth the exercise of faith in Christ, on a true knowledge of him, and show that knowledge to be not merely notional, but really experimental.

---

[324] Matthew 7:22.
[325] Matthew 7:23.
[326] Job 13:16.
[327] John 6:40.
[328] John 10:4, 5.
[329] 1 Peter 2:3.
[330] 1 John 1:1.
[331] Psalm 45:8.

This is also an *appropriating* knowledge, more or less; a soul that thus knows Christ, is able to appropriate him, in a measure, to himself, and sometimes arrives to such a confidence as to point him out, and say with the church, *This is my beloved, and this is my friend.*[332] And with Thomas, *My Lord and my God!*[333] and with the apostle, *Who loved me, and gave himself for me.*[334] The nature of the expression in the text is such, as when the apostle says, *We know that if our earthly house of this tabernacle were dissolved, we have a building of God:*[335] that is, we are assured of it; it is not a mere conjectural knowledge, but a thing we are quite satisfied about. So Job expresses his faith in a living Redeemer, in such language, *I know that my Redeemer liveth.*[336]

He not only knew there was a Redeemer, and that he would appear upon the earth another day; but he knew him to be his, 'I know that my Redeemer liveth.' Every degree of knowledge has something of certainty in it, or else it would be scepticism, a mere conjectural knowledge; but this is not the case with the knowledge of true believers, they can say with the apostles, We *believe, and are sure, that thou art Christ, the Son of the living God.*[337]

This knowledge, though it is imperfect in the present state, yet it is a *growing* knowledge. There is such a thing as growing in grace, and in the knowledge of Christ, by means of the ministration of the word, and the administration of the ordinances. The path of the just is as the shining light, which shines more and more unto the perfect day. Every degree of this spiritual knowledge of Christ has salvation inseparably connected with it. *For this is life eternal, to know thee, the only true God, and Jesus Christ, whom thou hast sent.*[338] And therefore it must be the most excellent of all knowledge, which made the apostle say, *I count all things but loss for the excellency of the knowledge of Christ Jesus my Lord.*[339] What signifies what a man knows, if he does not know Christ crucified: and the way of life and salvation by him? All his

---

[332] Canticles 5:16.
[333] John 20:28.
[334] Galatians 2:20.
[335] 2 Corinthians 5:1.
[336] Job 19:25.
[337] John 6:69.
[338] John 17:3.
[339] Philippians 3:8.

knowledge in things natural, civil, or even in religious matters, is of no avail. What if his eyes are opened as Balaam's were, who saw the vision of the Almighty, and who said, he should see him (the Saviour) but not nigh? What signified all the prophetic knowledge and light he had, while he was destitute of a spiritual knowledge of Christ? Nothing short of this will be of any avail: and if a man has but this, it is enough—If he has but the smallest degree of it, he shall be saved; for *every one which seeth the Son* (it is not said, whoever has such and such a degree of spiritual sight) *and believeth on him* (even though his faith be but small) *shall have everlasting life.*[340]

Now this spiritual knowledge comes from God, as faith does; it comes from God the Father, Son, and Holy Spirit. All the three Divine Persons are concerned in communicating this spiritual light and knowledge. The Father. To him our Lord ascribes it, when he says to Peter, *Blessed art thou, Simon Barjona, for flesh and blood,* (carnal sense and reason) *hath not revealed it unto thee, but my Father, which is in heaven.*[341] Sometimes it is attributed to God the Son, *We know* (says the apostle John) *that the Son of God is come, and hath given us an understanding that we may know him that is true, and we are in him that is true, even in his Son, Jesus Christ.*[342] And sometimes to the blessed Spirit, who is styled a *Spirit of wisdom and revelation in the knowledge of Christ.*[343] And it is a special gift of God's grace, and for which we should be thankful who have any share in it.

III. We may observe the firm persuasion the apostle had of the ability of the person he had believed in, to keep what he had committed unto him against a certain day.

We will here enquire what he committed to him. Not his labours and sufferings, expecting they would hereafter be brought forth to his advantage. They were, indeed, great: but they were performed by the grace of, and through strength communicated from God. As for his sufferings, they were many indeed, more than others of his fellow-labourers in the gospel; but then he knew that the sufferings of this

---

[340] John 6:40.
[341] Matthew 16:17.
[342] 1 John 5:20.
[343] Ephesians 1:17.

present life, were not worthy to be compared to the glory that shall be revealed in him.

Rather he may mean the souls of the persons he had been instrumental in the conversion of; and we find him sometimes commending such persons to God and to the word of his grace.[344] These he committed to Christ, and believed that he would keep them, and that he should meet them as his joy and crown of rejoicing in another day: or it may be interpreted, of his natural life which he had committed into the hands of his Redeemer; who he knew would take care of it, who told him, at first setting out, not to be afraid. And he had experienced many a time, that he had saved it when in imminent danger: though it seems best of all to understand it of his precious and immortal soul, and the everlasting concerns thereof. This he committed to his dear Redeemer at first conversion, when he first knew him, and he knew he was able to keep it safe against the day here referred to. So every true believer does the like; commits and commends his immortal soul into the hands of his Redeemer, and there he leaves it.

This act of committing it to Christ, supposes knowledge. No man that is wise, will commit any thing of worth into the hands of one unknown to him; and much less will any commit his immortal soul into the hands of one unknown. No, he must know him, *they that know thy name, will put their trust in thee,*[345] and it implies the giving the preference to Christ, above all others. We may consider the apostle as looking about among all the sons of the mighty upon earth, and angels in heaven, to see whether any of those were fit to commit his soul unto, and finding none of them were, he says, *Whom have I in heaven but thee? and there is none upon earth, that I desire beside thee.* He saw an in-sufficiency in all others; that they were unequal to the task of saving his soul; that salvation was not to be hoped for from the mountains; that truly in the Lord, and in him only, was salvation to be found. Such a view have all true believers, and therefore say they, *Asshur shall not save us; we will not ride upon horses; neither will we say any more to the work of our hands, Ye are our gods; for in thee the fatherless find mercy.*[346] Each of them addresses Christ, *as* Ahab did Benhadad, *I am*

---

[344] Acts 20:32.
[345] Psalm 9:10.
[346] Hosea 14:3.

thine, and all that I have.[347] 'I give up my soul, and all that I have, to be saved in thee, with an everlasting salvation.' It denotes trusting in Christ for grace here, and glory hereafter: leaving all with him, believing that he is able to save to the uttermost, all that come unto God by him.

As to the day here referred to, this may be understood of the day of death. Death is appointed by the Lord, to every man;[348] and against this day, the apostle committed, and so every true believer commits, his soul into the hands of Christ, when he hopes to meet with the Lord, and to be for ever with him, out of all danger from every enemy. Or it may be understood of the day of the resurrection. The first resurrection. The dead in Christ shall rise first, and happy will they be; for on them the second death shall have no power, and they shall be for ever with the Lord. Or it may be understood of the day of judgment, in which they must all appear before the judgment seat of Christ, in which he will make an open acknowledgment of them, and say, 'These persons are the gift of my Father unto me: I have redeemed them with my blood; and by my grace they have been enabled to commit themselves into my hand: lo! here am I, and the children which God hath given me.'

The ground and foundation of this trust in Christ, arises from his proper *Deity*. He being God over all, blessed for evermore, it is this that encourages a soul at first, and that from the declaration Christ himself has given, *Look unto me, and be ye saved, all ye ends of the earth*; for I am GOD, *and there is none else.*[349] He being the former and the maker of all things, forming all things by the word of his power, is another argument. 'He whose hands laid the foundation of the earth, and whose right hand hath spanned the heavens', may well be considered as able to keep the soul which is committed to him against that day. He having already performed the work his Father gave him to do, is another foundation from whence this trust and confidence in him arises. He came, and his own arm has brought salvation. The work is done. He has obtained eternal redemption for all his people; and seeing it is done, what encouragement is here for a poor soul to commit himself into the hands of Christ; believing that he is able to keep him. To which may be added, the consideration of God the Father trusting Christ with the souls

---

[347] 1 Kings 20:4.
[348] Hebrews 9:27.
[349] Isaiah 45:22.

of his people. He has put all his beloved ones into the hands of his Son; he has trusted him with all their persons, grace, and glory; and he is faithful to him that appointed him, and will at last say, 'Lo! here am I, and the children which thou hast given me.' 'Well then', (may a soul say) 'if God the Father hath trusted him with thousands of souls, surely I may trust him with mine. If he hath been faithful to him that appointed him, in keeping the souls that were committed to him; I may believe that he will keep mine.'

IV. I pass on now to the last thing, namely, that this is the support of every true believer, in life and in death; that they know whom they have believed. This was the apostle's support under all his trials, afflictions, and sufferings, for the sake of the gospel. Hear his own words, *For the which cause I also suffer these things; nevertheless, I am not ashamed.*[350] 'I am easy under them, I know whom I have believed.' So let the believer's afflictions and sufferings be what they will, if he knows whom he has believed, he is sure that they will all work together for his good; that ere long he shall be free from them, and be for ever with the Lord, into whose hands he has committed his immortal soul. This the apostle knew, that though men were able to kill the body, they could not reach the soul. That was in the hands of Christ, and therefore it was safe; bound up in the bundle of life; hid with Christ in God; laid and built upon that Rock of Ages, against which the gates of hell shall never prevail. The apostle was now in the view of death and eternity; and this was his support in the view of an eternal world. And the same upholds every true believer, more or less. O what a support must this be to a dying saint, that though he is leaving the world, and all things in it; though he has no more an interest in his worldly substance, relations, friends, and acquaintance, and soul and body are parting, yet still his interest in a blessed Redeemer continues! He knows whom he has believed. When flesh and heart, and every thing else fails him, God is the strength of his heart, and his portion for ever. Christ is his Redeemer and Saviour; who is the same yesterday, today, and for ever. What a supporting consideration must this be to him; that when he is brought to the streams of Jordan's river, that blessed Redeemer, who has been his God and guide through life, will not leave him now; but will be with

---

[350] 2 Timothy 1:12.

him through the valley of the shadow of death; therefore he fears no evil. Now he is not at a loss for a Surety and Saviour; he knows whom he has believed. He knows the Lord his Righteousness; and that he has a righteousness in him that will answer for him in time to come. How delightful the thought, when he is just upon the borders of another world, that now he is departing from hence, to be for ever with the Lord! to be lodged in those mansions his Saviour and Redeemer is gone before to prepare for him; that he may be with him where he is, and for ever behold his glory.

But these are but some short hints of what gracious souls more largely experience under present troubles, and in the views of death and eternity.

This knowledge of Christ was the support of our deceased friend, whose death has been the occasion of my discoursing on these words. His standing in this church has been but a short time; though an ancient professor and disciple of Jesus Christ. He belonged to other churches in the country; who gave him the character of an upright man. For the time that he hath been with us, he has behaved as one that made a good profession of the grace of God. He walked answerable to it; and appeared to have a great deal of affection to, and a liveliness in, divine and spiritual things.

In his last illness he was very comfortable. To one that visited him, he said, he had been many years walking through a dirty narrow lane; but hoped he was now come near the end of it: and he desired to depart, and be with Christ. He had no darkness nor fears upon his mind; all was bright and serene. He expressed his faith in Christ, as that foundation that will never give way: he knew whom he had believed. And so I find he continued, until he sweetly fell asleep in Jesus; and there we must leave him till the resurrection morn.

Upon the whole we may see, of what importance an interest in Christ is; to know whom we have believed, and to commit our souls to him. Of what use is this, both in life and in death! A soul may well say, 'Give me an interest in Christ, or I die.' There is no happiness without it: and a knowledge of that interest how comfortable it is! As to those of us who have made a profession, let us enquire what is the object of our faith and trust? Is it any thing of our own, or is it Jesus Christ? If we trust in a wrong object it will do us no good. We should also consider what our knowledge of Christ is, whether it is notional or experimental;

as it is the latter only which issues in eternal life. As to those of you who are trembling, doubting believers, I would say, Give not way to unbelief. Were not you enabled years ago to give up yourselves unto Christ: to venture your souls on him? And is he not the same yesterday, to-day, and for ever? Why then should you give way to an evil heart of unbelief, in departing from the living God? Leave all with him, and fear not. To conclude, what encouragement is there for poor sensible sinners, to commit their souls into the hands of Christ, who is able to save to the uttermost; and who hath assured us, that whosoever believeth in him shall not perish, but have eternal life.

Appendix II

Gill On Justification Through God's Eternal Love

From: *Of the Perseverance of the Saints*

For Gill, adoption, justification and pardon stemmed alone from the eternal love of God in Christ and were thus part and parcel of the doctrine of the perseverance of the saints, which means that they shall always continue to experience that eternal love. Explaining this doctrine, Gill writes:

> The argument in favour of the saints' final perseverance, receives great strength from the promises of God, which are sure, and are all yea and amen in Christ, and are always fulfilled; not one of the good things God has promised has ever failed; and many are his promises, as has been observed, concerning the perseverance of his people; as that they shall hold on their way, and be stronger and stronger; that he will not turn away from them; and they shall never depart from him; with a multitude of others; and, in general, he has promised, he will never leave nor forsake them: and therefore it is impossible they should perish; for then his promises and his faithfulness in them would be of none effect; which ought not to be said.

This truth may be further confirmed from the gracious acts of God, flowing from his everlasting and unchangeable love. The love of God to his people is an everlasting love, which it would not be should they perish; for none can perish and remain the objects of his love: but his love always remains, it is never taken away, nor does it ever depart, nor can there be any separation from it; and consequently those interested in it can never be finally and totally lost: and there are many acts of grace arising from this love, which show it; not to take notice of the act of election before observed, which secures their salvation; nor the covenant of grace, from the perpetuity of which this point has been argued; nor the act of putting the elect into Christ's hands, from whence they can never be plucked; there are several others which ascertain the same thing; two or three of which I shall mention.

1. The adoption of the children of God into his family; by which he takes them for his sons and daughters; which is a wonderful instance of his love, 1 John 3:1; now to this they are predestinated according to the good pleasure of his will; and this predestination and appointment of them to adoption is his will to adopt them; and his will to adopt them is the adoption of them; this is what is called a putting them among the children, Jeremiah 3:19; and whom God puts among the children, and accounts as such, it is not in the power of men or devils to put them out; nor can they put out themselves, should they even desire it, or express their contentment to be no longer sons but to be servants; it is impracticable and not to be admitted, as the case of the prodigal shows, Luke 15:19, 21; the blessing is bestowed in the covenant of his grace, and is irreversible; Christ by his redemption has made way for the reception of it, which makes his redemption a plenteous one, this with other blessings of grace, being included in it; and to them that receive him, and believe in him, he gives a power to become the sons of God; his Spirit witnesses to theirs that they are so, and by faith it becomes manifest. Now between sonship and heirship there is a close connection: if a son, no more a servant of sin and Satan, and the world, but an heir of God through Christ; if children, then heirs, heirs of God, and joint-heirs with Christ, Galatians 4:7; Romans 8:17; and can a child of

God become a child of the devil? shall an heir of heaven be seen in the flames of hell? or shall one that is a joint-heir with Christ, come short of the incorruptible inheritance? no, that is reserved for them, and they are kept to that by the power of God'—

2. Justification is another act of God's free grace, and the fruit of his ancient love, Romans 3:24 and 5:17; the sentence is pronounced in the mind of God by himself, and none can reverse it; it is God that justifies, and who shall condemn? such as are justified by him can never come into condemnation and everlastingly perish; otherwise how could he be just, and the justifier of him that believes in Jesus; if, after all, notwithstanding his imputation of the righteousness of his Son to them, and the justification of them by it, and their reception of it by faith, they should be condemned? or how would Christ's righteousness be an everlasting righteousness and answer for his people in a time to come, should they be condemned with the world and excluded from the kingdom of heaven? or how would this righteousness of his be unto justification of life? or what would signify their being made heirs of eternal life through it? or of what avail would their title to it be unto them, if after all they perish eternally? But the connection between justification and glorification is inseparable; whom he justified them he also glorified, Romans 8:30, and most certain it is, that the righteous, who are justified by Christ's righteousness shall go into everlasting life when the wicked will go into eternal punishment, Matthew 25:46.

3. Pardon of sin is another act of the riches of divine grace, and flows from unmerited and distinguishing love. Those whom God forgives for Christ's sake, on account of his blood shed for the remission of their sins, and upon the foot of satisfaction made for them by him, he forgives all their iniquities; not one sin is left unforgiven; and if so, how can they be destroyed or perish everlastingly? Is it possible that a man should go to hell with a full and free pardon of all his sins in his hands? Was ever any man executed, having received the king's pardon? and especially can it be thought that any whom the King of kings has pardoned, whose acts can never be made void, should yet suffer everlasting punishment for sin? no, when the iniquity of Israel shall be sought for, there shall be none to be laid to their charge, being

cleared of all; and the sins of Judah, and they shall not be found, nor any bill on account of them be found against them, and that for this reason; for I will pardon them whom I reserve, that is, for himself; and if reserved for himself, being fully pardoned by his grace, they shall be preserved from everlasting destruction.

The saints final perseverance in grace to glory, and security from ruin and destruction, may be concluded from the love of Christ to them, his interest in them, and theirs in him. Christ's love to them was from everlasting, his delights were with those sons of men before the world was, and from it nothing can separate them: having loved his own, which were in the world, he loves them to the end, John 13:1 to the end of their lives, and to all eternity; and therefore they can never perish. And they are not only the objects of his love, dear unto him, but they are his care and charge, who are committed to him to be kept by him; and he has undertook the care of them, has eternal life to give them, and does give it to them, and they shall never perish, but have it; yea, they have it already, a right unto it and earnest of it; and as they are his Father's gift to him, to be preserved by him, so they are the purchase of his blood, the flock he has purchased with it, and he will not lose one of them; should he, so far his blood would be shed for nought, and his death be in vain. They are members of his body, and can never be separated from it; should they, even the least member of them, his body, the church, would not be the fulness of him that filleth all in all; if any one member in a natural body should be wanting, even the least, it would not be a complete body; and this would be the case of Christ's mystical body, should any member in it perish; but as sure as Christ the head lives, so sure shall every member of his body live also, and never die. They are his children, his spiritual seed and offspring, to whom he stands in the relation of an everlasting Father; these are a seed that it is promised he shall see and enjoy for ever, and that they shall endure for ever; nor shall any one of them be missing at the great day; but Christ will present them to his Father complete and safe, who gave them to him, saying, Lo, I, and the children thou hast given me. They are his spouse and bride, whom he has betrothed to himself in loving-kindness, and that for ever, to whom he stands in the relation of an husband; and between whom there is a conjugal and indissoluble union; whom he has so loved as to give himself for, to sanctify and cleanse, and make them spotless and glorious in his sight; and after all the cost and pains he has been at to make her so, can it be thought he will suffer this choice one, and beloved spouse of his, or any of them that make up this spiritual body, to perish eternally? They are his portion, and the lot of his inheritance, his Father has given him, and he is well-pleased with; they are his jewels, and he will never lose any of them; they are a crown of glory, and a royal diadem in his hand; his Hephzibah, in whom he delights; his Beulah, to whom he is married, and he will employ all his power in the preservation and security of them. They are on him the foundation laid in Zion, which is sure and everlasting; on which all those who are laid are safe, and from whence they can never be removed by all the winds and waves, storms and tempests, raised by sin, Satan, and the world; they are built upon a rock immoveable, against which the gates of hell cannot prevail. They are interested in the intercession of Christ, which is always prevalent; for he is always heard; and he ever lives to make intercession for them; not only for all the necessary supplies of grace, for grace to help them in time of need; but for their eternal glorification, John 17:24.[351]

---

[351] *Body of Doctrinal Divinity*, vol. ii, Of the Perseverance of the Saints, pp. 894-897.

Appendix III

Of The Justice Or Righteousness Of God

CONCERNING this attribute of God, I shall,

First, Shew that it does belong to him, and is natural and essential to him. The scriptures do abundantly ascribe it to him; all rational creatures, angels and men, good and bad, acknowledge it in him, Revelation 16:5; Exodus 9:27; Jeremiah 22:3; Daniel 9:9; Psalm 145:7, and remove all unrighteousness from him, and affirm there is none in him, Psalm 92:15; Romans 9:14. And, indeed, without this attribute, he would not be fit to be the Governor of the world, and the judge of the whole earth; his government would be tyranny, and not yield that pleasure and delight to the inhabitants of it, it does; the reason of which is, because *righteousness and judgment are the habitation of his throne*, Psalm 97:1, 2. And from his love of righteousness, and constant performance of it, it may be concluded it is natural to him; as what is loved by men, and constantly done by them, shews it to be agreeable to the nature of them, Psalm 11:7 and 9:4, and, indeed, it is originally and essentially in God; it is in and of himself, and not of another; it is his nature and essence, and is not derived from another. *Adam* was righteous, but not of

311

himself, God made him upright, or righteous; saints are righteous, not by their own righteousness, but by the righteousness of Christ imputed to them. But God is righteous in and of himself; his righteousness is essential and inderivative, and is incommunicable to a creature; it is not that by which men are made righteous, as *Osiander* dreamed; for though he who is *Jehovah* is their righteousness, yet not as he is Jehovah; for then they would be deified by him: the righteousness of God being his nature, is infinite and mutable; the righteousness of angels and men, in which they were created, was mutable; *Adam* lost his, and many of the angels lost theirs; but *the righteousness of God is like the great mountains*, as high, firm, and stable as they, and much more so, Psalm 36:6. Righteousness in creatures, is according to some law, which is the rule of it, and to which it is conformed, and is adequate so the law of God, which is holy, just, and true, is a rule of righteousness to men; but God has no law without himself, he is a law to himself; his nature and will the law and rule of righteousness to him. Some things are just, because he wills them, as such that are of a posture kind; and others he wills them because they are just, being agreeable to his nature and moral perfections. This is an attribute common to the three Persons in the Godhead, as it must be, since it is essential to Deity, and they partake of the same undivided nature and essence: hence the Father of Christ is called by him *righteous Father*, John 17:25, and Christ, his Son; is called Jesus Christ the righteous, 1 John 2:1, and no doubt can be made of its being proper to the holy Spirit, who *convinces* men of *righteousness and of judgment*, John 16:8. But,

Secondly, I shall next consider the various sorts, or branches of righteousness, which belong to God; for though it is but one in him, being his nature and essence; yet it may be considered as diversified, and as admitting of distinctions, with respect to creatures. Some distinguish it into righteousness of words, and righteousness of deeds. Righteousness of words lies in the fulfilment of his words, sayings, prophecies, and promises; and is no other than his veracity, truth, and faithfulness; which will be considered hereafter, as a distinct attribute. Righteousness of deeds, is either the rectitude, purity, and holiness of his nature; which appears in all his works and actions, and which has been treated of in the preceding chapter; or it is a giving that which belongs to himself, and to his creatures, what is each their due. So justice is defined by Cicero[352], an affection of the mind, *Suum cuique tribuens*; giving to every one his own. Thus God gives or takes to himself what is his due; or does himself justice, by making and doing all things for his own glory; and by not giving his glory to another, nor his praise to graven images: and he gives to his creatures what is due to them by the laws of creation, and governs them in justice and equity, and disposes of them and dispenses to them, in the same manner. Justice, among men, is sometimes distinguished into commutative and retributive. Commutative justice lies in covenants, compacts, agreements, commerce, and dealings with one another, in which one gives an equivalent in money or goods, for what he receives of another; and when integrity and uprightness are preserved, this is justice. But such sort of justice cannot have place between God and men; what he gives, and they receive from him, is of free favour and good will; and what they give to him, or he receives from them, is no equivalent for what they have from him; *What shall I render to the Lord for all his benefits towards me?* Psalm 116:12. Nothing that is answerable to them. Besides, God has a prior right to every thing a creature has or can give; *Who hath first given to him, and it shall be recompensed to him again?* Romans 11:35. Retributive justice is a distribution either of rewards or punishments; the one may be called remunerative justice, the other punitive justice; and both may be observed in God.

1. Remunerative justice, or a distribution of rewards; the rule of which is not the merits of men, but his own gracious promise; for he first, of his own grace and good will, makes promises, and then he is just and righteous in fulfilling them; for God, as *Austin*[353] expresses it, 'makes himself a debtor, not by receiving any thing from us, but by promising such and such things to us.' And his justice lies in fulfilling his promises made to such and

---

[352] De Finibus, l. 5.
[353] Enarrat. in Psalm 109 tom. 8. p. 521.

such persons, doing such and such things; and not in rewarding any supposed merits of theirs. Thus, for instance, *The man that endures temptation shall receive the crown of life, which the Lord has promised to them that love him*, James 1:12. But the crown of life is not given according to any merit of it arising from enduring temptation, or loving the Lord; but in consequence of the promise of God graciously made to such persons, for their encouragement thereunto. Moreover, the reward is not of debt, but of grace; or God, in the distribution of rewards to men, rewards not their works, but his own grace; he first gives grace, and then rewards that grace with glory; called, *the reward of the inheritance*, Colossians 3:24. And this seems to be no other than the inseparable connection between grace and glory, adopting grace, and the heavenly inheritance; which, he having of his own grace put, does in justice inviolably maintain. Indeed, the remunerative justice of God is sometimes represented in scripture, as rendering to every man according to his deeds, or as his work shall be, Romans 2:5-7, 10; Revelation 22:12. But still it is to be observed, that the reward given or rendered, is owing to the promise that is made to them for godliness, whether as a principle of grace, or as practised under the influence of grace; or godly persons have *the promise of the life that now is, and of that which is to come*, 1 Timothy 4:8, which promise is punctually and righteously performed. Besides, God does not reward the works and godly actions of men, as meritorious in themselves; but as they are the fruits of his own grace; who works in them both *to will and to do* of his own pleasure; and therefore he is *not unrighteous to forget their work and labour of love*; which springs from love, is done in faith, and with a view to his glory, Hebrews 6:10. Moreover, the works according to which God renders eternal life, are not men's own personal works; between which, and eternal life, there is no proportion; but the works of righteousness done by Christ, of which his obedience and righteousness consist; and which being done by him, on their account, as their Head and Representative, are reckoned to them; and, according to these, the crown of righteousness is given them by the Lord, as a righteous Judge, in a way of righteousness, 2 Timothy 4:8.

2. Punitive, or vindictive justice, belongs to God; *It is a righteous thing with God to render tribulation to them that trouble his people*, 2 Thessalonians 1:6. and so to inflict punishment for any other sin committed by men; and this has been exercised by him in all ages from the beginning of the world; and has appeared in casting down from heaven to hell the angels that sinned; in drowning the old world; in destroying *Sodom* and *Gomorrah*; in the plagues on *Egypt*, on *Pharaoh* and his host; the righteousness of which was acknowledged, in some of the instances of it, by that wicked king, Exodus 9:27, in the several captivities of the Jews, and in the destruction of that people; and in the judgments of God on many other nations, in several periods of time; and as will be seen in the destruction of antichrist and the antichristian states; the righteousness of which will be ascribed to God by the angel of the waters, and by all his people, Revelation 16:5, 6, and 19:1, 2, and in the eternal punishment and everlasting destruction of ungodly men: and this righteousness is natural and essential to God; but this the Socinians deny, because they do not choose to embrace the doctrine of the necessity of Christ's satisfaction for sin, which, if granted, they must give into. But that punitive, or vindictive justice, is essential to God, or that he not only will not let sin go unpunished, but that he cannot but punish sin, is manifest,

1. From the light of nature: hence the accusations of the natural conscience in men for sins committed; the fears of divine vengeance falling upon them for it, here or hereafter; the many ways and means devised to appease angry Deity, and to avert punishment, some absurd, and others shocking; to which may be added, the name of δικη, vengeance, or justice, punitive justice, the heathens give to deity; see Romans 2:14, 15; Acts 28:4.

2. From the word of God, and the proclamation which God himself has made; in which, among other essential perfections of his, this is one, that he will by no means clear the guilty, and not at all acquit the wicked, Exodus 34:6, 7; Numbers 14:18; Nahum 1:3.

3. From the nature of God, 'who is of purer eyes than to behold iniquity;' cannot bear it, but hates it, and the

workers of it; which hatred is no other than his punishment of it, Habakkuk 1:13; Isaiah 1:13, 14; Psalm 5:5, 6. Now as his love of righteousness is natural and essential to him; so must hatred of sin be; to which may be added, that 'he is a consuming fire,' Hebrews 12:29.

4. From the nature of sin, and the demerit of it, eternal death, everlasting punishment and destruction. Now if sin of itself, in its own nature, merits such punishment at the hands of God, he is obliged to inflict it; or otherwise there can be no demerit in it.

5. From the law of God; the sanction of it, and the veracity of God in it: sin is a transgression of the law; which God, as a lawgiver, cannot but punish; otherwise his legislative power and authority is of no effect, and would be despised: he has annexed a sanction to his law, which is death; and his veracity obliges him to inflict it; nor is it any objection to all this, that then all sinners must be necessarily punished; since the perfections of God, though natural to him, the acts and exercises of them are according to his will; as has been instanced in his omnipotence and mercy. Besides, it will be readily allowed, and even affirmed, that no sin goes unpunished; but is either punished in the sinner himself, or in his Surety. The reason why some are not punished in themselves, is, because Christ has made satisfaction for their sins, by bearing the punishment due unto them. Hence,

6. From sin being punished in Christ, the Surety of his people, it may be strongly concluded, that punitive justice is essential to God; or otherwise, where is the goodness of God to his own Son, that he should not spare him, but awake the sword of justice against him, and inflict the whole of punishment on him, due to the sins of those for whom he suffered, if he could not have punished sin, or this was not necessary? and, indeed, where is his wisdom in being at such an expense as the blood and life of his Son, if sin could have been let go unpunished, and the salvation of his people obtained without it? and where is the love of God to men, in giving Christ for them, for their remission

and salvation, so much magnified, when all this might have been without it? but without shedding of blood, as there is no remission, so none could be, consistent with the justice of God; no pardon nor salvation, without satisfaction to that: could it have been in another way, the prayer of Christ would have brought it out, Father, *if it be possible, let this cup pass me*, Matthew 26:39.

But, Thirdly, I shall next consider the displays of the righteousness of God in his works; and vindicate his justice in them; *for the Lord is righteous in all his ways*, Psalm 145:17.

1. In his ways and works of providence: he governs the world in righteousness, orders and disposes of all things in judgment; and though he does according to his sovereign will and pleasure in heaven and in earth, yet he acts according to the strictest rules of justice and equity; *Just and true are his ways; he is the Judge of all the earth* who will *do right*, Revelation 15:3, Genesis 18:25 and does do it; nor is he chargeable with any unrighteousness in any of his ways and works: men may wrongly charge him, and say, as the house of Israel did; the way of the Lord is not equal; when it is their ways that are unequal, and not his, Ezekiel 18:29, nor is it any sufficient objection to the righteousness of God in his providences, that good men are often afflicted, and wicked men are frequently in very prosperous circumstances: these things have been stumbling and puzzling to good men, and they have not been able to reconcile them to the justice of God; Psalm 73:4-13; Jeremiah 12:1, 2. As for the afflictions of God's people, these are not punishments for sins, but chastisements of them; were they indeed punishments for sin, it would argue injustice, for it would be unjust to punish twice for the same sins; once in their Surety, and again in themselves: but so it is not; their afflictions come not from God as a judge, but as a father; and not from his justice, but his love; and not to their detriment and injury, but for their good. In short, they are chastened by the Lord, that they might not be condemned with the world, 1

Corinthians 11:32. And as for the prosperity of the wicked, though their eyes stand out with fatness, and they have more than heart can wish, yet they are like beasts that are fattened for the slaughter; their judgment may seem to linger, and their damnation to slumber, but they do not; sudden destruction will come upon them; the tables will, ere long, be turned, and the saints, who have now their evil things, will be comforted; and the wicked, who have, now their good things, will be tormented: justice, though it may not so apparently take place now, it will hereafter; when all things will be set to rights, and the judgments of God will be manifest. There is a future state, when the justice of God will shine in all its glory.

2. God is righteous in all his ways and works and acts of grace; in the predestination of men, the choice of some, and the preterition of others. While the apostle is treating on this sublime subject, he stops and asks this question, *Is there unrighteousness with God?* and answers it with the utmost abhorrence and detestation, *God forbid!* Election is neither an act of justice nor of injustice, but of the sovereign will and pleasure of God, who does what he will with his own; gives it to one, and not to another, without any imputation of injustice: if he may give grace and glory to whom he will, without such a charge, then he may determine to give it without any. If it is no injustice in men to choose their own favourites, friends, confidents, and companions; it can be none in God to choose whom he pleases to bestow his favours on; to indulge with communion with himself now, and to dwell with him to all eternity: if it was no injustice to choose some of the angels, called elect angels, and pass by others; and even to condemn all that sinned, without shewing mercy to one individual of them; it can be no injustice in him to choose some of the race of men, and save them, and pass by others, when he could have condemned them all. Nor can the imputation of *Adam's* sin to all his posterity, be accounted an unrighteous action. God made man upright, he made himself a sinner: God gave him a righteous law,

and abilities to keep it; he voluntarily broke it: God constituted the first man the federal head and representative of all his posterity; and who so fit for this as their natural head and common parent, with and in whom they were to stand and fall; and what injustice could be in that; since had he stood they would have partook of the benefits of it; as now he fell they share in the miseries of it? and since they sinned in him, it can be no unrighteous thing to reckon it to them; or that they should be made and constituted sinners, by his disobedience. It is not reckoned unjust, among men, for children to be punished for the sins of their parents, and particularly treason; and what else is sin against God? Exodus 20:5. The justice of God shines brightly in redemption by Christ; '*Zion*, and her converts, are redeemed in righteousness;' a full price is paid for the redemption of them; and in it 'mercy and truth meet together, and righteousness and peace kiss each other:' and though it is not for all men, no injustice is done to them that are not redeemed; for if God could in justice have condemned all, it can be no act of injustice to redeem and save some. Suppose one hundred slaves in Algiers, and a man out of his great generosity, lays down a ransom-price for fifty of them, does he, by this act of distinguished goodness and generosity, do any injustice to the others? or can they righteously complain of him for not ransoming them? In the justification of men, by the righteousness of Christ, the justice of God is very conspicuous; for though God justifies the ungodly, yet not without a perfect righteousness, such as is adequate to the demands of his righteous law; even the righteousness of his own Son, in the imputation of which, and justification by it, he appears to be *just, and the justifier of him which believes in Jesus*, Romans 3:26. Though God forgives sin, yet not without a satisfaction made to his justice; though it is according to the riches of his grace, yet through the blood of Christ shed for it; and upon the foot of the shedding of that blood, God is *faithful and just to forgive us our sins, and to cleanse us from all unrighteousness*, 1 John 1:9, and so it is both an act of grace and of justice; as is eternal glory and happiness, being the free gift of God, through Christ and his righteousness.

Appendix IV

Of Faith In God And In Christ[354]

FAITH is another branch of inward experimental religion and godliness, for *with the heart man believeth unto righteousness*; and of internal worship, and without which external worship cannot be performed in a manner acceptable to God, for *without faith it is impossible to please him*: there is no drawing nigh to God in any part of worship without it; if a man prays to God he must *ask in faith, nothing doubting*; for it is the *prayer of faith* that is availing and saving; if a man hears the gospel, unless the word is *mixed with faith* by them that hear it, it is not profitable; and both a profession of faith and the exercise of it, are necessary to a due subjection to the ordinances of the gospel. As to baptism, *if thou believest with all thy heart thou mayest*, said Philip to the eunuch desiring baptism; and so for the ordinance of the supper, a previous examination whether a man has faith, and the exercise of it, are requisite to eating of it; and without this a man cannot discern the Lord's body, nor answer the ends and design of that ordinance; concerning which may be observed,

I. Kinds of faith
The kind of faith to be treated of; for faith is a word of different use and signification, and there are divers kinds of faith.

---

[354] *A Body of Doctrinal and Practical Divinity*, The Baptist Standard Bearer, p. 730 ff.

1. It sometimes signifies the veracity and faithfulness of God; as when the apostle says, *Shall their unbelief make the faith of God without effect?* Romans 3:3, 4. Yea faith sometimes signifies veracity and fidelity among men, and is no other than a virtue belonging to the moral law, and is one of the weightier matters of it, Matthew 23:23.

2. It is sometimes used for the doctrine of the gospel, the word of faith, which the apostle preached, though he once destroyed it as much as in him lay, Galatians 1:23, and is the faith once delivered to the saints, which they should earnestly contend for, and build up one another in, Jude 3, 20, so called, because it contains things to be believed upon the credit and testimony of God; and because it directs to the great object of faith in salvation, the Lord Jesus Christ; and because it is the means of ingenerating and increasing faith in men, *for faith cometh by hearing, and hearing by the word of God,* Romans 10:8, 17.

3. There is a divine and an human faith; a divine faith proceeds upon a divine testimony, upon the authority and veracity of God the testifier; an human faith proceeds upon the testimony of man, and upon the authenticity and truth of the witness borne by him; concerning both which the apostle John says, *If we receive the witness of men, the witness of God is greater,* by how much the greater is his veracity and faithfulness; *for this is the witness of God which he hath testified of his Son,* 1 John 5:9, namely, that life and salvation are in him and by him; and to believe this witness, and to receive it within a man's self, is what is commonly called saving faith.

4. There is a faith of miracles which proceeds upon a revelation some way or other made by God to a man, which he believes; either that a miracle should be wrought by him, or should be wrought for him, for his benefit and advantage; of the former sort, and which is called faith in God, Mark 11:22, 23, the apostle is to be understood, when he says, *Though I have all faith, so that I could remove mountains,* 1 Corinthians 13:2, see Matthew 17:20, Luke 17:6, of the latter sort was the faith of the centurion, of the woman having an issue, of Jairus, and of the Canaanitish woman, Matthew 8:8, 10, and 9:18, 20, 22, and 15:28, and of the lame man at Lystra, Acts 3:9, 10. The one is

called active, the other passive faith; and this faith of miracles, in the first times of the gospel, was common to good and bad men, to the true disciples of Christ, Matthew 10:1; Mark 16:17-20, and to Judas, and to false teachers, Matthew 10:1, 4, and 7:22, 23.

5. There is what is called an historical faith, not because it is only giving credit to the historical part of the scripture, which is to be believed as well as other parts; nor because the scripture is read, and attention paid to it only as a common history or human testimony; for men, with this faith, believe it to be a divine testimony, and regard it as such; it may rather be called a *theoretic* faith, a speculative one, receiving all things in the theory but reducing nothing to practice; or a bare naked assent to the truth of what is contained in the word concerning God and Christ, and divine things; it is a faith common to good men and bad men; it must be and is where true faith is, and there can be no true faith without it; but if a man stops here and goes no further, it falls short of spiritual, special faith, or the faith of God's elect, and is no other than the faith of devils, and of bad men.

6. There is also a temporary faith, which continues only for a time, in some persons, as in the stony ground hearers, *Which for a while believe, and in time of temptation fall away,* Luke 8:13, this sort of faith differs from the former, in that it is not a mere assent to truth, but is attended with affection, joy, and gladness, as in Herod, who heard John gladly, and did many outward things, Mark 6:20, and in those the apostle speaks of, *who tasted the good word of God, and the powers of the world to come,* Hebrews 6:5, all of a natural and superficial kind, arising from a principle of self-love, and from the novelty, harmony, and connection of truths, and from a false presumptuous hope of future happiness in consequence of their assent unto them; and so is different likewise from the faith of devils, who believe and tremble, but have no joy; and it differs also from true faith, because it is without the root of grace in the heart, and is losable, is only for a time, for when trouble and persecution arise because of the word, such who have it, drop their profession of it; whereas where there is true faith, such do not *draw back*, but continue to *believe to the saving of the soul,* Hebrews 10:39.

7. There is a special faith, which is peculiar to God's elect, and is by some called saving faith, though strictly speaking salvation is not in faith, nor in any other grace, nor in any duty, only in Christ; there is no other name but his under heaven whereby we must be saved; he only is the author of eternal salvation; and yet there are some things in scripture which seem to countenance such a phrase; as when Christ said to the woman who repented of her sins, and had the forgiveness of them, loved Christ, and believed in him, *Thy faith hath saved thee; go in peace*, Luke 7:50, unless the object of faith should be meant; and certain it is that salvation is promised to faith, and connected with it, *He that believes shall be saved*, and is what faith issues in; true believers receive *the end of their faith, even the salvation of their souls*, Mark 16:16; 1 Peter 1:9, and this is the faith that is to be treated of; and next will be considered.

II. The objects and acts of faith

The objects of it, and acts of it on those objects. The objects of it are not bare axioms or propositions; for, as Dr Ames observes, the act of the believer does not terminate at an axiom but at the thing; for axioms are not formed, but that by them knowledge may be had of things; the principal term to which the act of a believer tends is the thing itself, which is chiefly regarded in the axiom; and so promises are not to be considered as objects unless in a tropical and metonymical sense, being put for the things promised; so the Old Testament saints, not having received the promises, the things promised, but having seen them afar off, that is, by faith, were persuaded of them, and embraced them, Hebrews 11:12, 13, nor even the benefits of Christ, or the blessings of his grace, no otherwise than as they are the end faith has in view in receiving him; he is viewed and dealt with as the object of faith in order to enjoy the good things which come by him: or they may be considered as motives encouraging to acts of faith on him, and are the fruits and effects of it received thereby from him. The proper and formal object of faith is twofold, God and Christ; God as the first primary and ultimate object of faith, and Christ as mediator is the mediate object of it, *Ye believe in God, believe also in me*, John 14:1.

God is the principal object of faith, Mark 11:22; Titus 3:8; 1 Thessalonians 1:8, which act of faith on him is not barely to believe there is a God, and but one; which is *credere Deum*, and which the devils themselves believe; nor is it merely to believe whatever he delivers in his word, as prophecies, promises, doctrines, &c. this is *credere Deo*, to give credit to God, believe what he says; but *credere in Deum*, by believing to cleave to God, lean upon him, and acquiesce in him as our all-sufficient life and salvation, Deuteronomy 30:20, and so it is not merely to believe there are three persons in the Godhead, but to go forth in acts of faith and confidence on them, in things relative to our welfare and happiness here and hereafter. And,

First, On God the Father, *Ye believe in God*, that is, in God the Father, the God of Israel, as distinct from Christ, for it follows, *in my Father's house are many mansions*, John 14:1, 2, and so our Lord further says, *He that believeth on me*, that is, not on him only, nor does his faith stop and terminate there, *but on him that sent me*, that is, on the Father of Christ, John 12:44, and it is also observed, that Christ was raised from the dead and had glory given him, that the faith and hope of his people might be in God, in God his Father, who raised him, 1 Peter 1:21.

1. On him as the creator, though not only on him as such; so runs the first article in the creed commonly called the apostles' creed, 'I believe in God the Father almighty, maker of heaven and earth'; to believe the creation of all things out of nothing by the word, even out of things which did not appear, is an act of that faith in God which is the substance of things hoped for, and the evidence of things not seen, Hebrews 11:1, 3, besides, a true believer in God fetches arguments to strengthen his faith in God, for relief, help, support, and supply from him with respect to things spiritual, as well as temporal, from his being the maker and creator of all things; *My help*, says David, *cometh from the Lord, who made heaven and earth*, Psalm 121:1, 2, and it is a special act of faith believers are directed to under sufferings, to *commit the keeping of their souls to God in well-doing, as unto a faithful creator*, 1 Peter 4:19, and so likewise on him as the preserver and saviour of men, for he *is the Saviour of all men, especially of those that believe*; and therefore saints put their trust in him, the living God, as such, 1 Timothy 4:10. But more especially,

2. Faith is exercised on God the Father as the object of it, as having loved his people in Christ before the foundation of the world; that the Father, as distinct from Christ, has loved his people with a free, sovereign, unchangeable, and everlasting love, is certain; *Now God, even our Father, which hath loved us, and hath given us everlasting consolation,* 2 Thessalonians 2:16, of which they may be most comfortably assured, and may most firmly believe, by his appearing to them as he did to his church of old, saying, *I have loved thee with an everlasting love,* Jeremiah 31:3, by his spirit witnessing it to their spirits, and by shedding it abroad in their hearts, and giving them some feeling sensations of it, so as to comprehend with other saints, the height and depth, the length and breadth of it; by remembering to them his former loving kindness, the favour he bears to his own people; and by acts of love done in eternity, as choosing them in Christ, &c. and by giving him for them in time, and by commending his love towards them through Christ's dying for them, while they were yet sinners; and by quickening them by his Spirit and grace when dead in trespasses and sins, and all because of the great love wherewith he hath loved them; and by drawing them with loving-kindness to himself, as well as by his word and oath, the two immutable things in which he cannot lie, Isaiah 54:9, 10. So that there is good and sufficient reason for the acting and exercise of faith, on the everlasting love of the Father; and what a strong act and expression of faith is that of the apostle with respect unto it; *I am persuaded,* I firmly believe it, that nothing, *nor any creature whatever, shall be able to separate us from the love of God, which is in Christ Jesus our Lord.* Romans 8:38, 39, this is to be rooted and grounded in love, Ephesians 3:17.

3. Faith is exercised on God the Father, as having chosen his people in Christ to grace and glory from the beginning, from everlasting, before the world began, Ephesians 1:3, 4; 2 Thessalonians 2:13, 14, this is the act of the Father of Christ, *Elect, according to the foreknowledge of God the Father,* 1 Peter 1:2, and this election of God is to be known by the gospel coming not in word only but in power, by being effectually called, for *whom he did predestinate, them he also called*; and by their having the faith of God's elect, for *as many as were ordained to*

eternal life believed, Romans 8:30; Acts 13:48, wherefore this may be most firmly believed, as it was by the apostle Paul, both with respect to himself and others, for which he blessed God, and gave thanks to him, Ephesians 1:3, 4; 2 Thessalonians 2:13, and our Lord exhorts and encourages his disciples to *rejoice because* their *names* were *written in heaven,* Luke 10:20, which supposes knowledge of it, and faith in it.

4. God, as the covenant-God of his people, is the object of their faith; the covenant runs thus, *I will be their God, and they shall be my people*; and this is made to appear in effectual calling, when they who were not the people of God, not known to be so, are openly such; then it is God makes good his promise, I will say, *It is my people; and they shall say, The Lord is my God,* Zechariah 13:9, as David did, *I trusted in thee, O Lord; I said, Thou art my God,* Psalm 31:14, and so may every believer say, and be assured, that this God is their God, and will be their God and guide unto death, for covenant-interest always continues; it was a noble act of faith in the sweet singer of Israel a little before his death, *Although my house be not so with God; yet he hath made with me an everlasting covenant, ordered in all things and sure,* 2 Samuel 23:5.

5. God, as he is the Father of Christ, so he is the Father of all that believe in him; *I ascend,* says Christ, *unto my Father and your Father,* John 20:17. So God, in the covenant of his grace, has declared himself, *and will be a Father unto you, and ye shall be my sons and daughters, saith the Lord Almighty,* 2 Corinthians 6:18, and as such faith is to be exercised on him with joy and wonder, saying, *Behold, what manner of love the Father hath bestowed upon us, that we should be called the sons of God,* 1 John 3:1, of the truth of which the leadings and witnessings of the Spirit are an evident proof, from whence he is called the Spirit of adoption; *for as many as are led by the Spirit of God,* off of themselves to Christ, and by him to the Father, *they are the sons of God*; and who also *received the Spirit of adoption, whereby they cry, Abba, Father; the Spirit itself beareth witness with their spirit, that they are the children of God.* Romans 8:14-16, so that their faith is grounded on good authority, on a divine testimony, true, sure and firm; this blessing of adoption is revealed to faith,

the witness of it is received by it, and so believers become openly and manifestly *the children of God by faith in Christ Jesus*; for to *as many as received him, to them gives he power*, authority, right, privilege, *to become the sons of God, even to them that believe in his name*, Galatians 3:26; John 1:12, and henceforward it is enjoined them that in the exercise of faith they call God their father, and not turn away from him, by giving way to an evil heart of unbelief, but say to him, *Doubtless thou art our father*, Isaiah 63:16, and they are directed in all their addresses to God at the throne of grace to say, *Our Father, which art in heaven*, Matthew 6:9.

6. God is the object of faith as a God forgiving iniquity, transgression and sin for Christ's sake; and in him he has proclaimed his name as such, and there is none like him on that account; he has promised pardon in covenant, saying, *I will be merciful to their unrighteousness, and their sins, and their iniquities will I remember no more*, Hebrews 8:12. He has set forth Christ in his purposes to be a propitiation through faith in his blood for the remission of sin; and he has sent him to shed his blood to obtain it, and has exalted him as a Saviour to give it, and to him give all the prophets witness, that whosoever believes in him shall receive it; and he applies it to them, saying, *Son* or daughter, *be of good cheer thy sins be forgiven thee; I, even I, am he that blotteth out thy transgressions for mine own sake, and will not remember thy sins*, Matthew 9:2, Isaiah 43:25. Hence upon such acts and declarations as these, the believer has sufficient ground to make God, as a forgiving God, the object, of his faith, and to call upon his soul and all within him to bless his holy name, Psalm 103:1-3, such an act of faith David put forth on God as a forgiving God, when, having acknowledged his sin, and confessed it before the Lord, added, *And thou forgavest the iniquity of my sin*, Psalm 32:5.

7. Faith deals with God as a justifier; its language is, *Who shall lay any thing to the charge of God's elect? It is God that justifieth*, Romans 8:33, and 3:30, and faith is exercised on him as he that *justifieth the ungodly*; and therefore not by works, nor on account of any good dispositions and qualifications in men; and they come to him not as workers, but as ungodly and sinners,

and believe on him as justifying them without works, and that by imputing the righteousness of his Son unto them; *even as David, also describeth the blessedness of the man, unto whom God imputeth righteousness without works,* Romans 4:5, 6. Christ of God is made to them righteousness; and they are made the righteousness of God in him; that is, by his gracious imputation of Christ's righteousness to them: and thus God appears to be a just God and a Saviour: just, whilst he is *the justifier of him that believes in Jesus*; and as such he is the object of faith; what Christ the federal head of his people, in whom they are all justified, said, his believing members may say, *He is near that justifieth me, who will contend with me?* Isaiah 50:8.

8. The God and Father of Christ is *the God of all grace*; it has pleased him, the Father, that all fulness of it should dwell in Christ as Mediator; he has made large provisions of it, and stored the covenant of grace with it; and is the author, giver, and implanter of all grace in the hearts of his people by his Spirit; and as he is able to make all grace to abound towards them, so he grants them a supply of it from time to time: now as such he is the object of faith; faith deals with him as such, and the believer applies to the throne of his grace, that he may obtain mercy, and find grace to help him in time of need.

9. Lastly, God, as a promising God, is the object of faith, he has made many exceeding great and precious promises, and these are all yea and amen in Christ, and God is faithful who has promised, and is able also to perform; and though promises themselves are not, strictly speaking, the object, rather the things promised, yet especially a promising God is the object faith is concerned with, Hebrews 10:23.

Second, God the Son is the object of faith; which faith lies not merely in believing that he is the Son of God, which is most certainly to be believed; it was not only the confession of the faith of Peter, *Thou art the Christ the Son of the living God*; which faith, or rather the object of it, is the Rock on which the church of Christ is built, and against which the gates of hell shall never prevail; but it was the faith of all the disciples, and which they express with the strongest assurance; *We believe and are sure that thou art that Christ, the Son of the living God,*

329

Matthew 16:16, 18; John 6:69, and it was with respect to this article that the eunuch expressed his faith in Christ previous to his baptism; *I believe that Jesus Christ is the Son of God*, Acts 8:37, and all things relating to Christ, his doctrines, and his miracles, were written by the evangelists, that *men* might *believe that Jesus is the Christ, the Son of God; and that believing, they might have life through his name*, John 20:31, but true faith is not barely a believing that Christ is the Son of God, but a believing in him as such; according to the question put by Christ to the blind man; *Dost thou believe on the Son of God?* John 9:35. *And this is his commandment*, the commandment of God, *that we should believe on the name of his Son Jesus Christ*. And again, *He that believeth on the Son of God hath the witness in himself*, 1 John 3:23, and 5:10. Believing in him is a going forth in acts of faith and confidence, and is called *faith towards our Lord Jesus Christ*, Acts 20:28. Christ, as the Son of God, is the true God and eternal life; he is God equal with the Father, and as such is equally the primary object of faith; which is strongly expressed by Thomas; *My Lord and my God!* and therefore our Lord says, *Ye believe in God*, in God the Father, *believe also in me* equally as in him, he being equal with him in nature, perfections, power, and glory. But Christ, as Mediator, Redeemer, and Saviour, is the mediate object of faith, or in and through whom men believe in God; thus the apostle Peter, speaking of Christ as Mediator, being foreordained before the foundation of the world; but made manifest in human nature in these last times for the sake of his people, described by him as such, *Who by him do believe in God*, 1 Peter 1:21. As Christ is the Mediator through whom all grace is communicated to his people, so it is through him that all grace is exercised on God, and particularly faith; Such trust have we through Christ to God-ward, says the apostle, 2 Corinthians 3:4. So believers reckon themselves *alive unto God through Jesus Christ our Lord*, Romans 6:11. Now faith in Christ as the Redeemer and Saviour includes in it the following things, and is expressed by a variety of acts, which shew the nature of it.

1st, I shall consider the several parts of faith in Christ, or what is requisite to constitute it.
   1. Knowledge of Christ is necessary to the exercise of faith on him, for *how shall they believe in him of whom they have not heard?* and if they have not so much as heard of him, they cannot

know him, and consequently cannot exercise faith upon him; and *How shall they hear without a preacher* to make him known unto them? Romans 10:14. When our Lord put the question to the man who had been blind, *Dost thou believe on the Son of God?* he answered and said, Who is he, Lord, that I might believe on him? upon which Christ made himself known unto him, Jesus said unto him, *Thou hast both seen him, and it is he that talketh with thee*; his eyes had been opened to see him, and his ears now heard him, and both being true in a spiritual sense he immediately expressed his faith in him, saying, *Lord, I believe*, and as a proof and evidence of it, *worshipped him*, John 9:35-38. Previous to faith in Christ, as a Saviour, there must be knowledge of the want of him; as such a man must be made sensible of the sinfulness of his nature, and of the exceeding sinfulness of sin, and of the just demerit of it, and of the miserable state and condition it has brought him into, out of which none but Christ the Saviour can deliver him; and therefore he then applies to him as the apostles in distress did, saying, *Lord, save us, we perish!* Matthew 8:25, he must be made acquainted with his impotency to save himself; that his own right-hand, his works and services, cannot save him; that if ever he is saved it must be by the grace of God, through the blood and righteousness of Christ, and not by them; he must have knowledge of the fulness and abilities of Christ as a Saviour; he must have seen him full of grace and truth, as having all the fulness of the blessings of grace in him suitable to his wants, whose redemption is plenteous, his salvation complete, he being made every thing to his people they want, and able to save to the uttermost all that come unto God by him; and he being just such a Saviour they need, and his salvation so suitable to them, *they that know his name*, Jesus the Saviour, *put their trust in him*; and the more ready they are to do this, as they are fully convinced there is no other Saviour; that salvation is in him, and in none else; that it is in vain to expect it from any other quarter from the works and services of the creature, and therefore determine upon it they shall not be their saviours; but say, with Job, *Though he slay me, yet will I trust in him: he also shall be my salvation!* Psalm 9:10; Job 13:15, 16. Hence knowledge being so requisite to faith, and included in it, faith is sometimes expressed by it,

Isaiah 53:11; John 17:3, both in spiritual knowledge and special faith, eternal life is begun, and with which it is connected; and so knowledge and faith are joined together as inseparable companions, and as expressive of the same thing; *And we have known and believed the love that God hath to us*, are firmly persuaded of it, 1 John 4:16, and some of the strongest acts of faith in the saints have been expressed by words of knowledge; *I know that my redeemer liveth, &c. I know in whom I have believed, &c.* Job 19:25; 2 Timothy 1:12.

2. An assent unto Christ as a Saviour, enters into the true nature of faith; not a bare naked assent of the mind to the truth of the person and offices of Christ; that he is the Son of God, the Messiah, Prophet, Priest, and King, such as has been yielded to him by men destitute of true faith in him, as by Simon Magus, and others, yea, by the devils themselves, Luke 4:34, 41. 'Of all the poison', says Dr Owen, 'which at this day is diffused in the minds of men, corrupting them from the mystery of the gospel, there is no part that is more pernicious than this one perverse imagination, that *to believe in Christ* is nothing at all but *to believe the doctrine of the gospel!*[355] which yet we grant is included therein.' Such a proposition, that Christ is the Saviour of the chief of sinners, or that salvation is alone by him, is not presented merely under the notion of its being true, and assented to as such, but under the notion of its being good, a suitable, acceptable, and preferable good, and to be chosen as the good part was by Mary; as being both *a faithful saying* to be believed as true, and as *worthy of all acceptation*, to be received and embraced as the chiefest good. Faith is an assent to Christ as a Saviour, not upon an human, but a divine testimony, upon the record which God has given of his Son, and of eternal life in him. Some of the Samaritans believed on Christ because of the saying of the woman; but others because of his own word, having heard him themselves, and knew that he was indeed the Christ, the Saviour of the world: true faith, in sensible sinners, assents to Christ, and embraces him not merely as a Saviour of men in

---

[355] A very important statement considering groundless modern accusations that Gill's view of faith is merely and solely 'an assent to the facts of the gospel'.

general; but as a special, suitable Saviour for them in particular: it proceeds upon Christ's being revealed in them, as well as to them, by the Spirit of wisdom and revelation, in the knowledge of him as a Saviour that becomes them; it comes not merely through external teachings, by the hearing of the word from men; but having *heard and learned of the Father,* such souls come to Christ, that is, believe in him, John 6:45, not the doctrine of him only, but in him himself.

3. Knowledge of Christ as a Saviour, and an assent unto him as such, is attended with love and affection to him; faith works by love, love always accompanies faith, at least follows it; Christ is precious to them that believe; they love him, value him, prefer him, to all others as a Saviour; and every truth respecting Christ is not barely assented to, but as they receive Christ, they receive the love of the truth with him.

4. True, spiritual, special faith in Christ includes in it a dependence on him, trust and confidence in him alone for everlasting life and salvation; it is a soul's venturing on Christ, resolving if it perishes it will perish at his feet; it is a resignation of itself to Christ, a committing its soul, and the important welfare and salvation of it into Christ's hands, trusting him with all, looking to him, relying on him, and acquiescing in him as the alone Saviour. All which will more fully appear by considering,

2nd, The various acts of faith on Christ, as described in the sacred Scriptures.

1. It is expressed by seeing the Son; this is one of the first and one of the lowest acts of faith, and yet eternal life is annexed unto it; *This is the will of him that sent me,* says Christ, *that every one which seeth the Son, and believeth on him, may have everlasting life,* John 6:40, it is a sight of the glories and excellencies of Christ's person, of the fulness of his grace and righteousness, and of the completeness and suitableness of his salvation. It is a looking to Jesus, the author and finisher of faith, a view of him as altogether lovely, the chiefest among ten thousand. Faith is a light struck into the heart of a sinner whose understanding was darkened, yea darkness itself, till God commanded light to shine in darkness; by which, though first but glimmering, he sees

himself a sinner, miserable and undone, without a Saviour, when Christ is held forth in the gospel to be looked at by him; that is a glass in which he is to be beheld, and where he is evidently set forth crucified and slain for sinners; and so is the hope set before them, both to be looked at and to be laid hold on by them, who was typified by the brazen serpent set upon a pole by Moses, for the Israelites bitten by the serpents to look at and live, John 3:14, 15. *And not only sensible sinners are directed to behold the Lamb of God which taketh away the sin of the world*,[356] as John's hearers were by him; and are encouraged by the ministers of the word, who shew unto men the way of salvation, to look to and believe on the Lord Jesus Christ and be saved; but they are encouraged by Christ himself; who says, *Behold me, behold me*, to a nation not called by his name, *look unto me, and be ye saved, all the ends of the earth; for I am God, and there is none else!* Isaiah 55:1, and 45:22, which sight of him fills their souls with love to him, as the most lovely and amiable one, with eager desires after him, and an interest in him, signified by hungering and thirsting after his righteousness, and panting after his salvation. And this sight of Christ by faith is nigh, and not afar off; now, and not hereafter; and for a man's self, and not another; he looks to him not merely as a Saviour of others, but to him as a Saviour and Redeemer suitable for him.

2. Faith is a motion of the soul unto Christ; having looked and gazed at him with wonder and pleasure, it moves towards him; this is expressed by coming unto him; *He that cometh to me*, says Christ, *shall never hunger; and he that believeth on me*, which explains what is meant by coming, *shall never thirst*, John 6:35, which coming to Christ is upon an invitation given, encouraging to it; not only by others, by the Spirit and the bride, who say *come*, Revelation 22:17, and by the ministers of the word; *Ho, every one that thirsteth, come ye to the waters; and he that hath no money, come!* and who, through the gospel-trumpet being blown with power, and the sound of it attended with efficacious grace, they that are ready to perish come, Isaiah 55:1, and 27:13,

---

[356] My emphasis. Modern critics of Gill stress that he has no message for sinners before they become 'sensible'.

but also by Christ himself, who says, *Come unto me, all ye that labour and are heavy laden, and I will give you rest!* Matthew 11:28, such souls come, being influenced and powerfully wrought upon by the grace of God; *All that the Father giveth me*, says Christ, *shall come to me*; efficacious grace will cause them to come, will bring them to him, through all discouragements, difficulties, and objections, and which are all removed by what follows; *and him that cometh to me I will in no wise cast out*, John 6:37. This coming to Christ as a Saviour, or believing in him, is owing to the Father's teachings, instructions, and drawing; *No man can come to me*, says Christ, that is, believe in him, *except the Father, which hath sent me, draw him*, draw him with his loving-kindness, and through the power of his grace, and of his divine teachings; *every man therefore that hath heard and learned of the Father cometh unto me*; yea, this is a pure gift of his grace, *therefore said I unto you, that no man can come unto me except it were given unto him of my Father*, John 6:44, 45, 65, and such souls come to Christ in a view of the blessings of grace, of righteousness, and strength, peace and pardon, salvation and eternal life; these are the goodness of the Lord, they flow unto him for, with great eagerness, swiftness, and cheerfulness. For,

3. This motion of faith towards Christ is expressed by fleeing to him; and such souls that believe in him are described as having *fled for refuge to lay hold up on the hope set before them*, Hebrews 6:18, and by *turning to the strong hold as prisoners of hope*, that is, to Christ, whose name is a *strong tower*, whither the *righteous run and are safe*, Zechariah 9:12; Proverbs 18:10, fleeing supposes danger, and a sense of it; Christ is the city of refuge, the strong hold and tower, they are directed to; whither coming, they find shelter and safety from avenging justice and every enemy, a supply of wants, and ground of hope of eternal life and happiness; and thus being come to Christ various acts of faith are put forth upon him; such as the following,

(1) A venturing act of their souls, and of their whole salvation on him, like Esther, who ventured into the presence of King Ahasuerus, saying, *If I perish, I perish!* faith at first is such a venture of the soul on Christ, not knowing as yet how it will fare with it; yea, a peradventure, perhaps there may be salvation in

Christ for it; as Benhadad's servants said to him; *Peradventure he* (the king of Israel), *will save thy life*; reasoning in like manner as the four lepers did when ready to perish with famine; *Let us fall into the host of the Syrians; if they save us alive, we shall live; and if they kill us, we shall but die*: so sensible sinners, seeing their perishing condition, resolve to venture themselves on Christ; if he saves them it is well, if not they can but die, as they must without him.

(2) A casting or throwing themselves into the arms of Christ, to be borne and carried by him as a nursing father bears and carries in his bosom a sucking child; so Christ carries the lambs in his arms, Isaiah 40:11, weak believers, who cast themselves and all their burdens, the whole care of their souls upon him; this sense חאמן has Numbers 11:12, from whence comes a word which in many places signifies to believe; see Isaiah 60:4 compared with Isaiah 66:12.

(3) A laying hold on Christ, who is *a tree of life to them that lay hold upon him*, Proverbs 3:18, from which tree they may pluck and eat all the fruits of grace and life. Christ is the hope of Israel, and the Saviour of his people; and there is great encouragement for sensible sinners to hope in him, because there are mercy and plenteous redemption with him; and he is in the gospel set forth before them as the ground of hope to lay hold upon, Hebrews 6:18, he is that Jew who sprang from the seed of David and from the tribe of Judah; and his righteousness *the skirt* ten men are said to *take hold of*, Zechariah 8:23, even the robe of his righteousness; which being revealed and brought near to faith, it lays hold upon and puts it on, as its justifying righteousness, seeing the insufficiency of its own, and the excellency of this. Socinus treats such an apprehension of Christ by faith for justification as a mere human invention, and a most empty dream; but the true believer finds abundance of solid peace and comfort in it. As Adonijah and Joab fled and laid hold on the horns of the altar for safety, and under a consciousness of guilt; so a sinner, sensible of its sin and guilt, and of its own incapacity to make atonement for it, flees to Christ, and lays hold on his sacrifice, and brings this offering in the arms of his faith, and pleads with God that he would be propitious to him through it,

and take away his sin from him. Faith lays hold on the covenant of grace, and upon Christ the Mediator of it, and upon the promises in it, which are yea and amen in Christ, and on the blessings of it, the sure mercies of David, redemption, justification, pardon, peace, reconciliation, and salvation, and claims interest in them. It lays hold on Christ for strength as well as righteousness; *Let him take hold of my strength*, to enable him to exercise every grace, perform every duty, bear the cross of Christ, persevere in faith and holiness to the end, Isaiah 27:5, 6.

(4) Faith is a retaining Christ, and an holding him fast; the soul being come to Christ, and having laid hold upon him, keeps its hold of him: it is said of Wisdom, or Christ, *happy is every one that retaineth her*, Proverbs 3:18, so the church having lost her beloved, and upon search found him, she *held him, and would not let him go*, as Jacob the angel that wrestled with him until he blessed him, Canticles 3:4, which denotes not only an holding fast the profession of the faith of Christ, but a continuance of the exercise of the grace of faith on him; an holding to him, the Head, and deriving nourishment from him, a walking on in him as he has been received; a being strong in the grace that is in him, firmly believing its interest in him. It is expressive of strength of faith in Christ, and of great affection to him; for it is sometimes with difficulty it keeps its hold of him when things go contrary, and Christ has withdrawn himself and is out of sight.

(5) Faith is sometimes expressed by leaning on the Lord, and staying upon him, *the holy One of Israel in truth*; and even those who walk in darkness and have no light, are directed and encouraged to *trust in the name of the Lord, and stay upon their God*, Isaiah 10:20, and 50:10, where trusting in the Lord, and staying on him, are manifestly the same; faith or trust in the Lord, is a staying or leaning on him for all supports and every supply; so the church is said to be *leaning on her beloved*, while coming up out of the wilderness, Canticles 8:5, which shows consciousness of her own weakness, a dependence on his mighty arm, and an expectation of all supplies of grace and strength from him. But,

(6) The grand and principal act of faith, or that by which it is more frequently expressed is, receiving Christ; *as many as*

received him, even that believe on his name, John 1:12, where receiving Christ is interpreted of believing on him. Christ is received, not into the head; for not all that say Lord, Lord, shall enter into the kingdom of heaven; but into the heart; for it is with the heart man believes in the Son of God unto righteousness; and in it Christ dwells by faith. A soul made sensible of its need of Christ and his righteousness, and of salvation by him, comes down from self-exaltation and self-confidence, and *receives Christ joyfully*, as Zacchaeus did. Faith receives a whole Christ, not in part only, but in whole, he is *altogether*, or *all of him lovely*; the whole of him is amiable in the sight of a believer, and acceptable to him. As the pass-over Lamb was to be eaten wholly by the Israelites, no part of it to be left, so faith feeds upon a whole Christ, Christ in his person, offices, grace and righteousness. *Is Christ divided?* He is not, not in his person; he is but one, God manifest in the flesh; nor in his doctrines; nor from his ministers; nor from his ordinances; where Christ is received all are received.

1. Christ in all his offices. Christ is received as the great Prophet in the church whom God promised to raise up, and has raised up, and sent to instruct his people; and by whom grace and truth, the doctrines of grace and truth, are come, and he is to be attended to; hear ye him, not Moses, nor Elias, but God's well-beloved Son, by whom he has spoken his whole mind and will in these last days; and who himself says, *Receive my instruction, and not silver; and knowledge rather than fine gold*; that is, his gospel published by him; and such who are spiritually enlightened in the knowledge of him by the Spirit of God, these receive the love of the truth; truth, with a cordial affection for it; receive the word gladly, with all readiness and meekness; they receive the ministers of Christ, and the doctrines preached and messages sent by them; which is interpretatively receiving Christ himself; *he that receiveth you receiveth me; and he that receiveth me receiveth him that sent me*, Matthew 10:40. And faith receives Christ also as a Priest, and the atonement which he has made; it views him as a merciful, faithful, and suitable one, who

has made reconciliation for sin, put it away by the sacrifice of himself, and made full satisfaction for it, and by his one offering has perfected for ever them that are sanctified. Faith regards him and receives him as the advocate with the Father, as ever living to make intercession; as always at the golden altar, ready to offer up the prayers of all saints with his much incense; and by whom, as their great high Priest, saints offer their spiritual sacrifices of prayer and praise, which become acceptable to God through him. And faith also receives him as King in Zion; *as ye have therefore received Christ Jesus the Lord*, Colossians 2:6, there seems to be an emphasis on that clause τον κυριov, the Lord; one that receives Christ, a true believer in him, acknowledges Christ as his Lord and Head, and gives homage to him as such, saying, as the Church did, *the Lord is our judge, the Lord is our lawgiver, the Lord is our king, he will save us*, Isaiah 33:22. Christ is received and owned by such, not only as a Priest, but as a Prince; not only as a Saviour, but as a Lawgiver; they take upon them his yoke, submit to his ordinances, and observe his commands; and walk as Zacharias and Elizabeth did, in all the commandments and ordinances of the Lord blameless.

2. Christ, and all the blessings of grace along with him, are received by faith; such as adoption; as Christ gives a power to them that believe in him to become the children of God, they by faith receive this power, right, and privilege from him; and hence we read of *receiving the adoption of children*, through the redemption that is by Christ, Galatians 4:5, and because faith receives it, believers in Christ become manifestly the children of God. They likewise receive the blessing from the Lord, even a justifying righteousness from the God of their salvation. They receive abundance of grace, and the gift of righteousness, by and from Christ, by which they are justified from all things, and put it on as their robe of righteousness, and glory in it. By faith they receive the pardon of their sins; as Christ is exalted as a *Prince and a Saviour for to give repentance to Israel, and forgiveness*

of sins, so *whosoever believeth in him shall receive remission of sins,* Acts 5:31, and 10:43, and that upon the foot of atonement made by him; hence they are said to *receive the atonement,* Romans 5:11, by faith they receive out of the fulness of Christ grace for grace, all supplies of grace needful for them; as they want more grace, and God has promised it to them, and provided it for them in Christ; so they apply to him for it, and receive it at his hands; and as he gives both grace and glory, they receive both; grace as a meetness for, and as the earnest of glory: not only do they receive the forgiveness of their sins, but also *an inheritance among them which are sanctified by faith,* Acts 26:18, they receive grace from God the Father to make them meet for it; and as the Spirit is given as an earnest of it, they receive him as the earnest of the inheritance until they are put into the full possession of it.

3. Christ is received as a free gift; he is the gift of God; *if thou knewest the gift of God,* John 4:10, and an unspeakable gift of his love he is, a gift freely given and unmerited; *God so loved the world that he gave his only begotten Son,* John 3:16, and he is received and owned as such; *unto us a Son is given,* Isaiah 9:6, and all blessings of grace are given, and freely given, along with him, and received as such, Romans 8:32.

4. Faith receives Christ in preference to all others; it receives him, and him only, as the one Lord and Head, as the one Mediator between God and man, and as the one and only Saviour of sinners; it chooses Christ, the good part that shall never be taken away, above all others: faith works by love to Christ in a stronger manner than to any creature-object whatever; than to the dearest and nearest relation and friend whatever; than to father, mother, brethren and sisters, houses and lands; yea, he that loves any of these more than Christ is not worthy of him. Nay, faith prefers the worst things belonging to Christ to the best in creatures; the believer is willing to do and suffer any thing and every thing for Christ; none of these things, as afflictions, bonds, and imprisonment for Christ's sake,

move the believer from Christ, and his faith and hope in him; he esteems reproach for Christ's sake greater riches than all the treasures in Egypt, and takes pleasure in persecutions and distresses endured on his account; and even reckons his own best things, his highest attainments in knowledge and righteousness, but loss and dung in comparison of the excellency of the knowledge of Christ Jesus his Lord, and of his righteousness, in which, and in which only, he desires to be found.

Third, God the Holy Spirit is also the object of faith; though we read and hear but little of faith in him, yet as he is God equal with the Father and the Son, he is equally the object of faith as they are; not only his being, perfections, deity, and personality, his offices as a sanctifier and comforter, and his operations of grace on the souls of men, are to be believed; but there are particular acts of faith, trust, and confidence, to be exercised upon him; as he is truly God, he is the object of religious worship, and this cannot be performed aright without faith. Baptism is administered in his name as in the name of the other two persons, and this is to be done and submitted to by faith in him; he is particularly to be prayed unto, and there is no praying to him nor in him without faith in him; yea a true believer trusts in him for his help and assistance in prayer, as indeed he does in the exercise of every religious duty, and of every grace; and besides all this there is a special act of faith put forth upon him, with respect to salvation, as upon the other two persons; for as we are to trust in God the Father to keep us by his power through faith unto salvation, and to trust in Christ for the salvation of our souls, so we are to trust in the holy Spirit for carrying on and finishing the work of grace in us, who is equal to it; we are to trust the whole of it with him, and be *confident of this very thing*, as we may, as of any one thing in the world, *that he* the Spirit of God *which hath begun a good work in us, will perform it until the day of Jesus Christ*, Philippians 1:6.

III. The subjects of faith
The subjects of the grace of faith, on whom this grace is bestowed, and in whom it is, in some more in others less, in all like precious faith.

First, The subjects of faith are not angels, neither good nor bad. Not the good angels; they live not by faith on God and Christ as believing men do, but by sight; they are possessed of the beatific vision of God, and are always beholding the face of our Father in heaven, and are continually in his presence, waiting upon him and worshipping him, and enjoy complete and inexpressible happiness in their access unto him, and communion with him, and in the service of him. They are ministering spirits to Christ, always attend him, ever behold the glories of his person and the fulness of his grace; one part of the great mystery of godliness respecting Christ is, that he is *seen of angels*, and being *received up into glory*, is the object of their vision continually, 1 Timothy 3:16, much less are the evil angels the subjects of this grace. There is a kind of faith that is ascribed to them, the belief of a God, and that there is but one; *thou believest that there is one God; thou doest well: the devils also believe, and tremble*, James 2:19, but then they have no faith on or towards God; no trust in him and dependence on him; they have cast off allegiance to him, and have rebelled against him; and much less have they any faith in Christ; for though they know him, and cannot but assent to the truth of things concerning him, yet can have no faith in him as their Redeemer and Saviour: and therefore they themselves very justly observed, *What have we to do with thee, Jesus, thou Son of God?* they had nothing to do with him as Jesus a Saviour, and could wish they had nothing to do with him as the Son of God, to whom all judgment is committed, and theirs also, and therefore dread him; but faith in him as a Saviour they could not exercise, for he was not provided as such for them; he took not on him their nature; he was not sent, nor did he come, to seek and save them, nor to die for them; when they sinned God spared them not, made no provision of grace for them, nor promise of it to them, but cast them down from heaven to hell, and has reserved them in chains of darkness to the judgment of the great day, to everlasting wrath and damnation; so that there is not the least ground for faith and hope in Christ concerning their salvation.

Second, Men only are the subjects of the grace of faith; and, not all men; *for all men have not faith*, 2 Thessalonians 3:2, that is, special faith in God and Christ; there are but few who have it; there are many who never heard of Christ, of his gospel, and of the way of life and salvation by him; *and how shall they believe in him of whom they have not heard?* And of those that have heard of him, and of the good news of salvation by him, *they have not all obeyed the gospel, for Esaias saith, Lord, who hath believed our report?* Romans 10:14, 16. There are some who do not belong to Christ, are none of his; and which is a reason why they do not believe in him; and is a reason which Christ himself gives, and a better cannot be given; *Ye believe not, because ye are not of my sheep*; they that are the sheep of Christ hear his voice, by which faith comes; they know him spiritually and savingly; they follow him, and yield the obedience of faith unto him, John 10:26, 27. There are some of whom it is said, *they could not believe*, because they were left of God to the blindness and hardness of their hearts; and whose minds, by permission, the god of this world blinds, lest the gospel should shine into them, and so they believe not, John 12:39, 40; 2 Corinthians 4:4. In short, none but the elect of God become true believers in Christ, and all these do, in God's due time, and through the efficacy of his grace; so it has been, and so it ever will be, until they are all brought to believe in Christ; *as many as were ordained to eternal life believed*, Acts 13:48, for, the belief of the truth, of Christ, who is the truth, and of the gospel of truth, that comes by him, is the means through which God has chosen men to salvation; and which is as certain to them thereby as the thing itself; for faith is given in consequence of this choice, and is peculiar to the objects of it; hence called *the faith of God's elect*, 2 Thessalonians 2:13; Titus 1:1, such only are the partakers and subjects of this grace, who are regenerated, called, and sanctified. Such that receive Christ and believe in him are described as *born of God*; yea, it is asserted, that *whosoever believeth that Jesus is the Christ is born of God*, John 1:12, 13; 1 John 5:1, whomsoever God calls by his grace with an holy calling, he bestows faith upon them; whoever are converted and turned to the Lord, believe in him; *faith* is one of the fruits of the Spirit in sanctification, Galatians 5:22, none but such who are made spiritually alive believe in Christ; whilst men are dead in trespasses and sins they are *in unbelief,* in a state of unbelief, as the apostle was before conversion, shut up in it till mercy is displayed in quickening and relieving them; there must be first spiritual life before there can be faith; hence says Christ, *whosoever liveth and believeth in me shall never die*, John 11:26. As well may a dead carcass fly, as a dead sinner believe in Christ, or have any will and desire to it. Such only who are alive see and hear in a spiritual sense, and believe in Christ with a special faith, and shall never perish, but have everlasting life.

Third, Those who are the subjects of this grace of faith, it is different in them as to the degree and exercise of it, though it is in all *alike precious faith* as to its nature, objects, and acts; and in such is the *common faith,* common to all true believers, of which they have a mutual experience; hence the apostle calls his faith, and the faith of the believing Romans, *the mutual faith both of you and me*; yet as to the measure and degree of it, it is in some more, in others less; see 2 Peter 1:1; Titus 1:4; Romans 1:12.

1. In some it is *great faith*; instances of which we have in the centurion, and in the woman of Canaan, Matthew 8:10, and 15:28, and many great and heroic actions are ascribed unto it in Hebrews 11 though all its greatness, power, and efficacy, are to be ascribed to the Object of it.

2. In some it is but small or *little faith*; in God, and in his providence, for the supply of their temporal wants; in Christ, as to his presence with and powerful preservation and salvation of them, Matthew 6:30, and 8:26, and 14:31.

3. In others it is very little, *least of all*; it is like a grain of mustard seed, which is *the least of all seeds*, Matthew 17:20, and 13:32, and as the apostle Paul calls himself less than the least of all saints, these are the least of all believers; the little ones, as Christ calls them, who believe in him; the lambs he carries in his arms; the smoking flax and bruised reed, the day of small things he does not despise.

4. In these it seems to be next to none, and as if there was none at all; hence these words of Christ to his apostles, *How is it that you have no faith?* and again, *Where is your faith?* Mark 4:40; Luke 8:25, that is, in act and exercise; otherwise they had faith as a principle of grace in them, though so little exercised by them as scarcely to be discerned; yet little faith, even that which is the least, differs from no faith. Where there is no faith there is no desire after God, nor after Christ, nor after salvation by him, and communion with him; such neither desire him nor the knowledge of his ways; but where there is ever so small a degree of faith there is a panting after God, a desire to see Jesus, and to have

fellowship with him, and a view of interest in him: where there is no faith there is no sense of the want of it, nor complaint of it, nor desire of it, and an increase; but where there is faith, though of the least degree, the soul is sensible of the deficiency of it, and complains of its unbelief, and prays for an increase of faith; as the poor man did, *Lord, I believe; help thou mine unbelief,* Mark 9:24.

5. In some faith is weak; in others strong: of Abraham it is said, that he was *strong in faith,* and staggered not at the promise through unbelief; but *believed in hope against hope*; these circumstances showed the strength of his faith. But of others it is said, *him that is weak in the faith receive ye; but not to doubtful disputations,* Romans 4:18, 20, and 14:1. See an instance of strong faith in Habakkuk 3:17-19.

6. Faith, as to its exercise, differs in the same individuals at different times; as in Abraham, the father of all them that believe, and who was so eminent for his faith; and yet what unbelief and distrust of the power and providence of God did he discover, as to the preservation of him in Egypt and in Gerar, which put him on undue methods for his security: and in David, who sometimes in the strongest manner expresses his faith of interest in God, and in his favour, and at other times was strangely disquieted in his soul, and ready to imagine that he was cut off from the sight of God: and in Peter, who not only strongly asserted his faith in Christ as the Son of God, but so confident was he, that though all men forsook him he would not; and yet, that night denied him thrice, intimidated by a servant-maid and others!

7. In some it arises to a plerophory, a *full assurance of faith*; as it is expressed in Hebrews 10:22, which signifies going with a full sail, in allusion to ships when they sail with a prosperous gale; so souls, when they are full of faith, as Stephen was, move on towards God and Christ in the exercise of it with great spirit and rigour, bearing all before them that stand in the way; being fully persuaded of the love of God to them, and that nothing can separate them from it, and of their interest in Christ, as having loved them and given himself for them; and therefore can say with Thomas, *My Lord and my God!* and with the church, *My beloved is mine and I am his*; but this is not to be found in all

345

believers; and where it is, it is not always in the same plerophory, without any doubt, hesitation, and mixture of unbelief.

Fourth, The seat of this grace, in the subjects of it, is the whole soul of man; it is *with the heart* man believes in Christ for righteousness, life, and salvation; says Philip to the eunuch, *If thou believest with all thine heart, &c.* It has been a dispute among divines, whether faith has its seat in the understanding, or in the will, or in the affections; it seems to possess the whole soul, or the whole soul is in the possession of it, and according to its various actings faith has a concern in each faculty; as it lies in the knowledge of divine things, and presents truth to the mind, and is the evidence of things unseen, it has to do with the understanding; and the apostle says of it as such, *by faith we understand, &c.* Hebrews 11:1, 3, and sometimes the strongest acts of faith, even assurance of interest in Christ as the Redeemer and Saviour, is expressed by knowledge of him; *I know that my redeemer liveth,* Job 19:25, as it is an act of choice, preferring Christ, as a Saviour, to all others; and of affiance, trust, and dependence on him, it is an act of the will; *though he slay me, yet will I trust in him: - he also shall be my salvation,* Job 13:15, 16, and neither of these acts can be without love to Christ, and a strong motion of the affections towards him, saying, *Whom have I heaven but thee? &c.* Faith works by love.

IV. The causes of faith

The causes of faith, from whence it springs, and how it comes to pass that any who are naturally in a state of unbelief, and shut up in it, should be possessed of this grace.

First, the efficient cause is God; hence it is called *the work of God,* John 6:29, which he works by his power and grace in the hearts of men; it is expressly said to be of *the operation of God,* Colossians 2:12, it is a very considerable part of the *good work of grace,* which is begun, carried on, and performed, by the Spirit of Christ; and from it the whole is denominated the *work of faith,* which is wrought and finished with the power of God, 2 Thessalonians 1:11, and it is also called *the gift of God,* who deals forth to every man the measure of faith as he pleases, Ephesians 2:8; Romans 12:3. All the Three Divine Persons, Father, Son, and Spirit, are concerned in it.

1. God the Father; as he is the God of all grace, so of this: *No man*, says Christ, *can come unto me*, that is, believe on him, as it is explained John 6:35, *except the Father, which hath sent me draw him*; and *except it were given unto him of my Father*, John 6:44, 45, 65, see Matthew 16:16, 17.

2. The Lord Jesus Christ the Son of God, has a concern in it, it is prayed and wished for, as from God the Father, so from the Lord Jesus Christ; and is obtained through the righteousness of God and our Saviour Jesus Christ; nay, Christ is expressly called, the *Author and Finisher of faith*, Ephesians 6:23; 2 Peter 1:1; Hebrews 12:2.

3. The Holy Spirit is, with the Father and the Son, the co-efficient cause of faith; not only faith is given by the Spirit, as it intends the faith of miracles, but the special grace of faith is reckoned among the fruits of the Spirit; and from hence he is called the *Spirit of faith*, because it is his gift, and of his operation, 1 Corinthians 12:9; Galatians 5:22; 2 Corinthians 4:13.

Second, the moving cause of faith is, the free grace of God; it is not of men themselves, the produce of their free will and power; but it is *the gift of God*; a gift of his pure grace, unmerited, and unmoved to it by any thing in the creature; hence those that believe are said to have believed through grace; it is a fruit of electing grace, and flows from that; the same grace that moved God to ordain any of the sons of men to eternal life, bestows the grace of faith upon them in consequence of it, Acts 18:27, and 13:48, and this is owing to sovereign and distinguishing grace, according to which it is bestowed on some and not on others, as it seems good in the sight of God, Matthew 11:25, 26.

Third, the word and ministers of it are the usual means and instruments of faith in the hand of God, and are used by him; the end of the word being written is, that men *might believe that Jesus is the Christ, the Son of God*, John 20:31, and the word preached is, *the word of faith*; and so called, with other reasons, because faith comes by it, Romans 10:8, 17, this has often been the effect and consequence of hearing the word preached, Acts 17:4, and 18:8, and the ministers of it are the instruments by whom and through whose word, doctrine, and ministry, others believe, John 1:17, 20; 1 Corinthians 3:5, but this is only when it is attended with the power and Spirit of God, 1 Corinthians 2:4, 5.

V. The effects of faith

The effects of it, or the various things which are ascribed unto it in some sense or another, which show the usefulness and importance of this grace. As,

First, Several blessings of grace are attributed to it; and with which it is, on some account or another, connected; by it access is had unto them, and an enjoyment of them, and comfort from them.

1. Justification; hence we read of being *justified by faith*, Romans 3:30; 5:1; Galatians 2:16, and 3:8, not by it, or through it, as a work of righteousness done by men, for then they would be justified and saved by works contrary to the Scriptures, Romans 4:2, 6; Titus 3:5. Nor as a grace of the Spirit of God wrought in men; for that is a part and branch of sanctification; and would tend to confound justification and sanctification, which are two distinct things; the one an act of God's grace towards men, the other a work of his grace in them: nor as a cause of it; for it is God, and not faith that justifies, Romans 8:33, for though men are said to be justified by faith, yet faith is never said to justify them: nor as a condition of justification; for God *justifieth the ungodly*, Romans 4:5, nor as a motive; for that is the free grace of God; *being justified freely by his grace*, Romans 3:24, nor as the matter of it; that is the righteousness of Christ: faith and righteousness are two different things, and are frequently distinguished; that by which men are justified are the obedience and blood of Christ, Romans 5:9, 19, but faith is neither of them; faith is a man's own, but justifying righteousness is another's; *not having on mine own righteousness*, Philippians 3:9, faith is imperfect; but the righteousness by which men are justified is perfect, or it cannot be reckoned righteousness, Deuteronomy 6:25, it is not the το, *credere*, or act of faith, but the object who, or what, is believed in, that is imputed for righteousness; it is Christ and his righteousness, the object of faith, by which men are justified; faith objectively, or the object of faith, Christ, who is sometimes called faith, Galatians 3:23, he is made righteousness unto them; faith only relatively

considered, as it relates to Christ, receives the blessing of his justifying righteousness from him, being revealed from faith to faith, and given to it, and put into its hands; which faith puts on as a robe of righteousness, and rejoices and glories in it.

2. Adoption; faith, as before observed, receives the adoption of children from Christ, the power he gives to become the children of God; and therefore said to be, *the children of God by faith in Christ Jesus*, Galatians 3:26, that is, manifestly so; faith does not make them the children of God, but makes them appear to be such.

3. The remission of sins; *God has set forth Christ to be a propitiation, through faith in his blood, for the remission of sins*, Romans 3:25, not that faith has any virtue or merit in it to procure it: nor is it for the sake of faith that God forgives sins; but for his own name's sake, for Christ's sake, whose blood was shed for it; but faith receives the remission of sins, as flowing from the grace of God through the blood of Christ, Acts 10:43.

4. Sanctification and purification are ascribed to faith. So it is said of such that receive the forgiveness of sins, that they also *receive an inheritance among them which are sanctified by faith that is in me*, in Christ, Acts 26:18, and again, *purifying their hearts by faith*, Acts 15:9, not that faith has such virtue in it as to sanctify and purify from sin; but as it has to do with the blood of Christ which cleanses from all sin.

5. Eternal life and salvation are connected with faith; yea, it is life eternal to know Christ, that is, to believe in him; nay, he that believes in him *has everlasting life*, John 17:3, and 6:47, not that faith is the procuring and meritorious cause of it; *for eternal life is the gift of God through Jesus Christ our Lord*, and faith looks unto the mercy of Christ for it, Romans 6:23; Jude 21.

Second, By faith souls have communion with God, with Christ, and with his people, in his word and ordinances.

1. They have access to God at the throne of grace, and can use freedom, boldness, and confidence with him, in asking of him what they stand in need of; *in whom*, says the apostle, *we have boldness and access with confidence by the faith of him*; that is, by faith in Christ, Ephesians 3:12. Christ is the way of access to

God; there is no coming to him but by Christ the Mediator, and by faith in him; faith gives freedom and boldness to speak to God; faith presents Christ's righteousness, pleads his blood, and brings his sacrifice in its arms, and boldly enters into the holiest of all thereby; and goes to God, even up to his seat, and lays hold on him, and claims interest in him, and will not go without a blessing.

2. The inhabitation of Christ in the hearts of his people is through faith; the apostle prayed for the Ephesians, that, says he, *Christ may dwell in your hearts by faith*, Ephesians 3:17, not in their heads by fancy and notion; but in their hearts by faith: there is a mutual indwelling of Christ, and believers in each other; he dwells in them by faith, and they dwell in him by faith; *he that eateth my flesh and drinketh my blood, dwelleth in me and I in him*, John 6:56, that is, who feeds by faith upon him; Christ and believers are not only inmates in the same house, and dwell under the same roof, but they mutually dwell in each other by faith, which is expressive of great nearness, intimacy, and communion.

3. Believers feed and live upon Christ by faith; he, says Christ, *that eateth me*, his flesh and blood by faith, *even he shall live by me*, a life of grace, which will issue in eternal life; yea, such as thus feed on Christ *have eternal life*, John 6:54, 57; and a most comfortable life this is, which a believer lives by faith on Christ, and so a very desirable one; *the life which I now live in the flesh*, says the apostle, *I live by the faith of the Son of God*, Galatians 2:20; nor did he desire any other; a better and a more comfortable life cannot be lived in this world; *the just shall live by faith*; not upon his faith; but by faith on Christ, Romans 1:17.

4. It is by faith that believers stand, and walk, and go on comfortably in their Christian race; *thou standest by faith*, in a gospel-church-state, in a profession of Christ, and in the enjoyment of his word and ordinances: *by faith ye stand*; keep your ground; turn not back, nor are moved from the hope of the gospel, Romans 11:20; 2 Corinthians 1:24. *We walk by faith, and not by sight*; so did the apostle, and so he directs others; *as ye have therefore received Christ Jesus the Lord, so walk ye in him*, 2 Corinthians 5:7; Colossians 2:6, go on believing in him till ye receive the end of your faith, the salvation of your souls.

5. Faith makes Christ precious to souls; *unto you which believe he is precious,* 1 Peter 2:7. Faith beholds the glories of Christ's person; the riches of his grace; the treasures and wonders of his love; which render him altogether lovely and the chiefest among ten thousands.

6. *Faith worketh by love,* Galatians 5:6, both by love to Christ and by love to his people; the clearer views a soul has of Christ by faith the more it loves him; and the more closely it cleaves unto him, leans upon him, and embraces him by faith, the more its affections are drawn out to him; and the more it feeds on him by faith, and the more tastes it has of him that he is gracious, the more are its desires to him, and to the remembrance of him; and it cannot but love all that bear his image, and partake of his grace; these precious sons of Zion are precious to whom Christ is precious, and are the excellent in the earth, in whom is the delight of such, even such who are Christ's Hephzibah and his jewels.

7. It is faith which makes the word useful and the ordinances pleasant and delightful. Where faith is wanting the word is of no use: *the word preached did not profit them, not being mixed with faith in them that heard it,* Hebrews 4:2, the word is compared to food, which though notionally received, yet if not heartily digested by faith, does not nourish; it is only when Christ is held forth, and seen in the galleries, and shows himself through the lattices to faith, that the ordinances are amiable and lovely, or when he is fed upon by faith in them; as the Israelites by faith kept the passover, a type of Christ our passover, sacrificed for us; so believers keep the feast of the Lord's Supper in commemoration of that sacrifice, and when they do it in faith, it is with joy and comfort, and to great usefulness.

Third, There are various other useful things ascribed to faith, as the effects of it: as,

1. It makes not ashamed. It is said, *he that believeth shall not make haste,* Isaiah 28:16, after another Saviour, or to lay another foundation, being satisfied with Christ. In some places in the New Testament the phrase is rendered, *shall not be ashamed and shall not be confounded,* Romans 9:33, and 10:11; 1 Peter 2:6, such who believe shall not be ashamed of their faith and hope in

Christ; nor of their profession of him; nor of the reproaches, sufferings, and persecutions they endure for his sake; nor shall they be confounded by any of their enemies; nor meet with a disappointment in their expectations here or hereafter, Psalm 22:5.

2. It fills the soul with joy on hearing the word, the good news of salvation by Christ; so the gaoler, on hearing the word of salvation preached, rejoiced, believing in God, Acts 16:31-34, and indeed, a sight of Christ by faith will fill a soul *with joy unspeakable and full of glory*, 1 Peter 1:8, hence we read of *the joy of faith*; for as faith increases joy does; wherefore the apostle prays that the Romans might be *filled with all joy and peace in believing*, Philippians 1:25; Romans 15:13.

3. It is by faith that saints get the victory over Satan, and the world, and every enemy; faith holds up Christ, the shield, whereby it keeps off every fiery dart of Satan, yea, quenches them; though he, like a roaring lion, goes about seeking whom he may devour; yet the true believer so resists him, being steadfast in faith, that he cannot get an advantage over him, but is obliged to flee from him, Ephesians 6:16; 1 Peter 5:9, and though the world is a very powerful enemy, yet *this is the victory that overcometh the world, even our faith; who is he that overcometh the world, but he that believeth that Jesus is the Son of God?*, 1 John 5:4, 5.

4. It is by faith that saints are kept unto salvation, and are saved by grace through it. *Salvation* is the *end* of their *faith*, and what it issues in; and they *are kept by the power of God through faith*; the power of God supporting their faith that it fail not, until they are brought unto salvation, to the full enjoyment of it, 1 Peter 1:5, 9, nor does this at all detract from the grace of God; since faith itself is a gift of grace, and gives all the glory to it, Ephesians 2:8, 9.

VI. The properties of faith

The properties or adjuncts of faith, which may lead more into the nature and excellency of it, and serve to confirm what has been said concerning it:

1. It is the first and principal grace, it stands first in order, and takes the precedence of other graces; *now abideth faith, hope, charity*, which last, though the greatest, yet not as to quality and use, but as to quantity or duration; faith is not only of the greatest importance in duty, service, and worship, without which it is impossible to please God; but it has the greatest influence on other graces, it sets them all at work, and as that is in exercise so are they more or less.

2. It is a grace exceeding precious, even the least degree of it; as it is in the least believer, it is *like precious faith*, as to its object, nature, and acts, with that in the greatest; it is more precious than gold that perisheth, for richness, brightness, splendour, and glory; it makes poor men rich, and is more bright and glorious than pearls and rubies, and all desirable things; it is more valuable than gold, because that perishes, but this does not; and it makes Christ precious, or shows him to be so, to them that believe, 2 Peter 1:1; 1 Peter 1:7, and 2:7.

3. It is but one; as there is but one Lord to be believed in, and to be subject to, so but one faith; as but one doctrine of faith, that faith once delivered to the saints, so but one grace of faith; though there are divers sorts of faith, there is but one that is special, spiritual, and saving, the faith of God's elect; though there are many subjects of it in whom it is, and many are the acts of it, and there are different degrees, as to the exercise of it, yet the grace itself is but one and alike in all, Ephesians 4:5; 2 Peter 1:1.

4. Though faith is called *common* faith, common to all God's elect, yet every man has his own faith; *the just shall live by his faith*, and not another's, Habakkuk 2:4. The faith of one man is of no service to another in the business of salvation; and no further useful to another than for imitation and encouragement to believe also; hence we read of *thy faith*, and *my faith*, as distinct from one another, James 2:18. Christ said to Peter, *I have prayed for thee that thy faith fail not*, Luke 22:32, meaning his particular, personal faith; not but that Christ has the same regard to all his people, and equally intercedes for them on the same account.

5. It is true, real, and unfeigned, 1 Timothy 1:5; 2 Timothy 1:5. There is an hypocritical faith, which lies only in profession, in saying that a man believes, when he does not, as Simon Magus;

and there is a believing with the heart, even with all the heart, as the eunuch did, Acts 8:13, 37, see Romans 10:9, 10.

6. It is a grace that cannot be lost; it flows from, and is secured by, the firm and immutable decree and purpose of election; it is given in consequence of that, and remains sure by it; it is a gift of God, and one of those gifts of his which are without repentance, is irreversible and irrevocable; it is confirmed by the prevalent intercession of Christ, and which he himself is the Author and Finisher of.

7. It is indeed but imperfect; yet may be increased; as knowledge is imperfect; *We know but in part*; so faith is imperfect; it has its τα υσερηματα, its deficiencies, or something *lacking* in it, to be perfected by prayer to God, saying, *Lord, increase our faith*; by the ministry of the word, and by a constant attendance on ordinances; and sometimes *faith grows exceedingly*; 1 Thessalonians 3:10; 2 Thessalonians 1:3.

8. According to the apostle's account of it, it *is the substance of things hoped for, the evidence of things not seen*, Hebrews 11:1, it realizes things, and gives them a subsistence, and makes them appear solid and substantial; it brings distant things near, and future things present; it makes difficult things plain and easy, and unseen things visible and gives a certainty to them all.

Appendix V

Of Repentance Towards God[357]

REPENTANCE is another part of internal worship; it is a branch of godliness which lies in the disposition of the soul Godwards; for in the exercise of this the sensible sinner has much to do with God; he has a special respect to him against whom he has sinned, and therefore it is with great propriety called Repentance toward God, Acts 20:21.

Concerning which may be observed,

I. The meaning of repentance
Its name, and the words and phrases by which it is expressed, both in the Old and in the New Testament, and by Jews, Greeks, and Latins, which may give some light into the thing itself.

1. The Jews commonly express it by השׁוּבה a turning, or returning, and it is frequently signified in the Old Testament by a man's turning from his evil ways, and returning to the Lord; the term from which he turns is sin, the term to which he turns is the Lord, against whom he has sinned; and what most powerfully moves, encourages, and induces him to turn, is the pardoning grace and mercy of God through Christ, Isaiah 55:7, and so in the New Testament, repentance and turning are mentioned together, and the latter as explanative of the former; see Acts

---

357 *A Body of Doctrinal and Practical Divinity*, The Baptist Standard Bearer, p. 713ff.

3:19, and 26:20. There is another word in Hebrew used for repentance נחם Hosea 11:8, and 13:14, which also signifies *comfort*; because such who sincerely repent of sin, and are truly humbled for it, should be comforted, lest, as the apostle says, they should be *swallowed up with overmuch sorrow*, 2 Corinthians 2:7, and it is God's usual way to bring his people into the wilderness, into a distressed state, to lead them into a sense of sin, and humiliation for it, and then to speak comfortably to them, Hosea 2:14, and the Spirit of God is first a reprover for sin, and a convincer of it, and then a comforter; he first shews men the evil nature of sin, and the just desert of it, and gives them the grace of repentance for it, and then comforts them with the application of pardon through the blood of Jesus, John 16:7, 8, 14, and blessed are they that mourn for sin in an evangelical manner, for they shall be comforted, Matthew 5:4.

2. The Greek word more frequently used in the New Testament for repentance is μετανοια, which signifies an after-understanding, or after-wit; as when a man takes into serious consideration a fact after it is committed, and thinks otherwise of it, and wishes he had not done it, is sorry for it, and resolves, through the grace of God, to forsake such practices; this is a proof of a man's wisdom and understanding; now he begins to be wise, and to shew himself an understanding man; even an heathen could say, 'Repentance is the beginning of wisdom, and an avoiding of foolish works and words, and the first preparation to a life not to be repented of.' It is a change of the mind for the better, and which produces change of action and conduct: this, as it is expressive of true repentance, flows from the understanding being enlightened by the Spirit of God, when the sinner beholds sin in another light, even as exceeding sinful; and loathes it, and abhors it and himself for it. There is another word the Greeks use for repentance, μεταμελεια, and though the noun is not used in the New Testament, the verb is, Matthew 21:29, 32, and signifies a care and anxiety of mind after a fact is committed, a concern with sorrow that it should be done, and a care for the future not to do it again; hence the apostle, among the genuine fruits of godly sorrow for sin, mentions this in the first place, *What carefulness it wrought in you,* not to offend more, 2 Corinthians 7:11. It also signifies a change of mind and conduct, as appears from Matthew 21:29, a penitent sinner has another notion of sin than he had; before it was a sweet morsel, now a bitter and evil thing; before his heart was bent upon

it, now determined through divine grace to forsake it, and cleave to the Lord with full purpose of heart.

3. The Latins generally express repentance by *poenitentia*, from *poena* punishment; hence our English word *penitence*, and the popish penance, which is a sort of corporal punishment for sin inflicted on the body by fastings, scourgings, pilgrimages, &c. but true penitence lies not in these things, but is rather an inward punishment of the mind, when a man is so displeased with himself for what he has done, and so severely reflects upon himself for it, that he takes as it were a kind of vengeance on himself within himself, which are the lashes of conscience; so the apostle observes of godly sorrow, *What indignation, yea, what revenge* it wrought in you, as in the above quoted place; and this inward revenge is sometimes expressed by outward gestures, as by smiting upon the thigh, and upon the breast, Jeremiah 31:19; Luke 18:13. There is another word which the Latins use for repentance, *resipiscentia*, which signifies a man's being wise again, a coming to his wits, to his senses again. Lactantius explains it of the recovery of a man's mind from a state of insanity; a man, whilst he is in an unconverted and impenitent state, is not himself, he is not in his right mind; not only his foolish heart is darkened, and he is without understanding, and to do good has no knowledge, but *madness* is *in his heart while* he *lives* in such a state; every act of sin is not only folly but madness, as all acts of hostility committed against God, which sins are, must needs be; the man that dwelt among the tombs, Mark 5:1-19, is a fit emblem of such persons: now when an impenitent sinner becomes penitent, he may be said to come to himself, as the prodigal did, Luke 15:17, so the apostle Paul before conversion was exceeding mad against the saints, and thought he ought to do many things contrary to the name of Jesus; but when he was converted he was recovered from his insanity, and appeared sober and in his right mind, and said, *Lord, what wilt thou have me to do?* when a sinner is truly convinced of sin, and thoroughly humbled for it, and has repentance unto life given him, and a comfortable application of the blood and righteousness of Christ unto him for his pardon and justification, and his mind is become sedate, serene and quiet, the man who before was mad, is an emblem of him, when he was seen *sitting clothed and in his right mind*, Mark 5:15.

4. The word *contrition*, or brokenness of mind, is sometimes used for repentance, and there is some foundation for it in the word of God;

we often read of a contrite heart and spirit; David says he was *feeble and sore broken*, Psalm 38:8, which seems to be under a sense of sin: a man's heart is naturally hard, as hard as the nether millstone, and therefore called a stony heart, and such an one is an impenitent one; hence *hardness*, and *an impenitent heart*, are put together, as designing the same thing, Romans 2:5. The word of God is made use of to break it in pieces, is *not my word like a hammer to break the rock in pieces?* that is, to make the heart contrite, which is like to a rock, and whereby it becomes soft and tender, as Josiah's was, like an heart of flesh, susceptible of serious impressions, and of a true sense of things; and though this contrition of heart seems to be a work of the law, by which is the knowledge of sin, and which works wrath in the conscience on account of it, smites and cuts and wounds it; yet hereby it is prepared to receive the benefit of the gospel, by which *the Lord healeth the broken in heart, and bindeth up their wounds*, Psalm 147:3; Isaiah 61:1. However, great notice is taken of men of contrite hearts and spirits; the sacrifices of such hearts are acceptable to God; he looks unto, is nigh unto, and dwells with those who are of such a spirit and saves them, Psalm 51:17, and 34:18, Isaiah 57:15, and 66:2, besides the heart may be broken, made soft and melted down as much or more under a sense of pardoning grace displayed in the gospel, than under a sense of wrath through the threatenings and terrors of the law.

5. Repentance is expressed by sorrow for sin. *My sorrow is continually before me*, says David, *I will be sorry for my sin*, Psalm 38:17, 18, and which is signified not by outward gestures, not by rending garments, but by rending the heart, Joel 2:13, it is a felt pain and inward sorrow of the heart for sin, and what the apostle calls a sorrow *after a godly sort*, κατα θεον, after God, which is according to the mind and will of God; and because of sin committed against God, a God of love, grace, and mercy, and which springs from love to God and hatred of sin, and is attended with faith in God, as a God pardoning iniquity, transgression, and sin, for Christ's sake; but of this more hereafter.

II. The kinds of repentance

The nature and kinds of repentance. Not to take notice of the penance of the Papists, which lies in punishing their bodies, as before observed; and in men making themselves, or in others making them, public examples in such a way; which though it may be called repentance before men, it is not repentance towards God, nor does it answer the end vainly intended by it, making satisfaction for sin; nor is an external reformation of life and manners repentance in the sight of God. Men may be outwardly reformed, as the Pharisees were, and yet not repent of their sins, as they did not, Matthew 21:32, and 23:28, and after such an external reformation men may return to their former sinful course of life, and their last end be worse than the beginning; besides there may be true repentance for sin where there is no time and opportunity for reformation, or showing forth a reformation of life and manners, as in the thief upon the cross and others, who are brought to repentance on their deathbeds; and reformation of life and manners, when it is best and most genuine, is the fruit and effect of repentance, and a bringing forth fruits meet for it, as evidences of it, and so distinct from that itself.

1st, There is a natural repentance, or what is directed to by the light of nature, and the dictates of a natural conscience; for as there was in the heathens, and so is in every natural man, a knowledge of good and evil, of the difference in some respects between moral good and evil, and a conscience which, when it does its office, approves of what is well done, and accuses for that which is ill; so when conscience charges a man with doing an ill thing, and he is convinced of it, the light of nature and conscience direct him to wish he had not done it, and, to repent of it, and to endeavour for the future to avoid it; as may be seen in the case of the Ninevites, who being threatened with the destruction of their city for their sins, proclaimed a fast, and issued out an order that every one should turn from his evil ways, in hope that the wrath of God would be averted from them, though they could not be fully assured of it. The Gentiles laid great stress upon their repentance to conciliate the favour of God unto them; for they thought this made complete satisfaction for their sins, and wiped them clean, so that they imagined they were almost if not altogether pure and innocent: there is a repentance which the goodness of God in providence might or should lead men unto, which yet it does not, *but after their hardness and impenitent heart treasurest up wrath against the day of wrath, and revelation of the righteous judgment of God*, Romans 2:4, 5.

2nd, There is a national repentance, such as the Jews in Babylon were called unto, to which temporal blessings were promised, and a deliverance from temporal calamities; as on the one hand, a living in their own land, and a comfortable enjoyment of good things in it; and on the other hand, captivity, and all the distresses of it threatened; *Repent, and turn yourselves from all your transgressions; so iniquity shall not be your ruin,* Ezekiel 18:30-32, and which has no connection with the special grace of God, and with spiritual and everlasting things. The same people were called to repent of their pharisaism, of their disbelief of the Messiah, and other evil works; and were told that the men of Nineveh would rise up in judgment and condemn them, who repented at the preaching of Jonah, and yet a greater than Jonah, even Christ himself, called them to repentance, Matthew 12:41. The same people were called upon by the apostles of Christ to repent of their rejection of Jesus as the Messiah, and to turn unto him, and to save themselves from temporal ruin, which for their impenitence and unbelief came upon their nation, city, and temple, Acts 3:19.

3rd, There is an external repentance, or an outward humiliation for sin, such as was in Ahab, which, though nothing more, it was taken notice of by the Lord, *Seest thou how Ahab humbleth himself before me?* and though it lay only in rending his clothes, and putting on sackcloth, and in fasting, and in a mournful way, yet the Lord was pleased to promise that the evil threatened should not come in his days, 1 Kings 21:29. And such is the repentance Tyre and Sidon would have exercised, had they had the advantages and privileges that some cities had, where Christ taught his doctrines, and wrought miracles; and of this kind was the repentance of the Ninevites which was regarded of God, Matthew 11:21, and 12:41.

4th, There is an hypocritical repentance, such as was in the people of Israel in the wilderness, who when the wrath of God broke out against them for their sins, *returned* unto him, or repented, but *their heart was not right with him,* Psalm 78:34-37, so it is said of Judah, she *hath not turned unto me with her whole heart, but feignedly, saith the Lord*; and of Ephraim, or the ten tribes, *they return, but not to the most High: they are like a deceitful bow,* Hosea 7:16, who turned aside and dealt unfaithfully.

5th, There is a legal and there is an evangelical repentance.

1. There is a legal one, which is a mere work of the law, and the effect of convictions of sin by it, which in time wear off and come to nothing; for

(1) There may be a sense of sin and an acknowledgment of it, and yet no true repentance for it, as in the cases of Pharaoh and of Judas, who both said, I have sinned, Exodus 9:27, Matthew 27:4, yet they had no true sense of the exceeding sinfulness of sin, nor godly sorrow for it.

(2) There may be a kind of sorrow for it, not for the evil of fault that is in sin, but on account of the evil of punishment for it, as appears in some cases, and in Cain's, Genesis 4:13.

(3) There may be a great deal of terror of mind because of sin, a great outcry about it, a fearful looking for of judgment for it, abundance of tears shed on the account of it, as were by Esau for the blessing, without success; the devils believe and tremble, but do not repent; there is weeping and wailing in hell, but no repentance.

(4) Such a repentance, if no more than a mere legal one, issues in despair, as in Cain, whose words may be rendered, *My sin is greater than that it may be forgiven*; it is a repentance that may be repented of and is not unto life, but ends in death, as it did in Judas; it is *the sorrow of the world which worketh death*, 2 Corinthians 7:10.

2. There is an evangelical repentance, which lies,

(1) In a true sight and sense of sin; in a sight of it, as in itself considered as exceeding sinful in its own nature, and not merely as in its effects and consequences ruinous and destructive; not only in a sight of it in the glass of the divine law, but as that is held in the hand, and seen in the light of the blessed Spirit; and in a sight of it as contrary to the pure and holy nature of God, as well as repugnant to his will, and a breach of his law; and in a view of it as it appears in the glass of pardoning love and grace.

(2) In a hearty and unfeigned sorrow for it; this sorrow for it is the rather because it is against God, and that not only as a holy and righteous Being, but as good, and gracious, and merciful, of whose goodness, both in providence and grace, the sinner is sensible; the consideration of which increases his sorrow, and makes it the more intense and hearty.

361

(3) It is attended with shame and confusion of face, as in Ezra 9:6, 8, 10; Luke 18:13, this shame increases the more, the more a sinner is sensible that God is *pacified* towards him *for all that he hast done*, Ezekiel 16:63.

(4) Such a repentance is accompanied with a loathing, detestation, and abhorrence of sin as the worst of evils; to truly penitent sinners sin appears most odious and loathsome; nay they not only loathe their sins but themselves for them, and the rather when most sensible of the goodness of God in bestowing both temporal and spiritual blessings on them, and especially the latter, Ezekiel 20:40-44, and 36:25-31, yea they abhor it as of all things the most detestable, when they are in the exercise of this grace; so it was with holy Job, when favoured with a special sight of the greatness and goodness of God, Job 42:6, see also Isaiah 6:5.

(5) Where this repentance is there is an ingenuous acknowledgment of sin, as may be seen in David, Psalm 32:5, and 51:3, in Daniel 9:4, 5, and in the apostle Paul, 1 Timothy 1:13-15, so the prodigal, as soon as he came to himself, and was made sensible of his sin, and repented of it, went to his father, and said to him, *Father, I have sinned against heaven, and in thy sight*, Luke 15:21, and to encourage such a sincere repentance and ingenuous confession, the apostle John says, *If we confess our sins, he is faithful and just to forgive us our sins, and to cleanse us from all unrighteousness*, 1 John 1:9.

(6) It is followed with a resolution, through the grace of God, to forsake sin; this the sinner is encouraged unto, as before observed, by the abundance of pardon through the mercy of God in Christ, Isaiah 55:7, and indeed it is only such who can expect to share in it; *Whoso confesseth* (sins) *and forsaketh them, shall have mercy*, Proverbs 28:13. Now such a repentance appears to be evangelical; inasmuch, as

1. It is from the Spirit of God, who reproves for sin and convinces of it, enlightens the eyes of the understanding to see the exceeding sinfulness of sin; and as a Spirit of grace and supplication works this grace in the heart, and draws it forth into exercise, to mourn over sin in a gospel manner at the throne of grace, Zechariah 12:10.

2. Such repentance, in the exercise of it, follows upon real conversion and divine instruction, *Surely after that I was turned I repented; and after that I was instructed, I smote upon my thigh*, Jeremiah 31:19, upon such a turn as is made by powerful and efficacious grace, and upon such instruction as leads into the true nature of sin, the effect of which is blushing shame and confusion.

3. Is what is encouraged and influenced by gospel promises, such as these in Isaiah 55:7; Jeremiah 3:12, 13, now when repentance proceeds not upon the terrors of the law, but upon such gracious promises as these, it may be called evangelical.

4. It is that which is attended with faith and hope: repentance towards God, and faith in our Lord Jesus Christ, go together as doctrines, and so they do as graces; which is first in exercise is not easy to say; our Lord says of the Pharisees, that they *repented not, that they might believe*, which looks as if repentance was before and in order to believing, Matthew 21:32, and elsewhere faith is represented as first looking to Christ, and then repentance or mourning for sin; repentance, as some have expressed it, is a tear that drops from faith's eye, Zechariah 12:10. However, that is truly evangelical repentance which has with it faith in the blood of Christ for the remission of sins; for repentance and remission of sins, as they go together as doctrines, so also as blessings of grace, Luke 24:47; Acts 5:31, for where true repentance for sin is, there must be faith in Christ for the remission of it, at least hope of pardon by his blood, or else such repentance would issue in despair, and appear to be no other than the sorrow of the world which worketh death.

5. It is such a repentance which flows not from dread of punishment, and from fear of the wrath of God, but from love to God, and of righteousness and holiness, and from an hatred of sin; they that love the Lord hate evil, and they love righteousness and hate evil because he does; and when tempted to sin reason after this manner, *How can I do this great wickedness, and sin against God*, so holy,

just, and good, and who has shown such love and kindness to me? Genesis 39:9. It was love to Christ, flowing from a sense of pardoning grace and mercy, that fetched such a flood of tears from the eyes of the penitent woman at Christ's feet, with which she washed them, and wiped them with the hairs of her head; and which caused Peter, under a sense of sin, to go out and weep bitterly, Luke 7:37, 38, 47, and 22:61, 62.

III. The object and subjects of repentance
The object and subjects of repentance; the object is sin, the subjects are sinners.

First, The object of repentance is sin, hence called *repentance from dead works*, which sins be; and from which the blood of Christ purges the conscience of a penitent sinner, and speaks peace and pardon to it, Hebrews 6:1, and 9:14. And,

1st, Not only grosser sins, but sins of a lesser size, are to be repented of; there is a difference in sins, some are greater others lesser, John 19:11, both are to be repented of; sins against the first and second tables of the law, sins more immediately against God, and sins against men; and some against men are more heinous and enormous than others, as well as those against God; as not only worshipping of devils, and idols of gold and silver, &c. but murders, sorceries, fornications, and thefts, which ought to be repented of, but by some were not, though they had deliverances from plagues, which was an aggravation of their impenitence, Revelation 9:20, 21, and not only those, but also sins of a lesser kind are to be repented of; and even sinful thoughts, for the thought of foolishness is sin, and to be repented of; for the unrighteous man is to repent of and forsake his thoughts, as well as the wicked man his ways, and turn to the Lord; and not only unclean, proud, malicious, envious, and revengeful thoughts are to be repented of, but even thoughts of seeking for justification before God by a man's own righteousness, which may be intended in the text referred to, Isaiah 55:7.

2nd, Not only public but private sins are to be repented of. There are some sins which are committed in a very public manner, in the face of the sun, and are known to all; and there are others that are more secret;

and a truly sensible sinner, as he desires to be *cleansed from secret faults*, or to have those forgiven him, so he heartily repents of them, even of sins known to none but God and his own soul; and this is a proof of the genuineness of his repentance.

3rd, There are sins both of omission and commission, which are to be repented of; when a man omits those duties of religion which ought to be done, or commits those sins which ought to be avoided by him; or omits the weightier matters of religion, and only attends to lesser ones, when he ought to have done the one, and not to have left the other undone; and as God forgives both, Isaiah 43:22-25, so both sorts of sins are to be repented of; and a sense of pardoning grace will engage the sensible sinner to it.

4th, There are sins which are committed in the most solemn, serious, religious, and holy performances of God's people, which are to be repented of; for there is not a just man that does good and sinneth not in that good he does; there is not only an imperfection, but an impurity in the best righteousness of the saints of their own working out, and therefore called filthy rags; and as there was provision made under the law for the bearing and removing the sins of holy things, as by Aaron the high priest, so there is a provision made for the atonement of these as well as all other sins, by Christ our high priest; and therefore these are to be confessed and mourned over the head of him our antitypical scapegoat.

5th, The daily sins of life are to be repented of; no man lives without sin, it is daily committed by the best of men, in many things we all offend, and even in all things; and as we have need to pray, and are directed to pray daily for the forgiveness of sin, so we are to repent of it daily; repentance is not only to be exercised upon the first conviction and conversion of a sinner, nor only on account of some grievous sin, or great backsliding he may after fall into, but it is continually to be exercised by believers, since they are continually sinning against God in thought, word, and deed.

6th, Not only actual sins and transgressions in thought, word, and deed, are to be repented of, but original and indwelling sin. Thus David when he fell into some grievous sins, and was brought to a true sense of them, and a sincere repentance for them, he not only made a confession of them in the penitential psalm he wrote on that occasion, but he was led to take notice of, and acknowledge and mourn over the original corruption of his nature, from whence all his sinful actions flowed, saying, *Behold I was shapen in iniquity*, Psalm 51:5. So the apostle Paul, though he lived a life unstained, and in all good conscience, free from any public, external, notorious sin, yet owned and lamented the sin that dwelt in him, and the force, power, and prevalence of it, as that it hindered him from doing the good he would, and put him on doing the evil he would not, Romans 7:18-24. Now when a sensible sinner confesses, laments, and mourns over the original corruption of his nature, and the sin that dwells in him, it is a clear case his repentance is genuine and sincere, since it is what he himself is only sensible of. Now all this is with respect to God; the sinner repents of sin with regard to God, and as it concerns him, and therefore is called *repentance towards God*, and a sorrow for it *after a godly sort*, Acts 20:21; 2 Corinthians 7:11, and he repents of sin because sin is committed against him.

1. All sin is against God in a sense, as it is against his will, yet there is distinction between sins against God and against men, 1 Samuel 2:25, now sin committed against God, and considered as such, is a cutting consideration to a sensible sinner, sensible of the greatness and goodness of God, and causes his sorrow and repentance for sin to rise higher, as it was to David, *Against thee, thee only, have I sinned, and done this evil in thy sight*, Psalm 51:4.

2. Because sin is a breach of the law of God, 1 John 3:4, of that law, which is itself, holy, just, and good; of that law of which God is the giver, and who is that lawgiver that is able to save and to destroy, and on whose legislative power and authority a contempt is cast by sin, and which therefore gives pain and distress of mind to the penitent sinner.

3. Because sin is contrary to the nature of God, as well as to his law; he is of purer eyes than to behold it with approbation; he is not a God that takes pleasure in it, but is displeased with it; it is the abominable thing his righteous soul hates, and therefore they that love the Lord must hate it, and it cannot but give them a concern, and cause sorrow when they commit it.

4. And the rather as by sinning a slight is cast on his goodness, grace, and love, and which occasions severe reflections on themselves, and much shame and blushing that they should sin

against so much goodness, and against God, who has shown them so much favour, loved them so greatly, and bestowed such blessings of grace upon them.

5. It appears that the sinner in repentance has to do with God, by confessing his sin and his sorrow for it; and also others glorify God for granting repentance to him as the Christian Jews did on the behalf of the Gentiles, Acts 11:18, and even there is joy in heaven, and God is glorified by the angels there, on account even of one sinner that repents, Luke 15:7, 10.

Second, The subjects of repentance are sinners, and only such; Adam, in a state of innocence, was not a subject of repentance, for not having sinned he had no sin to repent of; and such who fancy themselves to be perfectly righteous, and without sin in their own apprehensions, stand in no need of repentance, and therefore Christ says, *I am not come to call the righteous, but sinners to repentance*, Matthew 9:13, see Luke 15:7. Now,

1. All men are sinners, all descending from Adam by ordinary generation; all his posterity being seminally in him, and represented by him when he sinned, sinned in him, and they both have his sin imputed to them, and a corrupt nature derived from him; and so are transgressors from the womb, and are all guilty of actual sins and transgressions; and so all stand in need of repentance, even such who trust in themselves that they are righteous, and despise others as less holy than themselves, and think they need no repentance: yet they do; and not only they, but such who are in the best sense righteous need daily repentance, since they are continually sinning in all they do.

2. Men of all nations, Jews and Gentiles, are the subjects of repentance; for all are under sin, under the power of it, involved in the guilt of it, and liable to punishment for it, and God has commanded *all men every where to repent*, Acts 17:30. During the time of John the Baptist, and of our Lord's being on earth, the doctrine of repentance was only preached to the Jews; but after the resurrection of Christ he gave his apostles an instruction and order *that repentance and remission of sins should be preached in his name among all nations, beginning at Jerusalem*, Luke 24:47, in consequence of which the apostles first exhorted the Jews and then the Gentiles to repent, and particularly the apostle Paul *testified both to the Jews, and also to the Greeks,*

repentance towards God, as well as *faith toward our Lord Jesus Christ*, Acts 20:21.

3. Men are only subjects of repentance in the present life; when this life is ended, and the gospel dispensation is over, and Christ is come a second time, the door of repentance as well as of faith will be shut, and there will be no place found for it; no opportunity nor means of it; nor any subjects capable of it; as for the saints in heaven they need it not, being entirely without sin; and as for the wicked in hell, they are in utter despair, and not capable of repentance unto life, and unto salvation not to be repented of, and though there is weeping and wailing there, yet no repentance. Hence the rich man in hell was so solicitous to have Lazarus sent to his brethren living, hoping, that by means of one that came to them from the dead to warn them of the place of torment, they would repent, as well knowing they never would if not in the present life, and before they came into the place where he was; therefore repentance is not to be procrastinated.

IV. The Author, and cause, and means of repentance

1. The Author and efficient cause of it is not man himself, but God; *then hath God also granted repentance to the Gentiles*, Acts 11:18, it is not in the power of man to repent of himself, for he is by nature blind, and has no sight and sense of sin; his understanding is darkened with respect unto it, and he is darkness itself till made light in the Lord; and until he has a sight and sense of sin he can never truly repent of it; his heart is hard and obdurate, his heart is an heart of stone, and he cannot really repent of sin until that stony heart is taken away, and an heart of flesh is given; and whenever he becomes sensible of his need of repentance, he prays to God for it, saying, *Turn thou me, and I shall be turned*: nor do exhortations to repentance suppose it in the power of man to repent of himself; since these are only designed to bring him to a sense of his need of it, and of his obligation to it, and of his impotence to it of himself through the hardness of his heart, and to direct him to seek it of God, who only can give it; for,

2. Though God may give men space to repent, yet if he does not give the grace of repentance, they never will repent. Thus he gave space to the old world, threatened with a flood, which some think is meant by the one hundred and twenty years allowed them, when the longsuffering of God waited in the times of Noah, while the ark was preparing, but

without effect; so Jezebel, or Antichrist, is said to have space given her *to repent of her fornication, and she repented not*, Revelation 2:21, and this God sometimes gives to the children of men to show his sovereignty, that he will have mercy on whom he will have mercy, and give repentance to whom he pleases; and for the sake of his elect, not willing that any of them should perish, but that they should all come to repentance, and therefore his longsuffering towards them is salvation; and this also he sometimes gives to show his forbearance of the vessels of wrath, and to leave them inexcusable. Nay,

3. Though some men have the means of repentance, yet grace not being given them of God they repent not; the word, unless attended with power, is ineffectual; the most severe judgments inflicted on men are insufficient, as the plagues on Pharaoh, whose heart was the worse and more hardened under them, Exodus 11:10, and though the children of Israel were smitten with famine, with the pestilence, and with the sword, yet they repented not, nor returned unto the Lord, Amos 4:6-11, so the fourth and fifth vials poured forth on men, which will scorch and fill them with pains and sores, instead of repenting of their deeds they will blaspheme the God of heaven and his name, Revelation 16:8-11. And on the other hand, the greatest instances of mercy and goodness to men, and singular deliverances wrought for them, which should, and one would think would, lead men to repentance, and yet they do not Romans 2:4, 5; Revelation 9:20, 21, yea the most powerful and awakening ministry that a man can sit under, has no influence on the minds of men to bring them to repentance, without the power and grace of God; such as was the ministry of John the Baptist, who was the voice of one crying in the wilderness, preaching in a loud, vehement, and powerful manner, the baptism of repentance; and yet though some publicans and harlots believed, the Pharisees *repented not afterwards that they might believe*, Matthew 21:32 our Lord spake as one having authority, yet few believed; and many cities where he preached, and mighty works were done by him, yet repented not; and if one was to rise from the dead, and describe all the happiness of the blissful state of the saints in heaven he was capable of, or paint all the horrors of the damned in hell, it would have no effect, neither to allure nor frighten to repentance, or bring men to it, without the exertion of powerful and efficacious grace, Luke 16:31.

4. The sole efficient cause and author of repentance is God, Father, Son, and Spirit. God the Father, *if God peradventure will give them repentance*, 2 Timothy 2:25, Christ, the Son of God, as mediator, is exalted *to give repentance to Israel, and forgiveness of sins*, Acts 5:31, and the Spirit of God reproves for sin, convinces of it, and works repentance for it, John 16:8.

5. The moving cause of it is the free grace of God; it is a grant and favour from him, a gift of Christ, which he, as a prince and a saviour bestows, Acts 11:18, and 5:31, and an operation of the power and grace of the Spirit of God, and entirely flows from the sovereign will and mercy of God, *who hath mercy on whom he will have mercy, and whom he will he hardeneth*, Romans 9:18, not giving grace to repent.

6. The usual means and instruments of repentance are the word, and the ministers of it; as faith, so repentance, comes by hearing the word; the three thousand were pricked to the heart, and were brought to repentance, through the ministry of the apostle Peter; and as all the apostles were ordered by Christ to preach repentance in his name among all nations, so they went forth everywhere, and God in and by their ministry commanded all men everywhere to repent; and when and where the command was attended with power it produced the effect; and so the apostle Paul declared to Jews and Gentiles, that *they should repent and turn to God, and do works meet for repentance*; and the hand of the Lord being with him, great numbers everywhere believed and turned to the Lord, Luke 24:47; Acts 17:30, and 26:20.

V. The effects and consequences of repentance

Such effects as are evidences of it, and show it to be genuine; and such consequences which are salutary, and show the blessings of grace are connected with it.

1st, The effects of it, which prove it to be genuine; such as the apostle mentions as fruits of godly sorrow, 2 Corinthians 8:11.

1. *Carefulness* to exercise repentance in a proper way, and to bring forth fruits meet for it; carefulness not to sin any more in a like manner, or to live a sinful course of life, but to abstain from all appearance of evil; and carefulness not to offend God again, who had been so good and gracious to them.

2. *Clearing of themselves*; not by denying the fact, as Gehazi, nor by extenuating and palliating it as Adam, but by an ingenuous

confession of it, praying it might be forgiven, and that they might be cleansed from all sin by the blood of Jesus; so clearing themselves from the charges of hardness of heart, impenitence, and ingratitude, and of neglect of repentance when sin was discovered to them.

3. *Indignation*; against sin, expressing their abhorrence of it, and of themselves for it, as Job did, saying, what have we to do with it for the future? being filled with a loathing of it, and with shame and confusion for it; see Hosea 14:8.

4. *Fear*; not of the punishment of sin, of the wrath of God, and of hell and damnation, which is the fruit of legal and not evangelical repentance; but a fear of offending God, and of his grace and goodness in forgiving their sins, and of him for his goodness sake, Hosea 3:5.

5. *Vehement desire*; to be kept from sin, that they may not dishonour God, grieve their own souls, offend and stumble God's people, and bring reproach on his ways, doctrines, and ordinances; and that they might be indulged with nearness to God, communion with him, and fresh discoveries of his love to them.

6. *Zeal*; for God and his glory, for his doctrines and ordinances, for the discipline of his house, and for the performance of all good works.

7. *Revenge*; not on others but on themselves, and on their sinful lusts and corruptions, and on all disobedience, that their obedience might be fulfilled; striving against sin, acting the part of an antagonist to it, resisting even unto blood, not sparing but mortifying the deeds of the body, that they may live a holy life and conversation. But though these things are in a more peculiar manner applicable to the case of the Corinthians, yet they do more or less, and in a great measure appear in every repenting sinner.

2nd, The consequences of repentance, even blessings of grace, which follow upon it, and are connected with it, being promised unto it, and what it issues in; by which it appears to be salutary, and answers some valuable ends, and is of the greatest importance; as,

1. The pardon of sin; for though this is not procured by tears of repentance, by humiliation for sin, and confession of it, but by the blood of Christ only; yet to those who repent of sin sincerely, and are truly humbled for it, a manifestation and application of pardoning grace and mercy is made; and these two, repentance and remission of sins, are joined together in the ministry of the word, to encourage repenting sinners to hope in Christ for the forgiveness of their sin, who as he gives the one gives also the other, Luke 24:47; Acts 5:31, none that ever truly repented of sin and confessed it, but had his sins pardoned; such as forsake their sinful ways and turn to the Lord, he pardons and abundantly pardons; his justice to the blood and sacrifice of his Son, and his truth and faithfulness to his word and promises, leave no room to doubt of it, Isaiah 55:7; 1 John 1:9.

2. True evangelical repentance, which is God's gift, and a grant of his grace, is repentance unto life, Acts 11:18. It is not by repentance indeed by which men live spiritually, that is by faith in Christ; yet men begin to live spiritually when they are quickened by the Spirit of God, and have repentance from dead works given unto them; and though men by repentance do not procure eternal life, that is the free gift of God through Christ, yet true, special, spiritual, and evangelical repentance issues in eternal life, and is inseparably connected with it; though all impenitent sinners shall certainly perish, who by their hardness and impenitent hearts treasure up wrath against the day of wrath and righteous judgment of God; yet all that come to true repentance none of them shall ever perish, but shall have everlasting life.

3. Evangelical repentance, the work of godly sorrow, is *repentance to salvation not to be repented of*, 2 Corinthians 7:10, it is not the cause of salvation; Christ is the captain, cause, and author of salvation; but the means through and by which God saves his people; as they are saved *through faith*, so through repentance, and through both as the gift of God, flowing from his sovereign grace, Ephesians 2:8, as he *that believes* with the heart unto righteousness, so he that truly repents of sin *shall be saved*, Mark 16:16.

Bibliography

A more detailed bibliography is given in my book John Gill and The Cause of God and Truth. The works given below deal mainly with the topic in hand rather than Gill's wider testimony and works.

Primary Works

A Complete Body of Doctrinal and Practical Divinity (1 vol.) 1839 edition, reprinted 1989 by The Baptist Standard Bearer, Arkansas, USA.

Body of Divinity (3 vols), Subscription, 1769

Cause of God and Truth, The Collingridge, Waterford, 1855

Covenant of Grace: A Believer's Support in Trouble, The, Christian Bookshop, Ossett, 1995

Doctrines in the Supralapsarian Scheme impartially examined by the Word of God, London, 1736

Doctrine of Justification by the Righteousness of Christ, London, 1756

Doctrines of God's Everlasting Love to His Elect, and their Eternal Union with Christ, The, The Baptist Standard Bearer, 1987

Doctrine of the Trinity Stated and Vindicated, The, London, 1752

Exposition of the Old and New Testaments (9 vols), Baptist Standard Bearer, 1989

Mutual Duty of Pastor and People, The, London, 1734

Necessity of Good Works unto Salvation Considered, The, London 1739

Sermons and Tracts, (3 vols), Primitive Baptist Library, 1981

Song of Solomon, Sovereign Grace Publications, 1971

Truth Defended. Being an Answer to an Anonymous Pamphlet intitled Some Doctrines in the Supralapsarian Scheme impartially examined by the Word of God, London, 1736

Vindication of a Book Entitled The Cause of God and Truth, A, London, 1740 (also included in the Collingridge edition of TCOGAT).

Preface to *Hymns Composed on Several Subjects and on Divers Occasions*, Davis, Richard, London, 1748

Biographies
Broome, John R., *Dr John Gill*, Gospel Standard Publications, 1991

Coxon, Francis, *Christian Worthies* (2 vols) Gill in vol. 1, Zoar Publications, 1980

Craner, Thomas, *A Grain of Gratitude. A Sermon Occasioned by the Death of that Venerable, Learned, Pious and Judicious Divine The Revd John Gill D. D.*, London, 1771

Ella, George M., *John Gill and The Cause of God and Truth*, Go Publications, 1995

Fellows, John, *An Elegy on the Death of the Revd John Gill, D. D.*, London, 1771

George, Timothy and Dockery, David, *Baptist Theologians*, Gill in Chapter 4, Broadman Press, 1990

Harrison, Graham, *Dr John Gill and His Teaching*, Evangelical Library, 1971

Middleton, Erasmus, *Biographia Evangelica* (4 vols) Gill in vol. 4, Subscription, 1784

Rippon, John, *Life and Writings of the Rev. John Gill. D.D.*, Gano Books, 1992

Spurgeon, C. H., *The Metropolitan Tabernacle: Its History and Work*, Passmore & Alabaster, 1876, Gill biography in Chapter 4.

Wallin, Benjamin, *The Address Delivered At The Interment in The Burial-Ground at Bun-Hill, October 23, 1771*, London, 1771

Other Works Containing Relevant Material
Berkhof, Louis, *Systematic Theology*, Banner of Truth Trust, 1959

Berkhof, Louis, *The History of Christian Doctrines*, Banner of Truth Trust, 1969

Bicknell, E. J., *The Thirty Nine Articles*, Longmans, 1957

Brine, John, *An Antidote Against a Spreading Antinomian Principle*, London, 1750

Brine, John, *Christ's Active Obedience Imputed to His People*, Christian Bookshop, Ossett, England, 1995

Brine, John, *The Chief of Sinners Saved Through Jesus Christ*, Christian Bookshop, Ossett, England, 1995

Brown, John, *Life and Character of the Late James Hervey*, Ogle, Duncan & Co., 1822

Brown, Raymond, *The English Baptists of the 18th Century*, Baptist Historical Society, 1986

Buchanan, James, *The Doctrine of Justification*, Banner of Truth Trust, 1991

Calvin, John, *Calvin's Calvinism*, SGU, trans. Henry Cole, D.D., 1927

Calvin, John, *Institutes of Christian Religion* (2 vols.), Eerdmans, 1979

Crisp, Tobias, *The Sermons of Tobias Crisp* (with John Gill's notes), Tobias Crisp Series, Christian Bookshop, Ossett, England, 1995

Crosby, Thomas, *The History of the English Baptists* (4 vols), Church History Research, 1978

Dallimore, Arnold, *Spurgeon*, The Banner of Truth Trust, 1985

Daniel, Curt, *Biblical Calvinism* (pamphlet), Kenton L. Haynes, 1994

Daniel, Curt, *Hyper-Calvinism and John Gill*, Edin. Ph.D. 1884, (published privately, Dallas, 1984).

Dillistone, F. W., *The Christian Understanding of Atonement*, Library of Constructive Theology, James Nisbet, 1968

Doudney, David Alfred, *Retracings & Renewings*, W. Mack, London, 1880

Ella, George M., *Law and Gospel in the Theology of Andrew Fuller*, Go Publications, 1996

Ella, George M., *William Cowper: Poet of Paradise*, Evangelical Press, 1993

Ella, George M., *William Huntington: Pastor of Providence*, Evangelical Press, 1994

Ella, George M., *James Hervey: Preacher of Righteousness*, Go Publications, 1997

Engelsma, David, *Hyper-Calvinism & The Call of the Gospel*, Reformed Free Publishing Association, 1980

Foreman, John, *Duty Faith* (2 small vols), Christian Bookshop, Ossett, England, 1995

Fuller, Andrew G., *Life of the Rev. Andrew Fuller*, Religious Tract Society, Undated

Fuller, Andrew G., *The Complete Works of the Rev. Andrew Fuller*, Sprinkle Publications, 1988

Fuller, Thomas Ekins, *A Memoir of the Life and Writings of A. Fuller*, J. Heaton & Son, 1863

Fullerton, W. Y., *C. H. Spurgeon*, 1920

Goat Yard / Carter Lane Church Book 1719-1808, Metropolitan Tabernacle.

Goodwin, Thomas, *The Objects and Acts of Justifying Faith*, Banner of Truth, 1985

Hardwick, Charles, *A History of the Articles of Religion*, Cambridge, 1859

Hastings, James, *Encyclopaedia of Religion and Ethics*, Clark, 12 vols, 1908

Hawker, Robert et. al., *Sanctification in Christ Jesus: Sermons, Tracts and Writings*, Christian Bookshop, Ossett, England, 1995

Haykin, Michael A., *One Heart and One Soul: John Sutcliffe of Olney, his friends and his times*, Evangelical Press, 1994

Hendry, George S., *The Westminster Confession for Today*, SCM Press, 1960

Hervey, James, *The Works of the Rev. James Hervey*, Thomas Nelson, 1837

Hooker, Richard, *A Learned Discourse on Justification, Works, and How The Foundation of Faith is Overthrown*, The Silent Preacher Series. No. 1. London, 1814

Kistler, Don, (ed.), *Justification by Faith Alone*, Solo Deo Gloria Publications, Morgan, USA, 1996

Richardson, Samuel, *Justification by Christ Alone*, London, 1647

Rusk, John, *The Universal Invitation of the Gospel*, Gospel Standard Reprint, Pastor J. E. North, Lewes, England, 1995

Rusk, John, *Antinomianism Demolished and the Gospel of Christ Delivered from its False Charges*, The Huntingtonian Press, 1996

Historical and Theological Works which Shed Light on the Doctrine of Justification

Ivimey, Joseph, *A History of the English Baptists* (4 vols.), London, 1814

Kirkby, A. H., *The Theology of Andrew Fuller and its relation to Calvinism*, Ph.D., Edin., 1956

Lawson, Thomas, *Calvin: His Life and Times*, London, undated

Lumpkin, William L., *Baptist Confessions of Faith*, Judson Press, 1959

Morris, Leon, *The Apostolic Preaching of the Cross*, Tyndale Press, 1960

Murray, Iain (ed.), *C. H. Spurgeon: Autobiography* (2 vols.), Banner of Truth Trust, 1973

Murray, Iain, *The Forgotten Spurgeon*, The Banner of Truth Trust, 1986

Naylor, Peter, *Picking up a Pin for the Lord*, Grace Publications, 1992

Nettles, Thomas J., *By His Grace and For His Glory*, Baker Book House, 1990

Niesel, Wilhelm, *The Theology of Calvin*, Westminster Press, 1956

Pike, G. Holden, *The Life and Work of Charles Haddon Spurgeon*, Banner of Truth Trust, 1991

Reid, James, *Memoirs of the Westminster Divines*, Banner of Truth Trust, 1982

Ryland Jun., John, *The Life and Death of the Rev. Andrew Fuller*, Button and Son, 1818

Ryle, J. C., *Christian Leaders of the Eighteenth Century*, Banner of Truth Trust, 1978

Schaff, Philip (ed.), *Schaff-Herzog Encyclopaedia of Religious Knowledge*, Funk & Wagnalls, 894, 4 vols.

Seymour, R. E., *John Gill Baptist Theologian, 1697-1771*, Ph.D., Edin., 1954

Shedd, W. G. T., *Calvinism Pure & Mixed*, Banner of Truth Trust, 1986

Sheehan, R. J., *C. H. Spurgeon and the Modern Church*, Grace Publications, 1985

Smeaton, *Atonement According to Christ and His Apostles*, Sovereign Grace Publishers, undated

Spears, W. E., *The Baptist Movement in England in the late Seventeenth Century as reflected in the work and thought of Benjamin Keach, 1640-1704*, Ph.D., Edin. 1953

379

Thomas, W. H. Griffith, *The Principles of Theology*, Church Bookroom Press, 1945

Toon, Peter, *Hyper-Calvinism*, The Olive Tree, 1967

Toplady, Augustus Montague, *The Works of Augustus Toplady*, Sprinkle Publications, 1987

Turretin, Francis, *The Atonement*, Baker Book House, 1978

Wright, Thomas, *The Life of Augustus M. Toplady*, Farncombe, 1911

Journal, Magazine and Newspaper Items Appertaining to the Subject

Abbreviations:

Banner of Truth Magazine	BOTM
Baptist History and Heritage	BHH
Baptist Quarterly	BQ
Evangelical Quarterly	EQ
Evangelical Times	ET
Focus	F
Foundations	Fo
New Focus	NF
Strict Baptist Historical Society Bulletin	SBHSB
Transactions of the Baptist Historical Society	TBHS

Champion, L. G., The Theology of John Ryland, BQ, 28(1), 1979, pp. 17-29

Clipsham, E. F., Andrew Fuller: Fullerism, BQ, XX, 1963

Ella, G. M. Christ Alone Exalted in the life of Tobias Crisp, NF, Issue 3, 1996, pp. 13-16

Ella, G. M., A Gospel Unworthy of Any Acceptation, F, No. 8, Winter 1993/94

Ella, G. M., John Gill and His Successors, F, Spring, 1996

Ella, G. M., John Gill and The Cause of God and Truth, ET, April, 1994

Ella, G. M., Robert Hawker: Zion's Warrior, NF, Issue 5, 1996, pp. 11-14

Ella, G. M., The Atonement in Modern Evangelical and Liberal Thought, NF, Issues 1-8, 1996-1997

Fortner, Donald, S., The Distinctiveness of God's Love for His Elect, NF, Issue 1, 1996, p. 7

Gill, John, Come Unto Me: Commentary on Matthew 11:28, NF, Dec.-Jan., 1997, p. 14

Kirkby, A. H., Andrew Fuller: Evangelical Calvinist, BQ, XV, 1954, pp. 195-202

MacGregor, James, The Free Offer in the Westminster Confession, BOTM, 82, 83, 1970, pp. 51-58

Manley, K. B., John Rippon and Baptist Histography, BQ, 28 (3), 1979, pp. 109-208

Nuttall, G. F., Northamptonshire and the Modern Question, JTS, NS, XVI, 1965, pp. 101-23

Oliver, R. W., John Collet Ryland, Daniel Turner, BQ, XXIX, 1981, pp. 77-79

Oliver, R. W., By His Grace and For His Glory (Review/Nettles, BOTM, 284, 1987, pp. 30-32

Oliver, R. W., Historical Survey of English Hyper-Calvinism, Fo (Engl), 7, 1981, pp. 8-18

Oliver, R. W., Significance of Strict Baptists Attitudes to Duty-Faith, SBHSB, 20, 1993, pp. 3-26

Parker, T. H. L., Calvin's Doctrine of Justification, EQ, XXIV, 1952

Price, Seymour, Dr John Gill and the Confession of 1729, BQ, IV, 1928, pp. 366-371

Robinson, O. C., The Legacy of John Gill, BQ, XXVI, 1971, pp 111-125

Sheehan, R. J., The Presentation of the Gospel Amongst Hyper-Calvinists, Fo (Engl), 8, 1982, pp. 28-39

Toon, P., The Growth of a Supralapsarian Christology, EQ, XXIX, 1967

Toon, Peter, English Strict Baptists, BQ, 21, 1965, pp. 30-36

Weeler Robinson, H,. A Baptist Student: J. C. Ryland, BQ, III, 1926-27, pp. 25-33

White, B. R., Thomas Crosby, Baptist Historian I, BQ, 21, 1965, pp. 154-168

White, B. R., Thomas Crosby, Baptist Historian II, BQ, 21, 1966, pp. 219-234

White, B. R., John Gill in London 1719-1729, BQ, XXII, 1967, pp. 72-91

Young, Doyle L., Andrew Fuller and the Modern Missionary Movement, BHH, 17 (4), 1982, pp. 17-27

Index Of Persons, Places And Institutions

Index Of Topics

Index Of Scripture References

Old Testament

Psalms
5:5, 6, p. 316
8:5, p. 264 fn.
9:4, p. 311
9:10, p. 91, 295 fn., 299 fn., 331
11:7, p. 311
16:2, p. 223
18:2, p. 278
22:5, p. 101, 352
25:6, p. 278
31:14 p. 327
32, p. 106
32:1, p. 106
32:5, p. 105, 328, 362
32:5, 6, p. 115
34:18, p. 358
36:6, p. 312
38:8, p. 352
38:17, 18, p. 358
45:8, p. 296 fn.
51:1, p. 109, 111, 112, 117
51:1, 2, 7-9, p. 105
51:1, 9, p. 106
51:3, p. 362
51:4, p. 366
51:5, p. 264 fn., 366
51:7, p. 107
51:17, p. 358
71:3, p. 277
73:4-13, p. 317
78:34-37, p. 360
89:19, p. 226
89:38, p. 133
90:2, p. 224
92:15, p. 311
97:1, 2, p. 311
100:5, p. 278
103:1-3, p. 328

103:2, 3, p. 112, 113
103:3, p. 107
103:17, p. 278
109, p. 313 fn.
116:12, p. 313
121:1, 2, p. 88, 325
130:4, p. 112
139:7-13, p. 223 fn.
139:16, p. 228
143, p. 144
143:2, p. 130
145:7, p. 311
145:17, p. 317
147:3, p. 358

Proverbs
1:24-28, p. 272
3:18, p. 94, 336, 337
18:10, p. 335
28:13, p. 362

Ecclesiastes
7:20, p. 119
7:29, p. 264

Song of Solomon
3:4, p. 337
5:16, p. 297 fn.
8:5, p. 337

Isaiah
1:13, 14, p. 316
1:18, p. 107
6: 2, 3, p. 233
6:5, p. 362
9:6, p. 340
10:20, p. 95, 337

New Testament

Index Of Works Quoted

www.ingramcontent.com/pod-product-compliance
Lightning Source LLC
Chambersburg PA
CBHW060446100426

42812CB00025B/2710